MODERN CHRISTIANITY CORRUPTED

Authored By
Bob Klingenberg

Dedicated
To Our
LORD JESUS CHRIST

MODERN CHRISTIANITY CORRUPTED

Table of Contents

††††

Preface

† † †

"Here I Stand; I Can Do No Other. God Help Me. Amen." ~Martin Luther

I preface the book with this story. A preacher went to preach in a distant place. He was kind of lonely and depressed, as no one met him there when he arrived. The place where he was staying was a rather ratty motel, and he got up Sunday morning feeling kind of blue. He went to breakfast and he needed some encouragement. So he said to the waitress, "I want a poached egg and a good word." She came back a few minutes later and brought him the poached egg. She put the poached egg down and was about to leave. The preacher said to her, "Wait a minute. I said a poached egg and a good word. You haven't given me the good word." So she came back to him, stooped down and said, "Don't eat the egg." There are those times in history and in our lives that the best word we can receive is a word of warning and alarm. This moment in history is indeed one of those times.

Modern America is undergoing a massive spiritual and moral corrupting due to the invasion of Secular Humanism. Modern Christianity is undergoing a massive spiritual and moral corrupting due to the invasion of Religious Humanism. Secular Humanism has made great inroads into the very soul of American society through the influence of left-wing judges and politicians as well as the American Civil Liberties Union. Religious Humanism has made great inroads into the very heart of the American Church through the influence of humanistic preachers and man-centered/mammon-centered theologies.

In either case, whether it is Secular Humanism or Religious Humanism, the emphasis is on the human and not on the Divine – a humanized philosophy and religion. Moreover, while Secular Humanism replaces God with man, Religious Humanism equalizes man with God and prioritizes man before God. In both instances man has increased and God has decreased in stature and importance.

The philosophy of Secular Humanism replaces Divinity with humanity, while the theology of Religious Humanism elevates humanity to Divine status. This will become shockingly evident as this book unfolds. The catastrophic consequence is that in either case, God no longer stands exclusive, transcendent or sovereign. In short, in Religious Humanism, God is but the backdrop to the drama of life's main character – man.

As a result of Religious Humanism's deification of man, man's natural sinfulness and depravity are now being down-played, deodorized if not denied.

People are going to Religious Humanism churches not only to escape sin's punishment, but sin-consciousness in their lives. Religious Humanism's message is not atoning, just nicely antiseptic. God is no longer the pardoner of the guilty, but the patron of the worthy. Religious Humanism obscures man's villainies and denies his villain status. Religious Humanism helps people ignore sin and exalt self!

Secular Humanism presents man as independent, while Religious Humanism presents man and God as codependent. In Secular Humanism, "Independent Man" is self-enabling, while in Religious Humanism "Codependent Man and God" are mutually enabling. In the former, man doesn't need God. In the latter, man and God equally need each other. In Secular Humanism, man uses and commands other men to accomplish his desires. In Religious Humanism, man uses and commands God to accomplish his desires.

If you will, in Secular Humanism, man exists for himself, while in Religious Humanism, God exists for man. This is totally corrupting authentic Christianity in which man exists for God. In Religious Humanism God becomes the servant of man and not man the servant of God. God becomes man's helper, not his Master!

In my book *Is God With America?* I explain the lethality of Secular Humanism in American society, politics, and education. In this book *Modern Christianity Corrupted*, I explain the lethality of Religious Humanism in modern Christendom. Religious Humanism is the forced marriage of Humanism and Theism that has found its way into so much of religious network television programming today, as well as into major denominational and independent churches across America.

It stands to reason that Religious Humanism, given its priority emphasis on man, is carnal, temporal, and materialistic in its thrust and priorities. When man becomes the focus, the spiritual and the eternal are effaced and eventually erased. God becomes the means to man's material and temporal ends at best, and not Himself the eternal beginning and end of all things. Religious Humanism can be characterized as a modern epidemic of materialistic affluenza which supersedes spirituality and is blocking the flow of a holy, deep God awareness.

Entire congregations and vast TV audiences across the world are regularly listening to sermons on man's comforts rather than God's character, on cash rather than on Christ and the cross, on riches rather than righteousness, on giving to get rather than giving to bless God and His Kingdom, and on success rather than salvation. Am I saying that comforts, cash, riches etc. are taboo in the Christian life? Of course not! God graciously meets our needs and then some. What I am saying is that Religious Humanism majors in minors, and minors in majors. It has everything so horribly twisted and out of balance so that people's spiritual vision is being seriously knocked out of focus. In short, Religious Humanism obsesses about what man desires and deserves, not about what God demands.

It is complex! Religious Humanism is not a monolith. It has many heads and many faces. Muslims tell an ancient story about the time when the prophet Mohammed rode his horse to Heaven. When he got there, he saw an angel with seventy thousand heads. Each head had seventy thousand faces. And each face had seventy thousand mouths. And if that was not enough, each mouth had seventy thousand tongues. All of that on the neck of one angel! You talk about a multi-headed grotesque monstrosity! I have come to feel that way about the many heads of Religious Humanism. But you will find that they are all on the one neck of exaggerated and exalted man.

It is my fervent prayer that the Holy Spirit will use *Modern Christianity Corrupted* to expose this false religion that has infiltrated and is corrupting the modern church under the guise of Christianity. The historic Christian Church's foundations are being undermined, her laws discarded, her worship diluted, her doctrines shredded, her Gospel falsified, and her integrity impugned. It is not Christianity, but rather a dangerous counterfeit. It has reached pandemic proportions, and like a massive avalanche it is sweeping many downhill and burying them on the slippery slopes of temporality and carnality, and endangering their spiritual, moral and eternal lives.

I am deeply concerned about the children of modernity who are now being contaminated with Religious Humanism in their churches before they even get started in life. There is an Amish proverb that states, "We do not inherit the future from our fathers, rather we borrow it from our children." If we do not clean up the modern church from the toxic waste of Religious Humanism in a big hurry, we will poison the minds and the hearts of our children and future generations to the imperiling of their souls.

MODERN CHRISTIANITY CORRUPTED

Chapter One

THE CORRUPTING ROOTS OF MODERN CHRISTIANITY

†††

"If We Take Away This Foundation, That Man Is By Nature Foolish And Sinful, Fallen Short Of The Glorious Image Of God, The Christian System Falls At Once; Nor Will It Deserve As Honorable An Appellation As That Of A Cunningly Devised Fable." ~John Wesley

The roots of an insidious Religious Humanism have for some time now steadily been growing deeper and deeper and taking a firm hold in the modern Christian Church in America and across the world. The lethality of this rooting is that Religious Humanism is filled with false teachings which are historically known as heresies. Heresy is a word that isn't used much anymore, except in the Bible. Today the word heresy has been all but dropped from the church's vocabulary. That is the greatest heresy of all. And when heresy is rampant it is no longer recognized as heresy, but as normalcy.

The church of Jesus Christ has always been plagued by heresies throughout time. However, in many aspects, the modern invasion of heresies is unparalleled in all of church history. The Apostle Paul's warning about heresies to the first century Christian church has never been more poignant, as he writes in Galatians 5:19-20 (KJV),

> **"Now the works of the flesh are manifest, which are these…idolatry, witchcraft…heresies."**

Or again, the Apostle Peter's warning in II Peter 2:1 (KJV),

> **"But there were false prophets also among the people, even as there shall be false teachers among you, who privily shall bring in damnable heresies…."**

This book is about today's damnable heresies, which are being taught in the modern church not privily but blatantly, and are being accepted by the religious and non-religious gullible masses as orthodox Christianity. The English noun "heresy" comes from the Greek word "hairesis", which simply means "opinion" or "sentiment." In short, heresies are opinions not based upon and in direct conflict with fundamental Biblical truths. Opinions are just that – opinions and not facts! If you will, false doctrines which contradict Scripture and which this book systematically exposes and refutes.

Am I a heresy hunter? My answer to that question is that you don't have to hunt for heresies. They are so plentiful and thick these days that every time you take a step, you trip over another one. We are not hunting them, they are hunting us. Whether you and I like it or not, we are on the front lines of the biggest "Truth Vs Heresy War" in church history.

As in Martin Luther's day, few in the religious grassroots knew that there was even a cold war taking place in the Catholic priesthood and hierarchy until Luther's 95 Theses. For centuries the church had been in a slow doctrinal rot. That is how it goes historically, as it seems that history must run its rotting course until it becomes putridly unbearable. We are at the same point again, only worse. No one stood up and protested until courageous Martin Luther. Then it went from a cold war to a very hot war in no time flat. This led to Martin Luther in 1521 being "Dieted at Worms" where he was excommunicated by the church and then declared by the Pope to be an outlaw.

Truth is never defended and falsehood never corrected without a war, and there is always a price to pay. I am sure that through it all Martin looked around many times for like-minded priests and theology professors and asked, "Where is everybody? Why is everyone else so silent?" It all turned out to be much bigger than anyone could have then envisioned. From one faithful protestor Protestantism was born. It only takes one spark to get reformation fires burning. Martin Luther lit his reformation torch and Biblical Christianity was preserved.

The heresy propagators are never silent. They are always very vocal crusaders. In Washington D.C. the Left Wing Opinion Corps in the legislative, judicial and executive branches of government are more and more speaking their heresies into the Constitution rather than allowing the Constitution to speak into them. In the modern church, the Ecclesiastical Opinion Corps, i.e. Religious Humanists are more and more speaking their heresies into the Word of God, rather than allowing the Word of God to speak into them.

The Bible warns us about this under various metaphors. God warns us in Ephesians 4:14 not to be carried about by "Every Wind of Doctrine." Winds of doctrine! Not breezes, winds! Winds, not wind. We never know where they will be coming from next. They are blowing all over the place, and we are warned not to be carried away by them. Strong winds indeed, because you don't get blown away or carried away by balmy breezes. These are gale force false-doctrine winds. We are living in that day when the spiritual weather reports are forecasting 100% chance of "Strong Opinion Storms." More like "Heresy Hurricanes." Batten down the church hatches folks, for the powerful heresy winds are only going to increase to the end of time.

Multitudes are being carried away by these heresy hurricanes. It is all part of the great apostasy prophesied by the Apostle Paul in II Thessalonians 2:3, leading to the rapture of the church. We are right now smack dab in the middle of the end-time falling away, and we must resist it come Hell or high water.

Adding to all of this is the fact that we live in a day in which man believes that there is no objective truth, only opinions, and that each one's opinion is just as valid as everyone else's opinions. The modern day church has become a heresy wind tunnel. All Bible truth is now up for grabs. It was Peggy Noonan who said, "Man has never had a weapon that he didn't use." Not very comforting considering the maniacs that now rule North Korea and Iraq! But even more disturbing to me is this, "Man has never put forth a falsehood that was not believed."

To alarm the contemporary church about rampant heresies is as difficult today as it was for President George W. Bush to convince Europe about the need for their participation in the War on Terror. *Modern Christianity Corrupted* is a bright red flare shot into the ecclesiastical skies warning believers that the modern church is harboring heretics and heresies, even as Middle Eastern nations are harboring terrorists and terrorism. As in President Bush's case, you soon find out who your true allies are and are not. Great Britain proved to be America's strongest supporter. So we wonder just where support for reformation will come from, and can reformation fires burn again.

President Bush's warning about "Acts of Terror" has also been downplayed by the Obama administration with the far less alarming and far more generic "Man-Made Disasters." However, the Oklahoma City massacre and the 9/11 carnage were not man-made disasters. They were brutal acts of domestic and foreign terrorism and savagery. As if we are going to buy into the lie that the Islamic suicide bombers in cars and airplanes are now to be lumped together with careless forest-fire cigarette-butt droppers!

So too today warnings about "Acts of Heresy" fall on deaf ears. I ask many people in the church world if they have any hot-stove, hot-button issues relating to the modern church scene. Many say no, not one. All the while people are being propagandized by and are buying into the preachers, sermons and books of Religious Humanism. Mike Oppenheimer of "Let Us Reason Ministries" so accurately and insightfully writes: "One part truth shaken and stirred with two parts deception, then bottled in a new Divine revelation – produces a demonic cocktail sauce waiting to be sprinkled on impressionable, biblically illiterate Christians."(1)

Bible knowledge and doctrinal savvy among church-goers is at an all time low. Therefore, when people are warned about rampant untruths and false teachings in the modern Christian church, one can discern that not only are they ignorant of them, but what is worse, when they are told about them, they are not at all alarmed. When it comes to Biblical truth and contending earnestly for it, there is today a faint, passionless pulse in the Body of Christ. This is because much of modern religion is self and experienced based and no longer Biblically and doctrinally based. A lethal combination indeed! The perfect storm! In short, modern church-goers may carry their Bibles, but its full and balanced truth no longer carries them.

Please do not misunderstand me. I am not putting down experiencing God. Anything but! Oh how man needs a born-again experience with Jesus Christ and a moment by moment experience walking hand and hand with the living Christ. Only a personal and daily infilling of the Holy Spirit can do that! Why so important? Doctrine apart from the experiential-God is as dry as dust and cannot raise a worm from the dead. Frankly, over the years much of formalized and doctrinalized religion has been one of the greatest hindrances to a direct experience with God. You can't just memorize or theologize God and have it do you one bit of temporal or eternal good. But hear me, at the same time experientialism apart from a strong Bible-doctrine foundation will become a lose canon. And God only knows how many lose canons there are on the ecclesiastical-experiential stage today.

There is also a spiritual laziness in modern religious circles. Church folks not only don't want to be bothered with what's going wrong in modern Christianity, they don't have the slightest inclination to find out for themselves. The old mountaineer and his son were sitting in front of the living room fireplace. They weren't saying anything to each other, and after a long time of silence, the father said, "Son, go outside and see if it's raining." Without looking up, the son answered, "O Pop, why don't we just send out the dog and then call him back in and see if he's wet." Hey, let Bowser do it! Let George do it. It is just too nice here in front of the fire. Very few anymore feel the need to make themselves personally responsible for the truth.

To make things far worse, religious programming on American television is literally saturated with and contaminated by Religious Humanism. American religious networks have become landfills of Religious Humanism. For those of you who have been sucked in by the false teachings of Religious Humanism because you are not grounded in the Word of God, I am deeply concerned about your spiritual safety as believers in Christ. Media religion has never been so full of unscrupulous people who will manipulate vulnerable and spiritually gullible people for their own man-centered and mammon-centered ends. Religious television is a swamp full of self-dealing alligators as never before seen in church history!

We continue with the bull's-eye comments of Mike Oppenheimer: "Indeed, false teachers have existed for thousands of years, and are a recurrent, festering, ingrown toenail on Christianity's big toe. Now with the advent of modern technology, demonic doctrines span the electronic airwaves and tickle our ears day and night, with an orchestrated siren's song of, 'Trust in me and I'll set you free.'"(2) Heresies have never been so available to so many around the clock.

THE SELF-HELP CULT

Have you ever read or perhaps spoken the phrase yourself, "God helps those who help themselves?" Do a poll with your own church people and ask them if that phrase is found in the Bible. It will shock you how many say that it is. Or at the least, they are under the impression somehow that this is in fact what the Bible teaches. There is a Religious Humanism "Self-Help Cult" that has grown exponentially in the modern church and on religious television across the land. More than that, it again illustrates the enormous lack of Bible knowledge that now exists in the modern church.

Nowhere does the Bible teach that God helps those who help themselves! Nowhere! The Bible teaches the exact opposite throughout. The Bible is anything but a self-help manual. However, this self-helpism taken at face value is in a nutshell the essence of Religious Humanism. Why? Because it prioritizes man, and relegates God to a degrading auxiliary and assistant role. Man initiates and God supports. Proactive man and reactive God! Man the accomplishing genius and God the always-available assistant. Religious Humanism reduces God merely to man's servant rather than his Master.

The Bible records Jesus Christ's popping of man's ego balloon and the total exploding of man's fabricated self-sufficiency when He said in John 15:5,

"...apart from Me you can do nothing."

All of which simply means that apart from God man cannot initiate, sustain, or complete one thing. Nothing! Nada! Zilch! Zero! Zip! Helpless rather than a self-helper! I so appreciate the old Ziggy cartoon picturing Ziggy and his even smaller dog standing at the window of their second-story apartment and looking out at the busy city streets below. Then Ziggy says to his dog, "Well, it's you and me against the world, and I think we're going to get creamed."

The truth is that God only helps those who are totally helpless and know it. The Bible is strictly a "God-Help Book!" Those who talk of self-help are blowing humanistic smoke, and scores of people breathe it in every day.

Allow the Psalmist in Psalm 121:2 to blow the smoke away with the resounding confession of all of Scripture,

"My help comes from the Lord Who made heaven and earth."

Our help does not come from self. Man cannot blow his nose, blink an eye, make a buck, think a thought, or lift a finger without the Lord's empowering. It is the Holy Spirit alone Who gives us the ability to function successfully in the humdrum routine of our daily lives where most of our time is spent. It is the Holy Spirit alone Who gives us the power to be all that God calls us to be. Man apart from God's Spirit is powerless and helpless. That is why we read in Zechariah 4:6,

"...'Not by might nor by power, but by My Spirit,' says the Lord of hosts."

Man loves to be told that he can do anything he so desires. General Patton's soldiers were in awe of him. A member of General Patton's staff once asked a second lieutenant under Patton's command if he believed that General Patton could walk on water. The lieutenant replied, "Colonel, I know General Patton. If he had to walk on water, he would figure out a way, and within twenty four hours he would have me doing it as well." It is all part of the folklore that is rooted in the mythology of self-sufficiency. It is also the essence of Religious Humanism that religionized man can do anything that he jolly well sets his mind to. It is all part of the humanistic hype.

The Bible tells us something very humbling. Reminding man of his origin, God says in Ecclesiastes 3:20,

"...All came from the dust and all return to the dust."

It was said of the ancient King of Sicily, King Agathocles (317-289 BC), that he did something to constantly remind himself of his humble beginnings. He was by birth the son of a lowly potter. When he was served food at his kingly table, he demanded that there would always be very modest earthenware among the regal table settings, so that he would never forget his lowly and humble beginnings. It would be well for self-reliant Religious Humanists to have a bowlful of dust or dirt included in their elegant humanistic table settings to remind them of their humble and helpless origins as well. On second thought, Religious Humanists would need a truck load!

This is the desperately pressing truth of the Bible throughout that we must grasp, never let go of and constantly confess, "God, I'm helpless. I'm without help and without hope if I am without You." We begin our Christian life that way, for we can do nothing to save ourselves. We live our Christian life that way, for we can do nothing to sustain ourselves. We conclude our Christian life that way, for we can do nothing to complete ourselves. Helplessness before God and dependence upon God is lifelong, and not just in rare moments of crisis. Man is utterly helpless every moment without God's love, without God's forgiveness, without God's enabling, and without God's Christ. That is the Christian's lot in life temporally and eternally.

Pastor Don Emmittee tells the story of Bob Hodges, a Presbyterian minister in Rogersville, Tennessee. Bob Hodges was duck hunting with his friend, Riley, who had just given his life to Jesus Christ. Eventually Riley mustered up the courage and asked Pastor Bob, "Why is it that I am having more trouble since I became a Christian than I ever did when I was lost? I'm having such a struggle." Pastor Bob responded, "I'll tell you why, Riley. A couple of ducks fly over you and you shoot. You kill one and injure the other. They both fall into the lake. What do you do? You have to get out of the boat and go pick up the ducks, but which one do you go after first?" Riley answered, "That's easy! I would go after the injured one first. The dead one ain't going nowhere!" Pastor Bob said, "And that's the way it is with the Devil. He goes after injured Christians. He is not going to bother with the man who is dead in sin. The moment you give your life to Christ, get ready, the Devil is going to come after you."(3)

There is nothing in the Scriptures to indicate that it easy to follow Christ. It is always hard, and it is eternally worth it. I know from experience that Satan never, never lies down, rolls over and plays dead. He fights harder in the life of a Christian than he ever fought in the life of the same person when he was an unbeliever.

Satan will always confirm in your mind self-helpism and self-reliance. He loves to take on spiritually cocky people. Oh how many so-called mighty religious leaders have fallen in their self-conceived, self-assured invincibility and humanistic doctrines! We will not only be injured but we will spiritually be dead ducks, too if we rely upon our own capabilities.

Man is clothed in impotence! God is clothed in omnipotence! Psalm 93:1 tells us that,

> **"...The Lord has clothed and girded Himself with strength...."**

No doubt the Lord is here referencing the royal robes of earthly kings as they clothe themselves in regal splendor. The Lord tells us that His kingly wardrobe is strength. Man is clothed in weakness, which he wears everyday like a cheap T-shirt.

The truth is many think that because they uttered a quick prayer yesterday they have a reserve of strength today and they can handle tomorrow on their own. That is fatal thinking which sets them up for failure every time. So many are staggering around in defeat because they do not follow Christ on their knees! They stumble into pastoral counseling sessions again and again looking like those pathetic cars we see on the road with smashed-in fenders and bumpers with dead taillights. All beat up by Satan! Religious Humanism's self-helpism emasculates prayer, optionalizes God and causes the downfall of even the mightiest men and women of God.

In fact, so weak is man that Paul tells us in I Corinthians 1:25,

> **"...the weakness of God is stronger than men."**

This again is a play on words by Paul, for God has no weakness in any dimension. However, even if He did, His weakness would be infinitely stronger than the collective spiritual, mental and physical strength of mankind put together. Utter dependence upon God's power and wisdom is man's greatest strength. Dependence upon his own power and wisdom is man's greatest weakness. Self-help thinking has no place in Christian theology or living. Self-help is a totally false couplet. 100% unbiblical and Christians should never speak or think those words.

Psalm 70:1 must be our moment-by-moment cry,

> **"O God, hasten to deliver me; O Lord, hasten to my help!"**

The psalmist is in the heat of confrontation! Oh God, hasten Your deliverance! Hasten! Hasten! Help! God, please double Your speed to come to my side! The heat is on. This is a now-or-never prayer. There are those times that Satan sneaks up on us and broadsides us. It is a do or die moment! Call out to

God with the assurance that you will never get a voice that says, "Thank you for calling God. In order to serve you better, your call is being routed to a pastor or chaplain best able to help you. If Satan or a demon has broken into your home, press 1. If the intruder is armed, press 2. If the intruder is in the room from which you are making the call, press 4. If you are attempting to avoid detection and have turned off the lights, press 233920029372 followed by the pound side." No, no, no, for with God, He will be there to deliver you before you amen the call.

RELIGIOUS HUMANISM'S SELF-BELIEF

Where does this self-help philosophy which is now engrained in so much of the American cultural, educational and ecclesiastical thinking have its roots? The tap-root of this man-centered self-helpism is what has come to be known as "Positive and Possibility Thinking." At the head of the positive-thinking philosophy is Norman Vincent Peale, and at the head of the possibility-thinking philosophy is Robert Schuller. They are in fact flip sides of the same philosophical coin. Positive possibility-thinking is taught 24/7 on religious television as well as in many if not most churches and colleges across America and the world.

"Let Us Reason Ministries'" Mike Oppenheimer on his web-page entitled, *"Norman Vincent Peale-A Man Who Made Up His Mind,"* points out the teacher-learner relationship of Peale and Schuller in this quote from Schuller about Peale: **"THE MAN WHO HAD INFLUENCED AND IMPACTED MY THINKING AND MY THEOLOGY AND MY LIFE MORE THAN ANY OTHER LIVING PERSON."** (4)

Against that background it is revealing when we read in "Let Us Reason Ministries," - "In his (Peale's) book *The Power of Positive Thinking,* the theme and teaching is '**BELIEVE IN YOURSELF AND HAVE FAITH IN YOUR ABILITIES**.' The Bible commands us to have faith in God, to abide in Christ, because apart from Him we can do nothing. Peale teaches the opposite, that we can do all things through our mind. Not Christ. This is what the human potential movement (part of the new-age counterfeit) teaches."(5)

David Cloud is the Founder and Director of "Way of Life Literature" website and he writes: "Peale speaks much of faith, but it is not faith in God, but 'faith in faith,' which means in your capabilities…this is nothing more than self-help with a sprinkling of devout-plus-medical phrases." (6)

Self-help! Self-belief! Belief in one's vast abilities! Believe in self. It is really Secular Humanism's philosophy dragged into religion, i.e. Religious Humanism. It is secular psychology with a thin layer of God-frosting that is being eaten up by the church. It has done and is doing untold damage to people's relationship with God and their dependence upon Him. It has made them independent from God, and independence in the Kingdom of God is a dirty word. It has horozontalized rather than verticalized modern religion. It was the final line in the Harvard Law School commencement address spoken by Elle Woods, played by actress Reese Witherspoon in the film *Legally Blond.* In this case, smart blond Elle looks at the graduation class and tells them that the most important thing in their lives is to have faith in themselves. She could just as well have preached it as a sermon in Religious Humanism churches.

Religious Humanism's "Self Creed" has replaced the "Apostles' Creed" and the "Nicene Creed" in modern day churches. These historic creeds and doctrinal confessions have been silenced and are no longer known or spoken in unison by congregations. These confessions of faith in God historically have been the great repositories and reliable trustees of the Christian faith over the centuries. They have been shoved aside. They are now considered passé by the religious in-crowd. These principled schoolmasters of faith have had their classes cancelled.

You will seldom if ever hear recited any longer the Apostles' Creed which begins with the well-known words, "I believe in God the Father Almighty." As a result, modern Christianity has paid an awful price. The weeds of self-belief have grown to such heights in the church world that they now overshadow the so-called antiquated and outmoded faith-in-God creedal stuff. Self-belief is the Religious Humanist's creed – "I believe in Man Almighty." Those who are steeped in the self-help and self-belief cult, at the most can only pretend to believe in God. They will be the first to sign up for "Realize Your Potential Seminars," but they wouldn't be found dead at church prayer meetings.

To say to people in many ecclesiastical settings today, "God alone is able, put all of your trust in Him," is received with awkwardness and uneasiness. It doesn't register. It is much more compatible to say, "Go for it, you're the man, you're the main man, there is no limit, you're awesome." Or, "Go for it girl, you can do it. You are woman! You've got what it takes. You've got to believe in yourself!" It is not only the main theme of commencement speeches, but also of sermon-series and casual conversation. Only a return to historic creedal Christianity can purify what Religious Humanism has corrupted.

The Biblical fact is that nowhere does the Bible teach man to believe in himself. Nowhere! Not to be found! Scrap it! It is not Biblical Christianity, not in the least bit. Not even close! It is strictly the teaching of Religious Humanism. The Bible not only tells us not to put our trust in ourselves, but to trust in nobody else either. A double whammy! Don't put your trust in your neighbor or even your brother. Why? God says so! We read in Jeremiah 9:4,

"Let everyone be on guard against his neighbor, and do not trust any brother; because every brother deals craftily...."

Kind of narrows down the trust field, now doesn't it? There is an old adage that people use at times about one another, as someone will say about a friend, "I would trust him with my life." Bad idea! According to God, every brother deals deceitfully. Derek Prince once said that those who we think will be with us aren't, and those that we never thought would be with us are. Truer words were never spoken.

In God We Trust! That statement of national trust-in-God first appeared on America's currency in 1864. It became the official national motto by an act of Congress in 1956. President Obama recently said to the Turkish Parliament that America is not a Christian nation. I ask you President Obama, "What God do you think that is in our declaration of national trust?" I can guarantee you, Mr. President, that it isn't Allah, even though you recently declared that America is not a Christian nation and then later referred to America as a Moslem nation. It is the God and Father of the Lord Jesus Christ, even though you also recently demanded that the symbol of Christ to be covered over during your recent address to Georgetown University. That is an act of heresy in Christianity and a gross violation of the freedom of religion guaranteed by the First Amendment of the Constitution of the United States of America. So far, Mr. President, you are a presidential heretic.

Religious Humanists may let this go by, for they are the very same ones in the name of God who fight for human rights, including the right to burn the American Flag, and the right to kill non-human babies. But Bible-based Christian Americans will not let this go by. Never! In one act, Mr. President, you committed an act of heresy and violation of the Constitutional. You denied your "Christian" confession and you did not defend the United States Constitution as you pledged to all of us you would do.

America was founded by Trinitarian Christians. America's pilgrim forefathers and founding fathers were devoted to the Bible's God. They did not put their trust in presidents, senators, representatives, court justices, the military, the heads of foreign governments and above all not the economy. America is still being admonished by her money to get her eyes off the now failing dollar and back on Almighty God! She from her earliest years put her trust in God alone. Wise girl! Now she has fallen into the trap of self-trust, self-reliance and God-denial. Stupid girl!

The result of all of this has been that man's self-belief and self-reliance apparently doesn't leave him with a whole lot of health and strength after all. In fact, it is unsettling and sickening him. People suffer by the millions from severe stress and angst. Some of the best-selling drugs in America are Valium for relaxation, Inderal for high blood pressure, and Tagamet for ulcers. Billions of dollars are spent each year on drugs due to stress-related symptoms. Some doctors estimate that stress may be killing more people than AIDS. Belief in and reliance upon self is putting pressure on self which it is unable to bear. When self-belief takes center stage, the drama of life becomes the tragedy of an alcohol and drug-dependent society.

Well then, more pointedly, who are we supposed to believe in and put our trust in? The Bible tells us in Proverbs 3:5-7 in no uncertain terms,

> **"Trust in the Lord with all your heart, and do not lean on your own understanding. In all your ways acknowledge Him, and He will make your paths straight."**

As we say in modern English, "He will steer you straight." God is the only One who can lead us to the right paths to walk in, and give us the strong legs to walk on. That is about as clear as you can make it. Do not believe in yourself! Trust in the Lord with all that is in you. Do not lean on your own brains whatsoever! Religious Humanism as we shall see believes in human brain-power. Christianity believes in Divine omniscient-power.

When you trust in the Lord with all of your heart, then there is no trust left over to put in yourself, in your own mental ability, or in anyone else. God's instruction makes it crystal clear that to trust in self or others is virtually a total distrust of God. In Christianity trust is always vertical, never horizontal.

Allow me to become personal for a moment. The worst messes that I ever got myself into were those situations in which I thought that I had everything all figured out by myself. I had it nailed. It was in the bag. I trusted in my instincts. I was self-confident. Bad news! It was a huge flop! It reminds me of the story of Henry Ford who was asked how he came to be so successful. His response was that he became successful by making wise decisions. Then he was asked, "How did you learn to make wise decisions?" He responded, "From making stupid decisions." I don't doubt that we can all relate. And the most stupid decision we can ever make is to lean on our own understanding and not lean fully on God's understanding. Been there, done that!

SELF-TRUST – ABSOLUTE FOLLY

There is nothing accomplished for the Lord in our lives apart from the total adequacy of the Lord combined with the total inadequacy of ourselves. If the Bible makes anything clear, it is that self-trust and self-confidence are the marks of a fool. We read in Proverbs 28:26,

"He who trusts in his own heart is a fool...."

Jesus said in John 15:5,

"...for apart from me you can do nothing."

So much for the lie of self-confidence! All true confidence in the Christian life is "Christ-confidence." Christians are Christ-confident and not self-confident. How in the world can we have self-confidence when apart from Christ we can do nothing? Oh my, it is so difficult to get Christians these days to think and talk like Christians and not to think and talk like Religious Humanists and even Secular Humanists. Self-confidence is another man-made couplet that has no foundation whatsoever in Scripture, and no place in the Christian life. But like dumb, humanized parrots we continue to repeat the vocabulary of humanism in the church, and we don't even realize what we are saying. Religious Humanism has not only permeated our ranks but our minds! It has made the religious more self-reliant than God-reliant. Disaster!

I have finally learned to totally lean and rely upon the wisdom and power of God. We never have to inform omniscience, and we never have to rejuvenate omnipotence. God alone knows what path we must take, and He alone has the power to keep us walking on it. Furthermore, you cannot do both, that is, lean on self and lean on God at the same time, as Religious Humanism would lead you to believe. Religious Humanism's schizophrenia at its worst!

Finally, believe in self? Trust in self? Are you kidding? That is the very thing that has turned the world into the vestibule of Hell. That is the very thing that God is ordering man not to do. The reason for not believing and trusting in self is profound. It is stated about the human heart in Jeremiah 17:9,

"The heart is more deceitful than all else and is desperately sick; who can understand it?"

Man in Religious Humanism is presented as fully trustworthy, just as CNN claims to be "America's Most Trusted Network." And if you believe that, I have a bridge in Brooklyn that I will sell to you cheap. Follow your heart? Trust your instincts? Believe in self? All of that is horrible advice. Why? Because the human heart is sicker and more deceitful than anything else in the entire world! It is the most fallacious and unreliable of all guidance systems.

Jeffrey Dahmer was easily one of the most demented and brutal serial murderers in the history of the United States. He trusted the notions and promptings of his heart and followed his own sin-sick mind. He once said, "I lived the idea of evolution, and that there was no God. That made all morality meaningless and all my actions relative."

It was a love-sick Susan Smith who let her car slide into the lake with her four year old and two year old boys strapped in the back seat. She thought that she would be more attractive to the man she loved and so desperately wanted, if she was childless. I am sure that Susan Smith would have said, "At the time I thought it was the right thing to do." Man can do anything that he sets his mind to!? You can say that again. Signed by Oswald, Ray, Sirhan, the 9/11 terrorists and hosts of other sin-sick maniacs!

RELIGIOUS HUMANISM'S OTHER MANTRA – SELF-ESTEEM

Closely allied with the "Self-Helpers" and the "Self-Believers" are the "Self-Esteemers." Heading the list of modern self-esteem crusaders is Robert Schuller as embodied in his book *Self Esteem: The New Reformation.* What an astounding title for a book, namely, to link the concept of "Reformation" to "Self-Esteem!" That book is easily one of the worse distortions of Christianity I have ever read.

The 16th century Reformation was desperately needed because of the Roman Catholic Church's high estimate of man as being able to save himself by good works. It was that very elevated idea of man that corrupted Roman Catholic Church doctrine and practice, as well as marginalized the cross of Christ. Martin Luther and the reformers have already fought this battle. They brought us out of human self-esteem to Divine grace-esteem. Now the battle must be fought all over again. The dog has returned to his vomit.

Rick Miesel and John Beardsley in their website "Biblical Discernment Ministries" state, "He (Schuller) ascribes man's resistance to grace to a lost sense of self-worth... (Now quoting Schuller): **'EVERY HUMAN BEING MUST BE TREATED WITH RESPECT; SELF-ESTEEM IS HIS SACRED RIGHT.'**"(7) Of course we are to treat everyone including ourselves with respect. That is a no-brainer! But now to the real issues here!

First, the wife-abuser would agree with Schuller to be sure. It is an utterly common phenomenon for a man who has been apprehended after years of senseless cruelty, to look at the social worker or psychologist with an expression of only mild dismay and made the comment, "Hey, I know what you're thinking, but that wasn't me out there, not like me at all. She taunted me into doing what I did. I'm a caring type of guy. Anyway it's over now, and I've got to get on with my life." Nobody is guilty in prison, and no one is bad by nature. Everyone deserves respect.

Self-esteem is the key couplet today in churches where worship services and prayers of confession have been destigmatized by removing all guilt and guilt oriented references. As in, "Lord, we approach Thy throne of grace having committed acts which we do heartily acknowledge must be difficult for Thee to understand. Nevertheless, we do beseech Thee to postpone judgment and to give Thy faithful servants the benefit of the doubt until such time as we are able to answer all questions fully and clear our reputations in Heaven. Amen."

Second, man resists God and His gracious gifts of salvation and forgiveness not because he thinks so lowly of himself, but because he thinks so highly and haughtily of himself. The only people who are touched by and cherish the grace of God are those who can say with the Apostle Paul in Ephesians 3:8,

"To me, the very least of all saints, this grace was given...."

God's grace according to Paul can only be given to the least self-esteemers, not to the highest self-esteemers. If anybody learned that big time, Paul did, who before his conversion thought himself totally worthy of God's favor and blessings, and was continually having self-esteem celebrations. Furthermore, the male sex as contrasted with the female has great difficulty saying these five things – I don't know, I was wrong, I need help, I'm afraid, and I'm sorry. Paul as Saul was "Mr. I Can Do No Wrong."

Third, Religious Humanism's major concern is always rights. The Religious Humanist is always thinking and saying, "I've got rights – read me my rights." Self-esteem is here called a sacred right! Read us our rights! Claiming our rights! God, I demand my rights! Sounds exactly like the world. Human rights! Religious Humanism's message is about rights to the deserving. Christianity's message is about graciously bestowed gifts to the undeserving.

Of course we as Christians have our rights, to begin with John 1:12,

"But as many as received Him, to them He gave the right to become children of God, even to those who believe in His name."

However, even the fact that we are as believers called the children of God is graciously given to us. Through faith in Jesus we have the right to forgiveness, the right to not have a past, and the right to an eternal and glorious future. But all of our rights are based on what Christ graciously did for us on the cross. Religious Humanism goes to God and demands its rights. Christianity bows down beseeching and thanking God for His grace. Religious Humanism goes from rights to rights. Christianity goes from grace to grace. (John 1:16) All that the Lord bestows upon us are gracious privileges. That is what the Christian's rights are – gracious privileges. Amazing Grace versus Religious Rights!

That would be the day when I go to God and say, "Look here God, I demand my rights." The last person I read about doing that was the self-righteous, obnoxious elder son in Luke 15 who made it clear that he thought it was his right to have a party held in his own honor and not a party in honor of his long-lost loser brother who suddenly shows up on the doorstep.

Fourth, self-esteem is not the sacred issue in Christianity. Esteeming others and above all esteeming God are the central and sacred issues of Christianity. We are not commanded to highly esteem ourselves, but to highly esteem others, which by the way takes tons of Divine grace, how well we know. (Romans 12:3) Man's universal tendency is to over-esteem self, and to under-esteem others. God's grace to man is given for self-humbling, not for self-exalting. It takes a lot of grace to humble one's self. It takes a lot of gall to exalt one's self. When someone is high on self, he will be low on others, including God. That is why we read in Philippians 2:3,

"...let each of you regard one another as more important than himself."

Fifth, we have saved the most important point till now! Religious Humanism teaches: "Self-esteem is man's sacred right." Christian-ity teaches: "God-esteem is man's sacred duty." If we don't get that, we get nothing! So the Psalmist says in Psalm 99:5,

"Exalt the Lord our God, and worship at His footstool; holy is He."

End of story! Who receives the highest esteem here? Very obvious! The holy God! God gets the throne! Man gets the footstool. God receives the worship. Man does the worshipping. Religious Humanism is forever tripping over the footstool as it clumsily clamors its way to the throne of self-exaltation and self-worship. Religious Humanism is inebriated on the 100% alcohol of self-esteem. They send pictures of themselves – to themselves! Religious Humanists are staggering around in a world of "Selfaholics." So let's toast with our wine glasses and have another toast to ourselves. More Religious Humanism blow and show!

NOT ESTEEMNG SELF – THE CORE OF SIN

Hang on now, you haven't heard anything yet! So sacred is man's self-esteem in the mind of Religious Humanism that it actually goes so far as to teach that not to have a high self-estimate is the very essence of sin. Yes, you have read correctly! "Biblical Discernment Ministries" on their webpage entitled, *Robert Schuller, Quotes From Self-Esteem: The New Reformation*, states, "Schuller's theology is nothing but dressed up humanism – religious humanism. Religious Humanism is much worse than Secular Humanism because of the religious language used to convey the message…What is Sin? (Quoting Schuller) **'THE CORE OF ORIGINAL SIN…IT COULD BE CONSIDERED AN INNATE INABILITY TO ADEQUATELY VALUE OURSELVES. LABEL IT A 'NEGATIVE SELF-IMAGE.'"(8)** If you can fathom it, one thing clearly emerges is that original sin at the core is the lack of self-esteem. Sin according to Religious Humanism is a negative self-image!

Japan has Mt. Fuji. Religious Humanism has mountains of phooey. This is the tallest one of all. We could well call it "Mount Phooey." This is the monster of absurdities. Mind you, we are told here that not to esteem ourselves is not only sin, but it is the core of sin. Now you are at the summit of Mt. Phooey! To declare that the core of sin is the lack of self-esteem makes sin essentially a human matter and human offense against the human self. Sin then is primarily what man does against himself, not against God. Jesus likewise then died for sins committed not first of all against God, but for sins that man committed against himself.

However, Jesus did not die to reconcile us to ourselves. He died to reconcile us to God. (II Corinthians 5:20) Huge! If you will, Religious Humanism is about getting right with ourselves. Christianity is about getting right with God. Religious Humanism's definition of sin is a complete distortion of Biblical truth.

The fact is that all sin is ultimately against God. All sin is an offense against Divinity. No sin ultimately or at its core is against humanity! When David had committed adultery with Bathsheba and murdered Uriah, he does not in the least confess to God that he sinned against Bathsheba, Uriah, or himself for that matter. When he finally was brought to confession by the prophet Nathan, he cried out to God that he had sinned against Him and Him alone. He states in Psalm 51:4,

"Against Thee, Thee only, I have sinned …."

Was David wrong? No! Not in the least! Read it strong! Shout it out –
THEE ONLY! Christianity! The reason that he committed adultery with
Bathsheba was not because he lacked esteem of himself or Bathsheba. He did it
because he lacked esteem for the holiness of God. The reason that he committed
the murder of Uriah was not that he lacked esteem of himself or of that mighty
and faithful soldier. He committed murder because he did not in those moments
hold the God of life in high and holy reverence. The reason abortionists kill
babies is not because they do not esteem babies, though they do not. No, they
murder babies because they do not esteem the Giver of life.

That is what makes sin so dark, because it is committed against perfect light –
God! That is what makes sin so hateful, because it is committed against perfect
love – God! That is what makes sin so hideous, because it is committed against
perfect holiness – God! The Biblical truth is that the core of sin is lack of God-
esteem!

Religious Humanism sweeps aside the Apostle Paul's definition of sin as well.
Sin according to Paul is falling short of the glory of God. Romans 3:23 states,

> **"For all have sinned and fall short of the glory of God."**

Romans 3:23 does not say,

> **"For all have sinned and fall short of the glory of self."**

The Bible teaches that sin robs God of His glory. Religious Humanism
teaches that sin robs man of his glory. And by the same token, then when we sin,
we should ask ourselves for forgiveness and not God. Had enough?

I AM, I AM, I AM – RAH, RAH, RAH

Religious Humanism is a self-festival. All that's missing is Lawrence Welk's
bubble machine. It is 99 and 99/100% self. The rest is God. Christianity is a
Christ-festival. It is 100% God, with no self. The Apostle Paul never celebrates
himself, but only and always and forever the Christ who lives in him. In fact,
Paul considered himself to no longer be alive. He had been crucified with Christ.
The risen and reigning Christ living within him had become his total life. He
wrote in Galatians 2:20,

> **"…and it is no longer I who live, but Christ lives in me.…"**

That is why Paul never celebrates himself, but only Christ in him. He would

22

call self-celebration a pile of dung. (Philippians 3:8 KJV) Strong smelling stuff indeed! When people celebrate themselves, all they are really doing according to Paul is creating quite a stink.

When I was yet unsaved, I gloated in and celebrated myself regularly. It is even possible for preachers to preach for their own glory and not God's glory. I have done my share of that. But now I would feel like a heathen celebrating myself. I have no incentive whatsoever to celebrate me. I can't even get started now! None! It turns me off. Dullsville! Oh sure, we celebrate birthdays, anniversaries and the like. But when people celebrate and congratulate me on my birthday, I have to chuckle to myself. I didn't begin my life, I haven't sustained my life, and I won't complete my life. It has been all God from the beginning and will be God all the way to the end! Congratulate Him! Celebrate Him on my birthday and at my home-going! Don't celebrate me! Or as Acts 17:28 says,

"for in Him we live and move and exist…."

I am decreasing, and Jesus is increasing. (John 3:30) I am just starting to get the hang of it. Religious Humanists are also telling their congregations that one of the best ways to build up one's self-esteem and self-celebration is to repeat the "M" sound over and over again. As "Let Us Reason Ministries" points out, "Schuller writes: **THE MOST EFFECTIVE MANTRAS EMPLOY THE "M" SOUND. YOU CAN GET THE FEEL OF IT BY REPEATING THE WORDS 'I AM, I AM' MANY TIMES OVER…TRANSCEN-DENTAL MEDITATION OR TM… IS NOT A RELIGION NOR IS IT NECESSARILY ANTI-CHRISTIAN.**'" (Mike Oppenheimer then comments on this) "This is what people in the occult do (such as I AM groups like the Ballard's or Elizabeth Claire Prophet). TM is religious and is Hinduism, it is promoted by the Maharishi who is Hindu, and leads to union with the Hindu God Brahma and to eternal separation from Christ."(9)

Now to the issue at hand – the "M" sound stuff. Just keep on repeating the "I AM" mantra several times each day. Verbally charm yourself into an intense self-awareness and elevated self- estimation by walking around the house repeating this incantation over and over again, "I AM, I AM, I AM." It is all based upon the trinity of Religious Humanism – Me, Myself and I. There it is! Be your own cheerleader with the self-cheer of Religious Humanism which goes like this, "I am, I am, I am – rah, rah, rah – sis, boom, bah."

Religious Humanism's self-refrain sounds like the old Campbell Soup jingo! I loved that little ditty when I was a boy. Still do as a matter of fact! It reminds me of my mother. I remember thinking that she composed it. Toasted cheese sandwiches and Campbell's tomato soup were some of her favorite delicacies! It was "MMM" good! It still is! Some of you are too young to remember how it went. Some of you remember it well. This soup promo for many years was very successful also because of the "M" sound in the catchy phraseology, "M'mm Good, M'mm Good, That's What Campbell Soups Are, M'mm Good." To paraphrase and spoil the jingle with Religious Humanism's self-mania thrown in, it would go like this, "I'mm Good, I'mm Good, That's What I'mm, I'mm Good."

This entire "I Am" obsession is quite the opposite of the "M" sound in Christianity! It is totally unchristian! The Judeo-Christian celebration is not about "MEEE" and the fact that "I AMMM." Not at all! The "M" sound of Biblical faith is found in Exodus 3:14,

> **"And God said to Moses, 'I AM WHO I AM'; and He said, 'Thus you shall say to the sons of Israel, I AM has sent me to you.'"**

Now we are home again! No place like home! "MMM" good! Christianity is not the celebration of "I Am," but of "THE **GREAT I AM.**"

When God calls Himself the "I Am," He is telling us that "He Is, Always Has Been, And Always Will Be." As Revelation 1:4 puts it,

> **"...from Him who is and who was and who is to come...."**

He is the essence of immortality and eternal life. In fact, He is life, and no one can say "I am" apart from the fact that "God Is." Everyone and everything is only because He is! I think of that each time I see a baby or a little tike being carried or pushed around in a stroller by daddy or mommy in a shopping mall. Daddy is one of the reasons that the cute little bundle is. That is a picture of my Heavenly Father and me. – "I am" because "He is!" Of course, as in human life, so in Religious Humanism, the little human gets all of the attention, and daddy is just along for the ride.

Religious Humanism is centered in and focused upon "I AMMM." Christianity is centered in and focused upon "THE GREAT I AM." Religious Humanism is about self-esteem. Christianity is about God-esteem. By causing people to fixate upon "I Am," Religious Humanists cause people to lose sight of the "**GREAT I AM.**" You can't be full of "I AMMM" and "**THE GREAT I AM**" at the same time! NNNOOO!

RELIGIOUS HUMANISM'S MANTRA – I AM WORTHY

"Alright, enough already," some are saying. No, we haven't seen anything yet. As if things aren't distorted enough by all of this Religious Humanistic I AMMM madness, many Religious Humanists with their ego-centered doctrines are also preaching to people this: "**IT IS A TERRIBLE SIN FOR ANYONE TO SAY ABOUT HIMSELF, 'I AM UNWORTHY.'**" The world would completely agree, as we hear and see products being sold on TV with the words, "You are worth it girl," or, "I am worth it."

"Biblical Discernment Ministries" states, "As one noted reviewer of *Self Esteem: The New Reformation* (Word 1982) said, 'He (Schuller) sets man rather than God in the forefront…and thinks that we should tell sinners that they are worthy rather than unworthy…'" (Then quoting Robert Schuller): "**SIN IS PSYCHOLOGICAL SELF-ABUSE…THE MOST SERIOUS SIN IS THE ONE THAT CAUSES ME TO SAY, 'I AM UNWORTHY.' I HAVE NO CLAIM TO DIVINE SONSHIP IF YOU SEE ME AT MY WORST. FOR ONCE A PERSON BELIEVES HE IS AN UNWORTHY SINNER, IT IS DOUBTFUL IF HE CAN REALLY HONESTLY ACCEPT THE SAVING GRACE GOD OFFERS IN JESUS CHRIST.**"(10)

First, as we have already seen, sin is not psychological self-abuse. Religious Humanism is secular psychology with a God- twist. No, sin is spiritual God-abuse. Here we go again! Religious Humanists always have man so sickeningly prioritized that they teach that when we sin we are abusing ourselves, not God. For crying out loud, whose will are we sinning against, God's or ours? Religious Humanism has messed us up so bad psychologically that we can't even think straight about who we are dishonoring.

Second and more to the point! The most serious sin, mind you! And what is that? It is when anyone says, "I am unworthy." Can you begin to fathom the twisting and the warping of Christianity by Religious Humanism? Just another attempt on man's part to hide his sins with fig leaves! If man was truly worthy, Jesus would not have had to come and die as the totally worthy One for the totally unworthy ones, the just for the unjust, the holy for the unholy! This teaching of human worthiness makes Jesus' entire redemptive mission superfluous. It turns the cross of Calvary into a sham, for man then has no shame! Religious Humanism totally destroys the Gospel of Jesus Christ.

The truth is that the most deadly sin that Saul the Pharisee was infected with was his conviction that he was super-worthy. Jesus can't save people like that. The world is full of them, and now Religious Humanists are trying to fill the church with them, too. So the Lord had to knock Saul off from his self-worthy pedestal, blind him, and drill into Saul's oversized head just how unworthy he really was. Then and only then could Saul accept Christ and become Paul!

Saul the Pharisee brings to mind the story of the arrogant churchman who was trying to impress upon the young minds of a class of boys and girls the importance of leading a Christian life. The self-worthy man asked them while standing very erect and smiling down at them, "Why do people call me a Christian, children?" After a pause, a shrill little voice said, "Because they don't know you." Out of the mouths of babes!

Third, the total opposite of Religious Humanism's assertion is this thoroughly Biblical truth: "The most serious sin is the one that causes me to say, 'I am worthy.' For once a person believes that he is a worthy one, it is doubtful if not impossible that he can really honestly accept the saving grace that God offers in Jesus Christ." Why the most serious? Because walking around self-flattering oneself by chanting "I am worthy" makes man's sin-sickness harder to cure if not incurable. It is this self-worthy pretense that men will grasp at to their dying day in case there is a God that they have to stand before one day. They think that their self-worth and self- merit will make them fit to enter Heaven and fellowship with God forever. To call men to chant, "I Am Worthy" is to give them a false and damning hope. Stop it!

Fourth, Religious Humanism totally distorts the Bible when it teaches that man should never be called an unworthy sinner. Religious Humanism is putting an entirely opposite and false spin on Christianity, given the fact that all of us must confess that we are sinners, that we daily have sin in our lives, and that we need constant forgiveness to our dying day. (I John 1:8-9) What Religious Humanism then leaves itself embarrassed by are crazy oxymora such as "Worthy Sinners," or "Holy Hellians." The truth is, the only thing that we are worthy of is condemnation and eternal judgment.

A photographer took several pictures of a very proud woman. She complained to him that the photographs didn't do her justice. He replied, "To be honest with you, you don't need justice, you need mercy." Jesus mercifully became our unworthiness and shame that we might have His worthiness and honor. That is why the anthem of Heaven recorded in Revelation 5:12 will be raised up forever,

"…**Worthy is the Lamb that was slain**…."

Nowhere do we read of the song being sung in Heaven,

"Worthy are those for whom the Lamb was slain."

Even though that is the "Magnum Opus" of Religious Humanism – to make man appear worthy and wonderful!

MAN-CENTERED THEOLOGY

One of the most corrupting influences that Religious Humanism has had within modern Christendom is when it places man at the center of life, and God therefore on the periphery. Some brands of Religious Humanism actually believe, and hang on to your seat now, that one of the great errors of historic Christian theology is that it has been "God-centered" and not "Man-centered." Can you fathom that? I cannot! In Christianity, God is the Alpha and the Omega. In Religious Humanism, man is the alpha and the omega.

This is actually being taught in Protestant churches today! "Biblical Discernment Ministries" states: "He (Schuller) redefines the terminology of the Faith so as to produce an entirely different and false theology... (Then quoting Robert Schuller): **'CLASS-ICAL THEOLOGY HAS ERRED IN ITS INSISTENCE THAT THEOLOGY BE 'GOD-CENTERED,' NOT 'MAN-CENTERED.'"** (11) In other words, historic Christianity has always been at fault in its consistent and unvarying theocentricity. It needs to become anthropocentric. The moment you read something this bewildering, it is a screaming warning to you not to go one step further in that direction.

First of all, the phrase "Man-Centered Theology" is another Religious Humanism blue-ribbon oxymoron. If it is man-centered it is not and cannot be theology. Rather, it is then "Anthropology" or "Humanology" or "Manology." To assert that theology can or must be man-centered requires a huge "Apology" to God. Why do you and I call it theology in the first place? Because it is God-centered and God-permeated! The Greek noun "Theos" means "God." If you will, we call it theology because it is "Godology" and not "Manology."

The Creator is being more and more replaced by the creature. This is exactly what has happened in major churches and universities of America, even those that started out being theocentric such as Princeton University. Princeton in its origin was closely aligned with the Presbyterian Church. Humanism has replaced Theism, and man has replaced God, to the point that Princeton appointed Peter Singer as the chairman of the Bio- Ethics Department! Peter Singer, an avowed atheist, believes that apes are persons, and that parents should have the right to terminate a child's life up to 30 days after birth if the child is deemed to be too drastically retarded, deformed or handicapped. Remove God-centeredness as the guiding principle in education and everything goes Hellward and not Heavenward.

Second, it was man-centeredness in Adam and Eve's thinking that turned their lives into death and earth into Hell's vestibule. Man came down with the feverish myself-malaria and died. If Adam and Eve would have remained theocentric and not anthropocentric, Paradise would have never been lost, they would have not been tossed out of the Garden of Eden, and humanity would not have been corrupted. Instead, they focused upon themselves and what they wanted to become – God-equals, rather than God's servants.

It was man-centeredness, i.e. man turning in upon himself that messed the world up so bad to begin with. Man-centeredness never improves the human condition, it only worsens it. Man-centered theology is about as smart as the Republicans in the 2008 presidential campaign centering upon John McCain's "Joe The Plumber" and Sarah Palin's "Joe Six Pack" as their hope for victory. Joe-man just couldn't get the job done, no matter how many pipes he fixed or how many six packs he drank. The Republicans totally forsook God-centeredness for Joe-centeredness, and the Republican Party now has become so secular that atheists can easily vote Republican. The Republican Party has lost its identity and its Judeo-Christian core values. It has lost its Godly voice as has much of the contemporary church, and both had better find it back quickly.

Third, propounding a man-centered theology produces a religion which keeps man childish. You know how children are, don't you? Sure you do! They want to be the sole center of attraction, and when they are not, they scream and throw temper tantrums so that they can be the epicenter of their world and have their own way again. To put man at the center of his own belief system keeps man spiritually infantile, and turns the church into a screaming nursery of terrible two year olds. Most church fights and splits are rooted in man being at the center of his life and not God. It is becoming more and more noxious as we dig around in the diaper pail of this man-centered, childish Religious Humanism. Religious Humanism smells of dirty diapers on 40 year-olds.

SELF-ESTEEM – HORIZONTAL OR VERTICAL

The fact is that all of man's worth is centered in God and not centered in himself. Critically important stuff! We must state it again, namely that true self-esteem and self-worth do not come from one's relationship with or estimate of self, but from one's relationship with God.

More exactly, it is God's love for man, not man's love for man, or man's love for himself, that will alone enable man to live a self-respecting life in the midst of so much horizontal disrespect and rejection. Because we know that we are infinitely loved by God, it makes no difference that our picture will never be on the cover of *Time* magazine. It is perfectly okay that Charles Gibson on "World News Tonight" will never announce our name as person of the week. Few if ever are invited to dine at the White House with the president. So what! None of that matters. What alone matters is that the God of the whole universe loves us and holds us dear in the center of His heart. We are special people because God tells us in Jeremiah 31:3,

"…I have loved you with an everlasting love…."

Allow me to illustrate to you how true lasting self-esteem is realized. You may recall the time when Jesus and His disciples were going down to Jerusalem and they passed through Samaria. It is all recorded in Luke 9:51-56. There was a real problem between the Jews and the Samaritans. Samaritans were half-breed Jews who were the offspring of a Jewish parent who had married outside of Judaism. Simply stated, they were hated by the pure-blooded Jews and vice versa. Samaritans spit at Jews, and when the Jews went home, they would wash their clothes if they had touched a Samaritan.

It was now nightfall as Jesus and His disciples were approaching Samaria. They were understandably tired, needing a bath and rest, and in those days they rightfully were counting on eastern hospitality to provide them with both. It was cultural and customary then. Jesus sent some of His disciples ahead. They came to the first door and knocked, and a Samaritan opened the door and then slammed it in their faces. John, who had a testy temper, didn't need much to set him off. I can hear him as he turns to James and says, "Did you see that? Why, that half-breed!" Apparently they knocked on a lot of doors in Samaria, and every door was shut to them. It was insulting not only, but it was out and out discrimination.

James and John, known also as "The Sons of Thunder," had lightening shooting out of their eyes. Wherever they went they were like walking bottles of nitroglycerine that would blow up if you bumped or rubbed them the wrong way. They went back to Jesus and in Luke 9:54 asked Him the following,

"…Lord, do you want us to command fire to come down from heaven and consume them?"

Man oh man they were hot, and they wanted Jesus to make it even hotter for the Samaritans. They wanted to turn them into deep-fried Samaritans. Instant crispy-critter half-breeds!

What can explain James and John wanting to microwave the Samaritans? Simple really! This is what happens when man is at the center of his life. You see, James and John were at the center of their universe. Sons of thunder always are. They were the issue! And when man makes himself the central focus, then all doors must open to him, all people must serve him, and all circumstances must come into alignment with his demands. If one or all of these do not cooperate, then it is that man blows a gasket, and like James and John, he wants the non-worshippers of himself to be torched on the spot. Man must never be center stage, for he will always blow up the theater and everyone in it for lack of applause.

But we must learn the even greater lesson in all of this. Jesus' self-esteem did not depend on the treatment or the opinion of Him by the Samaritans or by anyone else on earth. The self-esteem in Jesus was always to be found in Who He was in intimate relationship with – His Heavenly Father. He was God's only begotten and beloved Son, and that was all the self-esteem and self-worth He would ever need. What more could He desire than the voice of the Heavenly Father at His baptism declaring out of Heaven in Matthew 3:17,

"...This is My Beloved Son, in whom I am well-pleased."

Boy would that make my day, my life, my eternity!

To be loved and complimented by the Heavenly Father and God of eternity, why, that would pretty much do it for all of us! Self-esteem unlimited! Frankly, when we are esteemed by the infinite God, who needs the esteem of finite man?

So Jesus literally caused James and John to drop their blow torches when He said to them in Luke 9:55,

"...You do not know what kind of spirit you are of."

I do! It was the spirit of Religious Humanism! It was the spirit of man-centeredness and not Christ-centeredness. When man is central, every-thing gets out of focus. When God is central, everything is in focus.

Tony Campolo tells of when he was asked to be a counselor in a junior high camp. Tony relates that a junior high kid's concept of a good time is picking on other kids. In Tony's experience, at this particular camp, they picked on a little boy who was suffering from cerebral palsy. His name was Billy. As Billy walked across the camp with his uncoordinated body, the other kids would line up and imitate his grotesque movements. Tony watched one day as Billy was asking other kids for direction. "Which...way...is...the... craft...shop?" he stammered with his mouth contorted. The other boys mimicked him in that same awful stammer, "It's... over...there...Billy."

The shamefulness of it all reached its lowest level on a Thursday morning when it was Billy's cabin's turn to be in charge of camp devotions. Tony wondered what would happen because he found out that they had appointed Billy to be the speaker. Tony knew that they just wanted to get Billy up there to make fun of him. As Billy dragged his way to the front, you could hear the giggles rolling over the crowd. It took him almost five minutes to say seven words. The words were these, "Jesus…loves…me…and…I…love…Jesus." When Billy finished, there was dead silence. Tony looked over his shoulder and saw junior high boys weeping all over the place. (12) It was more than enough for Billy. Jesus loved Billy and Billy loved Jesus. Jesus' love was all the self-esteem and self-worth that Billy could ever want. Billy was centered in Jesus and not in himself. Many of those boys accepted Jesus as their Lord and Savior that day.

It doesn't matter what bloodline you came from, how smart you are, or how skinny or fat you might be. It doesn't matter whether you are Jew or Greek, slave or free, male or female, black or white, Dutch or Hispanic. It doesn't matter if your degree is from Harvard or Podunk U. What alone matters is that we are loved and held dear in the heart of God. So we read in I John 3:1,

**"See how great a love the Father has bestowed upon us, that
we should be called children of God…."**

God's beloved children! How great is that? Who could ask for any more self-esteem than that?

SELF-LOVE –THE GREAT ENDTIME DANGER

The themes of self-enablement, self-belief, self-esteem and self-centralization keep coming up over and over again in Religious Humanism like cows chewing their cuds. But each time these self-enamored themes surface, they grow into other unbiblical self-fetishes and self-exaggerations. It was bound to happen, and that is another Religious Humanism mantra – self-love. It is the unending refrain of Religious Humanism. It sells books like hotcakes as well as packs pews and seminars.

"Let Us Reason Ministries" writes quoting Robert Schuller: "**SELF-LOVE IS A CROWNING SENSE OF SELF-WORTH…LOVE YOURSELF OR DIE – PHYSICALLY AND SPIRITUALLY.**"(13) What we have here is again just another Religious Humanism. It is not even close to being a Biblicism. Not even warm.

First, as we have already noted, God's love for man is the crowning sense of all self-worth, not his love for himself or others' love for him. It is more than obvious that professional athletes these days love themselves enormously. Lebron James of the Cleveland Cavaliers in the NBA is atypical and loves being called

King James. Every slam-dunk is another self-coronation as afterwards he often stands before his loyal subjects and welcomes their worship and applause with outstretched arms. Self-love and self-coronations are a way of life for those who are the sports gods in America. I must confess that Lebron isn't quite as in love with himself and self-coronating as Terrel Owens of the Buffalo Bills in the NFL. It makes me vomit.

No, God's people don't walk around in life blowing kisses at themselves and having self-coronation parties every day. They are crowned with love from someone much higher. We read of this glorious love-coronation in Psalm 103:4 where the Psalmist says about God and His children,

"...Who (God) crowns you with lovingkindness and compassion."

Crowned with love by God Himself, the King of the Universe! How is that for regal living? Any other crown in comparison, including self-crowns, makes us look like Burger King. Religious Humanism believes in the self-coronation of self-love. Christianity believes in the Divine coronation of God's love.

Second, love self or die? Are you kidding me? That is not the Gospel of Christianity. It is the gospel of Religious Humanism. The Bible teaches and the fact is that apart from God's love we are already dead in every way. And loving ourselves more than loving God killed each one of us.

The Prodigal Son in Luke 15 ran away from his dad for some wine, women and song fling-dings. When he came to the end of himself, and came to the realization that he was about as good as a dead man, he went back to the loving arms of his father who said about his returned son that he was dead but now had begun to live again. (Luke 15:32) Before, the son had taken his life into his own hands and died, but now experiencing the love of his dad he was alive again.

Dad then threw a love-party for him that made him feel like a king I tell you. That is true of all of us when we come back home to Abba God through the blood of Jesus Christ. That is the believer's crowning moment and it lasts forever. There is only room on the believer's head for God's love-crown and none else. You haven't been crowned until you have been love-crowned by God. Every other crown in comparison is a dud.

Third, let us make this clear as day! The love of self is not even close to being central in Christianity. Love for God is central in Christianity. Dietrich Bonhoeffer was a German theologian who was executed by Hitler during World War II. Years later, one of his students recalled the last classroom session he had with his teacher. Bonhoeffer, knowing that his arrest was imminent, asked his students a question that took them by surprise. He asked them, "Do you love Jesus?" This is not the typical question one hears in a modern seminary classroom today. Today's seminary classrooms are reserved for more academic issues. (14)

Someone might still respond, "I agree with the Religious Humanists and their strong emphasis on self-love. After all, God did command us to love ourselves!" Did God command us to love ourselves? True, God nowhere tells us to hate ourselves. He does imply that we should love ourselves. In fact, as we shall see in Jesus' words, self-love is presented by our Lord as the pre-condition in His children's lives for the expression of love for others. One cannot love his neighbor with God's love if he despises and abuses himself.

But we should also note this, that God never commanded us to love ourselves. Never! Self-love is the keynote of modern psychology, and has become the main theme of Religious Humanism. Religious Humanism marries secular psychology with theology. The result is self-love in a gross imbalance and over-emphasis. In Religious Humanism self-love is taken to extremes and becomes a narcissistic personality disorder.

We are commanded to love our enemies. (Matthew 5:44) Husbands are commanded to love their wives. (Ephesians 5:25) We are commanded to love our neighbors. (Matthew 22:39) God only implies self-love, no more, no less. What was it that Jesus said? Jesus did say in Matthew 22:39,

"...**You shall love your neighbor as yourself**."

The emphasis in that command is on our love for our neighbors. It is not an emphasis on self-love. Because God knows something only too well! God understands human nature's obsession with itself, and that self-love inherently abounds. It sticks so close to human nature, that neither religion nor regeneration can shake off its excess.

We live in a self-centered, self-absorbed, self-love world where everything is designed to cater to self, to meet self's wants, and to meet them lavishly. A self-centered, self-infatuated world has turned itself into a sickening, self-pleasing orgy. It is this pervasively self-centered, self-serving, self-satisfying philosophy that has turned the world into a selfish mess.

Now the church under this false ideology is being turned into a selfish mess, too. I know that this is happening when I hear church people telling themselves and others to buy this and do that and travel there because they have it coming to them. I can't count how often we have been told by church folks that we should buy that or travel there, because we have earned it, deserve it, have it coming to us, and that we must be good to ourselves for no one else will. El Puko!

God called such a world a dangerous place in which to live. He said in II Timothy 3:1-4,

> "But realize this, that in the last days difficult (dangerous) times will come. FOR MEN WILL BE LOVERS OF SELF, lovers of money, boastful, arrogant, revilers, disobedient to parents, ungrateful, unholy, <u>unloving</u>, irreconcilable, malicious gossips, without self-control, brutal, haters of good, ...lovers of pleasure, rather than lovers of God."

About as full and comprehensive a catalogue of sins that is found anywhere in the Bible. Could you not help but notice something glaringly obvious here? What is listed first as the causal factor for the end-time world being such a dangerous place to live in? Lovers of self! Having a love affair with self as the numero uno in our lives! From that condition flows all of the other horrors that have made life so precarious in this world today. IGM – I GOT MINE, no matter how much it hurts others.

The sin list that then follows in II Timothy 3:1-4 reads like the cast of characters from TV's recent hit series *The Sopranos*. Unholy! Unloving! Without self-control! Brutal! Treacherous! According to God, being lovers of self makes people unloving. Touche! In short, the entire foul list of rot in II Timothy 3 spews forth from the main culprit, the "Mafia Don" at the head of the entire mafia family – Self-Love. Inflated and exaggerated self-esteem and self-love are the great strongholds of every conceivable and inconceivable evil, for by nature we over-value and over-love ourselves, and under-value and under-love others. The rest is sinful history in the raw.

Let's try to shed some light on this darkness, and then see if self-love is the answer to cause a new spiritual sunrise to dawn upon this end-time darkening earth. You may recall an unmarried young couple of the 1990s. I believe that both of them were 18 years of age, and they lived in the Northeastern United States. They had a baby out of wedlock who they didn't want. The plea of the unwed mother to the unwed father after the baby was born was this, "Just get rid of IT." The young dad admitted to having put the baby in a plastic container and throwing IT in a garbage bin. The noise that he heard was apparently the crack of the child's head hitting the inside of the garbage container. The young man was sentenced to a hardly noticeable two years because he cooperated with the court. The young woman was sentenced to a mere two and half years.

All of this is what II Timothy 3 is talking about. Self-love affairs propelled this young couple into protecting their self-convenience, self-reputations, and self-status in their community at the expense of a precious newborn baby who was their own flesh and blood.

To summarize, Religious Humanism prioritizes the message of self-love. Christianity prioritizes the message of love for God and love for our neighbors. It begs the legend of a teacher who had a strange experience while walking through an orchard on a windy day. Coming to a fence which divided the grove from an adjoining forest, he imagined hearing the different trees of the forest talking to each other. Boastfully a maple tree said to a nearby fruit tree, "Why don't your leaves rustle in the breeze like ours so that you can be heard from a distance?" The fruit tree replied, "We don't need that useless fluttering to draw attention to ourselves. Our fruit speaks for us!"(15) People will know that we are Christians not by our self-love. That is the fluster and bluster of Religious Humanism. They will know that we are Christians by our love for God and our fellow man. That is authentic Christianity.

JESUS NEVER CALLED ANYONE A SINNER

The conflict between Religious Humanism and Christianity here reaches its sharp antithesis again. Religious Humanists do not want to preach about the fact that man, even redeemed man, is a sinner. They do not want to refer to man as a sinner, period! Candy-coated churches where the pastor says to those who have sinned their brains out, "Hey, don't get down on yourselves, I used to do some of those same things myself." Oh my, now we all feel better, because the pastor preaches, "I'm okay, you're okay."

I have actually been in churches where the pastor pledged to the congregation that he would never refer to people in the church service as sinners. I loved candy as a child, too, but eventually it rotted my teeth. These preachers are going to rot people's souls with their candy-coated preaching. More than that, to abandon the words sin and sinner will not only accomplish nothing in the getting rid of sin. It will make it worse as we enable sinners to hide from their sin. You can take the words sin and sinner out of your preaching, but that doesn't mean that sin will then be taken out of people's hearts. But horrifyingly this no-sinner preaching is common now, and the very heart of Christianity and the Gospel of our Lord Jesus Christ are being corrupted. Let us all be warned by the Word of God in Galatians 1:9,

"As we have said before, so I say again now, if any man is

preaching to you a gospel contrary to that which you received, let him be accursed."

"Let Us Reason Ministries" observes: "To accept his (Robert Schuller) philosophy one would have to throw out the entire New Testament which focuses around Jesus Christ and His purpose for coming to redeem mankind from sin by His work on the cross…He (Robert Schuller) affirms that, '**JESUS NEVER CALLED A PERSON A SINNER**.'"(16) Religious Humanism tries to release man as a beautiful and innocent bird from the cruel cage of classical Christian theology. Why? Nothing complicated really. As the King James Version says in Psalm 36:2 about sinful man,

"For he flattereth himself in his own eyes…."

Men, even religious men, think of themselves more like doves than vultures. They think of man as mounting up to Heaven rather than someone who is spiraling downward into Hell. Of all of the self-couplets in Religious Humanism, self-knowledge is not one of them – the true knowledge of himself as a lost sinner. But God's Word describes man in exactly those terms.

Jesus told the parable of a Pharisee and a tax-gatherer who were both praying in the temple. As His parable unfolds, Jesus chooses carefully the word characterizations of the persons involved. Jesus calls them like He sees them! The Pharisee, who would have made a devout modern Religious Humanist, didn't really pray in the Temple. He gloated! Over what! Over himself! Read it, and it will nauseate you. He didn't even come close to calling himself a sinner. He would fit well in today's Religious Humanism churches. He congratulated himself to God that he was not like other men. It wasn't prayer at all, but instead it was just another big blow-hard Pharisee trumpeting and worshipping himself.

As Jesus tells the story, there was also a lowly tax-gatherer off in the corner of that same temple praying the self-demeaning prayer in Luke 18:13,

"…God, be merciful to me, the sinner."

"The Sinner" is what Jesus called him and had him calling himself. Jesus pictures this praying sinner as unable to lift his eyes to Heaven, as well as beating his breast in self-denunciation. In Religious Humanism, self-worthy braggarts blow their horns. In Christianity, unworthy sinners beat their breasts.

Did you also notice that Jesus in the parable had the publican referring to himself not only as a sinner, but as "The Sinner?" Definite article! As if he was the only sinner in the whole world. The Apostle Paul called himself the chief of sinners. For that matter, the Lord in His Word calls us sinners to our face again and again as we read in Romans 5:8,

"But God demonstrates His own love toward us, in that while we were yet sinners, Christ died for us."

We must remember, as shown earlier, that Robert Schuller was impacted most in his life by Norman Vincent Peale. Listen to what Norman Vincent Peale once said about human beings: "**THEY ARE INHERENTLY GOOD. THE BAD REACTIONS AREN'T BASIC. EVERY HUMAN BEING IS A CHILD OF GOD AND HAS MORE GOOD IN HIM THAN EVIL. BUT CIRCUMSTANCES AND ASSOCIATES CAN STEP UP THE BAD AND REDUCE THE GOOD. I'VE GOT GREAT FAITH IN THE ESSENTIAL FAIRNESS AND DECENCY – YOU MAY SAY THE ESSENTIAL GOODNESS OF THE HUMAN BEING.**"(17)

I was talking to a loving sister just the other day whose brother is in the tough teen years of puberty, and is struggling as most of us did with acne. The bully-boys in his class are taking full advantage of it, pushing him around while calling him "nerd" and "pizza face." But after all, that is what good little doobies do, isn't it? The essential goodness of man!

I disproved the essential goodness of little Bobby as a young boy when my buddies and I threw railroad-track stones at hoboes who had jumped off freight trains near our house and hid in the ditches. Of course, what others thought of us was that we were cute, nice little kids who threw stones into puddles and blew soap bubbles. The very same darlings who ran through sprinklers forced "tramps" to run for their lives lest we stone them to death. We turned their lives into Hell so we could get our demonic kicks. We were the same kids from "good" homes who were told not to play with matches and to be polite at all times to all people. The essential goodness of man!

God calls homosexuality an abomination. It has and is destroying marriage and family thereby ripping apart the very fabric of society. It is a plague upon the human race. President Obama by official presidential proclamation declared June 2009 as "Lesbian, Gay, Bisexual, and Transgender Pride Month." Obama states, "LGBT Americans have made, and continue to make, great and lasting contributions that continue to strengthen the fabric of American society." The essential goodness of man and the sanity of the current American presidency!

While we read Peale's statement about essentially good man, criminal minds are trying to figure out how to steel your identity and mine, as well as everything else we own. My wife and I had an old pontoon boat that we used for fishing which we enjoyed very much. We kept it parked near other boats, but at night crooks were constantly ripping off anything that was not locked down with chains. It became a battle of wits, but like squirrels they always found a way to get what they wanted. Very talented varmints indeed! And of course as in all things, some are more talented than others. Around us homes are constantly being broken into and pilfered. The essential goodness of man!

Then of course on the global-terrorism scale there are the training camps of Al Qaeda where terrorists train others in the fine arts of suicide bombing, kidnapping and beheading. Then they appear on Al Jazeera with their victims who later show up on TV hanging from a bridge somewhere minus their heads. Islamic maniacs train their children in suicide bombing schools, where the alma mater is, "Our blessings to you who fight at the gates of the enemy and knock on heaven's door with his skulls in your hands." The essential goodness of man!

Charlie was sitting around the lunch table with a group of his fellow workers, and he said to them, "You know, I have come to the conclusion that man is basically good. There is so much good in all of us." One of the workers looked at him and said, "You know Charlie, there has to be a lot of good in you, for so little has ever come out." Ouch! The basic goodness of man!

Religious Humanism's statement about the essential goodness of man contradicts the Bible, word for word and line for line. We read in Romans 3:15-16 about all men by nature,

"Their feet are swift to shed blood, destruction and misery are in their paths."

The Bible says this about human beings: **"THEY ARE INHERENLTY BAD. THEIR BAD REACTIONS ARE BASIC. EVERY HUMAN BEING IS A CHILD OF SATAN AND HAS MORE BAD IN HIM THAN GOOD. CIRCUMSTANCES AND ASSOCIATES CAN INFLAME THE BAD AND INCREASE IT."** And I might add, **"I'VE GOT NO FAITH IN THE MYTHICAL, ESSENTIAL FAIRNESS AND DECENCY – YOU MAY SAY THE FICTIONAL GOODNESS OF THE HUMAN BEING."**

Religious Humanists attempt to present sinners as "The Brady Bunch." Jesus didn't. Not even close! Religion cannot cover up the basic badness of man either. Mind you, in Matthew 23 Jesus renames the religious Pharisees, who thought that they were the crème de la crème not only of humanity but of the religious world, and refers to them by such scorching names as hypocrites, blind guides, fools, blind men, serpents, brood of vipers and killers. Christ's rap sheet for the religious leaders of His day! My, my, for them to have been called sinners would have been an upgrade! God have mercy! Rather than reflecting Heaven, they rivaled Hell.

"Biblical Discernment Ministries" states, "In 1984, 'Christ- ianity Today' editors examined Schuller's theology, and amazingly concluded that he is not a heretic, claiming that he believes all the 'fundamental' doctrines of traditional fundamentalism… (quoting Schuller): **'BUT POSITIVE CHRISTIANITY DOES NOT HOLD TO HUMAN DEPRAVITY, BUT TO HUMAN INABILITY**.'"(18) Wrong! Dead wrong! The Bible does not hold to human inability, but to human depravity. Man is not disabled, he is totally depraved. Totally depraved means totally corrupt! So Romans 3:12 says about all men by nature,

"…**there is none who does good, there is not even one**."

It is by the denial of the total corruption of man that Religious Humanists are corrupting modern Christianity. If you don't believe that, then *Modern Christianity Corrupted* is not your kind of book, and you had better instead pick up a copy of *I'm Okay-You're Okay*. Far better, read the Apostle Paul's words about himself in Romans 7:18,

"**For I know that nothing good dwells in me**…."

Notice he says, "Nothing good dwells IN me." If you are to really know man, you have to follow him into the secret room of his heart. Paul allows us in, and says you will absolutely find no good in here. Total depravity! That means that all men by nature are as proud as Satan, as false as Judas, and as hateful as Hitler. That is why we all have to be born again with a brand new righteous nature, by being made brand new creatures in Jesus Christ!

Wherever there is the denial of man as sinner, there will be an inescapable weakening of the need to preach Jesus as the Savior from sin. It is massively happening. We don't have to be theologians to figure that out. When man the sinner is characterized as worthy goodie-two-shoes, then both the sin and the savior concepts are neutralized. When the black ink on man's spiritual rap sheet is erased by modern-day Religious Humanism preachers, the precious blood of Jesus becomes a pale and anemic pink. Because of Religious Humanism preachers throughout the American church, the cross of Christ is being shrunk and the blood of Christ is being diluted. Right now because of Religious Humanism in the modern church, in front of our very eyes, we are experiencing the "Decline and Fall of Historic Christianity" as we have known, believed and embraced it with our blood-bought Christian brothers and sisters over the centuries.

Now also being spawned by Religious Humanism is what is called "The Emerging Church Movement." The roots of "The Emerging Church Movement" today go deep into the basic-goodness-of-man philosophy of Religious Humanism. Because of the rejection of the man-is-a-rotten-sinner truth, we now have an emerging religion across the world teaching that you can encounter God in everyone you meet, regardless of what you or they believe. All men are God-revealers and not sin-carriers. Every man is a revelation of goodness and Godness, and Christ in essence ends up walking the plank for nothing. Lies, every bit of it! Stay away from anything to do with the Emerging Church, for what is emerging is not truth, but more heresies.

Jesus said in John 14:6,

"...I am the way, and the truth, and the life; no one comes to the Father but through Me."

We only meet God in Christ, and sinners only come to God, meet God and know God through the blood of Christ. Everything we know about God is through Christ, and everything we know about God apart from Christ is wrong. In Christ alone dwells the fullness of Deity in bodily form (Colossians 2:9), and in man apart from Christ dwells the fullness of sin bodily. But when man's fullness of sin is denied, then no longer will Christianity be full of Christ, the cross and the blood! Multitudes of modern church goers are letting this happen on their watch and will be judged by God for it one day soon.

Resources:

1. Let Us Reason Ministries, Mike Oppenheimer, "Internet Christian Bookstores: Havens for Non-Christian Materials"

2. Ibid.

3. Dynamic Preaching, "The Greatest Temptation of All" (Seven Worlds Corporation, Knoxville, TN, September/October1996, Volume XI, No.8) Page 6; Contributed by Pastor Don Emmitte

4. Let Us Reason Ministries, Mike Oppenheimer, "Norman Vincent Peal - A Man Who Made Up His Mind" (The Plus Factor, Published Excerpts From Schuller's 'Hour Of Power,' Copyrighted 1985, P. 3)

5. Let Us Reason Ministries, Mike Oppenheimer, "Norman Vincent Peale A Man Who Made Up His Mind (Norman Vincent Peale, Power of Positive Thinking, P.

1)

6. Way of Life Literature, David Cloud, Founder and Director, "Norman Vincent Peale: Apostle of Self-Esteem" (Christianity Today, November 11, 1957)

7. Biblical Discernment Ministries, Rick Miesel, John Beardsley, "Robert Schuller Quotes From Self-Esteem: The New Reformation" (p. 171)

8. Ibid, (p. 67)

9. Let Us Reason Ministries, Mike Oppenheimer, "Another Possible Gospel of Robert Schuller's" (Robert Schuller, Peace of Mind Through Possibility Thinking, 1977, pp. 131-132)

10. Biblical Discernment Ministries, Rick Miesel, John Beardsley, "Robert Schuller Quotes From Self-Esteem: The New Reformation" (pp 98-99)

11. Ibid. (p. 64)

12. Dynamic Preaching, "Two Parades" (Seven Worlds Corporation, Knoxville, TN, April, 1995, Volume X, No. 4) Page 13; Tony Campolo, Discipleship Journal, Issue Eighty-Four, Page 66

13. Let Us Reason Ministries, Mike Oppenheimer, "Another Possible Gospel of Robert Schuler's" (Robert Schuller, "Self-Love, The Dynamic Force of Success" pp. 32, 43)

14. Dynamic Preaching, "Does It Make a Difference Who Jesus Is?" (Seven Worlds Corporation, Knoxville, TN, July/August 1996, Volume XI, No. 7) Page 42

15. Dynamic Preaching, "With Your Head in the Clouds" (Seven Worlds Corporation, Knoxville, TN, February, 1996, Volume XI, No. 2) Page 23, Illusaurus

16. Let Us Reason Ministries, Mike Oppenheimer, "Another Possible Gospel of Robert Schuller's" (Self-Esteem: The New Reformation, pp.100, 126, 157)

17. Way of Life Literature, David W. Cloud-Founder and Director, "Norman Vincent Peale: Apostle of Self-Esteem (Modern Maturity Magazine, December-January, 1975, 76)

18. Biblical Discernment Ministries, Rick Miesel, John Beardsley, "Robert Schuller Quotes From Self-Esteem: The New Reformation" (p. 67)

Chapter Two

THE CORRUPTING FANTASYLAND OF MODERN CHRISTIANITY

†††

"Man's Mind Is Like A Store Of Idolatry And Superstition; So Much So That If Man Believes His Own Mind It Is Certain That He Will Forsake God And Forge Some Idol In His Own Brain." ~John Calvin

God makes it crystal clear in His Word that we are to be positive thinkers. He states in Philippians 4:8,

> **"Finally, brethren, whatever is true, whatever is honorable, whatever is right, whatever is pure, whatever is lovely, whatever is of good repute, if there is any excellence and if anything worthy of praise, let your mind dwell on these things."**

If that isn't a Biblical explanation of and an injunction to positive thinking, then there is none to be found.

This means for all of us that our minds must first be cleared of negatives and falsehoods, even as a garden is cleared of weeds. However, a room may be cleaned but still very empty. We then must fill our minds each day with thoughts of God's beauty and bounty like a garden planted with good seeds. In fact, so much does God require us to be habitually positive thinkers, that He concludes Philippians 4:8 with this exhortation,

> **"…let your mind dwell on these things."**

He instructs us not only to be good-news concentrators, but to linger there as a way of life. Let our minds concentrate on truth, honor, righteousness, purity, loveliness, good news, excellence, and praise-worthiness. These are the dwelling places of the Christian mind.

The story is told of a Presbyterian missionary who was for an extended period of time held hostage in Lebanon. While in captivity, every Saturday night he saved a piece of bread from dinner, and on Sunday morning he would celebrate "The Lord's Supper" by eating that treasured morsel. It was treasured because it filled him with thoughts of God's love, Christ's death for his sins, and the promise that Jesus made in the institution of the memorial feast of His coming again. He thought of God's people all over the world with whom he was joined in partaking of that holy symbol of the body of Christ. He filled his mind with the most positive thoughts and thereby was sustained. It is a lesson for all of us. Remembering Jesus as He commanded sustained his soul.

However, sad to say, that is not what modern Religious Humanists mean by positive thinking. Not at all! That is what is so tricky about the familiar couplet – Positive Thinking. For Religious Humanists, it means something quite different than what it at first glance seems to suggest. The positive-thinking philosophy is married to the possibility-thinking philosophy. They are flip sides of the same coin. In short, the marriage of the two means that if we positivize and possibilize our thinking, there is nothing that will be impossible to us. Let's take a much closer look.

THE POSITIVE-POSSIBILITY MIND – THE GREATEST POWER

Have you ever heard someone say to someone else, "It's all in your head?" Or again, "It's all in your mind!" According to Norman Peale and Robert Schuller, it is! That is, our lives and our futures with all of their exciting possibilities are contained within man's amazing, positive, cognitive powers, i.e. his reputedly unlimited creative mind with its supernatural capability. Mr. Super Mind! Man the mental giant! Religious Humanism believes in and teaches the supremacy of the human intellect. The human mind and imagination are the grandees of Religious Humanism.

"Let Us Reason Ministries" observes: "It was Peale's positive thinking that gave birth to Schuller's ever popular possibility thinking...(quoting Robert Schuller): **'POSSIBILITY THINKING MAKES MIRACLES HAPPEN...THE GREATEST POWER IN THE WORLD IS THE POWER OF POSSIBILITY THINKING.'"** (1) Religious Humanists are always having brain celebrations. Religious Humanism has regular parades down the main street of man's mind, with the positive thinkers blowing their horns, the possibility thinkers beating their drums, and the human brain as the drum major marching out in front leading the way.

Drug addicts take chemical trips through which they hope to enlarge their consciousness. Religious Humanists take positive and possibility brain trips through which they believe they can visualize and actualize all of their dreams, solve all of their problems, and create all of their fantastic futures! For Religious Humanists, the glue that holds their entire system together is this: **"NOTHING SHALL BE IMPOSSIBLE TO THE POSITIVE-POSSIBILITY THINKING MAN."**

Religious Humanists aren't serious, are they? Come now! Attributing miracles to the positive and possibility-thinking human mind!? Miracles are super-realities far exceeding the power of any created agent including man. Miracles come from Divine omniscience and omnipotence alone. Nothing about man makes miracles happen! Nothing! Not even his positive-possibility thinking. No matter how positive man's mind, he can no more make miracles happen that he can make God do them.

Man has always from the beginning of time wanted to be much bigger than he is. Hence we have the fantasy worlds of Superman, Batman, Spiderman and Aquaman. And now along with all of these fictional messiahs we have Religious Humanism's supernatural "Mindman."

Or again, calling positive-possibility-thinking Mindman not only the miracle worker but the greatest power in the world! I have heard of grandiose complexes before, but this beats them all. This is like calling a baby an adult! This is like calling a midget a giant. This is like calling a weakling an Atlas. This is like calling an idiot a genius. This is like calling man a god.

Ascribing mind-miracles and greatest-power capabilities to the creature and not exclusively to the Creator!? It would all be so silly if it weren't so sad. And calling the positive-possibility-thinking Mindman the greatest power in the world would be much sillier still if it weren't far sadder. Mindman replacing God as the number one mind-power in the world! Religious Humanism stuffs man's mind so full of himself, there is no mindspace left for God.

Two little boys were the terrors of their school. Particularly in their homeroom, as every time one of them would cut up, the other would about die of laughter. Their teacher had gotten fed up with both of them and sent them to the principal's office for the umpteenth time. The principal came out, grabbed one of them by the arm and took him into his office. He left the other boy outside. The principal shook his finger right up to the boy's nose and asked, "Where is God? Where is God? I want you to go out there and think about that?" The little boy was shaken. He came out and saw his cohort in crime. His buddy asked, "What did he say?" He said, "God is missing and the principal thinks you and I have something to do with it."

It is so important to note at this point that in much of modern Christianity the true God of the Bible has indeed gone missing and has been replaced by man and human contrivances. Can you imagine calling the human mind the greatest power on earth!? The fact that we will see over and over again in multiple ways in this book is that the only God has gone missing in much of modern Christianity, and that Religious Humanists have everything to do with it.

Jesus has already taught us that apart from God everything is impossible to man, naturally and supernaturally! Everything! But in total contradistinction, we read about God in Luke 1:37,

"For nothing will be impossible with God."

There are no impossibilities or improbabilities with God. But for man by himself apart from God, everything is highly improbable because everything is impossible. There is no greater argument for improbability than impossibility. All true possibility thinking is rooted in God, not in man.

God rains on this human brain-power ticker-tape parade as we read about God and man in the starkest contrast in Matthew 19:26,

"…With men this is impossible, but with God all things are possible."

After all, why would human possibility thinking be man's strong point when in fact everything is impossible to him? Man apart from God has no strong point, least of all his mind! Apart from God there are no possibilities for man, and this entire possibility-thinking thing is a myth.

WISHFUL THINKING

"Let Us Reason Ministries" observes: "Peale's spirituality was a blend of Christian Science and Mind Science teachings with a dash of Christian terminology. The world you live in is mental and not physical. Change your mind and you change everything… (Quoting Peale): **'YOUR UNCONSCIOUS MIND… [HAS A] POWER THAT TURNS WISHES INTO REALITIES WHEN THE WISHES ARE STRONG ENOUGH.'"**(2)

The conscious mind tapping into the unconscious mind with the strong seasoning of wishful thinking thrown in, and you have the recipe for wishamatic miracles. Here Religious Humanism builds a temple to the god not only of thinking, but to the god of wishful thinking. You can dreamily, imaginatively and miraculously wish your dreams into reality as long as you wish hard enough. So I ask, "How in the world do you wish hard enough? Brain strain and grunt when you are wishing and then turn red!?"

Religious Humanism reminds me of Disneyworld's theme song, "When you wish upon a star, it makes no difference who you are; your dreams will come true." Or again, it reminds me of making a wish before you blow out the birthday cake candles, as you tightly scrunch your eyelids shut and blow a wish for all your worth. Supposedly if your big-birthday blow leaves one candle lit, your wish goes up in flames and smoke. I have made a wish, blown all of the candles out, and it still was a big bust.

Positive-possibility thinking and strong wishing – Religious Humanism's dynamic duo! God is simply brought in to tie up any wishy-washy dangling participles or blow out that last stubborn candle. Excuse me, but it also reminds me of the often tugged-on chicken wishbone. If you end up with the thick end of the chicken wishbone, your strongest wishes will come true. Apparently the wishbone didn't help the chicken very much who not only got axed but eaten.

We have come to find out early in life that often the birthday wishes went up in puffs of smoke, and the pulled-apart wishbone caper was only a bunch of jokesters pulling our legs. This again is Religious Humanism's fantasyland at its fictional and corrupting worst. Religious Humanism is a wishing well. Christianity is a pray-ing heart. Religious Humanism is three coins in a fountain. Christianity is the three Divine Persons in the one Godhead.

BUILD IT AND THEY WILL COME

Peale also believed in what is commonly called "Imaging." Writes "Let Us Reason Ministries": "Peale's spirituality is not Christian but New Thought and is embraced among evangelicals who have not discerned its origin… (Quoting Peale): **'THERE IS A POWER AND A MYSTERIOUS FORCE IN HUMAN NATURE…A KIND OF MENTAL ENGINEERING…A POWERFUL NEW-OLD IDEA… THE CONCEPT IS A FORM OF MENTAL ACTIVITY CALLED IMAGING…IT CONSISTS OF VIVIDLY PICTURING IN YOUR CONSCIOUS MIND A DESIRED GOAL OR OBJECTIVE, AND HOLDING THAT IMAGE UNTIL IT SINKS INTO YOUR UNCONSCIOUS WORLD, WHERE IT RELEASES GREAT UNTAPPED ENERGIES.'"** (3)

"Let Us Reason Ministries" continues its quote of Peale: **"WHEN THE IMAGING CONCEPT IS APPLIED STEADILY AND SYSTEMATICALLY, IT SOLVES PROBLEMS, STRENGTHENS PERSONALITIES, IMPROVES HEALTH, AND GREATLY ENHANCES THE CHANCES FOR SUCCESS IN ANY KIND OF ENDEAVOR…."** (4)

Down through the years, this belief system of positive imaging has also been identified by terminology such as "Visualization." Human success all begins and ends with the visualizing and imaging powers of the human mind. Imagine it, picture it, dream it, mentally hold on to it, wish like mad for it, and you can make it happen through your own huge untapped energies. You have heard it said that a picture is worth a thousand words. Here, imaging is equal to a thousand prayers. This is the fantasyland of Religious Humanism!

It calls to mind the film starring Kevin Costner as Ray Kinsella, and Amy Madigan as Annie Kinsella, entitled *Field Of Dreams.* The persistent words that kept coming to Ray Kinsella in the corn fields of Iowa were as you may recall, "Build it and they will come." Kevin Costner played the role of an Iowa farmer who with his wife risked their farm and their family to follow Ray's mental-imaging hearsay. Then through the magic of modern movie-making, the viewers were led to believe that the imaginary will become reality if you just believe strong enough, hold on to the imaging long enough, and pursue it tenaciously enough against all opposition.

The "they" did eventually come to Ray Kinsella only after he destroyed several acres of his cornfield and built a baseball field instead. It wasn't long before Ray's baseballized cornfield was brought to life by long-ago deceased baseball players playing in Iowa the game they loved so much. They mistook Iowa for Heaven. I never have. I like Iowa very much, but not that much. Apparently they had not been to Heaven, for if they had, the thought of mistaking Iowa for Heaven would have seemed to them pretty corny. The film ends with Ray playing catch on the field of dreams with his deceased dad, John Kinsella.

Norman Peale and Robert Schuller could have well been the co-producers and co-directors respectively of *Field Of Dreams.* You really have to imagine it, desire it, persist in it, and then you can play catch with baseball's dead immortals. Excuse me, but it is long overdue for Religious Humanists to follow Dorothy back home to her farm, family and friends in Kansas, and leave Emerald City behind in never-never land. Oz looks so alluring from the outside, but from the inside Oz is never what it was imagined to be. There is no Heaven on earth. Heaven only exists in Heaven.

By the way, in case we have forgotten or never fully understood, Adam and Eve imagined that they could build their field of dreams, too. Satan put it into their heads. The parents of humanity followed their satanically inspired thoughts and imaginations. They grew to want them very badly. They wished for them real hard. They hung on to them until it became part of their conscious and subconscious minds. They came down with a fatal case of mental imaging, with Satan's visual aids of course. What was their imaging? They wished higher than Heaven's stars. They wished for Heaven's throne. They imagined that the forbidden tree would make them as wise as God. They hungrily pursued their imaging. In so doing they filled their lives and the world with misery, madness, and murder!

What is even worse, the world's first case of imaging all took place in the state of original innocence, not in a cornfield in Iowa, but in a place called the Garden of Eden, which was as close to Heaven on earth as you could get. Their imaging destroyed their lives and their Paradise before they had barely spent a day in either. If Satan can do that to man through mental imaging in man's state of innocence, I don't even want to think about what he can do in man through mental imaging in the state of sin.

In fact, what happened in the world of Adam and Eve's fantasyland of mental imaging was the exact opposite of Norman Peale's powerful and positive claims for mental imaging. *Field of Dreams* is the ethereal world of Hollywood's make-believe. Genesis 3 is the real world of actual human beings thinking and imaging themselves equal to God, and being separated from Him in a state (not Iowa) of sin and death. What really happened was this: "**WHEN THEY APPLIED THE IMAGING CONCEPT STEADILY AND SYSTEMATICALLY, THEY CREATED PROBLEMS, WEAKENED PERSONALITIES, PRODUCED SICKNESS, AND GREATLY ENHANCED THEIR CHANCES FOR FAILURE IN ANY AND EVERY KIND OF ENDEAVOR.**"

It was human imaging, wishing, and dreaming that populated earth not with dead baseball heroes come to life in a field of dreams, but with dead-in-sin men walking who have turned their world into fields of nightmares. Paradise was lost by man's cognitive and imaginative powers. Man left to his own thoughts and imaginations will lead himself not into a *Field Of Dreams*. Man's thoughts and imaginations are so sickened by sin, so lost in darkness, and so misguided by foolishness, that no matter how positive and possible it all might seem, to trust them will lead not only to the *Nightmare On Elm Street,* but to nightmares on every street. By the way, how many nightmares are there on your street?

All of this reminds me of the can of room air freshener on which appeared these words, "Bring the clean, natural freshness of a country meadow indoors – freshens the air in your home with a clean back-to-nature scent – as refreshing as the summer grass and fragrant flowers of a country meadow!" Following those words were these, "WARNING! Inhaling the contents can be harmful or fatal." Those words remind me of the rhetoric that comes out of Religious Humanism's fields of dream.

WICKED AND WILD IMAGINATIONS

To be sure, man's mind and imagination has been used and is being used in incredible creativity. Automobiles, airplanes and space vehicles etc. are just a very few evidences of man's mental and imaginative prowess. However, as we shall see, all of these inventions are due to the direct intervention of God. The Bible tells us that every good and perfect gift comes from God. (James 1:17) Only God's goodness could have over-ridden man's mind and imagination and its potential for unspeakable evil.

To reference man's mind and imagination as the great hope and future for mankind as Religious Humanism encourages us to do, is just as dangerous as telling a child to go into a barn and play with matches. All of this is repudiated by the Apostle Paul in Romans 1:21 where he says about all men's imaginations,

> "...but they became futile in their speculations,
> and their foolish heart was darkened."

"Futile" here means "Worthless," that is, "Void" and "Empty" of any meaning or virtue. A darkened heart means a total spiritual and moral eclipse! Imaginations empty of all Divine character and purpose, and hearts with only dark, evil shadows! That is how God describes man's natural mind and imagination. Religious Humanism in one fell swoop sweeps all of this aside. Nonetheless, Romans 1:21 in the KJV states about Adam and Eve's descendants,

> "...they...became vain in their imaginations, and
> their foolish heart was darkened."

A man by the name of Adolph Hitler thought and dreamed and imagined a super race, and in the pursuit of his demented mental imaging, shot, starved, butchered and burned 6 million of God's chosen people. When we think about the Hitlers of the world, our response often sounds like this, "We can't even imagine thinking, let alone doing such a thing." Oh yes we could, and if it weren't for the grace of God and the mind of Christ in us, we just as easily would.

When I was a young boy I heard vivid stories about World War II and the Third Reich in the post war 1940s. It was then freshly blood-red stained into people's mind. I vividly recall thinking and imagining that if the Germans ever marched down 32nd Street in Holland, Michigan where I lived as a boy, I would turn them all into buzzard bait. In my mind and imagination I really got into it, but I won't tell you how I planned it, except that it was gruesomely imaginative for a small boy.

On a different but tragic level, I have counseled too many married people who imagine that life with the other man or other woman will be far more thrilling than the life they are living with their "stale spouses." Like children they sit in their classrooms of life imagining and wishing that they were somewhere else to avoid the responsibility of the here and now. They think and imagine that they are headed for a dream-world where they will discover that illusive rush and gush. On top of that, Satan majors in "Virtual Reality." It looks real, but in fact it isn't. He makes things look bigger and better than life, but they are in fact death.

How often I have seen the adulterer or adulteress chase their dream, and the dream turned into a nightmare on Illusion Street, where they were now living in a haunted house which first appeared as a dream castle. The rush soon was flushed forever. Married people who play around often trade in their real houses for playhouses, but the playhouses so often become haunted houses – haunted by the memories of the marriage they destroyed for what proved to be a mirage. No matter how you cut it, and no matter what you call it, Romans 6:23 says,

"For the wages of sin is death...."

Haven't you ever asked yourself or wondered as you are being bombarded on television with previews to hideous upcoming movies and television shows, just who in the world are these people who have such corrupt minds and imaginations as to be able to come up with such unspeakably violent and lustful garbage? No, they are not looked upon in society anymore as sociopaths. They are instead embraced as your everyday neighbors next door. But we know this for certain, that their minds and imaginations are so vulgar that for the most part they allow no control from right reason or moral sensitivity. That is where all of the illicit sex and violence is coming from on TV shows such as *Desperate Housewives* and *The Sopranos*. Man's mind and imagination are overflowing sewers.

It is man's wicked imagination that leads him into the doing of the unimaginably horrific. Mankind's sin-sick minds and imaginations are what cause the Cho Seung Hui, Stephen Kazmierczak and BTK monstrosities of life to act out their vengeance and gore upon their fellow citizens, fellow students and faculty members at institutions of higher learning like Virginia Tech University and Northern Illinois University. It was Gary Ridgeway, the Green River mass-murderer, who viewed killing females as his calling, and each day went to work thinking and imaging how to do his job. They all thought about, imagined and planned their atrocities. They were not simply spur-of-the-moment blood-letting rampages. They were pre-meditated and pre-imagined all in sinful hearts that were darkened by Hell.

It is easy to see therefore that Romans 1:21 was not only an address to the ancient Romans, but even more accurately a characterization of modern man. The world has thought and imagined in the dark ever since the first sin of the first man. So much for Peale's words: "**IMAGING...IT CONSISTS OF VIVIDLY PICTURING IN YOUR CONSCIOUS MIND A DESIRED GOAL OR OBJECTIVE, AND HOLDING IT THERE UNTIL IT SINKS INTO YOUR UNCONSCIOUS WORLD WHERE IT RELEASES GREAT UNTAPPED ENERGIES.**" Man does it ever!

EVERY IMAGINATION ALWAYS EVIL

Dateline June 2009 – **THE DAYS OF NOAH HAVE RETURNED.** Noah's time in history became so bad that all of men's imaginations were completely vile. The King James Version of the Bible says in Genesis 6:5 about the entire human race of Noah's day before the flood,

> **"And God saw that the wickedness of man was great in the earth, and that every imagination of the thoughts of his heart was only evil continually."**

Not some, not most, but all of man's thoughts and imaginations were saturated with filth on a non-stop basis!

If you get the thrust of the text, you can also be assured of this, that man's evil deeds were just as numerous as his continually evil thoughts and imaginations. Get the picture? It was literally the original script for the film *New York Gangs.* It was a total meltdown of the entire moral fabric of society. In fact it was so horrible that we find God Himself regretting that He had made man at all. Who would have ever thought that they would hear God saying, "What was I thinking anyway?" The NASV says in Genesis 6:6,

> **"And the Lord was sorry that He had made man...."**

The KJV says in Genesis 6:6,

> **"And it repented the Lord that He had made man...."**

And while God was repenting that he had made man who had now gone so horribly bad, there was no sinner repenting of his horrendous badness. Humanity had become garbage fit only for the dumpster.

The Lord tells us that as the days approach His coming to judge the living and the dead, the world will once again be as it was in the days of Noah. (Matthew 24:37) It only takes half an eyeball to see that what Jesus prophesied is happening now. We are there! Our prisons are bulging with murderers and sex offenders. Erectile dysfunction products are now on display 7/24 in commercials that are nothing less than pornographic. Commercials for TV programs which shout sex and bloody murder from beginning to end leave our brains riddled with the shrapnel of lust and violence! Satan no longer majors in sniper fire as in the days when the moral walls of society still stood tall. It is in-your-face warfare for all to see. While watching TV, we can't get away from the feeling of being constantly degraded and defiled.

How does it work? Norman Peale stated: **"THERE IS A POWER AND A MYSTERIOUS FORCE IN HUMAN NATURE… A POWERFUL NEW-OLD IDEA…A FORM OF MENTAL ACTIVITY CALLED IMAGING."** Oh yes, it is powerful in human nature alright and very old. Here is how it really works, and follow this now. Men's thinking and imaging faculties are saturated with anger, hatred and lust. This corrupt stuff rolls around constantly in their minds, and then it reaches their imaginations, and they together unendingly obsess and picture how they can give vent to this rancor and rot. The natural mind deals in foul thoughts, while the imagination deals in vile images. The intercourse between the two conceives the licentious and grotesque. This is how the natural human mind and imagination deal and traffic in darkness.

But we are far from done. Men's sin-seething imaginations then reach and inflame their already raging and lustful passions! Their wrathful and lustful passions then boil over and gain control of their wills. There may be some initial resistance from the natural mind and the will of man because of the pressures placed upon them by the laws of civilized society. However when the natural mind and will are in conflict with the imagination, the imagination always wins. Then men knowingly and willfully commit murder, adultery and perversion which turn our world into an ongoing blood-soaked orgy. Hello Noah's Day!

So God sent a flood and drowned them all minus eight. Noah and his family were eight grains of salt sprinkled on earth's dunghill. The toilet of earth had to be flushed. That was the only way to give earth and man a new start! Men's minds and imaginations have polluted the earth again. Next time God will not destroy the earth with a flood. He will burn it, and with it all of these vain imaging philosophies of men. So we read in II Peter 3:10,

"But the day of the Lord will come like a thief, in which the heavens will pass away with a roar and the elements will be destroyed with intense heat, and the earth and its works will be burned up."

Why? Because according to Proverbs 6:16-18 in the KJV translation, there are seven things that the Lord hates, among them being,

"...an heart that deviseth wicked imaginations...."

CAST DOWN AND CAPTURE

According to Norman Vincent Peale, man is a "Mental Engineer." Mindman! The Apostle Paul describes man in radically different terms when it comes to his cognition and imagination. We read in II Corinthians 10:5 (KJV),

"Casting down imaginations and every high thing that exalteth itself against the knowledge of God, and bringing into captivity every thought to the obedience of Christ."

Do you see it? Do you feel it? Religious Humanism addresses man's cognitive and imaginative powers as magic carpet rides. Christianity addresses man's cognition and imagination as wild animals of prey that must be hunted down on a daily basis. Paul does not picture us as mental engineers, but rather as "East Africa Safari Hunters." And remember, Paul is talking to Christians here, not savages. Let's take a look.

The Apostle Paul employs some incredibly strong language when He tells us what we must constantly be doing regarding our thinking and imaging: **"CASTING DOWN IMAGINATIONS AND CAPTURING THOUGHTS."** The Greek word for "Casting Down" imaginations is "Kathaireo" which means "To Put Down" or "To Destroy." Bring down and destroy what? Every imagination that lifts itself up against the knowledge of God! They must be brought down and put to death as the dangerous animals of prey that they are. Open hunting season on our thoughts and imaginations year round. We are on a wild animal hunt in this book as well, attempting to bring down and destroy the vain imaginations of Religious Humanism that are lifting themselves up against the knowledge of God.

When it comes to bringing down and destroying imaginations that are being lifted up against the knowledge of God, where do we begin in all of this Religious Humanism that is inundating and corrupting the modern church? It is contaminating Christianity in every aspect. What follows is case and point! Be careful here because you are going to find yourself in deep mud that will try to suck your safari hunting shoes right off from your feet.

We know according to the Apostle Paul that holy marriage between a man and a woman is designed by God to be a sacred type, a holy illustration, a Divine show-and-tell of the marriage between Christ and His blood-bought bride the church. (Ephesians 5:31-32) Huge reality! Holy Reality! The husband and wife's oneness is a holy type of Christ and His church-bride's oneness. (Mark 10:8, I Corinthians 6:17) The husband's love and laying down his life for his bride is to be a living example of Christ's love and laying down His life for His bride the church. (Ephesians 5:25) Even as Christ is the head of His church, so the husband is the head of his wife. (Ephesians 5:23) The husband and wife's relationship is ultimately not about them, but about the Heavenly Bridegroom and His Church-Bride. (Ephesians 5:32)

How then is all of this conveyed in the marriage covenant? One Biblical, traditional and time- honored way in which the church, the bride of Christ, is pictured as having no life apart from Christ her husband is by being named with her Heavenly Bridegroom's name – Christian. Mrs. Christ! The name Christian shouts that she no longer has an independent existence, but has died to self, and lives only from and for her Husband – Christ Jesus the Head of the Church. In short, the wife loses her maiden name and takes her husband's name signifying that she has no life apart from him, even as Christians have no life apart from Christ. There is no double life or identity in Christianity on any level, including marriage. It's all about Christ who is our life. Or as the Apostle Paul puts it in Colossians 3:4,

"When Christ, Who is our life, is revealed...."

Got it? Not anymore! Every time-honored practice based on Biblical principle is now being dishonored. Particularly since feminism and women's rights, which are fueled by the spirit of Religious Humanism, have crept into the church! Now about-to-be wives in the Christian Church are demanding, just like the world does, that they be called by their maiden names as well as by their married names. Why? Because they imagine that they can hang on to their independent, single life and identity and at the same time enter into the Christian marital relationship. Sarah Jones is married to John Smith and now demands to be called Sarah Jones Smith. Who cares about this Christ and His Christian-Bride thing anymore?

And God forbid, as has been the case throughout the Christian centuries that she and her husband would ever be introduced as Mr. and Mrs. John Smith, thereby leaving her with only a "Mrs. Smith" identity with both her first and last name omitted. Horrors! That is an invitation to all-out warfare, as Mrs. Sarah John Jones Smith suddenly becomes a snarling feline who would like to sink her unfriendly claws into your face.

It has gotten so bad that married feminists today are now demanding that their children bear both their father's surname and their mother's maiden name, along with the first and middle name which they have been given. The poor kids will have names as long as freight trains and they will have to write a book every time they sign their names. Condemning a child to a lifetime of nomenclature nonsense! At the least what a waste of good ink!

What we have today are hybrid marriages, neither here nor there, but somewhere in between. In so doing, the husband and wife are living in an imaginary marriage world, and lifting up vain imaginations that are directly opposed to and against the knowledge of Christ and the Word of God.

This is just some of the stuff that must be cast down and destroyed as vain imaginations that are rising up against Divine revelation, against the knowledge of God, and are corrupting modern Christianity. And what is even worse, it is all being done in the name of Christ. Religious Humanism!

But we are not done yet! Not only must we cast down these high-minded imaginations that exalt themselves against the knowledge of God, but we must also bring every thought into captivity to the obedience of Christ. Yes, you are reading Paul correctly. Just the language of "Capture" and "Captivity" that Paul uses ought to tell you how wild the human mind with its untamed thoughts can be.

The Greek word for "Bringing Into Captivity" is "Aichmalotizo" which literally means "To Take By The Spear." Whoa! Again, very severe language! Mental engineers!? Are you kidding? Spear hunters and captive thought-takers! That is more like it. Either our thoughts will be taken captive by the law of God, or they will remain captive to the law of sin.

I was reminded of all of this when Alaska Governor Sarah Palin's pregnant, unwed daughter-mother, Bristol Palin, was interviewed on Fox Network by Greta Van Susteren about sex and teen pregnancy. Never once were the Biblical words such as sin or fornication used in Greta's questions or Bristol's answers. Bristol only indicated that it is far wiser to wait to have a baby until marriage. Wiser but not necessarily more moral than having a baby before marriage! She also stated that teenage sexual abstinence is unrealistic.

God talks about a rebellious people in Isaiah 65:2,

> "...**who walk in the way which is not good, following their own thoughts**."

Our natural thoughts have to be hunted down and taken captive like fugitives running from the law of God. Why? Because by nature they are rebellious and disobedient thoughts! It was obvious that Bristol's mind was not yet captive to the obedience of Christ, which captivity alone can be realized by a deep, personal relationship with Christ and being immersed in His Word on a daily basis. Or as the Psalmist states in Psalm 119:97,

"O how I love Thy law! It is my meditation all the day."

The best defense is a powerful offense in this case! Either take rogue thoughts captive to the Word of God or be taken captive by them.

To change the analogy for a moment, bringing our thoughts captive to the obedience of Christ may be likened to rounding up, corralling, breaking, and training a herd of wild stallions so that they are brought into submission and obedience to the rider through bit and bridle. A horse trainer wants his horse to think what he is thinking without even saying it, so that the horse will instinctively know, act, and react accordingly. There is nothing more beautiful than a rider and his horse moving together as if they were sharing one mind and heart. Just the slightest and most imperceptible flick of the wrist, nudge of the foot, or pressure on the reins is all that is needed. That is the way it should be between Christ and His followers. That is bringing every thought captive to the obedience of Christ. He wants us to instinctively think His thoughts after Him.

THE SOARING EGO OF BABEL

If man's mind, imagination, and emotions are not led captive to Christ, they will be taken captive by man's massive ego. Always! The huge human ego is God's incessant competitor. As "Let Us Reason Ministries" points out, "Robert Schuller had appeared on Larry King Live on 1/28/94 to promote his book *Achieve Your True Potential Through Power Thinking Or Power Thoughts.* He (Schuller) said: '**POSITIVE THINKING SAYS, 'HEY, I AM SOMEBODY. I CAN DO IT.' POSSIBILITY THINKING PICKS UP ON IT AND SAYS, 'OKAY, HOW IS IT POSSIBLE AND HOW CAN WE MAKE IT POSSIBLE?' AND POWER THINKING SAYS, 'OKAY, I AM. I CAN. IT'S POSSIBLE. OKAY, LET'S YOU AND I DO IT....'"** (5)

We are back to the mantra of "I Am" again. In Schuller's words, if we read them carefully, we hear a trialogue between "Positive Thinker," "Possibility Thinker," and "Power Thinker," the three persons of Religious Humanism's triune god – the human mind, which has been described earlier as the greatest power in the world. It is Religious Humanism's triune god that rivals if not replaces The Father, The Son and The Holy Spirit of true Christianity. In Genesis 1:26 we hear The Triune God saying, "Let us make man etc." In Religious Humanism we hear the triune mind-god saying, "Let's you and me do it."

But more than that, Religious Humanism is not a dialogue between totally "Weakman" and "The Most Powerful God." No, no, not that old fashioned, antiquated man-is-weak and God-is- powerful religion any more. Religious Humanism's god chants, "I am, I am somebody and I can do it!" Christianity confesses, "I am nobody apart from Christ, and I can do nothing apart from Christ. But I can do all things through Christ who strengthens me." Religious Humanism is man's trialogue with himself. Christianity is God's dialogue with man and man's dialogue with God.

In Religious Humanism, the biggest somebody is Mindman. In Christianity the biggest Somebody is Almighty God. This totally ego-centered, "Positive-Possibility-Power-I-Am-Somebody" thinking will lead inevitably to the building of what becomes an "Ego-Babel." Why do you think the story of the building of the city and the tower which came to be known as Babel is recorded in the Bible in Genesis 11? Simply because God wanted to illustrate to us that "Ego-I-Am-Somebody" man will always think, imagine, dream and build that which secures for his ego the resounding applause of self, of men, as well as his lasting fame in history that he so much desires. "Positive-Possibility-Power-I-Am-Somebody" thinking is nothing more or less than "Babel-Thinking." Man is out to prove that he is really something – the big somebody!

That is exactly what happened in the post-flood world as Egoman took over. We read of it in Genesis 11:4,

"And they said, 'Come, let us build for ourselves a city, and a tower whose top will reach into heaven, and LET US MAKE FOR OURSELVES A NAME....'"

Bingo! They wanted to build their own "Hall of Fame" in the form of a "Tower of Fame." In the final analysis, the tower blueprints had to be as big as the name they wanted to make for themselves.

The Babel culture of the early Old Testament wanted to beat all past, present and future competition on its way to the throne of historical supremacy. They wanted a monopoly of greatness. After all, that is what "Halls of Fame" and "Towers of Babel" are all about! Ego immortality! The truly noble among us give their lives in inconspicuous laboratories trying to discover a cure for cancer. The "Babelites" of modern sports give their lives to making a name for themselves illegally through steroids, and now play in billion dollar amphitheaters called state-of-the-art "Baseball Babels" (stadiums) with ridiculous ticket prices to support their obscene ego-salaries. Now the "Halls of Fame" are becoming "Halls of Shame."

It is all the same ego-addiction in every level of corporate America, and now in the modern church, as preachers pump their parishioners full of pseudo-spiritual steroids to enlarge their self-images, self-confidence and self-worth. And often those same preachers preach their human-steroid sermons to draw huge crowds and thereby build their own "Mega-man Babel Churches." They are filling them with Ego-man, Mind-man, Positive-man, Possibility-man, Power-man, Worthy-man, Esteem-man, Love-self-man, Good-man, I-am-man, Somebody-man, Miracle-man, Imaging-man, Wish-man, Dream-your-future-man and I-can-do-man. Religious Humanism's parishioners.

In short, Religious Humanism is building "Babel Churches" all over the country in tribute to "Mr. Awesome-man" and all of his buddies. There is barely any room to fit in the "Only Sovereign And All Sufficient God" anymore in this "Babel-Man Religion." Perhaps a seat in the back for Him with the aged and the infirmed, for He has now really gone out of date! And certainly there is no room for the antiquated and irrelevant Sinner-man, Unworthy-man, Depraved-man, Contrite-man, Repentance-man, Born-again-man, Confession-man, Forgiven-man, Saved-man, Redeemed-man, Saint-man, Dependent-man, Disciple-man, and Servant-man. Christianity's parishioners! We are finally rid of those old codgers. Now instead the praise goes forth, "Halle-mind-man-jah!"

This colossal Babel undertaking did not just pop up in early civilization's collective thoughts and imaginations all at once. No, mankind's inflated ego over a period of time caused them to think and think, imagine and imagine, dream and dream, and wish and wish about how best to make a name for themselves. There were no doubt those who marched in the forefront of this ego-parade, imagined a tower, and said to the others, "Hey, we are somebody, we can do this." It sounded more and more positive and possible, and it caught on in the thoughts, imaginations and desires of the general population. They psyched each other into holding that grandiose image of the "Ego-Tower" in their minds. It was a clear case of ego-imaging in early world history. This is the stuff that is boiling and bubbling in man's mind and imagination on the front burner called ego. Today we have a religion based on ego-imaging, and it is called Religious Humanism.

God is intolerant of this "Babel Egomania" in society, and especially in the church. We should tremble at God's stern warning when He says in Jeremiah 45:5,

"But you, are you seeking great things for yourself? Do not

seek them...."

God here shoots the soaring ego out of the sky, and with it "Positive-Possibility-Power-I-Am-Somebody" thinking. The city and the tower on the plain in the land of Shinar (Genesis 11:2) were both ego-eyesores to Heaven, because they were all about the glorification of man, and had nothing to do with the glorification of God. You cannot glorify God and man as the same time. Something has to give.

So God grew foreign tongues in their ego-mouths, and next thing we know they were all stuttering and stammering in total gibberish. We read in Genesis 11:7 God saying,

"Come, let Us go down and there confuse their language, that they may not understand one another's speech."

Before they could lay another brick, their tongues became multi-lingual and they became totally unintelligible to one another. No interpreters were provided by Heaven. Imagine that! The chaotic result was that they couldn't understand a word that they were speaking to each other no matter how loud they shouted. What a sight! What a sound! They were now fit for nothing. God then scattered them to the four winds, and the city as well as the tower were stopped by this nonsensical babbling. Hence it was called Babel (Genesis 11:9), which comes from a root word which means to "To Confuse" or "To Confound." God the ego-dream crasher arrived on the scene, and the skyscraper was scrapped. No Ego-Babel will be tolerated by God, most of all "Ego-Babel Religion."

Oh, by the way, fame doesn't really last anyway. Out of sight, out of mind! You know how it goes. There will always be somebody to take your place. Fame flies away like time. One day you are a "Who's Who," and before you know it, when your name is mentioned someone is bound to ask, "Who?" Johnny Carson related one night that a man came up to him after he had left television. The man asked Johnny, "Didn't you used to be somebody important?"

BE WARNED OF THE SWOOPING EGO

The soaring ego also swoops down upon and carries away the spiritually minded and the initially well-intentioned. It is possible to hear the call of God and obey it, but to do so for the wrong ego-reasons. You may right now be experiencing what J.B. Phillips once experienced in his life. He was a parish pastor in London in 1941. He had a noble dream. He took the Apostle Paul's letter to the Colossian Christians and translated it into modern English so that young people could better understand that part of the Bible.

Phillips then received a letter from of all people, C.S. Lewis, whom he did not know personally. Lewis wrote, "I congratulate you! It is as though there is an old picture that has been cleansed. Please continue to do it all." My, my, there is an ego-builder for you – a more than positive letter from C.S. Lewis, arguably the greatest Christian writer of the 20th century. As a result, J.B. Phillips' New Testament in modern English was finally published in 1951, and a revised edition came out in 1961.

So then, J.B. Phillips did exactly what C.S. Lewis suggested to him. Overnight, Phillips became a world sensation. He received invitations to speak which he had never received before. All of the trips were paid for. He got VIP treatment wherever he went. People everywhere were clamoring for him to write something more, something better. He authored *Your God Is Too Small* which was published in 1952. Book sales were booming all over the world. It wasn't very long before Phillips was led to discover the anguish of trying to live up to a false image of a man he simply was not. Before he knew it, he had gotten all caught up in ego, fame, and money. All of that of course in the service of God!

"For four years," Phillips once shared, "I was able to make it through the day. But at night, it was a nightmare. Fears and even false guilt about sins that I had never committed! For four years it was as though God wasn't there." He went on, "I never reached the point of nihilism, believing that there were no standards and that life was senseless. I never reached the point of despair. But every night was like a nightmare. Even my sense of God disappeared. That's what caused the four years of spiritual illness and the terror at night." He then declared, "When I came to grips with the false image of myself, I was terrified to destroy it, but when I realized that it had to be destroyed – then I again practiced the presence of God."(6)

The soaring ego once again had its wings clipped. God will allow no rivals to His Divine supremacy and genius. The wise man warns us in Proverbs 29:23,

"A man's pride will bring him low…."

GOD'S WILL MAY NOT ALWAYS SOUND POSITIVE

Let's get to a basic Christian-life principle here, and that is that there are those times that God's will for our lives may not strike us as positive or even possible. It may appear to us to be absolutely negative and impossible. God's will for us is not always our being deployed for dreamland. God's dream for Moses appeared to him as an absolute nightmare. As you may recall, when God told him that he was to lead God's people out of slavery and command King Pharaoh of Egypt to release his captives, it left Moses absolutely "speechless." At least that was the excuse he used to get out of God's will for his life – I am no good at talking, I am speech impeded.

Yes, you are reading correctly. Religious Humanism, exit stage left! Christianity, enter stage right! God's plans for His servants in the first instance have nothing to do with positive or possibility thinking and imaging. Man's thoughts and plans are designed for himself, often at other's expense. God's thoughts and plans for us are ultimately designed for Himself, always at our expense.

To be totally honest about it, many modern Christians can't conceive that God might want them to deliberately forego their present high standard of living in order to go to some miserable third-world environment to present the Gospel, or to be a member of a support team to build churches, schools, homes, hospitals etc. in some retarded, backward civilization. Religious Humanism has corrupted modern Christianity with the inability to believe that the Lord would lead us into some obscure, destitute, underprivileged, and even dangerous mission or endeavor.

Religious Humanism has permeated modern Christianity with the following panacea as its guiding principle, namely, that there is nothing on earth too good for the people of God. In total contradistinction, Christianity's guiding principle for life is that there is no sacrifice on earth too great for the people of God. Or as Isaac Watts puts it:

> **"Were the whole realm of nature mine, that were an offering far too small; love so amazing, so divine, demands my soul, my life, my all."**

You surely recall Jonah! When Jonah was informed by God of His will for Jonah's life, Jonah did not receive it as a positive, possible, dreamy and unimaginably wonderful prospect. It was to Jonah horribly unbecoming for an Israelite. It was the most unfit way for him to spend his life. To be fully honest, it was negative, preposterous, and just plain disgusting.

The Assyrians were a bloodthirsty people, and had been a nemesis to Israel for many years. God told Jonah to go to Nineveh and hold an evangelistic crusade amongst the Assyrians. Jonah was furious about God's positive plan for these ancient terrorists. Why, just the thought of them soured his stomach. The mention of their name gave Jonah a bad case of indigestion that no Alka-Seltzer would help. He was outraged at the thought of any Assyrian becoming part of the family of God. And more than that, Jonah felt totally justified in his outrage.

(Jonah 4:9) He would have rather died than become victimized by God's brand of positive, possibility thinking.

I have learned from men like Jonah that powerful emotions like anger, prejudice and fear will always paralyze our potential usefulness for God's purposes. I know of those who are running from the will of God for their lives because of those very powerful feelings of anger and fear. Because of anger and fear, they get ideas about the express will of God for them that are totally wrong and contrary to God's heart and mind. So they run from the call of God because they like to think that they are wise rather than be filled with God's wisdom. They would rather appear wise to themselves than be walking in the perfect wisdom of God.

The thought of God showing mercy to the Assyrians was as painful to Jonah as men being told that from now on they would have to give birth to babies. Men don't like childbirth, and Jonah didn't like Assyrian spiritual rebirth, and even worse that he would give birth to it. So Jonah ran full speed from the maternity room of the birthing of God's purposes in his life, in what proved to be one of the most famous and futile attempted escapes from God recorded in the Bible or anywhere else. Instead of going to Nineveh, Jonah took a ship over the Mediterranean Sea to Tarshish, a far-away ancient city in what is now Spain.

First of all it is never a good idea to disobey a direct order from God. Second, it is not a good idea to run away from God's will. Jonah sinned against God's clear command, and did so with a prejudiced heart and a defiant spirit. He disobeyed God knowingly and resolutely, and stared down his own conscience as well.

The result! Jonah ended up in "Motel Fish Belly" for three days and three nights. God did not leave the light on for him. Not exactly four-star lodging! Then when the time was deemed right by God, the very large fish puked Jonah into the will of God. The unbeliever would say that Mother Nature played Jonah for a chump. Believers know better, and because he was a proud blockhead, Jonah became God's example of what God's regurgitated will looks like when we disobey it the first time.

Why didn't God just write Jonah off? Listen, a creditor does not lose his right to his money, simply because the debtor is unwilling to pay it. God does not lose His right to obedience, simply because His subject is unwilling to give it. God ordered Jonah a second time, and this time Jonah obeyed God. You and I would too after such a dark, slimy, deep-sea excursion and yet living to tell about it.

Jonah then went on a multi-day missionary hike to the great city of Nineveh. He did not preach one word about self-love, self-esteem, or self-worth. Nor did he preach about the "M" sound. Instead, he preached the "J" sound –

Judgment." We read in Jonah 3:4,

> **"Then Jonah began to go through the city one day's walk;**
> **and he cried out and said, 'Yet forty days and Nineveh will**
> **be overthrown.'"**

I am sure of this, that Jonah loved threatening Nineveh with Divine judgment. That really was his cup of tea. And I am also sure that he counted on God doing just that, wiping Nineveh off from the face of the earth. We must add this, that while Jonah was enjoying in his heart preaching about the coming judgment of God upon these savages, he was the complete antithesis to the unfathomably merciful heart of God.

But horror of horrors, the Ninevites responded favorably to his message. The Spirit of God began to move upon the hearts of the Ninevites through Jonah's message of warning and impending destruction. The city of Nineveh was changed for the good. The people of Nineveh repented, turned to God and away from their wickedness, violence, and international mayhem because of Jonah's reluctant campaign. So much so that God spared the city from destruction, though Jonah was still pining away and mired in self-pity and bitterness under the unwanted success of it all! Thank God that He uses imperfect people to accomplish His perfect will.

Let's hasten to add here that God's purpose will not lead to "Assyrian Revivals" every time and everywhere. The Apostles of Jesus Christ sometimes had to run for their lives, and even be stoned and left for dead. Nowhere are we promised 100% success. We may lose a few battles, but God promises us that we will win the war in the end in Jesus' name. In fulfilling the will of God, we have every right to expect the best, and every obligation to prepare for the worst.

For Jonah, going to Assyria was not his dream, and the Assyrian Revival was not exactly a dream come true. It always comes down to this, as I quote now a dear pastor-friend of mine by the name of Vic Charnley who says, "We either will dream God's dream or man's dream, and we will either be running God's race or man's race." He goes on, "God's dream and man's dream aren't even close." I couldn't agree more. If you dream man's dream, in the USA it will no doubt be some version of the "American Dream" which is of course a really nice home with 4 bedrooms, 3 bathrooms, a 3 stall garage for two cars, 2 motor cycles, 2 snowmobiles and a large RV parked next to the garage. But to have the American dream you must run the American race, better known as the rat race, and it is hard to run the rat race without you and your wife becoming rats yourselves. I have no doubt that many Christians have had their dreams scripted for them by the prevailing culture and not by God. Many are not where God wants them to be, but where their environment taught them they should be.

However, in it all God knows what He is doing, where He is going and why. We may not be able to explain the why until much later. Amy Carmichael, the devoted missionary to India, when she was a child wanted to have pretty blue eyes just like many of her friends. One night she earnestly prayed to God that her brown eyes would be turned into blue eyes. That is what she wanted. Alas! When she woke up the next morning she discovered that those brown eyes were still the same boring color. She was very disappointed, and in her heart she questioned God and asked, "Why God? I prayed to you and I believed. Why are my eyes still brown?"

Years later, Amy Carmichael was called by the Holy Spirit to be a missionary to India. That is what God wanted. Through her experiences in this new land, she came to understand why when she was a child the Lord did not affirmatively answer her prayer for blue eyes. He answered negatively for a much higher and positive purpose. It was a no, but a no with a yes at the center. Since her eyes were brown, she was not looked upon as a foreigner in India. Instead, she was more easily accepted, and was able to minister much more effectively to the people of India. (7)

God's will and calling for our lives must be trusted, even though not initially understood. Many times the calling of God for my life, and therefore for the lives of my wife and family, scared me and them half to death. I could not fathom what God was up to. I want everything in my thinking to be decisive, orderly, rational, humanly doable and convenient. Christianity is not only peace that passes understanding, but more often than not, it is peace without understanding. Easier said than done!

Finally, so convoluted can this whole positive thinking and imaging thing become in man's mind, that negative realities in his way of thinking can appear as most positive and desirable, and vice versa. It was Saul who was controlled by a murderous rage which seemed to him to be both good and necessary. He thought that it was a holy calling to do many things contrary to the name of Jesus. (Act 26:9) Saul, the Pharisee of Pharisees, in his vengeful spirit against Jesus Christ, was so blinded and perverted in his reasoning, that he positively had convinced himself that his bloody crusade against Christians was both magnanimous and just. He ended up blinded by a light from Heaven which shown brighter than the noonday sun. The light was Jesus Christ Himself. He was led away by his seeing-eye companions to a house on Straight Street in Damascus where God would finally straighten him out once and for all.

We now know him as Paul. The name change was much easier than the heart change. He sat in a total stranger's house blinded and without food or drink for three days before his conversion to Christianity was complete. For three days and three nights both Jonah and Paul were in the dark before they could truly see the light. They were not so much persuaded as they were overpowered. God has His overmatching methods. Oh does He ever!

All of this illustrates to us that any man's life under the influence of his selfish thoughts, wild imaginations, and raging emotions can become a positively negative mess. It also illustrates that the mind of man, even of religious man, can be so deceived, that it considers God's good will to be very bad and its own rebellious thoughts and designs to be very good. This exposes the terribly dangerous fallacy of teaching man to rely upon what appears to be positive, possibility thoughts and images as his true and trusted guidance system in life.

GOD'S WILL – OFTEN MAN'S LAST RESORT

The reason that people get sucked into Religious Humanism's positive and possibility fantasyland is because in it all, they can still hang on to their own wills. Nothing to man is so torturous as having to pray that God-awful prayer of Jesus in the Garden of Gethsemane, when He prayed to His Father in Luke 22:42,

"...not My will, but Thine be done."

Not mine, Thine! What a raucous rhyme that is for many religious people when thinking about where that prayer led Jesus – to His suffering and death on the cross. The will of God really gets a bad rap when people, even church people, think and talk about the dreaded will of God. God have mercy! The will of God!? Why, that is the last thing that we would ever want for our lives. People forget of course that Christ's prayer led to His complete victory over sin, death, Satan, and Hell, as well as to our salvation, resurrection and ultimate glorification.

Still, the tragic fact remains that when Religious Humanists hear that phrase being prayed to God, namely, "Thy Will Be Done," they have seizures. When many people pray that prayer, the very tone of their voices while praying it suggests that they expect it to be something that they really don't want at all. It is almost a fatalistic sigh. It comes near to negative resignation. It is closer to a begrudging submission.

You perhaps have sounded that way as you prayed with negative thinking that said, "Well, okay then, God, if You absolutely must, Your will be done. We never wanted to even think that it would ever come to this." That is exactly why in many instances people prefer Religious Humanism to true Christianity which they view as totally encumbered by the "Sadistic Sovereign Will of God." They would rather think up some positive thoughts and dream some dreamy plans of their own, than ever entertain the bitter alternative of having to submit to that distasteful will of God. In short, Religious Humanism majors in human willing, while Christianity majors in Divine willing.

All of this of course is paganism, pure paganism. If we think dark, negative thoughts when we pray for God's will to be done and not our will, it is then that we are slandering the Heavenly Father, mistrusting Christ, and grieving the Holy Spirit. It is rank blasphemy to say, "Okay God, Your will be done, so just go ahead and wreck my life." We are taught in Romans 12:2 that the plans that God has for our lives are good, acceptable, and perfect. In other words, it doesn't get any better than God's perfect will. His will is the highest positive, the ultimate possibility, and the best there can ever be.

Because God's will alone is perfect, it is the only safe will to pray for, and the only safe will to be in. To pray to God, "Thy will be done," is the best and only secure prayer to base your life upon. Simply because it is a prayer to the all-wise God who is perfect love! The truth is this: "**GOD INTENDS INFINITELY BETTER FOR US THAN WE COULD EVER INTEND FOR OURSELVES.**"

RELIGIOUS HUMANISM – NEVER PRAY, "IF IT BE YOUR WILL."

Religious Humanists become very contentious and even irate when they hear someone say or pray the words to God, "Thy will be done**,"** or even worse, "If it be Your will." That is particularly true in many Charismatic groups within modern Christendom. I am deeply saddened to have to designate "Charismatics" in the Religious Humanism context. I believe in Biblical Pentecost with all of my heart, and am a product of the glorious Charismatic Renewal that cut across denominational lines in the 1970s and 1980s resulting in the restoration of the precious gifts (charismata) of the Holy Spirit which had been stolen from the Christian Church by religious tradition. I call it tradition, because it contradicts the Word of God. And anybody who tells you that we don't need the gifts of the Holy Spirit is himself infected with his own brand of Religious Humanism. Why? Because he would rather operate in his own wisdom and strength than in the demonstration of the Holy Spirit and power! (I Corinthians 2:4)

However, so much of that blessed Charismatic Renewal has now sadly become "Charismania" which is polluted by Religious Humanism. Religious Humanists develop a major religious rash when they encounter the words, "If the

Lord wills." Prominent Charismatic personalities such as Benny Him, Frederick Price and many others are of this school of thought. They believe categorically the following: "**IT IS UNBIBLICAL TO PRAY, 'IF THE LORD WILLS.'**" Entire ecclesiastical fellowships and churches are taught never to pray these words. Their entire theology is built on the rejection of that prayer. That prayer language is literally banned by thousands of modern-day Religious Humanists. It is denounced as anathema. It is considered a big no-no, because it allegedly creates doubt and weakness in faith. Religious Humanism!

Evangelist Benny Hinn is world renown for his healing crusades. "Let Us Reason Ministries" writes, "Benny Hinn said, '**NEVER, EVER, EVER GO TO THE LORD AND SAY, 'IF IT BE THY WILL'....'DON'T ALLOW SUCH FAITH DESTROYING WORDS TO BE SPOKEN FROM YOUR MOUTH.'**"(8)

Frederick Price is pastor and founder of Crenshaw Christian Center in Los Angeles, CA. "Apologetics Index," with its publishers Anton and Janet Hein-Hudson, is a vital resource in its crusade for orthodox Christianity. "Apologetics Index" writes, "Price claims he was brought up in a Jehovah's Witness family. After he converted to Christianity he experienced many different denominations This was all left behind him after he read K. Hagin's booklet *The Authority Of The Believer*. This developed him into being the chief exponent of name it and claim it, say it and frame it, speak it and keep it... (quoting Price): "**IF YOU HAVE TO SAY, 'IF IT BE THY WILL,' OR, 'THY WILL BE DONE,' IF YOU HAVE TO SAY THAT, THEN YOU ARE CALLING GOD A FOOL BECAUSE HE IS THE ONE WHO TOLD US TO ASK.**"(9) This would mean of course that Jesus Christ by praying exactly that was calling His Heavenly Father a fool. That is sheer blasphemy!

Jesse Duplantis is a comedic evangelist as well as a frequent speaker on Trinity Broadcasting Network. "Let us Reason Ministries" writes, "Jesse also boasts (quoting Duplantis): '**I CAN HONESTLY SAY THAT THE LORD HAS DONE EVERYTHING I HAVE PRAYED FOR.**'"(10) Let's take a look first of all at this alleged and astounding prayer batting average. When you are batting a thousand percent in your prayer life, there seems to be no need to add, "If the Lord wills." When you hit a homerun every time you pray, I would suppose that you equate your will with God's will.

That is exactly what Religious Humanists do. They believe that they have a direct pipeline into the secret council chambers of the Trinity, and are privy to all of the plans and purposes of God. That in spite of Deuteronomy 29:29! When they pray, they give you the distinct impression that it is the same thing as God speaking. How else could you hit the prayer ball out of the prayer ballpark every time you swing your prayer bat? A 1000% prayer batting average!? I have never met anybody before, including anyone in the Bible, who claims to have received everything that He asked God for. Not even Jesus!

To be totally honest with myself and you, I don't have a very high prayer batting average when it comes to praying for people with terminal cancer. I don't even think in that regard that I am even a solid .200 hitter. This of course means that I surely wouldn't make the "Religious Humanism Prayer Squad." If I did, it would be as a reserve and I would have to ride the prayer bench. For you see, in Religious Humanism, the chief emphasis is on the faith-production of the one doing the praying, and not on the faithfulness of the One being prayed to. Even though God's answer-average is 1000%, because He is the all-wise Sovereign God who never strikes out on our prayer fast-balls! He answers all of our prayers perfectly and hits a home run every time.

Let's go now to the Religious Humanist's denunciation and denial of the phrase, "If the Lord wills." Their teachings in this regard are flat-out rejections of and contradictions to the clear Word of God. Two truths cannot contradict each other. If they could, then two contradictions could be equally true at the same time. But Religious Humanists flat out contradict the Bible and call it truth.

The Lord speaks to us in James 4:15, and commands us in the following unmistakable words,

> **"...you ought to say, 'If the Lord wills, we shall live and also do this or that.'"**

The Apostle Paul lived and spoke that very same way, as evidenced by the fact that when he had gone to the synagogue in Ephesus and reasoned with the Jews, he made such a good impression that he was asked to stay longer. He said in Acts 18:21,

> **"...I will return to you again if God wills...."**

And again we read in Hebrews 6:3,

> **"And this we shall do, if God permits."**

The Bible is full of the "Sovereign If." If God wills! If God permits! Hello! Heaven to earth! Bible to Religious Humanists! Are you reading God's Word? No, you are not reading the full counsel of God! You are floating around in your Disneyworld Christianity which refuses to submit human reason and wishful thinking to God's sovereign and perfect will. But the Bible is clearer than clear on this critical matter. Run Dick run, go get the ball. It is as plain as a first-grade reader.

Did you see it? You ought to say, "If the Lord wills," says the Apostle James. What part of that don't we understand? It ought to be the Christian's normal daily conversation about the Lord's will as well as his constant submission to the Lord. This is the Biblical language that surrounded me from child-hood onward – we will be going there if the Lord wills, we will be doing this or that if the Lord wills, and we will live and do such and such if the Lord wills. Right on! Thoroughly Biblical! Why? Because He is God and we are not! As least until now!

Religious Humanists wouldn't be caught dead with those words on their lips, even though God alone wills our first and last breaths as well as every breath in between. Religious Humanists often walk around like they have life, the universe, the future and every circumstance in their hip pocket. They will never say or pray, "If it be God's will," or, "If it be Thy will," or "If the Lord wills."

There are no "Ifs" in Religious Humanism. Why? Because Religious Humanists have the last word, not God! In fact, they are God's Word! When they speak, declare and order, it is done! American radio stations used to sign off for the day with the National Anthem – "Oh Say Can You See!" Religious Humanist radio stations have their own Humanist Anthem with which they sign off on every issue – "I Say, And It Is So!"

Christians sign off for the day in this spirit – "Until Tomorrow, If The Lord Wills." Throughout the centuries, it has been common for Christians to sign their letters to each other with the letters D.V. Those two letters stand for the Latin "Deo Volente" which means, "The Lord Willing" which really means "If The Lord Wills." Religious Humanists today refuse such a salutation.

We must think, say, and pray, "If the Lord wills, we shall live and do this or that!" It is a Divine command. God orders it. Contrariwise, there are those in modern day Religious Humanism who actually practice and teach that when we pray, we should demand of God to give us our rights. Demanding and commanding God! I was watching one of these Religious Humanist evangelists do exactly that on television as he raised his hand toward Heaven, pointed his finger at God and said, "God, I command you!" El nutso! It's off the charts! I remember saying to that fella, "You better back off, dude, God is the Commander, and you are the commandee! And if you continue to try and push God around, He may well become the Consumer, and you will be the consumee, as He sends fire from Heaven to burn some truth in your haughty head."

This commanding and controlling spirit corrupts so much of what Religious

Humanists today call prayer. It is not prayer at all, for it turns prayer into an affront to God. It is not seeking God, but rather ordering God around like He is some sort of Kool-Aid and cookies God who distributes His goodies upon demand.

The denial of this one Bible truth, namely the refusal to pray, "If it be Your will," has opened up Religious Humanism's followers to more heresies, extremes, confusions, hurts and fatal damages than anything else I know of. I have more than once dealt with people who commanded the cancer in a loved one's life to leave in Jesus' name. The person died and so did the commander's faith, all because they were taught never to pray, "If the Lord wills." Then they blamed the dead one for not having enough faith, or having sin in his life, or both. I have seen entire churches lose their faith because they refused to submit to God and thereby played God. And when their commands were soundly disobeyed by God, their faith was destroyed. Hansel's and Gretel's faith was blasted, and they couldn't find their way home to God because the faith-fragments were eaten by the enemies of their souls.

Christians petition God. Religious Humanists order God. In Christianity, man submits to God's will. In Religious Humanism, God submits to man's will. In Christianity, man asks God and God responds with either "Yes" or "No" or "Later." In Religious Humanism, man orders God and God must say "Yes" and do it now.

Of course, that is never how it was in our home. There were many times as a father that I said "No" when my children declared "Yes." As a matter of fact, a significant percentage of the time my "No" trumped their "Yes," even though like all kids they would try to whine the "No" back to, "Oh, alright then." I don't know how many times I declined their request for this activity or for that goofing-off because they had to do their homework. I had the feeling at times that they imagined that the homework would somehow get itself done before they would have to do it.

In summary, in Christianity, Father knows best. In Religious Humanism, His children know best. Otherwise why would they refuse to submit to Him in prayer by saying, "If it be Your will." Religious Humanists remind me of children dressing up in their parent's clothes and playing house, as they assume the roles of Dad and Mom. It is cute and even hilarious as they stumble around in shoes big enough to put over their heads. However, it is not cute when Religious Humanists assume the role of the Heavenly Father which is infinitely too big for any human head. It is tragic!

Let me clue you in on something here. When you can't see Biblical truth and it is right there before your very eyes, or when you see Biblical truth and it bugs you because it won't fit into your belief system, it is the indicator that your belief system is out of order and out of balance. And truth out of balance will always be error. Of course, you can always make the Bible truth say something that it is not saying, so that you won't have to change your belief system. This is deception at work.

BOYCOTTING GOD'S WILL – WHY?

Why do Religious Humanists refuse to say or pray, "If the Lord wills?" First of all because it popularizes their ministries, enlarges their followings, and enriches their coffers. People love to support with their dollars those who tell them that they can unconditionally have from God whatever they want, without having to add that humiliating, degrading and very tentative phrase, "If the Lord wills." People devour this false teaching!

Religious Humanists preach Christmas every day of people's lives! God is Santa Claus 365 days of every year. In Religious Humanism God is jolly old Saint Nick asking Christians, "What do you want for Christmas? Come sit on Santa God's knee and tell Santa God what your will is for Me. Just give me your list. I'll take care of it!" Christianity is man bowing down before the throne of God and saying, "What do You want me to do, Lord Jesus? I am at your command, and by your power I will do it."

Second, and even more importantly, why do Religious Humanists detest praying to God, "If the_Lord wills?" I'll tell you why. Because ultimately: "**IT PUTS GOD IN CONTROL AND NOT MAN IN CONTROL**." Precisely! Religious Humanists want the throne. After all, who is the boss around here? They want to run their lives and the whole universe for that matter according to their own agenda. Total control! It is all inextricably bound up with man's age-old human desire to be the master of his fate, and the captain of his soul. Kings of the cosmos! Lords of the universe! Judge and jury! Frank Sinatra's "I did it my way," only this time with a thin veneer of religion brushed over the top. Religious Humanism!

There is an inscription that appears on the west wall of Winchester, Cathedral in England. It reads like this: "**THAT WAY THOU THAT PRAYEST – THIS WAY THOU THAT PASSEST BY**." The background of the Winchester inscription is most significant and fascinating. Many years ago, way back in 1632, a passageway was cut in the southwest corner of this great cathedral. The passageway was necessary because over the centuries, people had gotten into the habit of taking a shortcut through the nave of the cathedral and then out of a side door in the south wing. Merely using the cathedral as a walk-through might not have been so bad, except for the insensitivity of thoughtless people who were carting their produce from the market with them. The traffic and the litter became so bad that the Bishop of Winchester was forced to take action. Thus this passageway was carved out so people could pass through the southwest corner of the church without disturbing the worshippers in the sanctuary. Therefore over the passageway you will find those words, "That way thou that prayest – this way thou that passest by."

These are exactly the kind of signs that we need posted in the religious world today. Over the door of Christianity the sign should read: "**THIS WAY, THOSE WHO DESIRE TO PRAY.**" Over the door of Religious Humanism the sign should read: "**THIS WAY, THOSE WHO WANT TO RUN THE SHOW.**"

Third, then there are times that we refuse to pray for God's will to be done, because we know deep down the thing that we want, God will not give it to us because it is completely contrary to His Word. I recall vividly the married man who was having an affair. He said to me that he was praying to God that if He did not want him to have this other woman, then God would have to remove her. He was in fact praying from his own will and not for God's will. He would not pray, "Thy Will Be Done," for he knew that what he was doing was not God's will in the first place. His prayer was a farce.

Like the little boy who was overheard saying in his nightly prayers, "Please God, make Boulder the capital of Colorado." When he had said "Amen," his mother who overheard her son's prayer asked him, "Son, why did you ask God for that?" "Because," he said, "that's what I put down on my exam paper." The young son was asking God to create an examination fantasyland for him by changing the capital of Colorado before the teacher got around to correcting his exam.

DISCOVERING GOD'S PLAN FOR OUR LIVES

Christianity is not about positive or possibility thinking as they are defined by their proponents, but it is all about prayerfully discovering God's perfect plan for our lives. God has a glorious plan and purpose for each one of our lives, and for every day in our lives. We read in Ephesians 1:11,

> "**…having been predestined according to His purpose who works all things after the counsel of His will.**"

All things! Every moment! Therein is contained the entire point of our existence, and why we were created and recreated in Jesus Christ. God does not create and recreate without a design. The Lord doesn't want anyone to slip through the cracks. The Lord doesn't want anyone to die and say that his or her life didn't matter.

The issue then remains as to how we come to discover our Divine call in life and for every day in that life. Do we determine it by sitting down, thinking, dreaming, and imagining vocational thoughts, and then trusting in our own understanding and abilities to pull them off? When it comes to how to find our place in life, we have a lot of avenues to choose from. Somewhere in it all there is God. There is endless competition with God out there. You will hear Religious Humanists talk about visualization, positive imaging, positive thinking, possibility thinking, wishing, and sub-conscious empowering and on and on it goes. Religious Humanism leads people to believe that their successful future is in their cognitive crystal ball. It is what you think and imagine yourself being and becoming that is in fact what you can be if you wish hard enough and believe strong enough in yourself for it. Of course, always ask God to bless it.

There are several huge problems with all of this, and one of them Jeremiah tells us about in Jeremiah 10:23,

"I know, O Lord, that a man's way is not in himself; nor is it in a man who walks to direct his steps."

Whoops! This is a huge problem right from the get-go! It is not in us! This means that the plan that God has for us, including our life's work on a day by day basis, is not in our thoughts, our imaginations, or our dreams even though we are taught in Secular and Religious Humanism that it is. Our decisions do determine our destiny! We sure don't want to blow it here, and step out of the will of God. It is much easier to step into something that is not the will of God than it is to get out of it once we're in it! How well many of us know!

Well then, where is it? In God! Oh my, we are back to God and His will again! Those God fanatics! They make everything a God thing! I mean, a little bit of God will go a long way for many religious folks. But for most people, even religious ones, you can easily overdo this God-involvement stuff. A little dab of God will do ya! But after that, we are on our own. Life is about positive and possibility thinking. Life is about imaging. Life is about sweet dreams. Life is about wishful thinking. Just as people today in the world and in the church want to define their own moral codes, so they want to chart their own courses.

Sorry, it isn't what we imagine ourselves doing with our lives. It is what the Lord wants us to do with our lives. It is what the Lord has planned for us moment by moment. Jonah and Saul could not have imagined what God had planned for their lives. It was the farthest things from their minds. It was all in

God and not in them, and we, too, must find our way in God in order to find our way in life! And to many, that is about as foreign as cyber-sourcing. It makes about as much sense as satellite transmission. Someone says, "I have never heard of this before. I have never heard of anything like this. This is all new to me." Yes I know, and it is to lots of people who have bought into Religious Humanism's teaching that the way of man is in himself, that is, in his thoughts and imaginations. There is only one place to go to! Go to God! God commands us in Proverbs 3:5-6,

> "**Trust in the Lord with all your heart**, and do not lean on
> your own understanding. In all your ways acknowledge
> Him, and He will make your paths straight."

It is a complete wipe-out of all this positive-possibility thinking and magic-carpet ride imagination stuff as our GPS.

Trust in the Lord! Focus on and rest in His presence, and not primarily on His purpose. We must first live a Divine presence-immersed life and secondly a Divine purpose-driven life. The purpose is in His presence, and only when you practice His presence will His presence be in the purpose. I very much prefer to think and speak of a Divinely-directed life rather than a purpose-driven life. Christianity is not a cattle drive. Christianity is a shepherd-sheep relationship. Jesus the Good Shepherd said of Himself and His sheep in John 10:4,

> "…**he goes before them**, and the sheep follow Him because
> they know His voice."

Christians are not driven, they are led. He leads, we follow. Oh yes, he burns within us His purpose for our lives. I call it Holy Ghost heartburn. When He puts that call in your head and your heart, no amount of Alka-Seltzer will put the fire out. God first of all inspires us with the purpose, and then the purpose inspires us in service for God.

Trusting in God and constantly seeking His face for His will in our lives is infinitely more reliable than flying the uncharted skies of our imaginations. It is not the Christian, but it is the Religious Humanist who has his head stuck in the clouds of his cognitive fantasyland. Christians do not have their heads stuck in the clouds. They live far above them before the throne of God.

Don't trust in your own mind! God and God alone knows and makes the path that we are to travel in life clear and direct, if we rely totally and prayerfully upon Him. He alone has the map for our futures. He will speak to our hearts by the Holy Spirit, and mark the way by His still small voice and His opening to us doors of opportunities (Divine Providence). He alone can steer us straight. The Lord promises his children His faithful and sure guidance as we read about Him promising to us in Isaiah 30:21,

> **"And your ears will hear a word behind you, 'This is the way, walk in it,' whenever you turn to the right or to the left."**

PRAYING FOR GOD'S WILL IN OUR LIVES

Someone might ask, "Just how do I get tuned in and turned on to what God has for me? So far it all sounds pretty complicated – mental engineering, positive thinking, possibility thinking, imaging, holding things in my subconscious, wishing etc. I think I have tried it all, although I am not sure, and I have gotten nowhere. How does this Christian-guidance thing work and how do I get started?"

Yes I know, hearing you talk reminds me of a man who stopped by the computer store where he had recently purchased a PC. He said to the salesman, "I have a question about a computer that I bought here the other day." The salesman asked him, "What kind did you buy, sir?" The customer said, "A Crimean Extravaganza Nineteen Hundred." Asked the salesman, "Wow that is really a nice computer. Do you need some add ons? Do you need some more memory? Do you need an accelerator board?" The customer responded, "No, no, you don't understand. I just need to know how to turn the thing on!"

First of all then, we must be constantly praying and seeking God to show us what He made us to be and to do, and then ask from Him the wisdom and strength to carry out His will on a daily basis. We have not because we think not? No! We have not because we positivize not? No! We have not because we possibilize not? No! We have not because we imagine not? No! We have not because we dream not? No! We have not because we wish not? No! The Bible says that we have not because we ask not. (James 4:2)

Follow me now, because it becomes very embarrassing for us when we realize how often we miss the obvious. Do you remember the words of I Thessalonians 5:17? Sure you will when you see them, as the Holy Spirit through Paul commands,

> **"Pray without ceasing."**

That includes among other things constantly seeking God's will for our lives.

Perhaps there are some of you out there right now who are seeking God's purpose for your lives. You aren't yet getting a clear, Holy Spirit confirmed direction. Remember Jesus instruction to his disciples in Luke 18:1,

"…that at all times they should pray and not lose heart."

Those of you who are unsure about your future and God's plan for you, even though you have prayed and prayed, don't ever stop praying! Here is where the rubber hits the prayer road, and it is a long, long road. Unceasing prayer! You may be going through a dark tunnel, but the light will come. It may be that God wants to keep you right where you are. Remember, the grass is not first of all greener on the other side of the fence. The grass is greener where you water it. He will make it plain.

For others of you, God has been trying for years to get you from where you are to where He wants you to be. He has been attempting to birth his purpose in your life, and the good news is that it is never too late with God. Someone reading this has had a Holy Spirit heartburn in you for something your entire adult life, but you have never followed through. And now you are saying to yourself that by the time you get there, you will be too old. Might I ask you, "How old will you be when you don't get there?" Age is never the primary factor, the call of God is!

There was this lady who was very pregnant, went into labor and waited too long to go to the hospital. She didn't make it, though she did get into the hospital, but gave birth on the elevator. She was so embarrassed. She apologized again and again to the nurses. One of the nurses said, "Don't be embarrassed, for a couple of years ago there was a lady who didn't even make it to the elevator. She gave birth on the hospital lawn." And the woman said, "That was me, too." Better late than never!

On the other hand, there are those of you who have a deep and defined stirring, but nothing has opened up for you yet. Don't get impatient with God! Remember the words of Psalm 37:7,

"Rest in the Lord, and wait patiently for Him…."

The most harmful thing in the world is to try to speed God up. Abraham was guilty of trying to hurry things along. Abraham fathered Ishmael with Hagar and we have had the feud between the Arabs and the Jews ever since Abraham got in a rush. Quickie prayers are the sign that you are growing impatient. Quickie prayers lead to quickie decisions, and quickie decisions are generally bad decisions. This is not poetry, this is prose. This is not exaggeration. It is if anything an understatement. It cannot be overstated.

Listen closely now, we are to constantly pray our way through life first of all. We are not anywhere told by God to first of all think our way through life. How is that for a shocker to "Mindman?" We are not first of all to brain our way through life, but to bow our way through life. Braining our way through life is taking matters into our own hands, and that is when we get into big trouble.

Someone undoubtedly is saying, "How nuts is this? This author is telling us not to use our heads." Of course this author is not saying anything of the kind. We are to love the Lord with all out mind. What he is saying is what he heard a preacher once say, "If you have a brain in your head, you will pray at all times, and only when you pray at all times (Ephesians 6:18) can you even dare to use the brain in your head." He was right on! Only then will we hear the voice of God giving us a nudge in the right way, decision by decision. God's people were never meant to be primarily Mind-men! They were created by God to be "Prayer-men."

Then we can either choose to obey God's voice, or turn a deaf ear to Him and grope our way through the darkness. As William MacDonald observed, "For everyone who deliberately makes a choice, there are probably three who simply drift. They think of themselves as the pawns of chance or luck. They are fatalists. But, still, they have made their choice, and that choice is to drift along and take whatever comes."(11) Christians want to avoid the drift. Christians want with all their hearts only what God has for them. They want God's will more than life itself. Just like their Master, Jesus Christ. Not my will, but God's will be done!

Only those who yield their all to God will receive His guidance and avoid the drift. Here is how praying for the will of God for our lives truly sounds. As William MacDonald points out, "Betty Stam made life's great commitment nine years before she was martyred. She wrote in her Bible, 'Lord, I give up my own purposes and plans, and all my desires, hopes and ambitions (whether they be fleshly or soulish), and I accept Thy will for my life. I give myself, my life, my all utterly to Thee, to be Thine forever. I hand over to Thy keeping all my friendships. All the people whom I love are to take second place in my heart. Fill me with Thy Holy Spirit. Work out Thy whole will for my life, at any cost, now and forever. To me to live is Christ.'"(12)

God took her at her word. Betty and her husband, John, were called by God to be missionaries in a small town called Jingle near the eastern coast of China. Not exactly the stuff dreams are made of. Christianity is not a dream world. Christianity is in the real and raw world of life and death, love and hatred, light and darkness, befriending and beheading. John and Betty were killed by the communists. John was beheaded, and Betty was killed a few moments later. Because for John and Betty to live was Christ, for them to die was gain!

William Whiting Borden of Yale made his life's great commitment but a few years before he died of cerebral meningitis in Egypt while en route to China with the Gospel. In 1912, he offered himself to God for the China Inland Mission. He studied in Cairo, Egypt to learn Arabic. He was stricken with cerebrospinal meningitis. He died at age 26. He had once prayed, "Lord Jesus, I take hands off, as far as my life is concerned. I put Thee on the throne of my heart. Change, cleanse, and use me as Thou shalt choose. I take the full power of Thy Holy Spirit. I thank Thee."(13)

Only when we yield ourselves unreservedly to God will we be able to hear His voice calling us. In Religious Humanism, man uses God for his own purposes. In Christianity, God uses man for His own purposes. God, use me, just as You will, when and where! Do we have the courage to pray that prayer? That alone gets God's attention. That alone assures us that our lives will not be wasted, we will avoid the drift, and we will not be dreaming man's dream, but God's.

FASTING FOR GOD'S WILL IN OUR LIVES

Second, it is thoroughly Biblical to say that praying by itself is not enough. It must be accompanied by another spiritual discipline. Fasting! Prayer and fasting, the two wings of devotion! We cannot fly to the throne of grace on just one. That is the Bible's dynamic duo, not mental engineering and imaging. They not only empower us in our struggle against sin and Satan in order to overcome them, but to help us hear from God and powerfully walk the rugged road that He would have us to travel. Jesus said in Matthew 6:5, "And when you pray." He did not say, "And if you pray." Jesus said in Matthew 6:16, "And whenever you fast." He did not say, "If ever you fast."

Modern Christians overeat and under fast, if they fast at all. Most modern church people are more interested in gourmet cooking than they are in Biblical fasting. In fact, they have attended churches their entire lives and never once were taught about or challenged with the need for fasting. However, seldom was there anything great or holy accomplished in the Bible without fasting. Bodily abstinence with prayer is double strength to the spirit of man. The ways of Religious Humanism and Biblical Christianity are vastly different.

Prayer and fasting are true soul food. It goes all the way back to Moses. When Moses was being prepared to receive the law of God, it was with fasting. (Deuteronomy 9:9) When Jesus began His great earthly ministry leading to His atoning sacrifice on the cross, He did so through forty days of fasting. (Matthew 4:2) If Jesus had not denied His flesh, He would have been weakened in His spirit. If His table had always been spread with flesh food rather than spirit food, then I ask the Holy Spirit to allow me to adapt what the Psalmist said in Psalm 69:22 to Jesus Christ,

"The table would have been His snare."

Jesus would not have set His face to Jerusalem and ultimately to Calvary had He not fasted. Flesh must be denied before the spiritual can be embraced. We can only hunger and thirst for righteousness when we deny our hunger and thirst for everything else.

The Christian Church, from its very inception, heard from God and found its way by prayer and fasting. We read in Acts 13:2-3,

"And while they were ministering to the Lord and fasting, the Holy Spirit said, 'Set apart for Me Barnabas and Saul for the work to which I have called them. Then, when they had fasted and prayed And laid their hands on them, They sent them away."

Church history points to this moment as the time when "Christian Missions" was truly birthed, and the first Christian missionaries were sent forth by Christ through His church. Who these missionaries were to be and where they were to go in order to do the work that the Holy Spirit called them to, flowed from the spiritual disciplines of prayer and fasting. Without prayer and fasting in the Christian life, we are grasping at shadows. Without both of these as part and parcel of normal Christian living, we will not be able to hear God's voice amidst the crowded streets and seductive calls that will sweep us away and lure us in the wrong direction. Barnabas and Saul were swept along by the Holy Spirit, for we read in Acts 13:4,

"So, being sent out by the Holy Spirit, they went down to Seleucia, and from there they sailed to Cyprus."

LISTENING FOR GOD'S WILL IN OUR LIVES

Third, then we must listen to the voice of His Spirit speaking to us as we have just seen in Isaiah 30:21, and which must be repeated,

"And your ears will hear a word behind you...."

Lock coordinates into His guidance. Listening for and to His voice! Normal Christianity! Let's face it; God has a very hard time getting through to 21st century humanity, including Christians. They are too occupied, and I mean occupied, watching television to be able to hear from God. If they spent as much time before God as they do before their living room Cyclops, I have no doubt they would hear from God.

We live in a TV addicted society, and that includes church people. A man showed up at church with his ears painfully blistered. After the service, his concerned pastor asked, "What in the world happened to you?" The man replied, "I was lying on the couch yesterday afternoon watching a ballgame on TV and my wife was ironing nearby. I was totally engrossed in the game when she left the room leaving the iron nearby. The phone rang and keeping my eyes glued to the television, I grabbed the hot iron and put it to my ear." The pastor asked, "So how did the other ear get burned?" He said, "Well, I had no sooner put the phone down and the guy called again."

More than that, many old-line, mainline denominational church-goers in America in all of this are closer to Religious Humanism than to the authentic Christian experience. It is much more comfortable for them to be self-guided and self-reliant than to be God-guided and God-reliant.

Oh yes, church folks can be very religious about their religion. Doctrines! Traditions! Rituals! But this mysticism and fanaticism about seeking God at all times and about all things, and then literally hearing His voice speaking in response, well, that is just too super-spiritual and far too super-rational. This they feel makes men extremists as they are so viewed by typical self-reliant churchgoers. Though they will sing at Easter, not really knowing what they are actually saying, "He walks with me and talks with me along life's narrow way." They really don't believe that song. If they did, they would stop calling those who practice it the far-out mystically and emotionally affected ones.

However, don't think that you will hear from God one word when you persist in neglecting the Word of God. God is not a dog who barks when we say, "Speak!" The Voice behind you will only come when you are listening to the Word of God right in front of you – the Holy Bible. I find it hard to talk to those people who I can tell are not listening to me. Their eyes are all over the place, and all they are waiting for is for me to stop talking so they can start. I won't even try to give counsel or advice to such people even when they say they want it, for they don't really care about you or what you are saying. God feels the same way, as He says about such frustrating people in Matthew 13:15,

"...**and with their ears they scarcely hear**...."

Let your life show that you are attentive to the God of the Word before you can expect to hear a word from God. That is how it works.

Pilots, so I am told, must go through intensive training to retrain their minds and their instincts not to adhere to what they think and feel as to what is up and down, but to believe the instruments and to lock coordinates into them. So we must constantly and prayerfully believe what God is telling us, and lock coordinates into God and His guidance, and not into our own understanding. God-fixation is required!

God's promise to speak to us and guide us into His will for our lives is one of the most awesome assurances in the Word of God. And your ears will hear a word behind you, "This is the way, walk in it." Abraham, known as the father of all believers, lived by faith in the same way that all of us must live our lives. Eighteen hundred years before the birth of Christ, a man by the name of Abram who was 75 years old at the time, lived in a region of a country that today would be known as Iraq. God spoke to him and told him to get out of town. He believed God. He immediately set out for a new land which God had promised to show him.

Over and over again, we read in the Bible words like, "And God said unto him." For many devout denominationalists, that no longer takes place! They have God not alive and speaking into their lives, but embalmed in what they refer to as "Bible Times." Their faces stiffen when someone talks about God speaking to them. If they were honest, they would say, "I don't know much about that. I have a hard time believing that. I have never heard God speak. I really don't know what you mean by that." What a shame and a tragedy! It never occurs to them that the reason they don't hear God is that they are not listening for God. In fact, their spiritual hearing apparatus is not even turned on because they have been taught that God no longer speaks person to person.

But the harsh truth is that he who will not hear God will be in reality a disobedient servant. To be sure, we cannot do the will of God without hearing it from God. But equally true is that we can hear the will of God for our lives without doing it. In either case, **"MAN WILL BE HELD ACCOUNTABLE NOT ONLY FOR THE WORDS THAT HE HAS HEARD FROM GOD, BUT ALSO FOR THE WORDS THAT HE SHOULD HAVE HEARD, BUT DIDN'T."**

I have over the years come to understand more clearly why God speaks to us in the still small voice. It is because He wants to grow us up spiritually. He wants to strengthen our faith in Him and deepen our dependence upon Him. God could shout at us I suppose. But then we would not have to draw near to Him. We would only have to be in shouting distance, and our relationship with him would be distant, too. But now we must be still and close to Him in order to hear His voice. Draw near to Him and He will draw near to you. (James 4:8)

We must recognize both His voice contained in Scripture, and the voice that gives counsel in times of prayer and listening. Jesus said that His sheep know His voice. (John 10:4) That is Christianity! And remember, "**GOD WILL NOT SPEAK TO THOSE WHO AS A WAY OF LIFE DO NOT SPEAK TO HIM AS A WAY OF LIFE**." Moreover, "**THOSE WHO DO NOT SPEAK TO GOD WILL NOT BE LISTENING FOR GOD EITHER**." Furthermore, "**IF WE DO NOT SET ASIDE EACH DAY A SIGNIFICANT TIME TO SPEAK WITH GOD, NO DOUBT THAT NEITHER WILL WE SET ASIDE A TIME TO HEAR FROM GOD**." Finally, "**ALL OF THIS COMES DOWN TO THE FACT THAT MANY RELIGIOUS FOLK TALK AT GOD, BUT SELDOM IF EVER DO THEY TALK WITH HIM**."

You say, "I don't hear any of this in my church. All I hear about is self-belief, positive and possibility thinking, and tapping into my unlimited potential." Yes, I know! But now you know the choice. Positive thinking, imaging, and wishing hard – Religious Humanism! Prayer, fasting, and listening – Christianity! The choice could not be clearer. Does God then speak into our minds, imaginations and dreams? Of course He does, but only when we faithfully do the praying, fasting and listening.

Resources:

1. Let Us Reason Ministries, Mike Oppenheimer, "Norman Vincent Peale a man who made up his mind" (Schuller, Your Church, p. 85)

2. Let us Reason Ministries, Mike Oppenheimer, "Norman Vincent Peale a man who made up his mind" (Norman V. Peale, Introduction, Positive Imaging, p. 77, 1982)

3. Let Us Reason Ministries, Mike Oppenheimer, "Norman Vincent Peale a man who made up his mind" (Norman V. Peale, Introduction, Positive Imaging, p. 1)

4. Ibid.

5. Let Us Reason Ministries, Mike Oppenheimer, "Another Possible Gospel of Robert Schuller's" (Robert Schuller on Larry King Live, 1/28/94)

6. Ben Haden, "Changed Lives" (Ben Haden Evangelical Association, Inc., Chattanooga, TN) 1991

7. Dynamic Preaching, "Who Is God Anyway" (Seven Worlds Corporation, Knoxville, TN, June, 1996, Volume XI, N o. 6) page 6, Ralph E. Dessen, "Emphasis" (September/October,1992) Page 13

8. Let Us Reason Ministries, Mike Oppenheimer, "I Have What I Think and Say

I Have" (Rise and Be Healed! 1991, p. 47-48)

9. Apologetics Index, "Resources on Religious Movements, Cults, Sects, World Religions and Related Issues," Anton and Janet Hein-Hudson, Publishers (Frederick Price, "Ever Increasing Faith" Program on TBN, November 16, 1990

10. Let Us Reason Ministries, Mike Oppenheimer, "Jesse Duplantis, a Man with A Short Theology and Tall Tales" p. 44 Heaven: Close Encounters of the God Kind."

11. William MacDonald, "Think of Your Future," 1956, Page 25, © Walterick Publishing Ministries, Inc., Olathe, Kansas – Used By Permission

12. William MacDonald, "Think of Your Future," 1956, Page 37, (Quoted In "Were They Expendable?" By Clay Cooper, Brown Gold Publications, Chico, CA, Page 3) © Walterick Publishing Ministries, Inc., Olathe, Kansas – Used By Permission

13. William MacDonald, "Think of Your Future," 1956, Page 37, (Mrs. Howard Taylor, "Borden of Yale," 1909, Philadelphia: China Inland Mission, 1943, Page 123) © Walterick Publishing Ministries, Inc., Olathe, Kansas – Used By Permission

Chapter Three

THE CORRUPTING REVERSALS OF MODERN CHRISTIANITY

†††

*"When I Have Money, I Get Rid Of It Quickly, Lest It Find A Way Into My Heart." ~*John Wesley

There is an old adage which says that those who do not learn from history are bound to repeat it. I have been struck over the years by the total lack of attention given in many segments of modern Christendom to the Protestant Reformation begun in the 16th century and carried on by the great reformers such as Martin Luther, John Calvin, John Knox, John and Charles Wesley. As a matter of fact, I seriously doubt that the majority of modern Christianity could give a substantive, let alone impassioned account of what really happened on October 31, 1517 and why.

More than that, much of modern Christianity is far more focused on revival than on reformation, on experience than on doctrine, on innovation than on dogma, on tolerance than on truth. As a result, many if not most of the contemporary Christian churches have failed to learn the lessons of church history, and are now falling back into pre-Reformation heresies.

The dog has returned to its vomit. Martin Luther's 95 theses have been ripped off the modern church doors by Religious Humanism, opening the way to doctrinal chaos and corruption once again. The candlelight of the Protestant Reformation once burned brightly, but now is barely a flicker. And we all know about a candle that it burns brightly and warmly when it is first lit. But when it is allowed flicker and sputter, it soon clouds the atmosphere with smoke and then sheds light on nothing.

The truth about reformation that must be kept in clear focus is this: **"REFORMATION IS NOT JUST A TOKEN REMEM-BRANCE OF CHURCH HISTORY, BUT MUST BE AN ON- GOING PROCESS THROUGHOUT HISTORY."** Why must reformation be ongoing? Because Satan the liar and falsifier of truth is always writing new essays of untruth in the church and thereby deforming it! The Prince of Darkness never stops playing the light angel (II Corinthians 11:14) so as to deceive the children of God. His purpose is always to undermine and corrupt Christianity. He does so by perverting the Gospel of Jesus Christ, and causing men to lose their sense of evil.

He is universally doing both in the modern Christian Church today.

There is a much greater need today than in the 16th century for a new Protestant Reformation to correct rampant doctrinal heresy and human invention within Protestantism itself. Much of the present day revivalism is literally contaminated with Religious Humanism. What good is it to have sinners saved and then brought into deformity by becoming involved in churches permeated with doctrinal error? This is what is happening and will continue to happen unless a new reformation cleans up the spreading mess.

As always, Satan is sly and sneaky in his work of misleading people as he uses those who have prominent positions of impact in religious TV and inside the ranks of the so-called Christian Church to do his corrupting work. It was Martin Luther who made this statement: "**FOR WHERE GOD BUILT A CHURCH, THERE THE DEVIL WOULD BUILD A CHAPEL.**" I might add that in some church fellowships Satan's chapel has become the main church, and what was once the Orthodox Church has become a small chapel of hangers-on who are deeply grieved and yet cannot make their voices heard above the denominational leadership. This author hears your voices! Many stay in their ancestral churches from dedication and deep sentiment, but are in total disagreement with the higher ups. Today because it looks like a church, feels like a church and smells like a church does not necessarily mean it is the Church of the Lord Jesus Christ.

You have heard I am sure the old "Change The Light Bulb" stories about how many it takes to change a burned-out bulb. How many ecclesiastical liberals today does it take to change a light bulb? At least ten as they need to hold a debate on whether or not the light bulb exists. Even if they can agree upon the existence of the light bulb, they still might not change it, to keep from alienating those who use other forms of light.

How many neo-orthodoxes does it take to change a bulb? Who knows, because the truth is today that they can't tell the difference between light and darkness?

How many TV evangelists does it take to change a light bulb? Only one, but for the light to continue, send in your donation today. It is the last one here that that we must now deal with. Oh God do we ever?

GOD OWES ME ONE

It is disheartening to watch people in public eateries and fast-food restaurants when food is served to them. They dive right in like animals without bowing their heads to say thanks to God Who has provided it all. The Apostle Paul alludes to this very thing when he comments on these pig-trough thankless grunters and devourers in Romans 1:21,

"…they did not honor Him as God or give thanks…."

No thanks to God. Just oink-oink, chomp-chomp, and later burp- burp! Not one word of gratitude to or thought of God before or after their feeding frenzies. Concerning natural man it is accurate to say that he has only a mouth to eat but never to say thanks – all teeth to chomp and no tongue to praise God. And when his stomach is full of food, his heart is an empty hole of ingratitude.

People who live close to God are invariably thankful people. We read of that in Psalm 75:1,

"We give thanks to Thee, O God, we give thanks, for Thy name is near; men declare Thy wondrous works."

The words "Thy name is near" means to the Psalmist that God is near to His people. Out of that sense of Divine nearness and God's wondrous acts on their behalf, double thanks swells within their hearts. However, people who live far from God are invariably thankless people. They may be poor or wealthy. Monetary circumstances are not the deciding factors. Some of the wealthiest people I have known have been the most unthankful to God. Some of the poorest people I have known have been the most thankful to God. Yes, and vice versa as well.

It is curious to note however that when the heathen person goes through a series of hardships or afflictions, or when he starts to feel picked on, it is then that you will either hear him curse God, or you will hear him say, "**GOD OWES ME A BREAK**." Or, "**COME ON OLE MAN, GIVE ME A BREAK**." (In both cases, expletives deleted) He not only then reveals the fact that deep in his heart he acknowledges the existence of God, but he also gives indication that he lives with the inner conviction that God exists to change his run of bad luck! After all, that's what God, if there is one, is for! God exists to give to man and man exists to get from God. That is how it is supposed to work. Much of the contemporary church is confirming his pagan God concept.

Man by nature is such a voracious getter and taker that he will use and even abuse his fellow man to get what he wants. That is why greedy American corporate executives outsource the manufacturing of their products to grossly underpaid Asians, and they refuse to hire and pay their fellow countrymen and women a fair, living wage. They are takers and not givers. Life owes them! The world owes them! God owes them! Get it in any way that you can, no matter who you hurt! They owe it to themselves!

We have a grandfather clock in our house, and we so enjoy the soft tick-tock, tick-tock, tick-tock of the clock's faithful rhythm. The rhythm of greedy, executive, corporate America is by no means soothing, but instead it has become most irritating and offensive with its get-got, get-got, get-got beat. The rhythm of Religious Humanism is equally a complete turn-off with its unending give-get, give-get, give-get self-dealing. The rhythm of true Christianity is life-giving with its give-give, give-give, and give-give loving heartbeat. The world lives by the mantras, "Life Owes Us" or perhaps "God Owes Us," in the event there is a God. Religious Humanism lives by the Words, "God and I equally owe each other." Christianity lives by the words, "We owe everything to God."

The absurdity of God owing man is like none other if you really think it through. It is like a colony of ants saying to the landowner, "You owe us this turf." It is like fleas saying to a dog, "You owe us room and board." It is like mice saying to the baker, "You owe us the whole loaf, and while you are at it, throw in a slab of cheese."

Especially when the chips are down, or when men are gambling and rolling the dice for high stakes! Mankind then counts on God coming through for them as their lucky rabbit's foot, and coming through for them big time. If He doesn't come through with the big break, it is not uncommon to hear them say something like, "God is busting us and getting even with us for the bad stuff that we have done." Or, "See, this God stuff is phony." God cannot win with such people.

It is characteristic of all men, believers and unbelievers alike, to feel that God owes them one, or maybe even two. It calls to mind the story about a vendor who sold bagels for 50 cents each at a street corner food stand. A jogger ran past and threw a couple of quarters into the bucket, but did not take a bagel. The jogger did the same thing every day for many months. One day, as the jogger was passing by, the vendor stopped him. The jogger asked the vendor, "You probably want to know why I always put money in your bucket, but never take a bagel, don't you?" "No," said the vendor, "I just wanted to tell you that the bagels have gone up to 60 cents."

The fact is, God doesn't owe us; He owns us. God addresses this very thing in Job 41:11 where He asks,

"Who has given to Me that I should repay him? Whatever is under the whole heaven is Mine."

God owes us nothing because He owns everything. Everything we have we borrow from God. Since when does the owner owe the borrower?

ACCOUNTS RECEIVABLE – ACCOUNTS PAYABLE

Do you have those in your life who owe you one? Funny how that works! You did something significant or maybe even insignificant for someone, and sure enough, given human nature, it goes on your subconscious books as an item in your "Accounts Receivable." Not only that, but when that person crosses your path one day, something inside you comes up, goes off and says, "He owes me one."

It might even go further than that, as you verbally remind the person of what you have done for him with that wry look on your face that shouts, "Now remember, you owe me." You want to be certain that he puts it on his "Accounts Payable" to you. It may be a favor. It may be money, for at the top of the list that would be the most likely scenario. For some, money can literally burn a hole in their pocket. Money being owed to us in the accounts receivable department can also literally eat a hole in our attitudes toward the person who owes us.

Of course, people never do that with God, do they? They do not put things on some sort of "Accounts Receivable" to them from God Who owes them, do they? Oh my, do they ever! It is bad enough that man's sinful, selfish human nature is a "God Owes Me" nature. Now we have a modern religion under the guise of Christianity being based upon it, too.

As matter of fact, it is now out of control, as Religious Humanists today keep a personal running "Accounts Receivable" from God Himself. Yes, major segments of modern Christianity today teach that very thing, giving people the notion that God in Heaven has an "Accounts Payable" of things that He owes them. It may be money, good health, success, or any of a number of things. Why? Because of services they have rendered to God, or money they have given to Christian causes! When the hard truth is that we all have an unending "IOU" indebtedness to God from Whom all undeserved blessings flow into our lives.

We owe God everything plus, and He owes us nothing period, because everything we have and are comes from Him. In fact we came from Him to begin with. We read in Psalm 100:3,

"...It is He Who has made us, and not we ourselves...."

How can anyone who has been made by God think that he can always be on the make with God, when the very skin on his body came from God? We came into the world nude as a cue ball, and we shall leave this world nude as a cue ball. (Job 1:21) And in between we have on these naked carcasses only what God clothed us with. (Matthew 6:30)

Modern Christianity corrupted by Religious Humanism has become totally blind to these facts. Not only that, but Religious Humanists preposterously think that they stand on an equal footing with God, and that therefore there is an equality between the good they confer upon God and the good they deserve from God. The Apostle Peter was infected with the same mentality and gives clear voice to it in Matthew19:27,

"...Behold, we have left everything and followed You; what then will there be for us?"

You say, "Come on now, you don't mean it, you have to be kidding." Yes, I do mean it, and no, I am not kidding. Of course, true Biblical Christianity is all about man's "Accounts Payable" to God, and about God's "Accounts Receivable" from man. The fact is that we could never pay God back. When you and I sin against infinite holiness, we become infinitely indebted to God. Infinite debt owed by the finite sinner to the Infinite Holy One! Yet God in His infinite grace sent Jesus Christ to pay the infinite price of our infinite sin-indebtedness to God, and thereby satisfy infinite justice. That is Christianity!

Of course, God doesn't owe man one thing, and man owes God everything for every undeserved blessing that we had no claim to in the first place. Even our next breath and heartbeat are gifts from God. God did not owe you or me life itself. He did not even owe us the slightest existence. He could have created us to be rocks or fish, and we would have had to be eternally indebted to Him for it. Instead, He created us in His image to be reflectors of His glory.

G.K. Chesterton summarizes it all so well when he said, "Here dies another day, during which I have had eyes, ears, hands and the great world around me. And with tomorrow begins another. Why am I allowed two?"

Has it ever occurred to one Religious Humanist that the reason God blesses us is because He is good, kind and loving? It has nothing to do with our deserving, but everything to do with God's giving heart. A "Dennis the Menace" cartoon caught my attention. As you know, Dennis was known as a menace indeed to his next-door neighbors, Mr. and Mrs. Wilson, and yet Mrs. Wilson continued to be kind and gracious. This particular cartoon shows Dennis and his little friend leaving Mrs. Wilson's house, their hands full of cookies. Joey says, "I wonder what we did to deserve this?" Dennis answers, "Look, Joey, Mrs. Wilson gives us cookies not because we are nice, but because she is nice." Hello!

LET'S MAKE A DEAL

Rampant in modern Christianity is the following creeping corruption: **"RELIGIOUS HUMANISM IS TURNING MERCY SEEKERS INTO SHREWD MERCHANTS, SUPPLICANTS INTO INVESTORS, AND THE THRONE OF GRACE INTO A HEAVENLY STOCK EXCHANGE."** While Christians historically and humbly asked God for the undeserved blessings of Divine grace, now Religious Humanists come to make lucrative deals, drive hard bargains, and sign binding contracts with the great Banker of Heaven. Religious Humanism has become the 21st century version of the game show of the 1960s and 1970s called "Let's Make A Deal" hosted by Monty Hall. Monty Hall rides again as Religious Humanism's "Let's Make A Deal" contestants trade in their blessings from God for hopefully bigger prizes behind doors number one, two or three.

The religious now bargain with God for what they used to humbly petition Him for. They fully expect to get back more than what they give, for after all, they are making their deposits in the "Bank of Heaven," where the interest rate is the highest anywhere, and gives far greater returns on their investments than any banking institution on earth. Religious Humanism teaches that because we have done such and such for God, or given this or that amount of money to God, God now is duty-bound to come through for us in spades. When it comes to making deals with God, modern Religious Humanists are wheeler-dealers – the real deal.

Cleveland has a newspaper called "The Plain Dealer." It is Ohio's biggest and most successful newspaper. People want plain dealing, no spin, just up-front reporting. Most newspapers and networks today are so far left of center that they can only be read and viewed with the left eye. The right eye cannot find anything that is readable or viewable.

What the religious world needs to day is a "Plain Talker." Let me make it as plain and clear as possible. What has happened is this: **"GOD IN THIS RELIGIOUS HUMANISM HERESY NO LONGER GIVES GRACE-GIFTS TO SUPPLICANTS, BUT INSTEAD HE PAYS BACK OWED RETURNS TO INVESTORS."** Offering time in churches now takes place on "Wall Street" and not on "Grace Street." It reverses everything, for now instead of thanking God for what He in Christ has so graciously given to him, man thinks chiefly of what he in his investment-giving will potentially get back from God. Greedy investors are not just on Wall Street but on Church Street!

It is as if the tectonic plates of Christianity have violently shifted, and a 7.0 earthquake has destroyed the entire structure of the Christian faith. Divine Grace has been replaced by human merit. Local pastors have been replaced by celebrity-status media preachers. Biblical exegetes have been replaced by economists. Prophets have been replaced by profiteers. Giving has been replaced by deal making.

Deals! Deals! Deals! Modern Christianity under the influence of hordes of Religious Humanists has become all about money – money deals with God. Money, money, money! 24/7 around the clock! People watching religious TV networks today get the strong impression that Christianity is all about money. Just the other day my wife and I bumped into some dear friends at Hobby Lobby who said to us that they hear so many say that they don't watch religious TV anymore because all they talk about is money. It is sickening the body of Christ. By the way, big kudos to the Hobby Lobby Company and the beautiful Christian music they were playing in their store. I was truly blessed.

Someone will always say something like, "But the Bible talks more about money than this, that or something else." Why of course, because nothing in the world besides sex and food enslaves man like money and mammon. God has to give it major treatment in His Word because it can so easily become man's major snare. We read about man in Ecclesiastes 4:8,

"Indeed, his eyes were not satisfied with riches...."

Because money has that strong propensity to cause man to always need more, God must teach more about it. Money and people, people and money! They spend money they don't have to buy things they don't need to impress people they don't like. Because man cannot get enough, God can never say too much about its dangers.

When I was a youngster and people talked about wealth, they spoke of the Vanderbilts, the Firestones, the Rockefellers and people such as that. Now money has defined an entire religion, and Jesus Christ is being preached about by the Religious Humanists as the world's greatest financier rather than the world's only Redeemer. He is the modern religion's Donald Trump! He is being made to take on the aura of some mysterious Howard Hughes, rather than God's only begotten Son sent to die for a lost and perishing world. And they are getting away with it basically unchallenged. Until now!

I must quickly say here to those whose minds have been poisoned by this false gospel that true Christianity is not about money. It is about Jesus Christ who did not ask that we pay Him, but Who Him-self paid the full penalty – the full price on the cross for the sins of the whole world including every sin you have ever committed and every sin that I have ever committed. No, Jesus Christ is not about money, but He is about Heaven and Hell – suffering your Hell and my

MODERN CHRISTIANITY CORRUPTED

Hell that we might live in His Heaven and have a taste of Heaven on the way. That is a price that you and I don't want to pay, and that you and I could never pay. Why?

It is recorded in Romans 6:23,

"For the wages of sin is death, but the free gift of God is eternal life in Christ Jesus our Lord."

What all of us sinners have earned by our sins is eternal and spiritual death. That is our deserved wage from God. That is what God's justice owes us! Every man's paycheck is the same, for all have sinned and fallen short of the glory of God. (Romans 3:23) If we want what is owed to us, then we can pick up our paycheck at the end of our lives and cash it in Hell and there suffer an eternal dying agony. Still want to make a deal with God?

On the other hand, gifts are not merited and are completely unearned. If gifts could be earned they would not be gifts. For those who accept Jesus Christ as their Savior and Lord, He gives them the totally free gift of eternal life beginning now and in Heaven forever. So, what's it going to be, deal with God and collect our damnation wages, or humbly kneel before God today and receive His free gift of eternal life with Him in perfect glory? Deal or no deal!

HOW IT IS PULLED OFF

Let me assure you that when you get involved in Religious Humanism television, they will be inside your billfold before you can count to ten dollars. It all reminds me of the story of the sharp lawyer who paid attention to and defined every word. It is said that one time someone came up to him and said, "If I give you $100.00, will you answer two questions for me?" The lawyer immediately replied, "Sure, and what is your other question?" The questioner already owed the lawyer $50.00 before he knew what hit him. That is how it goes in media religion these days.

On televised "Religious Money-A-Thons" these days, the TV viewers are confronted with this come-on, namely, that if they send in a Divinely and mysteriously revealed and specified amount of money to some religious network – let us say a gift of $59.00 every month for the next 12 months, **"GOD WILL THEN PAY OFF ALL OF THEIR DEBTS, AND BRING A GREAT FINANCIAL BREAK-THROUGH INTO THEIR LIVES."** That's the pitch.

The television ministers and evangelists then promise the viewers that they will have a "Burn The Debts Ceremony" on their behalf. If they send in their first of 12 checks for $59.00 along with a statement of all of their debts, then on national television at an appointed evening and time, the debtors will see their debt sheets being thrown into a container of fire and going up in smoke, with the promise that God will miraculously pay off all of their debts because of the money they have sent in to the network. Walla! Debts go up in smoke. Poof! Money comes in like magic! Of course, the money which people send in is in many cases money they do not have in the first place, for it is all owed to creditors. It is actually therefore dirty money which they had been told would clean up their indebtedness. That is how it works.

First of all, how awesome all of this sounds to those who are in credit card debt over their eyeballs and can't see their way out of it? Here is being presented by those who supposedly are representing God Himself, a sanctified sounding way of getting yourself out of debt and advancing the Kingdom of God at the same time. The principle however that is really at work is this: **"DESPERATION IS THE BREEDING GROUND FOR DECEPTION."**

America is a credit card nation which has lost all of its immune system against the temptation of plastic currency. We live in a credit card economy. Too much on the books, way too much! The consumer has too much on the books, and the issuing bank or organization has too much on the books. It is the modern American money trap.

In the light of all of this, there are many very savvy Religious Humanist TV ministers, evangelists and motivational speakers who promise the hugely indebted and desperate masses that God will spring them from their financial plastic prison if they send in their non-existent funds. Add to all of this the sad fact of P.T. Barnum's observation that there is a sucker born every minute.

The whole thing is a reproach upon the name of Christ and the Christian Church. However, given the freedom of speech and freedom of religion guaranteed by the United States Constitution, they continue to get away with it year after year, as religious TV personalities pad their purses and upgrade their luxurious lifestyles with the monies of frantic debtors.

Second, it undermines the true foundation for serving Christ, and that is our great love for Him and our deep gratitude to Him for all that He has done and continues to do for us. Religious Humanism does not produce pure, selfless worshippers. It produces customers. Religious Humanism does not produce pure, selfless thankers. It produces shoppers. It is the old "Polly Wants A Cracker" routine. Polly goes through the motions and says the right words only because there is a cracker at the end of the deal. Seals will clap their flippers, too, but let's face it; their instincts are telling them that there is a fish to clap for.

Christians do not give to God for what they can get out of God, but because of Who He is and what He has so graciously, undeservedly and enormously given to them in Jesus Christ! This is captured so beautifully in the case of David when he asks in Psalm 116:12,

> **"What shall I render to the Lord for all His benefits toward**
> **me?"**

If you will, "What on earth can I give to Him who has given so immeasurably to me?" Nothing seems adequate! Here is a person overwhelmed with such enormous gratitude to God for the great kindnesses that God has showed him. David sounds like a woman in the travail of birth pangs. He is trying to bring forth an adequate expression of love, and no matter how hard he pushes, what he brings forth all seems so painfully miniature and inadequate. Not a hint in his thinking of giving to get, but rather a strong sense of his grossly inadequate giving.

When people are told that if they send in X amount of dollars, God will get the creditors off from their backs, as well as bring them into great financial advancement in their lives, then something deceptive and destructive begins to happen to the grateful heart of Christianity. It is this: **"THEY MAY THINK THAT THEY ARE THANKFULLY FOLLOWING CHRIST, BUT WHAT THEY ARE DOING IS FOLLOWING AFTER THE LOAVES THAT THEY HAVE BEEN TOLD CHRIST WILL MULTIPLY FOR THEM."**

Children are so very impressionable. Kids brought up in such a give-to-get environment will learn to think about Christianity as a package deal – what's the price of a ticket to get the big payoff from God? If you will, giving will become to them a matter of bargaining with God.

And lo and behold, when the bread truck doesn't come up their driveways, and their ship does not come in, the falsely taught and disillusioned will dump Christ and turn against the church. Then often their behavior can be described by the words of Isaiah 8:21,

> **"...and it will turn out that when they are hungry, they will**
> **be enraged and curse their king and their God as they face**
> **upward."**

In short, Religious Humanism corrupts the spirit of love for and gratitude to God. The very heart of Christianity is being poisoned. What makes it even more lethal is that we are not born as giving beings. We are born as takers! Then on top of it all are these contemporary Religious Humanists who are retarding people's spiritual growth and keeping them immature by luring them backwards into self-seeking, self-satisfying and perpetually sucking infancy.

EXPECT NOTHING IN RETURN

"Well then," you may ask, "what do these Religious Humanists base all of this on?" You will find that Religious Humanists salivate over verses in the Bible like the one found in Luke 6:38,

> "Give, and it will be given to you; good measure, pressed down, shaken together, running over, they will pour into your lap. For by your standard of measure it will be measured to you in return."

Religious Humanists absolutely go bonkers over Scriptures like this. "See," they say, "If we give, we can do so fully expecting to receive back far more than we gave." Pressed down, shaken together and running over. That becomes then the driving motivation for giving – give-Get, give-Get, give-Get.

But they constantly quote Luke 6:38 out of context, which practice is called isogesis! The way that this is done today is to quote snippets of Scripture out of context, and present them as full and balanced Bible truth. However, each time you study the context, their lie masquerading as truth becomes naked to the eye and bare to the bone.

To begin with, if you study the Luke 6:38 passage in its context, Jesus is talking about the loving and selfless spirit of true giving which defines Christ and His followers. He says in Luke 6:34,

> "And if you lend to those from whom you expect to receive, what credit is that to you? Even sinners lend to sinners, in order to receive back the same amount."

If we lend, that is, give to get back as our definition of giving, then there is nothing in that case that separates Christians from the world. That is how the world does business. That is what makes the world go round. But Christianity is not a business that gives only for returns. There is no real virtue in that, for then we have not really given even a small part of ourselves. Giving is only true giving when we give not to receive or get back, but simply to give. Then alone are we givers! Then alone are we Christians.

You see, to be authentic givers, we must give gifts, not loans with interest. And for a gift to be a bona fide gift, it cannot be taken or received back. The true giver surrenders all rights to that which he has given. To give a gift and then take it back is not giving, but rather it is stealing. For what has been given now belongs to the receiver and no longer to the giver.

For most people, giving is like the taxicab ride. The taxicab driver is taking you on, not giving you, a ride from point A to point B. But all the while there is that little box by the dashboard that is constantly flipping numbers. That little box is not simply measuring distance to tell you how far you have traveled. It is doing that, but what it is telling you mostly is what it is going to cost you at the end of the ride. Come on now, admit it, you have watched that little box during the entire trip, and you were not able to take your eyes off the thing, hoping that it would break down, or that the driver would speed us as you play beat-the-clock in your mind. In the world, the meter is always running. But in Christian living and giving, the meter is never running, for there is no meter. Christians truly give people a ride, while Religious Humanists today are taking people for a ride always with the meter running.

Then Jesus goes on in Luke 6:35 and what He says there clearly unfolds the true meaning of Luke 6:38. He says,

> **"But love your enemies, and do good, and lend, expecting nothing in return; and your reward will be great, and you will be sons of the Most High; for He Himself is kind to ungrateful and evil men."**

There it is! Christianity is: "**GIVE AND EXPECT NOTHING IN RETURN**." Religious Humanism is: "**GIVE AND EXPECT EVERY-THING IN RETURN**." A complete reversal!

You see, everything Jesus teaches us goes contrary to human nature. You know, like when someone bops you on the head, and Jesus tells us not to bop the bopper back. In fact, let him get in another bop if he needs to. Jesus put it this way in Luke 6:29,

> **"Whoever hits you on the cheek, offer him the other also...."**

That sounds absurd! The most that natural man can begin to understand is not to hit anyone unless he is hit first. Even that at times is a real stretch for him.

In man's way of thinking, everything must be reciprocal, whether it is good or bad. Don't pick a fight, but fight back when someone has picked a fight with you. In other words, when you have been picked on, pick back! Being bopped but no return bop allowed? Absurd! It all goes against the grain of man's natural instincts.

Is Jesus kidding? A right roundhouse to the face and no return roundhouse to even the score! No, He is not kidding. No retaliatory boppers in the Kingdom of God. That is exactly what He is saying, and that is exactly how He lived and died.

What then is Jesus' real focus in Luke 6:27-38? Wild and wacky stuff to most people's way of thinking! Love your enemies! Here He goes again! How do we like them apples? Not only do you not hit or lip back at your enemies, but you love them. How? You give to them and do so liberally. And after you do, tie your hands behind your back. Never give in a receiving attitude or getting-back posture. The plot thickens! Dear Lord, it is hard enough at times to love our friends, let alone our enemies. And on top of it giving to them – which in itself hurts – without expecting something in return. Love our enemies and give to our enemies. By nature we have no strong inclination in either case. Outlandish!

But there it is! Who in the world invites enemies to their birthday party, let alone send gifts to their enemies on their birthdays. Many of us secretly wish that they were never even born, but we keep those thoughts to ourselves. Get chummy with our enemies? Most folks would rather fly solo across the Atlantic!

Luke 6:38 in its context has nothing to do with investment giving, and everything to do with the giving of ourselves for our enemy's needs. Yes, even for the enemies of Christ who in the name of Allah are killing Christians in Sudan, Darfur, and Nigeria! (For years Christians have been slaughtered there, or kidnapped and sold on the slave markets for five bucks.) Then you will be sons of the Most High God, for He is always being kind and giving to people who never thank Him, who sin against Him and defy Him every day of their lives. Like Father like sons! So our Lord observes about Himself in Luke 6:35,

"...for He Himself is kind to ungrateful and evil men."

In other words, giving for the purpose of getting in return is categorically denounced by Jesus in the very context in which the statements of Luke 6:38 are made by our Savior. He is telling us to never allow receiving to be the slightest motive in giving. Bam!

Therefore, the teaching and practice that even implies sending in your money to these modern religious TV networks or anywhere else for the purposes of debt cancellation and increased returns, is in direct conflict with and a total contradiction to the clear and unmistakable spirit and teaching of our Lord. To use Luke 6:38 to lure people into "Giving to Get" is a rape of the text, its context, as well as of the entirety of the Bible.

In Religious Humanism "**GIVING IS FOR THE PURPOSE OF RECEIVING**." That is a total reversal of Christianity where "**RECEIVING IS FOR THE PURPOSE OF GIVING**." In Religious Humanism, even when I give, it is in effect not only to keep what I gave, but to get more besides. If you will, in Religious Humanism, "**MEUM EST MEUM!**" That is to say, "What is mine is mine." In Christianity, when I receive from God, it is for the purpose of giving it away. If you will, in Christianity, "**MEUM EST TUUM!**" That is to say, "What is mine is yours."

Here are some summary lessons we must learn from the Luke passage. First, Luke 6:27-38 is about Who God is! It is about how an abundantly merciful God operates. God by nature is a blessing and giving God. God is such a giving and blessing God that He states from His giving and blessing heart in Acts 20:35,

"…**It is more blessed to give than to receive**."

Giving excites God! He really gets into it! For God, receiving is dull in comparison to giving. Being blessed is dull in comparison to being a blessing. The State of Virginia we are told is for lovers. The Kingdom of God is for loving givers.

Second, He wants His sons and daughters to reflect His character. As He states in Luke 6:36,

"**Be merciful, just as your Father is merciful**."

Being merciful to friend and foe alike! Especially to the foe! If we are in misery and hard times, how deeply touched we are when people come to our rescue. Jesus here teaches that we are to rescue others from their misery, especially those who delight in making us miserable. That is what Luke 6:38 is all about. The big-blessing and the big-giving God and His big-blessing and big-giving children! Big givers and big blessers to big enemies! Shazaam!

Third, when His children give like He gives, they expect nothing in return. He however assures us that we will be blessed for our giving hearts and hands. Big time blessed! Pressed down, shaken together, and running over. It is God's modus operandi. It is how the giving God works. It is invariably true! Test Him, as Malachi 3:10 tells us to. Bring your tithes and offerings into His storehouse and see that He will deluge you with blessings from Heaven so over-flowingly that you will not be able gather them all in. You will be blessed so profusely that you will have to give most of it away.

Jesus in Luke 6 promises us that when we give to our enemies, we will freely receive. But don't ever forget the Master's words in Matthew 10:8,

"...freely you received, freely give."

And so the Christian rhythm goes on – give-give, give-give, give-give. To stall on receiving totally ruins the cadence. Where does receiving fit in? In Christianity receiving is merely the hyphen to bring us to the next giving act.

Fourth, God not only multiplies His giving to givers, but He multiplies the gift of the givers as well. The story about John Bowes while he was chairman of the parent company of Wham-O, the maker of Frisbees, bears this out. He sent thousands of those flying plastic discs to an orphanage in Angola, Africa. He thought that the children there would so much enjoy playing with those Frisbees. Several months later, a representative of the Bowes' company visited the orphanage. One of the nuns thanked him for the wonderful "plates" that his company had sent them. She told him that the children were eating off the Frisbees, carrying water with the Frisbees, and even catching fish with the Frisbees. When the representative explained how the Frisbees were initially intended to be used, she was even more delighted that the children would be able to enjoy them as toys. (2)

We should always give, asking and believing God to multiply our gifts in His miracle love, even as Jesus did the young lad's five loaves and two fish in the feeding of the 5000. (John 6:1-14) That, too, is our God! He multiplied the gift of the flying Frisbees, and turned them into tableware, fishing nets, water containers, and fun toys. Religious Humanism wants the Frisbees multiplied for the purposes of being flown back to them. God hates that.

PROTESTANT INDULGENCES

Tragically, the Religious Humanist's twisting and reversing of the Bible has turned back the clock of the Christian Church to the pre-Protestant Reformation era of the Roman Catholic Church. The last time that the Christian Church had such a tidal wave of "Giving To Get" and "Selling of God's Graces" was in the practice of "Selling Indulgences" by Roman Catholic churchmen the likes of Johann Tetzel (1465-1519). Johann Tetzel was a German Dominican Friar who was authorized and empowered by the Pope to sell indulgences using the catchy phrase: **"AS SOON A COIN IN THE COFFER RINGS, THE SOUL**

FROM PURGATORY SPRINGS." Spring loaded indulgences!

Indulgences were monies paid to the Roman Catholic Church for the sins of those languishing in the agonies of "Purgatory." As a matter of fact, indulgences would have had no place or value in the Catholic Church if it were not for the equally unbiblical teaching about a mythical state of a "Halfway-Hell" for the punishment of "Half-Way Sinners" called "Purgatory." Rest assured: "**THE DESIGN OF PURGATORY WAS PEOPLE'S POCKETS, AND INDULGENCES WERE THE INSTRUMENTS FOR PICKING THEM**." A really smooth operation!

As it is with most people, they do not identify the enemy until it is too late. Such was the case of the Japanese and Pearl Harbor, Al Qaeda and 9/11, Bernie Madoff and the investors, and Johann Tetzel and the indulgence purchasers. Not only don't people, yes very sincere people, see the enemy approaching, but they don't recognize the enemy in their midst even as they shake his hand. The common-man Catholic of Tetzel's day was no exception.

Tetzel, Pope Leo X's indulgence wheeler-dealer and hit-man, went so far as to contrive a chart that listed the monetary prices that had to be paid for each type of sin in order to release loved ones from purgatory. He even claimed to be able to sell indulgences that could save a soul that had sexually abused the Virgin Mary. I can't imagine the huge price tag on that one!

A ducat was a gold coin worth about $2.25. It was first coined in A.D. 1150, and used by several countries in Europe. "The Trinity Foundation," a most scholarly website dealing with Reformation history and theology writes, "Tetzel had a fee schedule for the forgiveness of sins: *Witchcraft, 2 ducats; Polygamy, 6 ducats; Murder, 8 ducats; Sacrilege, 9 ducats; Perjury, 9 ducats*. And so on. Other indulgence sellers in other regions charged different fees depending upon the gullibility of the people. Gold and silver flooded into the pope's treasury." (3)

Tetzel would pressure the uneducated and the peasants the hardest, for they were often the most gullible and vulnerable. The more ignorant the better, for the more uninformed of truth they were, the more ducats they handed over. They also had the least amount of money to spare, so that the sale of indulgences hit them the hardest. To free their loved ones from Purgatory, they bought a false comfort and hope from church leadership charlatans, and they laid down their money for lies.

Not only did John Tetzel prey upon people's ignorance of the Scriptures which was not yet translated into German, but he applied enormous pressure. Like a skilled drummer Tetzel beat on the emotions of the offspring of parents, whose dead parents he portrayed as crying out in pain to their children to free them from the woes of Purgatory and usher them into the wonders of Paradise.

They did so of course through buying "Free-Your-Loved-Ones-From-Purgatory Indulgences." He created within their descendants an awful sense of guilt if they didn't rescue their fathers, mothers and others. Another lesson being that if you're going to sin, make sure that your descendants will and can pick up the tab.

Listen to this quote from one of Johann Tetzel's indulgence sermons: **"DON'T YOU HEAR THE VOICE OF YOUR WAILING DEAD PARENTS AND OTHERS WHO SAY, 'HAVE MERCY UPON ME, HAVE MERCY UPON ME, BECAUSE WE ARE IN SEVERE PUNISHMENT AND PAIN. FROM THIS YOU COULD REDEEM US WITH SMALL ALMS, AND YOU DO NOT WANT TO. WE HAVE CREATED YOU, CARED FOR YOU. WHY ARE YOU SO CRUEL AND HARSH THAT YOU DO NOT WANT TO SAVE US, THOUGH IT ONLY TAKES A LITTLE?'"** (4)

When Martin Luther posted his "Ninety Five Thesis" on the Castle Church door in Wittenberg, Germany on October 31, 1517, one of most drastic consequences for the Roman Catholic Church was that the sale of indulgences dropped off considerably. Luther crippled the indulgence scam by teaching that sinners are justified by faith in Jesus Christ (Romans 5:1), and not by coughing up their money for the Roman Catholic coffers. That was close to 500 years ago.

Now five centuries later, this time mind you in Protestantism, tragically indulgences have experienced a huge come back. Tetzel's Indulgences have in modern times resurfaced in vast segments of the Christian Church under a different label. If Rip Van Winkle had been Johann Tetzel who was awakened 500 years later after a multi-century nap in the mountains of Germany, he would now conclude that the indulgence racket had made a strong comeback and was going strong.

As we have seen, Tetzel's Roman Catholic Indulgences were payments to buy your loved ones out of purgatory. Modern Protestant Indulgences can be defined as payments to buy oneself out of debt. If you will, buying from God debt-cancellation indulgences which will free you from the purgatorial torment of threatening creditors. Buying your way out of a financial Purgatory! Indulgences with a 21st century flair, but with a very strong 16th century echo.

The Protestant Tetzels of today might well have this as their rather catchy come-on, **"AS SOON AS A DOLLAR IN THE OFFERING PLATE LAYS, ANOTHER FINANCIAL DEBT THE HEAVENLY FATHER PAYS."** We live in an age in which once again, **"HEAVEN'S GRACES ARE BEING RETAILED."** Whether it is "Roman Catholic Indulgences" or "Religious Humanism Indulgences," they are in principle and practice the same disgusting heresy, namely, the purchasing of God's blessings and the selling of God's graces.

By the way, I love and appreciate Oral and Richard Roberts. They have been used mercifully by God to do so much good for so many. I have visited Oral Roberts University with dear friends some years ago and experienced the presence of God there. But, as sincere as they are, they are sincerely wrong when it comes to raising funds. There are countless others as well promoting the indulgence scam who love the Lord, but they have lousy theology. They have it all masked under the disguise of what they call "Seed Faith." What is that? People are encouraged to send in money to "Oral Roberts University" or to "The Hour of Healing." That money sent in is what is called a "Seed Faith" sown to God. With their money, people also send in requests for healings, miracles etc. Their gift of money is the "Seed Faith" that will sprout forth and grow the needed miracle from God. Seed Faith Indulgences!

No matter how you cut the check, it is nothing more or less than another "Protestant Indulgence." It is again buying God's gracious miracles through a complete misapplication of the sowing and reaping principles in the Bible. Never in Jesus' earthly ministry did He solicit so-called seed-faith money from people in order for them to believe for and receive a miracle. Never! It did not exist in Jesus earthly ministry. It does not exist in the Bible. It does not exist in true Christianity.

What a mess this stuff is! What a gross counterfeit of Christianity. Much of modern Christianity today has become a mongrel Catholic-Protestantism which has betrayed the legacy of truth handed down to us from the reformers.

Mike Murdock, another popular media-religion TV personality today, states: "**GOD HAD A SON AND NEEDED A FAMILY. SO HE USED HIS SON AS A SEED TO GET A HARVEST…I'M ASKING FOR 300 PEOPLE WHO NEED BIG MIRACLES (WHEN YOU CALL AND GIVE $1000.00.**)" (5) Are you kidding? God has no needs! Not one! If He did, he would be finite, i.e. not God! How can infinite perfection and completeness have a lack? God didn't need us, we needed God! God did not send His Son into the world as a seed-family planting for His desperately needy and lonely heart, but as a sacrifice for desperately needy and lost sinners. God wasn't lost, we were. God wasn't lonely, we were. God wasn't needy, we were.

Then on top of it all, Murdock uses this totally distorted concept of God seed-sowing His Son for reaping His family harvest, as a means to get people to buy $1000 indulgences to get their big harvest of miracles! So it goes, and people by the tens of thousands fall for it every day.

It was Judas Iscariot who sold Christ's person. It was the Catholic Pope who sold Christ's pardon. Now it is "Christian" preachers who are selling Christ's gracious gifts and blessings. The Roman Catholic Church in Martin Luther's day, through its indulgences, was the quick market for spiritual pardons. Vast segments of the Christian church of our day, through indulgences, have become the quick superbank for financial pay-offs. History is repeating itself in that religion is once again being merchandised.

If people examined the indulgence issue closely, they would see on it the blood-spattered scars and gouges of the indulgence wars of hundreds of years ago. Martin Luther, as did his followers, paid a great price for his devotion to the Word of God and his stand against indulgences and many other falsehoods. But Martin and his disciples did not back down. Many gave their lives for the cause of truth. It was at the Diet of Worms on April 18, 1521 that Martin uttered his famous, "Hier stehe ich. Ich kann nicht anders. Gott helfe mir – Here I stand. I can do no other. God help me. Amen."

PRICES "SCRIPTURALLY" SET

How are the prices for "Protestant Indulgences" determined today? Johann Tetzel had devised a pay scale for various sins. It becomes very arbitrary at best, and it depends upon who is doing the selling. On a Trinity Broadcasting Network Praise-A-Thon in 2004, it happened to be Pastor Paula White. She is not really the issue. It could have been anyone of a host of others. Paula White is just the tip of the iceberg. Protestant Indulgence marketing-gurus abound! She was a guest speaker and fund-raiser on TBN, and she ministered from a psalm of David in which he prays to God in Psalm 71:21,

"Mayest Thou increase my greatness and turn to comfort me."

Whenever Religious Humanists see the words "increase" and "greatness," their eyes light up like flashing neon dollar signs. As if greatness is only measured monetarily.

First of all, that is not what Psalm 71 is about at all. What is the setting of this Psalm? The now aging King David had gone through some really tough times with his son Adonijah's attempt to usurp his father's throne. Apparently Adonijah was fully aware of his father's intention to make Solomon his successor. In his weakened condition, King David felt that his kingly status was being threatened. His enemies from within and without made him feel so vulnerable now. He asked the Lord to raise him up to a formidable kingly status again. (Psalm 71:20) So he prays that God will increase his greatness. The Hebrew word for greatness here is "gadol," which means the restoration of his standing as the King of Israel.

King David's eyes in this Psalm were on the God of righteousness, not on himself. His prayer for a strong kingly standing in the opinion polls in Psalm 71:21 was not motivated by self-interest! Not in the least! What was his motivation then? Firmly established in his kingly status, he would then be able to speak effectively of God's righteousness all the day long. (Psalm 71:15, 16, 24) No separation of church and state here. That was unthinkable. Oh how we need the voice of God's righteousness in the national leadership of America today. As David puts it in Psalm 71:16,

"I will make mention of Thy righteousness, Thine alone."

Instead, as James Dobson recently said on his daily radio program, "There is utter evil coming out of Congress. I have been on the air 32 years, and I've never seen a time quite like this."

Second, "Forgotten Word Ministries" then goes on to quote Paula White as to her take on Psalm 71:21. She states: "**I BELIEVE TONIGHT THAT GOD WILL DO A MASTER BREAKTHROUGH IN YOUR LIFE. WHEN GOD SPEAKS TO YOU TO GO TO THE PHONE AND GIVE $71.21 FOR 12 MONTHS, GOD WILL INCREASE YOUR GREATNESS AND DO SOMETHING GREAT IN YOUR LIFE.**" (6) David's concern was for a revival of righteousness amongst God's people, not personal breakthroughs and increased greatness all for twelve easy payments of $71.21! Flex-Pay Indulgences! How convenient! When Christianity is reduced to a business proposition as it has been today, there are always down payments and monthly payments. You cannot distinguish the modern church anymore from a car dealership.

And mind you, making the psalm number and the verse number the basis of the indulgence price! Unbelievable! I have never preached on the numbers of a Bible chapter and verse and made it the essence of my sermon. Like saying to your congregation, "Turn with me this morning to Psalm 71 and verse 21, and the title of my sermon is 'Seventy One-Twenty One.'"

Roman Catholic indulgences were designed to be the "**SPRING A LOVED ONE OUT OF PURGATORY INDULGENCES.**" Religious Humanists are selling for $71.21 a month the "**SPRING YOURSELF OUT OF SMALLNESS AND INCREASE YOUR GREATNESS INDULGENCES.**"

Third, staying with Psalm 71:21 for just a moment! When David asked God for the increase of kingly stature for the sake of God's righteousness being established in the land, he did so through prayer! He did not send in to God $71.21 on a 12 month basis to buy kingly status. He prayed to God. The last time I checked, James 4:2 says:

"...You do not have because you do not ask."

It does not say:

**"You do not have because you did not fulfill your twelve
month indulgence pledge."**

It all depends upon what Scripture has been picked out and preached on during any given Indulgence-A-Thon. On another occasion it was Psalm 66:12 which states,

**"Thou didst make men ride over our heads; we went
through fire and through water; yet Thou didst bring us out
into a place of abundance."**

Abundance! Oh my, Religious Humanists hone in on that word like radar. Everything else on the radar screen disappears. That will get the Religious Humanist's adrenalin flowing faster than anything. That is like saying fox to a hound. What David is celebrating, however, is how God brought His ancient people, Israel, out of Egyptian slavery into a land of freedom and plenty. They truly became "One Nation Under God," even as the 4th of July is America's celebration of national identity and freedom in the new land of abundance as "One Nation Under God." This has absolutely everything to do with God bringing His people out, and nothing to do with buying their way out or into.

Nonetheless, Paula White again stated: "**SO THE INSTRUCTION OF THE LORD IS FOR THE NEXT 12 MONTHS TO SOW $66.12.**"(7) Cut-rate indulgences! They were mercifully on sale on that particular day. As they say, "Just wait a little longer, the price is sure to come down." But if you pony up the dough each month, you will be living on "Abundance Avenue," better known in our day as "Easy Street." What an utter rape of Scripture!

Even as indulgences were the most profitable means of income in the Roman religion, so indulgences are the most profitable means of income in modern church and media religion. Millions upon millions of dollars flow in through indulgences annually.

TETZEL'S PRESSURE-TACTICS REPEATED

Is pressure today applied to the people who are gullible enough to buy into it all? Oh yes indeed! Pressure to the extent that it makes Johann Tetzel's coercive tactics appear to be tame. Remember how he played upon the heart strings of sons and daughters concerning their purgatory-trapped parents? After all, just the mention of my dear-departed parents makes my eyes tear up without some of their purgatorial smoke being blown into and stinging my already misty eyes.

Indulgence trafficking is never passive or gentle. Moreover, from a marketing point of view, you have to first create a sense of guilt and fear to make indulgence sales profitable. The bully pulpit is always at work in the sale of indulgences. It gives the practitioners of this craft the edge if they know how to use it. On one telethon, these warnings and threats were given to the viewers by Paula White: **"AND SO THE PRINCIPLE HERE IS IF I TAKE FOR MYSELF WHEN IT IS TIME TO GIVE TO THE KINGDOM, I CAN BRING A CURSE UPON MYSELF...YOU WILL DIE! YOU WILL DIE UNLESS YOU GO TO THE PHONE AND DO WHAT GOD SAYS TO DO...DON'T JUST LISTEN TO THE WORD OF THE LORD, YOU'VE GOT TO DO THE WORD OF THE LORD...YOU WILL DIE! YOU WILL DIE UNLESS YOU GO TO THE PHONE AND DO WHAT GOD SAYS TO DO."** (8) This makes Johann Tetzel sound like a pussycat. The indulgence bully-pulpit at work! Modern indulgence pressures are far greater, and the pay scale much higher. We are now in the major leagues of indulgences which make Tetzel's indulgences look like the minor leagues.

We hear about death threats from Al Qaeda in the name of Allah all the time these days. Now we are getting death threats from the Religious Humanist indulgence-sellers in the name of Jesus. One cries, "Death to infidels." The other cries, "Death to the non-indulgers." Go to the phone and make your 12 month pledge or you are dead meat. And so many break their already broken banks so that God will not break their necks!

The mafia over the years has gotten rich through extortion, i.e. threatening and forcing storeowners and businessmen to buy protection from destruction. Destruction from whom? From the mafia! Either fork it over or get beat up. I am appalled when indulgence salesmen make God sound like a mafia extortionist. As if we must buy protection from God or die. But protection from whom? From God or course! These "Protection Indulgences" really give God the starring role in a new film series entitled *The Godfather of Indulgences*.

Listen, Jesus paid for our protection! It is included in our salvation. We don't pay for it, He did. Whom God saves, He defends. We read in Psalm 62:1-2 in the KJV,

"Truly my soul waiteth upon God: from Him cometh my

salvation. He only is my rock and my salvation; He is my defense; I shall not be greatly moved."

I shall not be greatly moved either, especially not to the indulgence phone. I shall not get shook up, because God alone is my rock, my salvation and my defense, and therefore I refuse to pay up.

We read in Psalm 91:11,

"For He will give His angels charge concerning you, to guard you in all your ways."

Now there is Heaven's protection policy — God Himself and an angelic entourage of body and soul guards for His children! What great good news that is, realizing that Satan and his demons are always swirling overhead ready to descend upon and attack us like starving hawks. We don't hire God or His "Secret Service Angels." They are appointed by God. His children are always under Heaven's surveillance. You can't buy protection like that, no one could afford it. The U.S. President's kids have nothing over God's kids. The noun "Angel" means "Messenger." Mighty messengers sent from God to shadow and protect us in everything we do and every place we go.

Today, on these Money-A-Thon-Indulgence sales, statements are made that if people do not go to the telephone and pledge their money, they will lose God's protection. So there is always that feeling that they should peel off another buck for added protection. You can't be too careful! I have even heard it said that if the listener does not pick up the telephone and make a pledge, sickness will not leave his body. Pay up or puke! For me it is quite the opposite. When I think of buying one of these indulgences, I become nauseated and feel the need to upchuck. When I denounce the indulgence, the nausea leaves and I feel totally healthy and protected once again.

Finally, not only do these indulgence salesmen and women put pressure on the purchaser, but they even put pressure on God to come through with what the indulgence buyer has bought. Like this quote from Pastor Jamal Bryant of Empowerment Temple in Baltimore, Maryland. He states to the TV audience: **"I'M BELIEVING GOD THAT WITHIN 24 HOURS ANY PERSON THAT SOWS A SEED (PLEDGES MONEY), YOU ARE GOING TO SEE A SIGN, A WONDER, A CONFIRMATION HAPPEN IN YOUR LIFE. ELBOW YOUR NEIGHBOR, SAY, 'I'M GIVING GOD 24 HOURS.'"** (9) Same day delivery guaranteed! By whom? By the indulgence salesman! I am not surprised that he didn't add, "Or your money back!" Oh no, they are slick but not stupid.

Mind you, binding the sovereign God to man's timetable! God, You have 24 hours to get it done. Tell your neighbor sitting next to you that you are putting God on 24 hour notice as follows, "The clock is ticking! Hop to it, God! Precious time is a-wasting! Your deadline is 24 hours from now!" Christianity teaches according to Psalm 31:15 that:

"MAN'S TIMES ARE IN GOD'S HANDS."

Religious Humanism teaches that:

"GOD'S TIMES ARE IN MAN'S HANDS."

CHEAPENED GRACE

It was Dietrich Bonhoeffer who warned us about what he called, "**CHEAP GRACE.**" By that he meant a concept of grace that many people have that does not take the judgment of God seriously. "I sin, God forgives," is their attitude. Easy sin, easy forgiveness! That is the concept of Christianity that people had in the Apostle Paul's day as well. Cheap grace! This very attitude was warned against and soundly rebuked by the Apostle Paul in Romans 6:1-2,

> **"What shall we say then? Are we to continue in sin that grace might increase? May it never be!..."**

Many have the feeling that if they miss a deadline, God will graciously extend it. If they fail to keep a promise, God will graciously overlook it. If they constantly fall back into the same old sinful patterns, God will graciously ignore it.

Cheap-grace type people treat sin exactly how they treat credit-card spending. It is so easy to buy things today when you are told that you are not going to see the statement for another 30 days. And then you have another 30 days to pay off your debt. If you do get up to the limit on the card, no big deal! Just get another card. You get offers all the time. So with sin! No big deal! Sinned again? Just get another dose of grace to cover it. Tomorrow affords another whole new supply of forgiving grace. The Apostle Paul said, "May it never be." The King James Version of the Bible says, "God forbid." (Romans 6:2)

Today, under the influence of Religious Humanism, we are seeing something that is equally tragic. It is "**CHEAPENED GRACE.**" Grace is God's amazing, unmerited and totally undeserved favor that is made available to us only in the inestimably costly death of Christ for ours sins. As if you can buy one of God's gracious and blood-bought blessings in Christ for $71.21 or $66.12 a month for twelve months! Cut-rate grace! Cheapened grace! This whole travesty today demeans and degrades the gracious and incalculable price that Jesus paid on Calvary.

Listen, the Christian life is in a state of perpetual free grace. I know that "Free Grace" is a redundancy, but sometimes you have to be redundant to make your point. The very thought of grace being retailed or wholesaled is not only a complete contradiction, but a grievous disgrace to the God of all grace. No grace-promise of God is ever fulfilled in our lives because of monies being given or from some fictitious meritorious earnings. Let no one be duped into thinking that they can buy what Christ has already graciously purchased for us. Let us get this deep into our spirits, namely that no benefit or blessing from God in the Christian life is on a co-pay basis.

Now read very carefully II Corinthians 1:20,

**"For as many as may be the promises of God, in Him
(Christ) they are yes; wherefore also by Him (Christ) is our
Amen to the glory of God through us."**

I personally have never counted the number of promises that God makes to His children in the Bible. Someone researched it and found 1,260. Sounds undercounted and understated to me. In any event, each and every promise of God is an absolute "Yes" to the believer because of what Christ has graciously done for and given to him on Calvary's cross. Every promise in Scripture would be an absolute "No" if it were not for the super-gracious death of God's Son for our sins. Christ is the sole and sufficient reason for every one of God's promises being a "Yes-Promise."

But Christ is not only our "Yes," He is also our "Amen." This means that all of God's promises in Christ are not only "Yes," but they are also "Sure." Amen means, "So it will be, count on it." Whether it is the promise of His forgiveness, or cleansing, or victory over sin, or protection, or provision, or eternal life, or healing, or His very presence with us, we are in a positive (Yes) and confident (Amen) relationship with God to receive the fulfillment of those promises only because of Christ. In fact every promise that God makes to us in the Word would without Christ be "No" and "Forget It."

But now people are being told that the nails in Christ's hands and feet really nailed nothing down for sure. From "It Is Finished" to "We Are Not Quite There Yet." If the Christian Church continues to allow these Religious

Humanists to go uncorrected and unchallenged, we will end up with folks everywhere in modern Christianity saying, "We used to be sinners, but now we are not. We used to desperately need Divine grace, but now we are on a give-and-take basis with God." And the great Reformation truths of the Bible will be discarded again as they were in pre-Luther Roman Catholicism.

If we allow Religious Humanists to have their way in modern Christianity, we can say goodbye to Sola Gratia – By Grace Alone; Sola Christus – By Christ Alone; Sola Fide – By Faith Alone; and Sola Deo Gloria – Glory To God Alone. As a matter of fact, they have already disappeared in much of modern Christendom which is constantly trying to add their something to Christ's everything, to finish what He has already completed, and to add their two cents to His full payment for our being brought into favor with God. All they are doing is trying to add worthless tar paper and scrap lumber to a finished mansion. We desperately need a new Reformation in modern Protestantism on a worldwide basis, for Religious Humanism has literally polluted the "Protestant Fundamentals of Faith." It is time for Protestants to vigorously and loudly protest again.

Finally, how on earth then did so much of modern evangelical Christianity get so perverted? By losing sight of the fact that the Christian life is all about God's grace in Christ from beginning to end, and that not one promise of God would be fulfilled in our lives if it were not wrapped up in Divine grace and bathed in Jesus' blood. That is why we read in John 1:16,

"For of His fullness we have all received, and grace upon grace."

There it is! Do you see it? Not from indulgence to indulgence. Rather, from grace to grace. Not from grace to merit. No, but from grace to grace. That is Christianity from beginning to end, because Christ is the Alpha and Omega of grace and all the way in between.

JUST DOING OUR UNWORTHY SERVANT DUTY

Alright, enough already! It becomes scandalous when carried to its ultimate role reversal. God, the Giver of all, in Religious Humanism ends up owing man, the real debtor, who got from God all that he is and has in the first place. Please, get us out of this insanity!

The Bible does just that. Jesus tells us that unforgettable story about a servant and his master in Luke 17. The details of the story are rather commonplace, but its riveting quality comes from the most striking and profound point which He makes at the end of an otherwise simple narrative. Jesus, the story-teller par excellence, unfolds it in Luke 17:7-10, where He says,

> "But which of you, having a slave (servant) plowing or tending sheep, will say to him when he has come in from the field, 'Come immediately and sit down to eat'? But will he not say to him, 'Prepare something for me to eat, and properly clothe yourself and serve me until I have eaten and drunk; and afterward you will eat and drink'? He does not thank the slave because he did the things which were commanded, does he? So you, too, when you do all the things which are commanded you, say, 'We are unworthy slaves; we have done only that which we ought to have done.'"

I really do not have to retell the story which we have just read, given its clarity and forthrightness. But I like the story so much that I will retell it to you anyway. Suffice it to say that the servant was plum tuckered out. He had been working his head off, plowing fields and tending flocks all day long for his master. The servant comes to the ranch house at the end of the work day sweaty and dirty, wiped out, starved for food, and desperately needing rest.

At this point, the least that one could expect for the worn-out servant would be that his work would now be considered completed for the day by his boss, and that he could finally sit back and relax. Sorry! Not so quick! His master demands that before he can eat and crash for the night, he must clean himself up, properly clothe himself, and then he has to prepare his master's supper not only, but serve it to him as well. The aroma of the food is tormenting him, but he cannot yet satisfy his cravings. Just when he thinks he has completed his duties, the master calls for another cup of coffee and another piece of that irresistible pie. Yes, I know, I am Americanizing the story.

Boy, by this time one would think that the least his boss owes the servant is a great big "Thank You." Think again! You've got it all wrong, you Religious Humanist you! You see, that is instinctively how human nature thinks, and man drags that self-serving and self-deserving attitude into his religion as well. It is all about human merit! But Jesus tells us that the servant of God doesn't deserve any "I Owe You Gratitude" of any kind from his Master. Why? Here comes the rub! Jesus is really saying in Luke 17:10 that when we've done for God everything that He commands us:

"...we have done only that which we ought to have done."

Whoops! Jesus just pulverized the entire Religious Humanism system with one short phrase!

Did you notice what else God says here about all of His servants? He says that when we have served our Master and done everything that He has commanded us to do; we are not to be called simply servants. No, no! That is still too high of a classification. Rather as in Luke 17:10, we are to refer to ourselves as "**UNWORTHY SLAVES!**" Yikes, what a slap in the face. It sounds cruel! The King James Version expresses it in this way: "**UNPROFITABLE SERVANTS**." Point! Set! Match!

Oh yes, for most if not all of us at first reading, this is a most abrasive thing to hear, even harder to accept; let alone looking in the mirror and telling ourselves that after all of our obedience to God we are still only unworthy servants. As a matter of fact, this entire story for the Religious Humanists is as uncomfortable as trying to put a size 10 shoe on a size 18 foot, and a size small cap on an XXL size head.

It is one thing to be called unworthy. It is quite another to call ourselves that. As we have already seen, Robert Schuller tells us that the most serious sin is one that causes me say that I am unworthy. The exact reverse is once more the truth. It is this, that the most sincere spirit is one that causes me to say that I am unworthy. Jesus commands us to attach to each and every act of obedience to God the words, "Performed for God by His unworthy servants." Service is our God-given duty from which we merit nothing! Somebody is wrong here, and it is not Jesus. I wonder who it could be!

Unworthy servants! Unprofitable servants! The word for "Unprofitable" used by our Lord in Luke17:10 is very, very strong. It is the Greek word "Achreios" which means "Useless" or "Worthless." Wow! It means essentially this, not that we are simply unworthy or undeserving servants, but that as His servants we can do nothing worthful. Zapparoo to the entire Religious Humanism mindset!

What this really means is that because God is complete and perfect in Himself, He will never be better off or have His state improved because of what we have done for Him or given to Him. There is no way that we can benefit God or enhance His condition. That is to say, He has never and will never be profited by one thing that we have done. How can He be bettered when He is already infinite perfection? Everything we do for God is imperfection serving perfection, impotence serving omnipotence, creature serving Creator, finiteness serving infiniteness, and human unworthiness serving Divine worthiness.

When each day is done, we have simply done what He commanded, fulfilled our duty, and when it is done, we are still unprofitable. It is infinitely gracious of

Him to even accept our service. Wham! So we read words like the following Scriptures (KJV) which summarize all that we have been saying. David said to the Lord in Psalm 16:2 (KJV),

"...my goodness extendeth not to thee."

That is to say, "No matter what good I perform, it falls far short of God's worthiness. It doesn't even come near Him." Or again, Elihu's words to Job in Job 35:7 (KJV),

"If thou be righteous, what givest thou him? Or what receiveth he of thine hand?"

In other words, "If we were righteous in ourselves, which we are not, what could we possibly give to God that would measure up to His worthiness and acceptance of it?"

I am reminded of my dear wife's father. His name was Harry. He is in Heaven now with his dear wife, Jennie, and they lived there a great deal before they went there. On my very first date with Ruthie, she asked me to come into the house because her Dad, Harry, wanted to speak with me. I had not come to talk with Harry, I had come for Ruthie. I was uneasy to say the least. However, Harry was waiting for me as I was invited into the living room where he was sitting with the open Bible across one knee and the Christian Reformed Church periodical *The Banner* across the other knee. He asked me to sit down, and engaged me in some friendly small talk for a short time.

Then quickly he became very serious and spiritual, and he began to tell me how the Lord had so abundantly blessed him over the years of his life, and that he felt so unworthy of God's blessings because he was such a sinner. What is more, he then began to cry as he told me about his marvel at Jesus' love for Harry the sinner. Harry's heart and tears overflowed in unspeakable gratitude and a deep sense of unworthiness that the Lord had not only so abundantly blessed him over the many years, but that Jesus would go through that horrible suffering and death on the cross for such an unworthy sinner as himself. That is when he really began to weep. Now I could date his daughter.

This happened most every time I picked up Ruthie for a date. I had to go through Harry's crying time first at Calvary. I can still hear his voice and see the tears coursing down his weathered cheeks. Harry always took me to Calvary. That will change anyone's dating behavior, let me tell you.

What I have just described to you in Harry's life has always been the humble and grateful heart of historic Christianity. Notice that I said, "Has Been!" Where have all the Harrys gone? They are a disappearing breed. Much of modern Christianity has developed a critical, if not fatal "Religious Humanism Heart Disease." Its arteries have been plugged with Religious Humanism's killing cholesterol of "God Owes Me" and "I Am Worthy."

Instead of falling down and weeping before the Holy God with an overwhelming sense of sin and unworthiness, and with an inexpressible gratitude for God's totally undeserved goodness and mercy, Religious Humanists are teaching modern religionists to stand before God like gold diggers staking their claims. People in these heartsick Religious Humanistic churches are being taught to make deals with God who then owes them; and they are no longer falling down with Harry before God in humility and brokenness of spirit with the deepest sense of unworthiness before God and eternal indebtedness to Him.

RELIGIOUS HUMANISM'S OTHER GLARING REVERSALS

Hang on now! Listen to the words of Jesse Duplantis, who is one of the mainstays on religious television today. Jesse Duplantis makes this statement: "**I HAD A MAN SAY, 'YOU LOOK SO PROSPEROUS, BROTHER JESSE.' I SAID, 'WELL, I'M BACKED BY A VERY RICH JEW. YEAH!! YES I AM! HIS NAME IS JESUS. I'M BACKED BY HIM.'**" (10) This statement of course comes from the "Prosperity Gospel" that has defiled and twisted the Word of God and metastasized like cancer throughout much of modern Christianity.

First, to refer to the ascended and reigning King of Kings and Lord of Lords as a "Rich Jew" is absolutely a flagrant and blasphemous violation of II Corinthians 5:16,

> **"...even though we have known Christ according to the flesh, yet now we know Him thus no longer."**

This reference to Jesus now as a "Rich Jew" is to reverse His ascension and exaltation to the right hand of God, and bring Him back down to His earthly state of incarnation and humiliation. We do not know Christ in fleshly terms any longer. This is to miss the reigning, glorified Christ in Heaven by as far as our feet are from our heads.

We are not backed by a "Rich Jew", but ruled by the "Righteous, Omnipotent Lord" of eternity. Jesus is no more a "Rich Jew" on the throne than I will be a "Penny-Pinching Dutchman" before the throne in Heaven. Jesus is not the "King of the Jews" but the "King of Kings and the Lord of Lords" over all nations.

Second, it is amazing how words stated in certain ways operate upon the minds of men. Words once taken in by the ears imprint themselves indelibly in either material or spiritual concepts upon the human mind. So here for instance, our Savior is called a "Rich Jew." Those words enter people's brains, and they form a picture of an opulent Jesus in their imaginations. Sort of like an instamatic camera, yes, the figure is taking shape. Oh yes, there He is, I can see Him now – "Money Bags Jesus," and "Jesus the Jewish Tycoon!" And here is the bogus lesson that is being taught by Religious Humanists: "**SINCE JESUS WAS AND IS A RICH JEW, (AND WE ARE TO BE LIKE JESUS), THEN EACH OF US WHO FOLLOW JESUS SHOULD BE RICH WHATEVERS, TOO.**"

Had enough? What a truckload of baloney! It is a completely false image of Jesus Christ! Nowhere in the Bible is Jesus in the slightest degree referred to or pictured as a "Rich Jew." Nowhere! In fact, He was born in a borrowed stable. He lived and was brought up on the wrong side of the tracks. He had to eat and sleep in borrowed homes as an itinerant teacher. He had to ride on a borrowed donkey. He had to be buried in a borrowed tomb.

What strong poison words can inject into the minds and imaginations of men! Satan bites with his tongue. Rich Jew! You've just been bitten and infected with the deadly poison of a false, materialistic gospel. Tens of thousands are suffering from the "Rich Jew" virus. Many of them are critically ill with Religious Humanism's spirit-killing affluenza, and are sick unto death.

Third, Religious Humanists will twist and distort the Scriptures to teach that we can and even should live for two worlds simultaneously. That is what the couplet "Rich Jew" applied to the ascended Lord is all about. Now we can live for two worlds. Now we can have our cake and eat it, too. Jesus is a rich Jew and He wants us to be rich Christians. Get it? That is to say, we can have our sights set on the temporal and the eternal, the material and the spiritual, the earthly and the heavenly. Religious Humanists teach not only that it can be done, but that it should be done. Religious Humanists attempt to join them as one. Christians separate them as two distinct and antithetical choices. Why?

Jesus taught us that living for the material and the spiritual is an absolutely impossible state of being. In other words, serving God and serving mammon at the same time wasn't presented by Jesus as a prohibition. He simply declared it to be a contradiction and an impossible state of being. He put it this way in Luke 16:13,

"No servant can serve two masters; for either he will hate

the one, and love the other, or else he will hold to one, and despise the other. You cannot serve God and mammon."

Mammon! What in the world is mammon? Is it a first cousin of manna? Or perhaps mammon is mummy food. Not so fast here. Mammon is not quite as mysterious or Egyptian as one might think. The Greek word for mammon is "Mammonas" which means "Wealth," "Riches" etc. Jesus boldly, clearly and unequivocally states that God and money, God and riches, God and wealth are two masters whose interests are so opposed to each other, that it is impossible to serve both at the same time. Master Jesus and Master Mammon are so contrary to one another, and work at such cross purposes in the human heart that you cannot serve them both. To serve the one will of necessity mean the cessation of the service to the other.

Come now! Are His words of exclusivity really that much of a shock to us? If they are, it is most likely the case that we are trying to love and serve both God and mammon at the same time. I love my wife Ruthie with all that is in me. She has captured my heart, and there is nothing left in me to be able to love another woman at the same time. That is an impossible state of affairs! It is no different with God, but even more so. He wants no competition in our lives from other lovers (gods), and He is very jealous over us.

But more than that, He knows that a divided heart is an impure heart, and that the river of love that flows between God and ourselves will be contaminated with raw sewage and unprocessed garbage if we allow other love affairs to be dumped into the flow. No species of fish can live long in a polluted stream. They will eventually die. So, too, a poisoned river of competing loves will infect and kill the relationship we have with Jesus. It will kill true Christianity in our lives. It is inevitable!

More pointedly, when we attempt this dualism, it will result in loving one and hating the other. That shouldn't shock us either. How often I have seen that very thing, when the husband supposedly falls in love outside of the marriage covenant, he leaves his wife for another woman, and ends up divorcing and hating his wife in the end. Especially when it gets into earth's courts! Hell on earth!

Is Jesus love/hate dichotomy extreme? Not in the least, for it happens all the time. That is how this inescapable dualism-dynamic works. Jesus isn't being overly dramatic here. He is stating obvious facts which are immediately understandable if we just allow ourselves to be honest with ourselves as to how close love and hate really are. So Jesus says that if we fully delight in Master Mammon we will despise Master Jesus, and if we fully delight in Master Jesus we will despise Master Mammon.

This is Jesus' "Mammon Whammy!" We cannot live a life of mammon bingeing and at the same time a life of blessing God. This strikes a death-blow to Religious Humanist's desire to live for the material and the spiritual. If you will: **"RELIGIOUS HUMANISTS THINK THAT THEY CAN SERVE BOTH, BECAUSE THEY DON'T UNDERSTAND THE NATURE OF EITHER."**

The Apostle John was discipled well by Master Jesus. That is why we read in I John 2:15,

> **"Do not love the world, nor the things in the world. If anyone loves the world, the love of the Father is not in him."**

We can't have earthly and Heavenly, material and spiritual love affairs simultaneously. If we love stuff, i.e. earthly treasures and the like, then the love of the Savior is not in us. Here we go again! We can't have it both ways. We cannot love the world and God at the same time, for if we do, then we do not love God whatsoever. The Kingdom of God allows no spiritual polygamists amongst its citizens.

In summary, worldly things and Godly things are such that we would need two hearts, two souls, two selves in order to give one heart to Master Jesus and another heart to Master Mammon. The problem is that none of us have any spare hearts. We each only have one. Therefore, don't become a materialistic Religious Humanist, for you will then end up loving mammon and hating God.

DESIGNER JESUS – CADILLAC MAN

Let's take a look at a few more of these reversals being perpetrated by today's Religious Humanists upon Christians and Christianity. To validate their mammon-mongering, as we have already seen, they have totally redesigned and perverted the Biblical Lord Jesus. They do so to legitimize their flesh-gratifying, self-ingratiating religion!

Religious Humanists, exactly like the world, is all about appearances. It is all in the look! It is so important to appear rich and successful. Religious Humanism is an external religion. There was an article in the papers some time ago about a fake antenna that was on the market for cellular telephones. It cost $19.00. This antenna gives the appearance of the real thing, but it is a fake. It is for people who can't afford cellular telephones, but don't want their friends to know it. The amazing thing is that more than 200,000 people bought the bogus things. As we shall see, Religious Humanism is a fake antenna, too, for it is all about appearance.

For instance, Religious Humanists tell their audiences that the reason the soldiers on Calvary's Hill were gambling for Christ's robe is because it was a very expensive, customized, designer garment. After all, they tell us, you do not gamble and risk your finances for mere rags. States comedic preacher Jesse Duplantis: "**YOU DON'T GAMBLE FOR RAGS. YOU GAMBLE FOR CLOTHES THAT COST**, DON'T YOU?" (11)

Religious Humanists, if you can imagine this, remake Jesus into some sort of hip, "Mr. Fashion Statement" of the 1ˢᵗ century. Not only that, but they do so at Calvary where He is suffering, bleeding and dying for the sins of the world. Materialism has never reached a more contemptible low than this. It isn't first of all that our Lord was the "Suffering Servant" on Calvary's cruel hill. The lesson at the cross according to Religious Humanists then comes down to this: "**THAT IF YOU DRESS LIKE JESUS, THEN AS THE ENTREPRENEUR OF MEN'S WAREHOUSE SAYS ON HIS TELEVISION ADS, 'YOU WILL LIKE HOW YOU LOOK, I GUARANTEE IT.'"**

Let the prophet Isaiah tell us how Jesus really appeared on the cross as described in Isaiah 52:14,

> "...**So His appearance was marred more than any man, and His form more than the sons of men**."

Jesus, after being beaten and abused, having His back whipped and shredded, His beard ripped out of His cheeks, and His head bloodied with a crown of thorns that had been jammed down into His forehead and skull, now dies with His hands and feet nailed to a cross. In it all He is in Hell's torments. His appearance was so marred that He was beyond recognition. Believe me, "**YOU WOULD NOT HAVE LIKED HOW HE LOOKED, I GUARANTEE IT**."

As to Jesus' garments, it takes a thorough-going Religious Humanist and exegetical manipulator to use sacrilegious souvenir-hunting and gambling soldiers to fabricate some nonsense about Jesus' Christian Dior or Yves Saint Laurent wardrobe. (Wouldn't you know it, men's clothing designers called Christian and Saint? It is a Religious Humanist's dream come true!)

The fact is that Jesus had become the laughing stock of the Jewish and Roman populace. The King of the Jews Who had created such a stir with His claims of Divinity and His miracles, is now being crucified as a common crook along with two other criminals! Something to remember this charlatan by perhaps! So the soldiers tore his outer garment into four parts, and for His seamless tunic they cast lots. (John 19:23-24) That way they all could have a piece of the action, and show their families and friends these laughable conversation pieces.

For the fun of it, they gambled for the Christ's inner garment as the real sporting prize for the day. You know how guys can be, making a game out of everything, and to spice it up some wagering as a kicker. Nothing new here! Furthermore, they had nothing better to do but to gamble their time away while they waited for Jesus and the others to die. It was their final insult to the "King of the Jews."

That's all it was, nothing more, nothing less. Just a diversion for the bored and calloused "hangmen!" In the final analysis: **"THEY WERE NOTHING MORE THAN VULTURES PREYING UPON AND DEVOURING A CARCASS; SHARKS WHO SMELLED BLOOD IN THE WATER, AND SO THEY REACTED IN A FEEDING FRENZY FOR WHAT SPOILS THEY COULD FIND."**

As if presenting Calvary's sacrificial Lamb as some sort of "Glamour Boy" is not repulsive enough, Religious Humanists actually go so far as to use the Palm Sunday donkey on which Jesus rode into Jerusalem as a way to somehow try to spread their affluenza and justify their materialism. To do so there are no boundaries that they will not cross!

The mammon-mongers in Religious Humanism try to convince us that because Jesus chose to ride on a donkey that had never been ridden on before, so we should all drive cars that had never been driven before. How is that for a million mile stretch? As Jesse Duplantis states: **"HE WANTED A DONKEY THAT HAD NEVER BEEN RODE. AS I SAID EARLIER, YOU MIGHT WANT A CAR THAT HAS NEVER BEEN DROVE."** (12) The point being, an unused donkey for Christ, and no used cars for Christians! That's God's Palm Sunday lesson! Jesus, "The King of the Cars!"

We are supposed to learn from this humbling moment on Jesus' Via Dolorosa that because He rode on an unused donkey, therefore, it would be beneath His followers to ride in or drive used automobiles. The truth is that Jesus on purpose humbled Himself by riding into Jerusalem on a lowly donkey, when He could have ridden on a majestic white horse, or in a regal chariot drawn by majestic steeds, thereby presenting Himself in royalty as some mighty, conquering, earthly king. But His Kingdom is not of this world. He would have none of it. None of it I say! Religious Humanists miss the entire point of His far less than a grand entrance. They twist the entire thing into a fairytale.

So the Religious Humanist makes it sound like Jesus was riding in the newest first-century luxury car available, because the donkey had never been ridden before. However, if it means anything, this donkey-colt had never been ridden before, was untamed and would have rebelliously bucked off anyone else. But He Who has all power to calm the sea has the power to tame a raw, ornery donkey, and stubborn jackasses like you and me. Even Religious Humanists! Instead we not only have our Lord being portrayed at Calvary as "Designer Jesus," but we also have Jesus being portrayed on Palm Sunday as "Cadillac Man."

Religious Humanism is all about man's trinkets and toys. It has been said that in Judaism he who buys toys at the lowest price wins. In Atheism there is no toy maker. In Evolutionism the toys make themselves. In Jehovah's Witnesses the one who places the most toys door to door wins. And in Religious Humanism he who has the most, the newest and the biggest toys wins.

Religious Humanists are creating a sensual religion in the name of Jesus, which in essence states that the Christian should have the best of everything and the most of both worlds. They should not have simply reliable transportation, but rather the sleekest sport's car on the market. They should not settle for just having their spouses rub their backs, but they should have weekly massages at the most socially elite spa. If you are going to enjoy a beautiful sunset, you owe it to yourself to see one in Acapulco, Mexico from the balcony of your five-star hotel. Physical exercise should be carried out with the latest aerobic attire at the most posh health club. It is not enough to eat gourmet food unless it is served with the proper and most costly ambience.

Jesse Duplantis goes on: "**I HAVE NEVER HEARD THE LORD SAY, 'JESSE, I THINK THAT CAR IS A LITTLE TOO NICE.' I'VE HAD VEHICLES AND THE LORD SAID, 'WOULD YOU PLEASE GO PARK THAT AT YOUR HOUSE. DON'T PUT THAT IN FRONT OF MY HOUSE. I DON'T WANT PEOPLE TO THINK THAT I'M A POOR GOD.'**" (13) According to this malarkey, if you have a run-down car, you are not welcome to the House of the Lord, or for God's sake, park your clunker down the street far away from church so that you don't embarrass the Lord. Religious Humanists are rewriting and corrupting Christ's beatitudes, so that now Matthew 5:3 reads:

"Blessed are the rich, for theirs is the Kingdom of Heaven."

That is where all of this leads, and it all stands in complete opposition to the teachings, principles, priorities and earthly life of Christ. It is an abomination.

We must leave this now and go on to other madness. Suffice it to say that when a fleshly preacher takes in the pure Word of God, what comes out of him is a carnally corrupted word. Religious Humanists remind me of a lions' den in front of which there are many footprints of unsuspecting animals going in, but none of their footprints coming out. These false teachers supposedly study and take in the Holy Word of God, but it never comes out of them in its true meaning. Before the Holy Word of God can come out of them and be preached, it is corrupted so badly, that they would have us believing that Jesus stepped out of *Esquire Magazine* and a *Mercedes Benz Showroom* onto the stage of history. When in fact He came from a Virgin's womb in a lowly stable being born to die on a criminal's cross and buried in another man's tomb so as to unhook His followers from anything in this world. They were seeing the Kingdom of Heaven enacted before their very eyes. We must not allow Religious Humanists to blind our eyes to the true lesson being taught by our Lord, and that is that while we are in this world, we are not of this world.

Resources:

1. Dynamic Preaching, "Good News for Broken Hearts" (Seven Worlds Corporation, Knoxville, TN, June, 1995, Volume X, No. 6) Pages 24-25; "The Hymnbook" (Philadelphia: John Ribble, 1950) Page 12

2. Dynamic Preaching, "A Cup of Cold Water" (Seven Worlds Corporation, Knoxville, TN, June, 1996, Volume XI, No. 6) Page 30, Gary B. Swanson, "Frisbees and Guerillas" (Light and Life, July, 1994) Pages 14-15

3. The Trinity Foundation, "Civilization and the Protestant Reformation" © 1998-2008 (Post Office 68, Unicoi, TN 37692, 423-743-0199)

4. Bible Light Homepage, Michael Scheifier, "Johann Tetzel, Grace for Sale Through Indulgences" (Hans J. Hillebrand, "The Reformation" Harper & Row, New York, NY, 1964) Pages 41-46

5. Forgotten Word Ministries, Robert E. Wise, "Mike Murdock – False Preacher/Teacher" (Mike Murdock, LeSea Television, Miracle Telethon, April 20, 2004)

6. Forgotten Word Ministries, Robert E. Wise, "Paula White – False Teacher, Prosperity Preacher" (Paula White, TBN, Praise-A-Thon, March 29, 2004)

7. Forgotten Word Ministries, Robert E. Wise, "Paula White – False Teacher, Prosperity Preacher" (Paula White, "Spring Praise-A-Thon," TBN, April 5, 2005)

8. Forgotten Word Ministries, Robert E. Wise, "Paula White – False Teacher, Prosperity Preacher" (Paula White, Benny Hinn Telethon, LeSea Network, April 16, 2004)

9. Forgotten Word Ministries, Robert E. Wise, "Michael C. Gaudiosi – The Noble Berean Fund Raising Report" (Jamal Bryant – TBN Spring 2007 Praise-A-Thon – 04/13/07)

10. *Let us Reason Ministries, Mike Oppenheimer, "Jesse Duplantis, A Man with a Short Theology and Tall Tales" (Jesse Duplantis, TBN, September 21, 1998)*

11. *Forgotten Word Ministries, Robert E. Wise, "Jesse Duplantis – False Preacher" (Jesse Duplantis, Marcus Lamb, and Joni Lamb, Daystar Fall "Share-A-Thon", September 15, 2004)*

12. *Ibid.*

13. *Forgotten Word Ministries, Robert E. Wise, "Jesse Duplantis – False Preacher" (Jesse Duplantis, "When Will We Yield To the Anointing of Wealth II, April 10, 2005)*

Chapter Four

THE CORRUPTING SELFIANITY IN MODERN CHRISTIANITY
†††

"I Am More Afraid Of My Own Heart Than Of The Pope And All His Cardinals. I Have Within In Me The Great Pope, Self." ~Sir Thomas More

Thankfully, there are still strong remaining pockets of the true Gospel where this man-centered, comforts-oriented Religious Humanism is being repelled, and where Mark 8:34-35 is still preached, believed, and practiced. Do you remember the following words of Jesus? He said,

> "...**If anyone wishes to come after Me, LET HIM DENY HIMSELF, AND TAKE UP HIS CROSS, AND FOLLOW ME. For whoever wishes to save his life shall lose it; but whoever loses his life for My sake and the gospel's shall save it.**"

Religious Humanism's priority is the self-focused life! Me, myself, and I! Self-prioritization, self-promotion and self-centralization! How-ever, what Jesus is saying is that there is absolutely no room for both the self and the Savior in the Christian life. It is either or, for we shall either be following after self, or we shall be following after the Savior. We cannot follow after both! To follow after Christ, self must be denied completely, and Jesus affirmed completely. In Religious Humanism, the focus is self-satisfaction. In Christianity, the focus is self-denial. In Religious Humanism self is enthroned. In Christianity Christ is enthroned. A total antithesis! Religious Humanists are self-followers. Christians are Christ-followers.

The comprehensive duty in Christianity is self-denial. The comprehensive duty in Religious Humanism is self-gratification. This is another one of the great divisions between Religious Humanism and Christianity. And be assured of the following, that no one opposes Christ but for the purpose of serving self. Likewise, no one ever truly affirms Christ without the willingness to deny self. We cannot have it both ways. It is either **HAIL KING JESUS** or **HAIL KING SELF**.

Is self-denial an easy thing to do? No, not at all! Denying self is not a simple goodbye to self. Hey self, see yah! I wish it were that easy. Not so. Not in the least. After all, we have lived with and served self for as long as we can remember. Self came into the world with us and has stuck to us like glue ever since. Self is the dominating force in our lives.

Each one of us is a unique self which is as distinctive as a fingerprint. But each self is like every other self in that all selves are self-centered and self-serving. From the very beginning of self's life, let any other self try to snatch self's toys or rattlers, and self becomes a raging monster. Suddenly it is obvious that the much-heralded baby can become a little hellian named "Selfish." For that matter, every other self is considered by self as a rival and a hostile force that must be constantly guarded against.

We get up with self and we go to bed with self. We have fed the open mouth of self's voracious appetites all our lives, and now we are going to have to starve self. Self has been at the center of all our preferences and pleasures, and now we must prefer and please someone else – God Himself. In short, to deny self is like putting a knife to the throat of our Isaac.

Let us not pass over this too easily or quickly at the outset. Self-denial is particularly difficult in a society whose motto is: "**LET THE REST OF THE WORLD BE DAMNED, YOU'VE GOT TO LOOK OUT FOR SELF, FOR BIG # 1, FOR NO ONE ELSE WILL!**" To deny self in this world therefore is the very hardest of all of the commands given to us by Jesus Christ. It is not simply a matter of undressing, as if it is no more than the removing of the old garment of self, and putting on the new garment of selflessness. This is not like changing clothes. No, no, no! To be disrobed of self is more like tearing, not your sweatshirt, but your body skin up over your ears and head. In short, it is like being skinned alive. To deny self is something like that, and for sure, it is an extremely painful matter. The Religious Humanist reading this is by this time on the floor writhing in skinned agony.

RELIGIOUS HUMANISM'S SELFIANITY

As we have already seen, and it bears repeating over and over again, it is precisely here that Religious Humanism and Christianity are 1000% antithetical and sharply irreconcilable. Their points of reference are completely at odds, for Religious Humanism's point of reference is self, and Christianity's point of reference is Christ. These reference points are as far apart as Heaven is from Hell.

The state highway department in Pennsylvania once set out to build a bridge, working from both sides. When the workers reached the middle of the waterway, they found that they were thirteen feet to one side of each other. Albert Steinberg, writing about this fiasco in the *Saturday Evening Post,* went on to explain that each crew of workmen had used its own reference point. That is why they could not connect. (1) Neither can Religious Humanism and Christianity. They are far more than thirteen feet apart. Rather, they are eternally apart, for their reference points are polar opposites.

You will never, I repeat, you will never hear Religious Humanists preach, let alone with fervor, about the core disciple-ship truths of Mark 8:34-35. Never! To speak of self-denial would for them be like committing suicide and killing their entire religious system. Self-denial! No, rather, "Viva Self!" Long live self! "Halle-self-jah!"

Religious Humanism calls to mind the story of the pig and the chicken. They were walking past a church one Sunday morning. The chicken said to the pig, "You know over the years those people in there have been pretty nice to us. I think that we ought to do something nice for them." The pig said, "Good idea, what do you have in mind?" The chicken responded, "I think we ought to have a big banquet." The pig said, "I am all for that. But what shall we serve them to eat?" The chicken said, "What about bacon and eggs?" The pig said, "Are you kidding? For you that is only giving something of yourself. For me it is total self-denial."

You will find an emphasis throughout Religious Humanism which makes sure that self is protected, promoted, and pampered. Self is packed into all of its thinking. What you will hear are self-couplets galore such as self-love, self-worth, self-esteem, self- potential, self-discovery, self-forgiveness, self-acceptance, self-reliance, self-realization, self-confidence, and self-admiration. None of these self-consciousnesses are even slightly Biblical themes or fruits of the Holy Spirit. The Bible has its own and far fewer self-couplets, such as man by nature being self-willed and therefore in need of self-control and self-denial. That pretty well takes care of self from God's perspective.

On and on it goes in Religious Humanism. No short supply of self here. It has created a completely different language in the church. It is the modern self-linguistics of Religious Humanism. In short, Religious Humanism is nothing more or less than "**SELFIANITY**."

SHE IS WOMAN – HEAR HER ROAR

Where does this modern self-litany of Religious Humanism lead to? In many directions, and all of them lead further and further away from the mandates of God's Word. For instance, that is exactly what has happened in the Episcopalian Church and many other churches as well. Since 1979, the official name of this denomination has been *The Episcopalian Church in The United States of America.* (ECUSA) The Episcopalian Church met in General Council in Columbus, Ohio in June of 2006 during which a woman by the name of Katharine Jefferts Schori was elected Presiding Bishop and Primate of the Episcopalian Church by the House of Bishops on June18, 2006. A woman elected to the highest seat of leadership and authority in a major historic Christian denomination.

The feminist movement in America celebrated! Women's rights reached the ecclesiastical summit of "Mt. Positional Equality." All that remains is for a woman to be elected president of the United States. As Hillary Clinton stated to her 18 million supporters in her non-concession concession speech to Barack Obama, "Although we were not able to shatter the highest, hardest glass ceiling this time, thanks to you, its got about 18 million cracks in it. And the light is shining through like never before, filling us with the hope and the sure knowledge that the path will be a little easier next time." She is woman, hear her roar.

God's Word clearly states for His church however in I Timothy 2:12,

"But I do not allow a woman to teach or exercise authority over a man, but to remain quiet."

God says "But!" But what? The opposite of "to allow" is "to disallow." Women teaching or exercising authority in the Church of Jesus Christ is disallowed by God. No "Unisex" positions in the church when it comes to teaching or ruling over the general church which includes men. Sorry! God disallows it! There is only one Head of the Church, and that Head is Jesus Christ even as the husband is the head of the wife. (Ephesians 5:23) Male headship is Divinely ordained! Female headship is Divinely disallowed.

The church could have saved itself a lot of forced research and wrangling if it would have submitted to God's clear-as-crystal Word and disallowed what God says must be disallowed. Since when does "Not Allowed" need study committees? But then again, the same modern churches appoint study committees to determine if Genesis 1 literally happened, as well as if homosexuality and same-sex marriages should be allowed by and in the church. There is theological and moral schizophrenia spreading throughout modern Christendom because it will not embrace the Bible's clear choice in Romans 3:4,

"Let God be true (Theism) and every man a liar (Humanism)."

But oh no, humanists today, both secular and religious, want to leave open the possibility that not only did the world evolve over millions of years, but also that man came from apes. Not only is all of that completely unbiblical and therefore a lie, but it's a joke, for it is as possible for man to come from an ape as it is possible for an ape to come from applesauce. They want us to accept from the goo to the zoo to you. Or again, eternal matter times evolving monkey equals mankind. But then again, I guess humanists ought to know their ancestors better than anyone else.

So, too, I Timothy 2:12 is as clear as crystal, but of course it goes completely against the grain of modern society and the modern church in absolutely every direction. But then, since when is the Church of Jesus Christ to be dictated to by society? Since when is the church supposed to be "Socially Correct?" Or again, Paul in I Corinthians 14:34 writes:

> **"Let the women keep silent in the churches; for they are not permitted to speak, but let them subject themselves, just as the Law also says."**

Taking it all together we come up with the following. Women are not allowed to teach men in the church! Women are not allowed to exercise authority over men in the church! Women must remain quiet in the church when it comes to teaching and ruling the general congregation!

By this time the religio-feminists are screaming and screeching and getting ready to burn down the church kitchen. But what part of 2+2=4 don't they understand? It should quiet the roar now shouldn't it? No, reading this they cry, "Foul!" They shout, "More Male Domination." No, it is not. It is "Divine Order!" It is "Divine Domination." And the religio-feminists resist all domination, even God's.

David once said about God's Word in Psalm 119:130,

> **"…It gives understanding to the simple."**

You have to be educated in a liberal college or seminary to be able to muddy the crystal clear waters of God's Word. God's will in God's Word for women in the church is crisp and totally unambiguous, and you really have to work hard to mess up and dull its meaning. You might just as well try to make the sunlight at high noon represent white things as black and black things as white. I Timothy 2:12 and I Corinthians 14:34 do not need explanation. They frankly read like a first grade reader.

When I am asked to explain passages like that, I feel like Beethoven who once played his latest sonata for a group of friends. The music filled the room. As the last note lingered, the friends asked Beethoven, "What does it mean?"

Beethoven's only answer was to return to the piano and play the entire sonata again. When he finished, he said to his friends, "That's what it means." When I hear people asking what I Timothy 2:12 and I Corinthians 14:34 mean, I simply read them again, and then I say, "That's what they mean?"

Listen, it is not the human understanding's inability to comprehend the truth, as it is its unwillingness to submit to the truth. What we have here is not misunderstanding, it is mutiny. It is not indecisiveness on God's part, as it is insolence on the church's part. Do we come to the Word of God to learn or to argue? It was Abraham Lincoln who once said, "Without this book, the Bible, we would not know right from wrong." But in modern Christianity, we do have the Bible, and we still cannot tell right from wrong. No, it isn't the ambiguity of the Word of God; it is the stubborn self that will not submit.

For women to obey I Timothy 2:12, they must first have the spirit of I Timothy 2:11,

"Let a woman quietly receive instruction with entire submissiveness."

Entire submissiveness? Paul, won't you settle for half and half, and we will call even? That is exactly what has happened today? But entire submissiveness, are you serious, Paul? We would be thankful today for partial submissiveness. In today's world that would be like demanding every pit bull to be totally obedient, benign and harmless. In today's world it would require total female hypnosis and the complete reprogramming of the non-submissive female psyche. But then God condemns things like hypnosis (Deuteronomy 18:10-12), and rather tells us to have the mind of Christ Who emptied Himself and became a servant.

But what is so shocking about all of this? Nothing really for Jesus said in Matthew 24:12 (KJV) that in the last days iniquity shall abound. What is iniquity? It is rebellion. It is lawlessness. If you will, there will be widespread rebellion against God's created and ordained order. It is obvious everywhere. It used to be that when children were naughty and disobeyed their parents, Dad would take the little rebels out to the woodshed. Now the little rascals cry foul, call a press conference and charge Dad and Mom with parental cruelty.

Iniquity, which is the across-the-board end time spirit of rebellion, has metastasized throughout society, marriage, family and the church, and God's order has been overthrown and everywhere we look there is disorder. God-ordained and God-ordered marriages, families and churches are now looking like deserted farmhouses on windswept prairies. All books on church order are being rewritten by man or just plain dumped. Religious Humanism! Modern

Christianity Corrupted! And God help those today who try to insert God's unspoiled truth into the conversation.

A woman is now the Presiding Bishop and Primate of the Episcopalian Church! Almost sounds like a Pope, only in this case it would be a Popess. For your information, "Primate" means someone who is first in rank and authority. Whoops! The Word of God has just dealt with that head on!

Let's deal now with the word "Bishop." Some reading this might be asking themselves, "Bishops? What are those? We don't have bishops in our church. We have a pastor, elders and deacons. The only Bishops I know of are in a chess game." At least to that extent, you are not far off, for everything today in the church is being moved around like pieces on a chess board, and male leadership is being checkmated. Elder retreats used to be "Guys Only" weekends. The only things that remain "Guys Only" these days, even in the church, are public restrooms. Mark my word that this, too, will change. Dear Lord, help us. Who knows what the next move of the feminist lobby in America will be?

But I must tell you, seeing that you have followed the Biblical pattern of pastors, elders and deacons in your church, this means that you do have "Bishops" in your church. You just do not call them that. Allow me to explain.

Let us concentrate on the "Elders" in your church to understand this. When the Apostle Paul visited with the elders of the church at Ephesus, we read in Acts 20:17,

"And from Miletus he sent to Ephesus and called to him the elders of the church."

The Greek word for "Elder" is "Presbuteros."

Later we read in the same setting in Acts 20:28 as Paul now speaks to these elders:

"Be on guard for yourselves and for all the flock, among which the Holy Spirit has made you overseers...."

The Greek word "Overseer" is "Episkopos" which can mean "Overseer" or "Bishop."

Then Paul goes on in Acts 20:28 and says to these elders or bishops:

"to shepherd the church of God which He purchased with His own blood."

The Greek word for "To Shepherd" is "Poimaino," which means that "Elders" or "Bishops" are also "Shepherds."

So then, we have this one-in-the-same office in the church being described in three ways. First, Elder-Presbuteros, which refers to the spiritual maturity of the "Elders." It does not refer to age. Age and maturity are not synonyms by any means. For instance, I have known younger men who were more advanced in the character of Christ as well as in Bible knowledge and wisdom than some older men.

Second, Bishop-Episkopos, which refers to the elder's spiritual authority over the flock. They are really spiritual fathers who must be accountable for the souls of God's family as they stand before Christ one day. Congregations must listen to the "Bishops" and receive and obey their Biblical counsel, correction and encouragement which they give to church members in love. (Hebrews 13:17)

Third, to Shepherd-Poimaino, which refers to the spiritual feeding as shepherds that they must give to the sheep of the Good Shepherd. That is why II Timothy 2:2 tells us that elders-bishops-shepherds must be apt to teach. This is their job description. Neither bishops nor deacons are called to take the complaints of parishioners in the church and nail the pastor with them in the board meetings. Parishioners must go to the pastor personally, for elders and deacons are not called to be go-betweens and congregational hit-men. Such a church is totally out of order, is sick, and will go through pastors like water.

So then, here we have three words and concepts for the same office. Where does the pastor fit into all of this? He is an elder, a bishop and a shepherd as well, but with this distinct difference and addition. He is referred to in Ephesians 4:11 and his unique calling is described in I Timothy 5:17,

"Let the elders who rule well be considered worthy of double honor, especially those (pastors) who work hard at preaching and teaching." "For the Scripture says, "You shall not muzzle the ox while he is threshing," and, 'The laborer is worthy of his wages.'"

The pastor is the one called to the ministry of preaching and teaching the whole counsel of God. He is a preaching elder-bishop-shepherd. He is to be paid for his ministry, while the other elders are not.

Now then, the Scripture remains totally consistent. God requires of the elder-bishop-shepherd in I Timothy 3:2, among many other mandated qualifications, the following:

"An overseer (bishop) must be the...husband of one wife."

Not only must the elder-bishop-shepherd be a man, but the husband of one wife. The same is true for deacons! (I Timothy 3:12) Bishop Katharine Jefferts Schori is the wife of one husband. The Bible knows only male elders-bishops-shepherds.

What then is causing Religious Humanism's distortion of the Word of God? Self-interest! The feminist lobby of Religious Humanism in modern Christianity is all about the female self, not about the Word of God. It is all about her, not about Him! It is about equal rights, not about rightly dividing the Word of Truth. The fact of the matter is that self-interest is the wheel which moves the world and is now moving the modern church. Undenied self, self-interest will always outweigh truth.

Therefore, let God speak whatever He may in His Word, if self-interest translates it, the result will be the "New Religious Humanism Twisted Version." The truth of God's Word will be shaded, distorted, ignored and trampled to accommodate self-interest. It is all about Selfianity and not about Christianity.

Today, churches across the spectrum are ordaining women to be elders, bishops and shepherds. Many of these churches have become weary of the constant nagging, hassles and in-fighting caused by the feminist lobby, as well as the threat of losing church members to other denominations who do ordain women as elders-bishops-shepherds. Some churches have held out longer than others against the persistent and powerful feminist lobby, and have tried to remain true to Biblical mandate. But little by little they have caved in so that they might enjoy again at least some semblance of peace by conceding defeat to the women's rights activists.

Accommodate self-interest! Override Divine mandate! Religious Humanism's Selfianity! Much of modern Christianity in so doing is no longer the New Testament Church. It is not being formed by the Holy Spirit, but by the humanistic, self-centered spirit of the age.

HEALING OR SAVING THE WORLD

Birds flock! Fish school! Deer herd. People mob! Heresies mass! Where the door has been opened to one heresy, others will always gather around it. When one Biblical mandate has been violated, other violations are sure to follow. Biblical truths begin to fall like dominoes. Count on this, heresies colonize like bees, and before we know it we are being swarmed by them.

The enemy then comes in like a flood, even though it started out as only an annoying drip. And where there is tolerated disorder, it will not be long and it will be impossible to maintain order anywhere. Once we start to drift, there is no end to drifting as to where it will take us. That is how it works. This is what is happening in modern Christianity. That is why we read in Hebrews 2:1,

"**For this reason we must pay much closer attention to what we have heard, lest we drift away from it.**"

We read this statement about God's mission for the world by Bishop Katharine Jefferts Schori: "**WE ARE BLESSED WITH LEADERS, LAY AND ORDAINED, WHO ARE INCREASINGLY AWARE OF THEIR GOD-GIVEN MINISTRIES TO LEAD THIS PEOPLE INTO FULLER PARTICIPATION IN GOD'S MISSION OF HEALING THE WORLD.**"(2) It all sounds so kind and compassionate. However it is a complete redefinition and distortion of Christ's purpose for coming to earth. The Bible tells us this: "**JESUS DID NOT COME TO HEAL A SICK WORLD.**" Au Contraire! Rather: "**JESUS CAME TO SAVE A SINFUL WORLD.**" Jesus' name means "Savior," not "Healer." At face value, Bishop Schori's definition of the Divine mission for the world is false. The Apostle Paul defined Christ's mission to Timothy in I Timothy 1:15,

"**It is a trustworthy statement, deserving full acceptance, that Christ Jesus came into the world to SAVE sinners, among whom I am foremost of all.**"

What is meant by the phrase, "Healing the World?" It becomes tricky at this point. First, we have to be acutely aware of the power of words, and the mind-manipulation that can be achieved through misapplied words. Wholesome words are used both to convince of truth and falsehood. When many religious leaders today talk about healing the world and not saving the world, it is because they have dropped the word "Sin" from their theological vocabulary. "Sin" has now become "Weakness," and "Iniquity" has become "Inability." "Healing" then becomes Christ's mission, not "Saving."

Likewise, "Theology" has become "Psychology," for what really is needed, we are being told by many religionists, is the healing of man's mental and emotional disorders and distortions. You know, man is mentally and emotionally maladjusted, not malevolent. Man is disoriented, not depraved. Man is misguided by his environment, not malicious by nature. He needs his mental and emotional nuts and bolts tightened and tweaked, and then society can be healed one man at a time and brought into harmony and order. Preachers become psychologists and sociologists in their communities, not the agents of the reconciliation of lost sinners to God through the blood of Jesus Christ.

More exactly: "**MAN NEEDS TO BE CURED OF MENTAL AND EMOTIONAL ILLS NOT CLEANSED OF SOUL-DAMNING SINS. MAN MUST BE REPROGRAMMED, NOT REGENERATED. MAN MUST BE REWIRED, NOT RECREATED. MAN NEEDS TO REFOCUS, NOT REPENT**." This is the first meaning of the concept of "Healing the World" rather than "Saving the World." It is rampant today as the panacea gospel for healing a sick world and the proposed new world order. When a Gospel preacher of the "Old Time Religion" preaches about sin, salvation and service anymore, he is viewed in many church circles as a religious prehistoric dinosaur.

Just one huge problem! "Healing The World" completely redefines and corrupts the true Gospel message of the Bible. As Mike Oppenheimer of "Let Us Reason Ministries" points out about the Apostle Paul's theology: "**WHILE SALVATION OF THE LOST WAS PARAMOUNT TO PAUL, HE RECOGNIZED THE FACT THAT A PERVERTED GOSPEL LEADS THE UNSAVED TO A FALSE CHRIST; NEITHER OF WHICH HAVE THE POWER TO SAVE**." (3)

Sinful man can no more recover or redirect himself away from sin than a no-spin bowling ball headed straight for the gutter can change its course. Only Jesus Christ can give an old rutted sinner a totally new heart and a completely new direction in life. The world does not need to be healed, it needs to be saved. The dead-in-sin human race (Ephesians 2:1) does not need to be tweaked, but it does need to be raised from spiritual death to new spiritual life in Jesus Christ.

Secondly, and it is married to the first, generally what religious leaders also mean when they talk about "Healing the World" and not "Saving the World" is the removal of prejudice, bigotry, intolerance and divisiveness from the human mind and spirit. Now follow along closely.

We are living in "The Age of the Self" as never before in human history. I am talking about the doctrine of the priority of self that now has taken deep root in the modern world and church. Self-affirmation! Self-acceptance! Self-endorsement! Whatever that self may be! Different strokes for different selves! I'm okay, you're okay! The diversity of human selves must be affirmed and celebrated.

Whether it is the morally relativistic self, the homosexual self, the bisexual self, the transsexual self, the pro-abortion-rights self, the partial-birth-abortion-rights self, the same-sex-marriage self, the fornicating self, the divorce self, the adulterous self, the common-law self-etc., etc, etc! Room for everyone! Live and let live! Free to be yourself and do your thing in society and in the church! Is everybody happy? After all, God is love and Jesus died for everyone. A Chevrolet and apple pie gospel! Now we have a "Healed Society," healed of "prejudice," and "intolerance" and everyone is free to be them-selves and accepted by all.

It used to be that in the church there was strong teaching against pre-marital sex. Now the United Church of Christ, once an offshoot of historic Puritanism, as part of their supposed war on AIDs and STDs, has decided to hand out condoms in their churches and faith-based educational institutions. Now a teenager can go to church, put a dime in the offering plate and take out a condom. Cash in – condom on! The modern church has traded unvarnished truth for protected sex. I wonder what their teens do after youth group is dismissed. They ride away from youth group on smooth tires, as smooth as condoms with no moral traction. Thank God that the United Church of Christ's membership is declining.

This is what is known as healing the world of intolerance. That is Secular Humanism's gospel, and now has become Religious Humanism's gospel as well. The truth is that the gospel of tolerance in the world and in the church is nothing more or less than a license for sinful self-indulgence. Tragically but predictably the more society and the church are "healed" of intolerance, the more sin-sick they have become. The phrase, "We won't tolerate that around here" is no longer tolerated. Therefore, very few things except intolerance are viewed as intolerable any longer!

SEEKER FRIENDLY – CHURCH LITE

True Christianity in obedience to Christ teaches that self must be totally denied, disowned, and summarily dismissed. Jesus articulated not only the non-prioritizing of self, but the total denial of self with as much emphasis and transparency as He possibly could. Self can no longer be a factor at all in Christian decision making. It is not just as if self does not exist. Rather, in Christ it actually and factually doesn't! All Christ and no self! That is Christianity. All self with Christ added on! That is Religious Humanism.

Only when there is all Christ and no self can we even begin to be His disciples, that is, learners under discipline. Why? Jesus commands us to make disciples of all nations, and to teach them to observe all things that He has commanded us. (Matthew 28:19-20) But with self still in place, people can learn next to nothing from Christ. Self cannot listen to or learn from Jesus. Self can only listen to and learn from self. By nature all sinful men are self- taught, i.e. sin taught and Satan taught. So Jesus commanded in Matthew 16:24 that if anyone wanted to follow Him, that is, be His learners under discipline, then this is what would have to take place before anything else:

"...let him deny himself...."

Religious Humanists won't admit to their posture being "Selfianity" and not "Christianity." They cover that all up by calling themselves "Seeker Friendly." You may even attend a so-called "Seeker-Friendly Church," and not be aware of it. Yet you sense that something is out of whack, but you can't quite lay your hands on it.

It's the latest craze. Seeker-Friendly Churches are a sub-division of Religious Humanism. I have attended churches like that. Everything is designed to appeal to visitors who are now being called seekers. Seeking what? Very simple! Seeking anything and every-thing that will affirm, indulge, soothe, entertain and satisfy self, all in the name of God of course! These are not seeker-friendly churches in the final analysis. They are "Self-Friendly Churches."

"Way of Life Literature" writes: **"NEWSPRING CHURCH'S BAPTISM CEREMONY ON SEPTEMBER 8 FEATURED A TAILGATING PARTY. THIS CONTEMPORARY, SEEKER-FRIENLDY SOUTHERN BAPTIST CHURCH IN ANDERSON, SOUTH CAROLINA BAPTIZED 562 PEOPLE THAT DAY, AND CHURCH MEMBERS WERE ENCOURAGED TO EMULATE A FOOTBALL TAILGATING PARTY. TONY MORGAN, THE CHURCH'S CHIEF STRATEGIC OFFICER, SAID, 'PEOPLE BROUGHT THEIR RV'S AND SET UP TENTS. THERE WERE TELEVISIONS GOING WITH PEOPLE WATCHING FOOT- BALL GAMES BEFORE THE BAPTISM SERVICE WAS STARTED' ...IT WAS PRETTY FUN.'"** (4)

"Way of Life Literature" then comments: **"FOOTBALL AND BAPTISM. WHAT AN UNHOLY AND CARNAL MESS. A BAPTISM IS NOT A WORLDLY PARTY. A BAPTISM IS A TIME TO PRAY AND A TIME TO REFLECT AND A TIME TO REPENT AND A TIME TO RE-DEDICATE, BUT IT IS NOT A TIME FOR WORLDLY SPORTS."**(5)

The goal of Religious Humanistic seeker-friendly churches is to convey compatibility between the world and the church, so that the leap of faith won't be that much of a leap after all. Just a small baby step so that self's cadence will not be interrupted!! There it is, that way the seeker can put his feet in two places, one foot on earth and the other foot in Heaven. We could call it "Straddle Religion!" The message is that we can have God and keep our sport's gods, too. Welcome also to "Super Bowl Sunday Night Church Blast" in the same hour when churches formerly held evening Divine worship services.

There is a large church in America that provides beer at their church picnics as one of the beverages of choice. Hey, why not? Different selves have different taste buds. Some like soft drinks and some like hard drinks. In this Religious Humanism church picnic, the King of Kings serves the King of Beers to His self-indulging non-subjects. In the modern world not only is there the "Banquet Beer," but in the modern church there is now the "Church Beer." We already have tailgate football bashes at baptismal services. Now we have beer bashes at church picnics. Hey, the perfect venue for "Church Beer" which can also be called "Church Lite."

Come to think about it, how would you like to tell your people who are coming to the church picnic to take along a designated driver and to please drink responsibly? Not funny! Or, the church and the home now in partnership in training up a child in the way he should drink. When did we first begin to lose our hops-picking minds?

These self-friendly churches should be aptly named after their beer, "Church Lite." That is more exactly the case! Nothing heavy! No meat! Just pablum! Peppy, stimulating, hand-clapping music to make the self-seeker feel upbeat! Then the preaching of self-affirming messages! Of course, all of that with Bible proof- texts taken out of context and lightly sprinkled in along the way in blatant isogesis – Sermon Lite. Nothing uneasy, unsettling or deeply convicting! Low key and undemanding!

Writes W. E. Vine, "**THE NEW CHURCH MODEL IS TO BE INOFFENSIVE, NOT TO SPEAK ON SIN OR MENTIONTHE CROSS OR SUFFERING, THUS AVOIDING ANYTHING THAT WOULD MAKE PEOPLE FEEL UNCOMFORTABLE.**" (6)

Religious Humanism has watered down the Christian Gospel. It has popularized the Gospel; wrapped it all up in entertainment, drama, and a lot of humor to take the cutting-edge off the sword of truth. Add some strobe lights, you know, some psychedelic mesmerizing, and you have an environment that will keep the seeker coming back, because he is made to really feel at home, and above all at home with himself.

So just keep on making everyone feel happy and good about themselves. Then all of those cute little "S-elves" will be dancing all over the sanctuary. We have all heard of Santa and his Elves. Well, this is "Pastor Santa Religious Humanist" and his "S-elves!" Always find the good and praise it, but never deal with the bad and pierce it. Then those cute little "S-elves" may even bake the pastor some Selfmas cookies, or better yet, take him out for Selfmas dinner.

Christianity in total contrast is about telling those very selfish little "S-elves" – **NO!** In Religious Humanism, the controlling principle is to soothe the selves and pack the pews. In Christianity, the guiding principle is to deny the selves and make disciples.

THE CROSS – RELIGIOUS HUMANISM'S FAULT LINE

This is where genuine Christianity begins. Complete self- denial! Fail here and no one will be able to carry out faithful Christian discipleship, at least, not for very long. It won't last! Why? Because the very next thing that Jesus commands His would-be disciple in Mark 8:34 is to,

"…**take up his cross**…."

The logic of Christ is flawless as always, and is illustrated by the discipleship principle that only those who say no to self will be able to say yes to the cross. We cannot hang on to ourselves and carry our crosses for Christ at the same time. Self is far too self-protecting for cross-bearing.

The cross of course for Christ ultimately speaks of death. It is obvious that only those who deny self will be willing to die for Christ. He who is reluctant to deny self will deny Christ to save his own neck. That's just the way it is. Self-denial is the prerequisite for cross-bearing. Count on it, self-friendly churches and the selfianity gospel will of necessity produce cross-avoiders at all cost. They will drop their crosses quicker than an ice cream cone melts in the sun of the Arizona desert in July.

These fundamental Gospel truths of self-denial and cross-bearing were spoken by our Lord before His own death on the cross. But His hearers caught some of the blunt force of what He was saying. Criminals and martyrs in the Roman Empire carried their crosses to their deaths. Following Jesus as one of His disciples was no small decision or Sunday morning diversion from the rest of the week. It was not exactly a harmless but satisfying sideline or hobby. It could cost His followers their lives. That is what taking up your cross means. Jesus would soon become the literal illustration of cross-bearing. All of his disciples, except Judas, would follow in His footsteps.

Jesus wanted His listeners to think through the consequences of discipleship before they made a commitment to Him. Those who leap before they look and do not count the cost will be the most likely ones not to stay with the program. Their commitment will always be superficial. He wanted people who were willing to put their lives on the line. Already here Jesus was separating the wheat from the chaff, for He knew that once the chaff got wind of what it really had gotten itself into, it would get blown away. Weigh the self-denial and the cross-bearing issues very carefully!

Three pastors got together for coffee one morning. Much to their surprise, they discovered that all of their churches had trouble with bats infesting their belfries. The bats were making a terrible mess. One pastor said, "I got so mad the other day that I took a shotgun and fired at them. It made terrible holes in the ceiling, but did nothing to the bats. Now with the holes they are worse than ever." The second pastor said, "Well, I tried trapping them alive. Then I drove them 50 miles before releasing them, but they beat me back to the church." The third pastor said, "I haven't had any more problems. What did I do? I simply trapped them, then I preached a sermon to them on self-denial and cross bearing, and ended it by baptizing them. I haven't seen any of them since."

There is a geological fault line that runs all the way down the Pacific Coast from Alaska through California and down to the Baja Peninsula. It is called the San Andreas Fault. Along that fault line there have been many earthquakes, one of the worst being the infamous San Francisco quake of 1906. A man in the sugar business by the name of Spreckles decided to construct a building in a way that had never been done before. He went a long ways down into the earth for the foundation of that building to what is better known as "Hard Pan" – the bed rock that is very deep. His critics told him that he was pouring all of that money and mortar needlessly into those holes. He was the laughing-stock of the contractors of his day. Then at 5:12 PM, on April 18, 1906, the earthquake hit San Francisco, and the one building that remained was the huge "Spreckles Sugar Building." If it is to be built correctly, the foundation of a building will be the most costly of all.

"Self-Denial" and "Cross-Bearing" alone provide the hard-pan foundation of enduring Christian discipleship. Otherwise the church will produce disciples that are wavering wobblers, and they will crumble in the violent shaking of opposition and persecution that is coming to American Christians. They will not stand the test!

Today's sugar-daddy Religious Humanistic preachers are creat- ing weak generations of church-goers who are totally unaccustomed to self-denial and self-sacrifice. They will be unwilling to give up their comforts for Christ, and will avoid inconvenience and pain for Christ at all cost. It is producing a most anemic and frail situation in the modern church. The result will be cowards and not champions! Pushovers rather than persevering soldiers of Christ! Those who are easily intimidated rather than those who are invincible! Casper Milquetoasts rather than mighty conquerors! When the storms of opposition begin to rage, they will be as seaworthy as a dingy in a violent ocean.

It is going to become more and more dangerous and life-threatening to be a witness for Christ in these last days of human history, which are increasingly characterized by anti-God atheism, anti-Christ secularism, and fiendish Islamic and Hindu radicalism. It is going to become cross-costly to stand up for Christ and Christian values in America and around the world. We will be hated by all nations! Jesus said in Matthew 24:8,

"Then they will deliver you to tribulation, and will kill you, and you will be hated by all nations on account of My name."

The only way that Christians will be able to stand tall for Christ in the 21ˢᵗ century is to deny self, and to put self on the cross of personal expendability for Christ.

I recall an old Mercedes-Benz commercial which shows one of their cars colliding with a concrete wall during a safety test. Someone then asked a Mercedes engineer why their company does not enforce the patent on their car's energy-absorbing structure. The Mercedes' design has been copied by almost every other car maker in the world in spite of the fact that they have an exclusive patent. The engineer replied in a very distinguishable German accent, "Because in life, some things are just too important not to share."(7)

What I am writing about is too important not to share either. It is Christ's exclusive patent for authentic, enduring discipleship. The true discipleship patent in Christianity is to deny ourselves and take up our crosses for Christ. Without doing so on a daily basis, our courage will collapse, and we will veil our cowardice in the name of prudence and caution. As Rick Blinson of KneePrints, Inc. writes: **"HE (JESUS) WANTED LIVING SACRIFICES THAT WOULD NOT ALWAYS BE TRYING TO CRAWL OFF THE ALTAR."** (8)

THE CROSS – A HEAVY LOAD

While guest-lecturing in Continental Theological Seminary in Brussels, Belgium, I was humbled and awed to get to know courageous Christian students from all over Europe. Do you recall what they did to Christians and Christian pastors in the old Soviet Union? If you were an evangelical Christian, you did not go to college. If you were an outspoken evangelical Christian, and you preached the Gospel of Jesus Christ, they would send you to a concentration camp. The Soviets didn't shoot you. Instead they just worked you to death.

I particularly recall one young male Romanian student whose father was a preacher in Romania and was thrown into prison for preaching Jesus Christ. After several years, his father was released, and he went right back to preaching the Gospel of salvation, for which he was thrown into prison again. His son, my theology student, was preparing for the ministry, and was going to go back home to Romania to take up his father's work in the ministry. Or should I say, "Take up his cross."

Carrying the cross can be a killing load. Paul Kengor's article entitled *Carrying The Cross In Iraq* is posted by International Christian Concern (ICC) on their website. ICC's calling is to bring assistance, advocacy and awareness for the persecuted and suffering church around the world. Kengor writes: "One very alarming report by the Assyrian International News Agency cites hundreds of killings and an exodus of hundreds of thousands of Iraqi Christians…Under Saddam, the importation of Christian literature to Iraq was limited or halted altogether, as was evangelization. Christian schools were confiscated by the state…Like today some Christians in Iraq had it worse in certain parts of the country, largely depending upon the concentration of extremist Muslim thugs. Christians in Basra, for example, throughout the 1990s complained of threats they would be raped, kidnapped, or killed for their faith. Some Christian minorities faced forced relocation…Indeed, in the general sweep of things, Iraqi Christians were just as likely…to have their children locked up in dog cages, to have their wives raped or beheaded or hung upside down in front of their families for hours as they menstruated (an actual interrogation technique under Saddam), to have their ears surgically amputated for refusing military conscription, to be subjected to chemical baths or the attachment of electrodes to their genitals, to be fed feet first into large industrial meat grinders, or to be lynched from lampposts or simply machined gunned." (9)

I am reminded of the story of a man who for many years played the part of Christ in the "Passion Play" of the Black Hills of South Dakota. He was being interviewed because, among other reasons, he had turned 70 years old and was still carrying out his theatrical role as Christ. With make-up and garb, they managed to transform the older man to appear to be the age of Christ. The man who was to do the interview watched the whole thing with intrigue, as the old man portrayed Christ with dramatic excellence. There was a special quality about his life as he represented Christ walking up the Via Dolorosa. The crucifixion was enormously moving; the resurrection was so thrilling!

At the end of the presentation, the reporter walked behind all of the props to a long corridor that led to the dressing room. In the corridor was the large cross that the man portraying Christ had carried up the Via Dolorosa to Calvary's Hill. He looked at it and thought, "It probably is a Styrofoam cross or perhaps a hollow one." He put his shoulder underneath it and tried to move it. It was huge and heavy, weighing close to 200 pounds. He couldn't believe it – this elderly man, 70 years old, had carried this cross night after night in acting out the life and death of Christ.

The reporter had a moving interview with the man who each performance passionately captured the character of Christ, and at the end of the interview, he said to the seasoned actor, "I have just one more question for you, I saw the cross out there – was that the same cross that you carried up Calvary's Hill?" The actor said, "Yes." "Well then," said the reporter, "I just do not understand, for that cross is huge and heavy. How on earth could you, a man nearly 70 years of age, carry that cross? I could hardly budge it." The old man looked at the reporter and said, "It is very simple, if you don't carry the cross, you don't get the part."

It would be a gross overstatement to in anyway imply that all of modern Christendom is unwilling to deny self and take up the cross for Jesus. There are many young and old alike who today treasure Jesus far above themselves. They are willing to lay down their lives for their witness to Christ. I am aware that more people across the globe are being martyred for Jesus in my lifetime, than in all of previous history put together. You would only have to subscribe to the most moving and convicting magazine *Voice of the Martyrs* to understand that fact. Our brothers and sisters in Christ have been and are giving their lives for Him in Communist lands, in Muslim lands, and in Hindu lands on a daily basis across the globe.

But let us bring it closer to home. I am not taking you back very far into history when I think of Columbine High School in Littleton, Colorado. You may remember their last names – Harris and Klebold. One of them asked a 17 year old girl, Cassie Bernall, with his gun pointed at her head, "Do you believe in God?" She replied with a strong voice, "Yes!" And then with instant cynicism the would-be killer asked her, "Why?" Then he shot her through the temple.

As the horrific event was more thoroughly investigated, it revealed that the real targets of the high school massacre were Christians. She was one of those that the late Dr. Jerry Falwell described as, "A Young Champion For Christ." They live in the cities, suburbs and farmlands across America, and their faith in Christ has not succumbed to or been contaminated by the self-serving spirit of Religious Humanism that is now poisoning and weakening the church.

Twenty-first century martyrdom in the United States of America! It was the badge of 1st century Christianity worn proudly by the great army of martyrs for Christ. It states in Philippians 1:29,

"For to you it has been granted for Christ's sake, not only to believe in Him, but also to suffer for His sake."

Martyrdom for Christ was received as a gift, a special grant from Heaven for Christ's sake. In radical Islam those who die while blowing up infidels are the honored ones. In Christianity those who die for Christ in sharing His Gospel are the privileged ones. In essence, martyrdom for Christ is more than a heroic act of faith, though it indeed is that. Martyrdom is considered in the Bible the highest of privileges given to God's chosen ones. Many of us reading this book will be granted that privilege from and for Christ.

We do well to learn the lesson from the annals of the United States Coastguard. Ten miles off the coastline, there was a ship with its captain and crew that had been smashed against an island of protruding rocks. The S.O.S. had been received, and a captain in the Coastguard ordered his crew to set out on the rescue mission. One of the young men said, "Captain, we may go out, but we will never get back." The Captain looked at the young man and said, "Son, we have to go out, but we do not have to come back. Nowhere in the oath does it say that we have to come back, but it does say that we have to go out." Nowhere in the Bible did Jesus say that we have to come back. But He did make it very clear that we have to go out and make disciples of all nations. (Matthew 28:19)

Rick Blinson summarizes it all very well when he writes: "**HE (JESUS) COULD HAVE PROMISED MAGNIFICENT, SWEET-SOUNDING FORMULAS OF PERSONAL GAIN TO THOSE WHO LISTENED TO HIS TEACHING. IT DEFINITELY WOULD HAVE ATTRACTED LARGER CROWDS. BUT HE PROMISED PRIMARILY A LIFE OF SELF-DENIAL AND A CROSS.**" (10)

RELIGIOUS HUMANISM'S MUSH – CHRISTIANITY'S MUST

This is the new age in which we have come to the wide-open spaces of the "Liberated Self." Self-expression! Self's room to roam! The age of Religious Humanism in which self doesn't have to feel so hemmed in anymore! We are now in the day of the self-freeing religion that self has always longed for. Self need no longer strictly adhere to and observe God's laws, and yet it may remain in good standing with God. It is a religion of mostly mush and very little must. Here a man can have his soul saved and keep his sins, too!

So why in such a mushy ecclesiastical environment would anyone feel compelled to exert moral self-control? Many years ago, there was a TV commercial for the soda drink called Orange Crush. An older brother is drinking a bottle of Orange Crush on the sidelines of a friendly neighborhood football game. He is invited to join in the game, and gives his little brother the ¾ full bottle of orange drink. He tells his brother to hold it and not to drink a drop of it. The little boy tries to resist, but eventually goes behind a tree and drinks all of it. Big brother after the game comes to the little brother for his bottle of Orange Crush. It isn't long and he can tell that the drink had been drunk. He is angry at first and his kid-brother says to him, "I tried, but I couldn't help it." The big brother softens and says to his brother, "That's okay, for I often can't control myself either." The message being that we all have these basic drives and needs, and you just have to do what you have to do." We understand!

One of the gravest situations today is the matter of marriage and divorce. I am not just talking about society in general. I am talking now about marriage and divorce in the Christian Church and amongst the Christian clergy. What is more disturbing still is how it is being dealt with, or should I say, how it is not being dealt with.

Jesus makes it first-grade-reader clear when He said in Matthew 19:9,

"And I say to you, whoever divorces his wife, except for immorality, and marries another woman commits adultery."

The only Biblical basis for divorce is the ongoing immorality of a spouse. By immorality Jesus means that if the husband or wife is having sexual relationships outside of the marriage union, the offended and faithful marriage partner has the God-given right to divorce the offending and immoral marriage partner.

I recall the husband who had to face the fact that he had married a nymphomaniac. She was having random sexual encounters on an ongoing basis, and he found out that he had married an alley cat. Sexually he was fortunate to get the crumbs that rolled off the table. He was a devoted Christian, and like Hosea, he took back his Gomer again and again. She then turned to lesbianism to get her desperate, twisted sexual kicks, and moved in with another female pervert. He was forced to divorce her and pursue child custody to protect his children from this Hell. In his case, divorce was absolutely mandatory as a child protection measure. Except for immorality!

I do not believe that Jesus in Matthew 19:9 is here issuing carte blanche licenses for divorce because a spouse was found out to have been unfaithful once. Jesus commands us to forgive 7 times 70. The Bible is totally opposed to our easy-divorce culture. Biblical Christianity is being destroyed in our day and with it the Biblical institution of marriage. We are in the middle of a marriage Pearl Harbor. The Lord's "Must Not" never changes as He states in Matthew 19:6

"...What therefore God has joined together, let no man separate."

There are however those times in this carnal, moral-mush culture when, for example, a godly Christian woman will marry the man she loves in good faith and total trust, only to find out that she has married a flesh-head who has the morals of a stuffed animal. These are the type of guys (and gals) whose eyes are always roving, and are constantly comparing their wives with younger, hard bodies and looking for fresher cuts of meat. Then she finds out that her husband is addicted to pornography, and that his recently discovered multiple affairs make his history look like the debris in a house after the flood waters have receded. He refuses to get help, for he is addicted to women and sex, and just keeps on, as they say today, "fooling around." These type of guys and gals are a dime a dozen, and are the marriage and family wrecking crews of the world. She has a Biblical right to divorce him and marry another, but never the right not to forgive him and not to pray for his salvation.

More than that, if the immoral husband ruins his marriage and marries another to-be-pitied woman, that immoral husband is committing adultery, and in that second marriage he is living in a state of adultery according to our Lord in Matthew 19:9. It isn't marriage at all. It is an adulterous relationship. Understand this please.

Sin is not determined by George Gallup. Sin is not determined by what people in California or Massachusetts say or do. It isn't determined by Hollywood, Washington DC, Paris or Amsterdam. It is determined by God. Someone who messes around with another woman, divorces his wife and marries the other woman not only has committed adultery, but is now living in adultery. Adulterers will not enter the Kingdom of God. (I Corinthians 6:9, 10)

Immorality! Adultery!? Whoever hears those sins preached against anymore? Religious Humanism preachers today are not preaching absolute morality, but instead are filling the air with wind, noise, shallow platitudes and pulpit-prattle. All mush and no must.

It is no wonder then that kids today do not even know anymore what immorality or adultery mean! I think of the young boy in school who with the rest of the class was asked to write a sentence with the word "adult" in it. Here is what he wrote: "Adults don't have any fun. Adults just sit around and talk. They don't do anything. Nothing is duller than adultery." The little boy didn't know what adultery means, but millions of little boys and girls are suffering today because their parents are immorally breaking their marriage vows and adulterously marrying another. Their children's lives are being scarred for a lifetime. An old Chinese proverb puts it well: **"THERE ARE NO WHOLE EGGS IN A BROKEN NEST."**

In the midst of Religious Humanism's weakening of the marriage covenant, I have seen again and again adulterers and adulteresses leave their spouses not only, but also leave their churches where they had been placed under church discipline (censure) because of their living in immorality. (Matthew 18:15-17) Church discipline today has become for the most part non-existent as well. Then these adulterers and adulteresses go to other churches with their newly married adulterous partners, generally churches of the large variety where they can blend in without too much notice. They are wholeheartedly welcomed with no questions asked. Hey, let bygones be bygones.

In many cases, I have witnessed first-hand that the pastors of their original churches found out that these immoral, adulterous and censured members were attending another church in the city. Telephone calls were made and letters sent by the original pastors to the new pastors of these sinning and offending parties, and the new-church pastors refused to return the telephone calls and letters, or to cooperate in any way in the enforcement of church discipline to bring the sinning parties to repentance. (Matthew 18:15) Christianity never sanctifies sin, but Religious Humanism does. Romans 1:7 says,

"...beloved of God...called as saints (holy ones)...."

Religious Humanism just says,

"Beloved of God...."

I have also seen more than once the adulterous husband divorce his wife, live with another woman, and enter into an adulterous marriage which wedding ceremony was then conducted by an adulterous pastor who himself had broken his marriage vows and married another. What an immoral zoo! Of course the pastor blesses them at the end of the marriage ceremony in the name of the Father, the Son and the Holy Spirit, and thereby makes the Holy Triune God look like the Three Stooges.

What Religious Humanism ministers today are looking for is warm bodies, increasing membership roles, bigger crowds, and fuller offering plates. Religious Humanism churches are more concerned about people feeling welcome than they are that God is being obeyed. All mush and no must or must not. Churches that carry on like this are not the Christian Church. They are pseudo-churches who sanction pseudo-marriages, just as Religious Humanism is a pseudo-religion that is embracing pseudo-members. The underlying rule in such pseudo-religion is, "Don't rock the boat. Don't disturb the peace." Mush! Offenses to God occur, but nobody talks about them. To accomplish this, they practice the business principle, "The customer is always right." Wrong! God alone is always right!

We live in a world that makes the dumping of a spouse as easy as flicking a bug off your knee. There are now companies that will electronically remove former spouses from family pictures. Now, with a few clicks and maneuvers of the computer mouse, graphic artists can manipulate an old print or negative and erase just about anyone. Not only can former spouses be zapped from marriage and family photographs, but the thrown-away spouse can be replaced with the new lover and spouse in the same photographs. Out of sight, out of mind! Now you see her or him, now you don't! Quick zap! One chain of photograph developers came up with a name for the service and called it, "Divorce X." (11) All that the adulterers have to do these days is find a Religious Humanistic mega-church, blend in with their new partners, get old photographs of their former spouses zapped by "Divorce X" and pictured with their replacements. Photo-marriage adultery!

Then on top of all of this mush-slush, while the true church of Jesus Christ seeks to exalt righteousness with "Biblical Musts" and come against sin with "Biblical Must-Nots," Religious Humanists redefine sin and invent sins in their own mushy-slushy carnal favor. In this connection, Robert Tilton, who is a television prosperity preacher and money-raiser for himself, has been married and divorced three times. Frankly, it gets very confusing because he divorced his third wife to remarry his second wife. But the sin that Tilton is most concerned about is what he calls the sin of poverty. He states: **BEING POOR IS A SIN, WHEN GOD PROMISES PROSPERITY. NEW HOUSE, NEW CAR, THAT'S CHICKEN FEED. THAT'S NOTHING COMPARED TO WHAT GOD WANTS TO DO FOR YOU.** (12) This gives a whole new meaning to "The War on Poverty" which to Tilton is "The War on Sin."

Religious Humanists today reinvent the entire ethics of the Bible. They practice sin as righteousness, and what is not unrighteousness they call sin. It isn't the guy who goes through women and wives like water that is morally bankrupt. Rather it is the poor fella on the wrong side of the tracks who is living in the sin of poverty. Please would someone call time out, I am out of breath.

I must add a quick clarifier here though I am reluctant to do so and thereby waste your time and my time on this nutsville stuff. It is a common theme in Religious Humanism to say that poverty is a sin, i.e. being poor is sinful. More corrupting mush! If this were the case, then the poor man Lazarus, who was sick and covered with sores which were licked by dogs, would have gone to Hell, and the rich man who ignored him would have gone to Heaven. But the Bible in Luke 16 tells us just the opposite in that the beggar-man's poverty did not qualify him for Hell, nor did the wealthy man's riches qualify him for Heaven.

In fact, the penniless pauper went to Heaven, and the prosperous man went to Hell. Religious Humanism is full of materialistic spin, and is about as fair and balanced as CNN.

THE ABUNDANT LIFE – BIOS, PSUCHE, OR ZOE

I have noticed over my span of 42 years of ministry that many churches call themselves by the name, "Abundant Life Church." Very appealing seeing that everyone in the world and the church is looking for abundance. However, Jesus clearly teaches that the truly abundant life has nothing to do with money or things or possessions. Nothing! Zilch! Zero! How is that for a game stopper? Did you know that? That is why we read words in the Bible like those in Ecclesiastes 5:10,

> **"He who loves money will not be satisfied with money, nor he who loves abundance with its income. This too is vanity."**

We read the equally powerful words of Jesus in Luke 12:15,

> **"...Beware, and be on your guard against every form of greed; for not even when one has an abundance does his life consist of his possessions."**

Powerful words! Man's great love affair, the love of money! Never has such an intense love affair been so unfulfilling. Not only is the love of money the root of all evil (I Timothy 6:10), but it appears to be the root of all human dissatisfaction. Other truths from the aforesaid passages are that while earthly riches are able to make a man greedy, greed has never made a man truly rich. Another is that the truly abundant life has absolutely nothing to do with earthly abundance. This shoots the core value system of Religious Humanism right out of the water.

It appears that the more money and possessions man acquires, the emptier he feels and the more he needs to try to fill his emptiness. It is a vicious circle. It brings to mind the tragic reality that the only reason drunks continue to drink more is that they drank too much already. And the only reason that people continue to buy is that they bought too much already. It is so sad but so very true that even as drunks drink themselves thirstier and the obese eat themselves hungrier, so the covetous buy themselves greedier. In short, the covetous and greedy person is always feeling himself in want of more.

Corporate and consumer greed has gotten America into her economic woes, and greed will continue to be her undoing. And so, the world is more sharply than ever divided into creditors and debtors who are presently guarding themselves against each other. And if you are not one, then you are surely the other.

What then according to Jesus is the abundant life? Jesus said in John 10:10,

"...I came that they might have life, and might have it abundantly."

In short, Jesus is the abundant life! Not Jesus plus! Jesus only! Life's abundance comes immediately from Christ Himself, and is not mediated from Him through cash or stuff or anything else. Every man in this world has all or nothing depending upon the presence or absence of Jesus Christ in his life. For you must understand that only the Son of God is the abundant life, and He is all of that and more, in ways that the fullest bank accounts, biggest houses, the most luxurious cars, yachts, and jets cannot begin to be.

All of this is exactly why the Apostle Paul in II Corinthians 6:10 wrote these astonishing words,

"...as having nothing yet possessing all things."

You've got to be kidding! Paul, are you serious? Are you trying to be clever with your words? Are you, Paul, caught up in some reckless verbal exaggeration like we are all prone to do? Having nothing and yet having everything? Paul is talking about an amazing life in which it is possible to look at our neighbor's mega-stuff when by contrast we have little, and yet never once covet any of it. He is describing an actual state of being in which it is possible to look at all that the world has to offer, and though we have zero, yet we do not need or desire it. He is describing an actual place in life where it is possible to have a body and a bank account both in poor health and yet have fullness of life. There it is! A life called in the Bible, "The Abundant Life."

The English language has only one word for all kinds of life, whether it is physical life, psychological life, or spiritual life. In many ways the English language is an impoverished language. Not so in the much richer Greek language in which the New Testament was written. It is critically necessary for us to understand that the Greek language uses three different Greek words which we translate by our one English word – life.

First, one word that is translated "life" in the Greek New Testament is the noun "**BIOS**," from which we derive the English word "Biology." However, the Greek word for bios-life has a much wider meaning, and does not only refer to our physical life, but also to our material life in general. It not only refers to matters of the human body, but also to investments, holdings, things, possessions etc. Bios!

The human self always tries to find the abundant life in bios. Always! The carnal self will always major in bios. Man's natural self is totally bios oriented. The human body has good enzymes that work in the stomach to break down food into nutrients that the body must have. The human soul has bad bioszymes that break down money and stuff faster than man can consume it. Because of his out-of-control bioszymes, he must always have more.

We must understand this truth! It is true of the bios-selves of all men who by nature think that eureka is found at the end of the bios rainbow. It is called in the Bible the lust of the flesh, the lust of the eyes and the pride of life. (I John 2:16) By nature, the human self-craves sex, stuff and fame.

But according to Jesus bios is an abundant-life bust. We read of Him saying in Luke 8:14 about those who are swimming in bios that they are,

"...choked with worries and riches and pleasures of this life (BIOS)...."

Choked, mind you! What an awful word! Nothing really pleasurable about being choked! Have you ever choked or been choked? People can choke on a piece of meat. They can also choke on bios. How? Choked with worries and cares! You know how it goes! The stock market's frightening roller-coaster ride! Always having to protect and insure your investments for more and more, while they are becoming worth less and less these days. Equity has become liability. My house is being devalued while my property taxes are constantly going up. Inflation! Paying more for less! Just when you think you are gaining, you are losing. Then on top of all of that, as Jesus said would be the case, moths and rust destroy our stuff if crooks don't rip it off first. (Matthew 6:19) You buy a beautiful bedroom set and you find out that it has Dutch Elm Disease. Sooner or later bios always puts a strong choke hold of angst on its devotees.

Worries! Cares! Fears! Very interesting! In this worry-filled, fear-filled society, the American Kennel Society tells us that at the beginning of the last quarter of the 20th century, cuddly poodles were the most popular purebred dogs in America. There were 139,750 registered poodles, and only 952 registered rottweilers. Rottweilers are of course a fiercer breed of dog, often used as guard dogs. Nearing the end of the 20th century, the poodle population had been cut in half to 61,775, while the rottweiler population had increased a hundred times to 102, 596. (13)

Fear and worry have gone up as people's standards of living have become more and more bios oriented. America is not only going to the dogs, but to the mean dogs as well. The fat cat needs the mean watchdog! That is why more and more American children and adults are being attacked by predator-pets. In short, the bios-focused life has the greatest potential to produce fears, worries, migraines and even sleeplessness. We read in Ecclesiastes 5:12,

> **"...But the full stomach of the rich man does not allow him to sleep."**

As one man put it, "I buy things on the 'lay awake' plan. I lay awake each night trying to figure out how I am going to pay for it."

Far more tragic are the Religious Humanism TV personalities and church pastors who are deceiving people into thinking that the "Abundant Life" is the "Bios Life." One pastor among the growing modern day horde of "Bios Preachers" is Creflo Dollar who is the pastor of World Changer's Church International in College Park, Georgia. Creflo Dollar states to his congregation this amazing contrivance: **"YOU AIN'T GONNA HAVE NO LOVE AND JOY AND PEACE UNTIL YOU GET SOME MONEY...YOU GOTTA GET SOME MONEY."**(14) The fact is that this teaching isn't worth two cents. Just some more hyperventilating humanistic material- ism in the name of religion!

True, we "gotta" earn some money to be able to live in this world and fulfill the calling of God. That is a no-brainer! The Bible tells us that if we don't work, we don't eat. (II Thessalonians 3:10) And of course if we don't eat we will not last long in our work. In the church at Thessalonica, there were some lazy busybodies mooching off other people's work and eating other people's bread. God takes a dim view of moochers. He commands them to live a disciplined life which means working without complaining and eating their own bread. (II Thessalonians 3:12)

But we do not work, eat and get money to have love, joy, and peace! Astonishing! Here we go again! Religious Humanists are full of bios, and I mean full of it! They falsely teach that love, joy, and peace are the exclusive results of getting and having bios. Not according to Jesus! Not according to Paul! Not at all! The Word of God tells us that love, joy, and peace are the fruits of the precious Holy Spirit in the believer's life. (Galatians 5:22) If you want overflowing love, joy and peace in your life, then "get" filled with the Holy Spirit. But you "ain't gonna" have love and joy and peace by getting filled with money and stuff. It "ain't gonna" happen.

Furthermore all of the Holy Spirit's love, joy and peace in the believer's heart are supernatural. That is why the Bible tells us that God's love is incomprehensible (Ephesians 3:19, His joy is unspeakable (I Peter 1:8), and His peace is not understandable (Philippians 4:7). We are talking about supernatural love, joy and peace that do not come through natural bios. Not a chance! Bios might give you a feeling of a surface peace after a storm, but only God can give us true peace in the midst of the financial storm that is buffeting America's economy.

So full of bios are these Religious Humanists, that they even teach that wholeness and completeness in life are based upon having lots of bios. Creflo Dollar states: **"WE ESTABLISHED LAST NIGHT THAT YOU ARE NOT WHOLE UNTIL YOU GET YOUR MONEY."** (15) In short, **"YOU AREN'T WHOLE UNTIL YOU GET YOUR DOUGH."** The poor person therefore is only half a person unless and until he gets his money.

The Word of God tells us something totally different. It tells us that Christ is our completeness, not cash. Colossians 2:10 says:

"And in Him you have been made complete...."

Can we fathom people who call themselves Christians believing and preaching that Christ plus cash equals personal wholeness, but Christ without cash equals personal incompleteness? Therefore, when you find Christ, you have not found all that you need to be a whole person. If you will, there is only totality of personhood beyond and in addition to Christ. Religious Humanism teaches that only Christ plus bios can make you whole. Christianity teaches that Christ plus nothing makes you whole. This means that you are a whole person when you are joined to Christ, but you are only a shell of a person when you are joined to mega-bios alone!

You see, everything and everyone's worth in many branches of Religious Humanism is now being measured by money. It corrupts absolutely everyone involved in it and their entire perspective on life. A husband/father was standing over his baby's crib, staring down very intently with the baby sound asleep in the crib. His wife entered the room and silently watched her husband. She thought she saw on his face the wide range of emotions – rapture and wonder, admiration and awe, love and concern. Deeply touched, she moved close to him and put her arm around him. And with glistening eyes and with a trembling voice she said to her husband, "A penny for your thoughts." Without hesitation the husband blurted out, "For the life of me, I can't see how anybody can make a crib like this for $129.95." She obviously thought that his heart was full of baby. Sorry, his head was full of bios. A parable of much of modern Christianity!

Second, another Greek noun for life in the New Testament is "**PSUCHE**" from which we derive the English word "Psychology." Psuche refers to our soul life, that is, what we think, what we want, and what we feel! Jesus said in John 10:15,

"…I lay down My life (PSUCHE) for the sheep."

He laid down self's thinking, wanting and feeling for His sheep as the Good Shepherd. If He hadn't laid down His psuche, He would have never gone to the cross, and we could never be saved.

There is no life in what self thinks, wants or feels. End of story! End of psuche! End of self! We have to lose all of that for Christ before we can find real life in Christ. Jesus tells us that in order for us to find life, we must lose psuche. (Matthew 10:39) So then, right now, whether you understand it all or not, say to your psuche, that is to self's natural thinking, wanting and feeling, "Get Lost!" Good! Now you are a candidate for the abundant life in Christ.

Third, it is essential to note that when the Bible talks about the "Abundant Life," it uses neither the noun bios nor the noun psuche. Let the Religious Humanists put that in their gold-rimmed wine glass and sip it. When the New Testament speaks about the "Abundant Life," it always uses a totally different noun. It is the word "**ZOE**" from which we get no English derivatives whatsoever. None! Why? Because there is nothing like this Zoe-Life in the entire world! Nothing!

I therefore intentionally repeat the verse of supreme importance when Jesus said in John 10:10,

"…I came that they might have life (ZOE), and might have it abundantly."

Jesus said in John 14:6,

"…I am the way, and the truth, and the life (ZOE)…."

And there is that magnificent truth in I John 5:12 which states:

"He who has the Son has the life (ZOE); he who does not have the Son of God does not have the life (ZOE)."

There is no misunderstanding of God here. It's all about the true and full life which is alone found in the Son of God. I have heard it said hundreds of times in my life if I have heard it once, "If you have your health, you have everything." Well folks, I haven't had good health for years, but I am loaded with life because I have Christ in me.

Also when men speak of the "Haves" they mean those who are rich and have lots of bios. And when they speak of the "Have Nots" they mean those who are poor and have very little bios. The Bible has a completely different definition of the "Haves" and the "Have Nots." If you have the Son of God in your life, you are an abundant life "have." If you do not have the Son of God in your life, you are an abundant life "have-not." Without God's zoe-life in us, life is not life, but a bare, empty existence. In other words, it is not "what" a man has that constitutes life, but "Who" he has that constitutes life. And we must remember that only those who are emptied of self can be full of the Savior – full of life.

Dynamic Preaching some years ago carried an article which has become even more relevant today. It was about the dramatic increase of Fundamentalist Islam in the nation of Turkey, a country that had been relatively secularist in its philosophy of life. The article quoted a young Muslim Turk who said to the western interviewer: "Our view of religion is different than yours. According to your rules, religion counts only in the place where you pray. Our religion is a way of life. I have no time at all, not one minute without Islam." (16)

A revealing commentary on how another world religion views the Christian faith. Would that it could be said of more Christians, to paraphrase the young Muslim, "I have no time at all, not one minute, without Christ." That is after all what the Apostle Paul meant when he said in Colossians 3:11,

"…but Christ is all, and in all."

SOLA SCRIPTURA – OR – THE LATEST SCOOP

We now discuss a critical issue. There are multitudes today who want modern day preachers and teachers to dazzle them with the newest exciting revelations. Hot off the press! The latest scoop! Thrill us! Shock us! Dazzle us! How they are riveted on the man or woman who says, "I have got a brand new revelation from God never before shared with man." Extra! Extra! Read all about it! Oooooh! Aaaaah! You heard it here first! Religious Humanism majors in extras.

You see, the human self, especially the religionized self, must always have the newest, the latest, and the hottest! Wanting and demanding newness in every dimension is the hallmark of the human self. It is no surprise therefore that in Religious Humanism, which majors in self and not self-denial, the old Bible translations have been judged as primitive. They have given way to constantly newer, briefly popular and some unrecognizable models like next year's cars. The old hymns of the centuries have been silenced and shoved aside by new and always newer choruses and ditties which do not have enough theological content to fill a thimble. Many of them are easily birthed and quickly pushed into the past. The old pipe organs, pianos and choirs have been pronounced dead and buried in classical graveyards in favor of the latest high-tech synthesizers, guitars and strobe lighting systems. The old doctrinal and moral absolutes sermons have all been chopped down like great felled oaks, and have been replaced by easy-believisms and a new morality that is more tolerant and therefore much more easily tolerated.

In Religious Humanism everything must be new and improved, kind of like the products we buy in stores these days. I have wondered many times how in the world the same product can constantly be new and improved and still remain the same product. But the manufacturers know full well that this is what people crave, and that it sells their products. For that matter, who in the world wants an old shirt and an old suit of clothes anyway? Many people wouldn't be caught dead shopping for used clothes at Good Will or Salvation Army. Let's admit it, for the "Newiacs," if it ain't new, it just won't do.

But the undenied self's need for and love affair with the newest and latest has taken it all a lethal step further. Religious Humanists now no longer view the Bible as the final word from God either. Revelation as viewed by Religious Humanists is always evolving. Always unfolding! New models every year! Religion is now being designed to be like the newest and most daring roller coasters at amusement parks. In Religious Humanism, people hang breathlessly on every word that the latest, most dynamic and exciting prophet or prophetess preaches, who begin by saying, "God told me, God showed me, God spoke to me, God revealed to me. I've got a brand new word from God."

This is a complete departure from and contradiction to historic Protestant Christianity which always and exclusively has followed the example of Jesus Christ in Matthew 4:4,7,10 where He quoted Scripture and said to Satan over and over and over again:

"IT IS WRITTEN, IT IS WRITTEN, AND IT IS WRITTEN."

That has been the strong heartbeat of the Protestant Reformation. It is also the strongest assurance that you are in a Bible-believing, Bible-preaching, and a Bible-based church. Not the now common, "The Lord revealed to me." Rather, "It is written."

Religious Humanism attends to the mind of God revealed in the preacher. Christianity attends to the mind of God revealed in His Word – the Holy Bible. The Christian Church is where the pastor preaches the written Word of God, word for word, verse by verse, precept upon precept, and line upon line. Exegetically! Textually! Contextually! Relevantly! It is written! It is written! It is written! Then and only then can we be assured of "Thus Says the Lord." If you are listening to a preacher without ever having to reference the Word of God, leave!

We must today also understand the words "Sacred Canon" as never before. "Sacred Canon" has been historically another couplet for the "Holy Bible." The English word "Canon" comes from the Greek word "Kanon" which means "Rule." In other words, the 66 books of the Bible have been throughout the centuries the only sacred and infallible rule for doctrine and conduct in the Christian life.

However, all of that is up for grabs today. Christianity believes that the Sacred Canon is closed. Religious Humanism believes that the Sacred Canon is open. Christianity believes in completed revelation. Religious Humanism believes in continuing and therefore incomplete revelation. This is a huge issue! In Christianity, you always know where you stand. Rock solid! In Religious Humanism, you never know where you stand. Shifting sand! "It is written" never changes. "The Lord said to me" is always changing.

I have preached the precious Gospel of the Lord Jesus Christ for over four decades before health issues took me off the evangelistic field. By God's grace I have thrilled to see innumerable people come to Christ as their Lord and Savior. I have preached countless sermons, and yet not one of them was equal to the inspired, infallible Word of God. How is that for a shocker? I have preached the inspired, infallible Word of God, but my sermons were not inspired or infallible. In fact the Bible calls it "The Foolishness of Preaching." (I Corinthians 1:21)

Perhaps you are asking by now, "Bob, what are you saying?" We read in II Timothy 3:16,

"All Scripture is inspired by God, and profitable for teaching, for reproof, for correction, for training in righteousness."

Where we read the word "Inspired," it is the Greek word "Theopneustos" which means most literally "God Breathed." It means that God breathed into the Bible writers His Word by the Holy Spirit, and what the Spirit of God breathed into their spirits and minds, they breathed out as the inspired and infallible Word of God. "Theopneustos" is used only once in the Bible and never applied elsewhere. Period! Holy Spirit-breathed, infallible revelation is only contained in the Bible and anybody else who tells you differently is blowing bad breath and not God's Breath.

My sermons were not little Bibles, though I was at times, as some would say, long winded! My sermons were prayed over, studied and I trust Spirit-guided explanations of the Bible. I hope and pray that they were inspirational to at least a few folks along the way. However I have never been "Theopneustosed." Nor has Pope Benedict even when he claims to speak "Ex Cathedra."

Nor are the gifts of the Holy Spirit little Bibles. They are tools given by the Holy Spirit to the church to empower the work of the ministry of the Gospel. For the church to carry out its salvation and discipleship mission without the blessed gifts of the Holy Spirit is like a preacher standing on the pulpit without his pants on. What a nightmare, for I have dreamed that very horror. Without the gifts of the Holy Spirit, the church is unclothed and unequipped! However, they are not to be used as replacements for the Bible or for Bible preaching.

The Sacred Canon of the Holy Spirit's inspired and infallible Word of God is complete and closed. Any modern preacher or prophet who stands before you constantly foaming at the mouth about what the Lord showed to him or spoke to him as the inspired and infallible basis for his ministry; all he is breathing on you is also bad breath. The gifts of the Holy Spirit are meant to illustrate and enforce the Bible, but never to be equated with the Bible. Never!

What people today fail to realize is how religious cults begin. One of the main trademarks of religious cultism is that its leader and founder has supposedly received, in addition to the Bible, a special revelation from God person to person, which then becomes the basis for the cult's belief system. This is evidenced in Mormonism and Joseph Smith, Jehovah's Witnesses and Charles Taze Russell, Christian Science and Mary Baker Eddy etc. The Bible, or just part of the Bible, is only thrown in for good measure. But the cult is based upon their founder's dreams, visions, and private revelations from God, just as the Roman Catholic Papacy gave rise to the heresies of Purgatory, indulgences, and papal parolees – ex-purgatorians. Cults have two Bibles, as in Mormonism's "The Book of Mormon" and "The Holy Bible." The Roman Catholic Church also has two Bibles – "The Holy Bible" and "The Apocryphal Bible." In each and every case, their distinctive doctrine is based on "The Extra Bible" and not exclusively on "The Holy Bible."

A cult is never solely based upon the great Protestant Reformation principle that has guided and guarded the Christian Church through the ages: "**SOLA SCRIPTURA – SCRIPTURE ALONE!**" There are two basic measuring sticks to determine cultness. What does this group do with Jesus and what do they do with the Bible. If they teach that Jesus is God's Son, but not God the Son, you are dealing with a heretical cult. If they teach that the Bible is God's Word, but not the only infallible and inspired Word of God, you are dealing with a heretical cult.

Right here is the basic cause for the many heresies that we are coming against in this book. Men and women basing their religion not on Sola Scriptura, but on personal revelations that they or others ostensibly have received from God! That is the major reason why modern Christianity in so many areas and churches has become such a cultic mess. You never know what you're going to hear in churches these days. Going to Religious Humanism churches and watching Religious Humanism TV networks is like playing the slot machines in Las Vegas, except by the time they are done with you Religious Humanists will cost you more money than Las Vegas ever did.

I am talking about those who are constantly claiming to have some inside hotline to God through which they are receiving never-before-known or revealed Holy Spirit-inspired truth. Benny Hinn states: "**PLEASE, PLEASE, PLEASE, DON'T THINK WE'RE HERE TO REPEAT SOME-THING YOU'VE HEARD FOR 50 YEARS…IF WE QUIT GIVING YOU NEW REVELATION, WE'RE DONE.**" (17) This is a cultic statement! And it is exposing multitudes to extremely high and unsafe levels of cultic Bible-Plus revelators. It is exactly because of such "New Teaching Revelators" that God's Word admonishes us in Jeremiah 6:16,

> "**Thus says the Lord, 'Stand by the ways and see and ask for the ancient paths, where the good way is, and walk in it; and you shall find rest for your souls….'**"

Did you notice that we are commanded by God to ask for the ancient paths? He knows something that we better learn fast today. It is this, "**THE NUMBER OF NEW THINGS WE NEED TO KNOW IS VERY SMALL COMPARED WITH THE NUMBER OF OLD THINGS THAT WE NEED TO BE CONSTANTLY RETAUGHT AND REMINDED OF.**"

What do the ancient paths tell us about the time of the coming of Jesus Christ and the rapture of the church? Simply this, as stated by our Lord in Mark

13:32,

**"But of that day or hour no one knows, not even the angels
in Heaven, nor the Son, but the Father alone."**

Mike Oppenheimer of "Let Us Reason Ministries" writes, "On the
November 9, 1990 Praise-A-Thon, (Benny) Hinn told (Paul) Crouch his new
revelation...quoting Hinn, 'Paul, I can say this – Are you ready for this? We may
have two years before the rapture...Can I be blunt with ya? I don't know if we
have two years left...I'm gonna prove to you from the Word of God tonight,
that we have less than two years.'"...Oppenheimer continues, "Two years makes
it 1992, but five years after when it was to occur, on the July 1997 fund-raiser
telethon on TBN Benny Hinn said a newer revelation for those who forgot the
other new one, but this is 7 years later, 'Jesus is coming again within the next two
years.'" (Trinity Broadcasting Network) (18)

Stop it already! Today it won't really suffice to ask your pastor for the ancient
paths. You have to demand them! The ancient paths alone will lead us into that
which is good for us. They alone are where we will find inspired truth and
therefore true rest for our souls. So the true preachers of God's Word must state:
**"PLEASE, PLEASE, PLEASE UNDERSTAND THAT WE ARE HERE
TO REPEAT WHAT THE SCRIPTURES HAVE TAUGHT FOR
THOUSANDS OF YEARS...IF WE QUIT GIVING YOU THE
ANCIENT SCRIPTURES, WE'RE DONE."**

THE SUN, THE LIGHT, AND THE BURNING RAY

In short, the self-generation is the latest-fad generation. The religionized
human self, always needing the new and most shocking, is no longer satisfied
with Who God has revealed Him-self to be in His Word either. It needs to
reinvent God as well. This is exactly why the delegates to the Church Policy
Making Body of the Presbyterian Church USA in 2006 presented to the General
Assembly a study done on new and fresh nomenclature for the Trinitarian
Godhead of Biblical Christianity.

The Bible tells us that God is the Triune God, the Three-In-One God, and
that He is called in Matthew 28:19 by the name of,

"...the Father and the Son and the Holy Spirit."

That is Who God is, and that is how He names Himself. I don't want anyone
messing with, changing or even slightly mispronouncing my name. What about

you? Come now, let's admit it! We are super-touchy about name-tampering or slaughtering! Well then, what about changing God's name. Of all the sacrilegious gall! God presents Himself in nomenclature that is perfect, clear, personal, and to be believed just as it is written. It is the thrice holy and profound mystery of the Trinity, yet presented with personal exactness and specificity. It is into that God, and into His threefold Name, that we are told to baptize converts to Christ – in the name of the Father, the Son, and the Holy Spirit.

However, the Presbyterian Church USA in a denominational study committee has come up with some other designations for the Father, the Son, and the Holy Spirit. The newest God names! Name that God! The "Religious Humanistic Self" finds it all so very alluring. R. Albert Mohler Jr., a guest columnist for "The Christian Post," writes the following in an article entitled, *The God Who Names Himself*: "On June 17 (2006), the 217th General Assembly of the church (Presbyterian Church USA) voted to 'receive' and commend to the church for study the paper entitled 'The Trinity: God's Overflowing Love.' The paper is now part of the official proceedings of the General Assembly and it is now forwarded to local congregations for study and application." (19)

R. Albert Mohler then shares some of the new Trinitarian designations for the Presbyterian Churches USA to consider. I hope that you are sitting down, so that you won't fall over when you read the suggested list. He writes:

"IN THE MOST CONTROVER- SIAL SECTIONS, THE REPORT SUGGESTS NEW TRIADS OF LANGUAGE THAT CAN BE USED IN PLACE OF THE BIBLICAL LANGUAGE FOR THE TRINITY – NAMELY, THE FATHER, THE SON, AND THE HOLY SPIRIT. THE NEW TRIADS, SUGGESTED FOR EMPLOYMENT IN WORSHIP, INCLUDE; 'RAINBOW, ARK, AND DOVE,' 'SPEAKER, WORD AND BREATH,' 'OVERFLOWING FONT, LIVING WATER AND FLOWING RIVER,' 'COMPASSIONATE MOTHER, BELOVED CHILD AND LIFE GIVING WOMB,' 'SUN, LIGHT AND BURNING RAY,' 'GIVER, GIFT AND GIVING,' 'LOVER, BELOVED AND LOVE,' 'ROCK, CORNERSTONE AND TEMPLE,' 'FIRE THAT CONSUMES, SWORD THAT DIVIDES AND STORM THAT MELTS MOUNTAINS,' 'THE ONE WHO WAS, THE ONE WHO IS AND THE ONE WHO IS TO COME.'" (20)

R. Albert Mohler then sharply and accurately reacts by saying: "There is absolutely no Scriptural warrant for the church to interpret, amplify, and expand upon the ways of naming the Triune God...The Christian faith is based exclusively in the understanding that God alone has the right to name Himself...He does not invite His creatures to experiment in worship by naming Him according to their own desires." (21)

I totally agree with Mohler's insightful condemnation of renaming God. I will carry it much further. When we are dealing with God's name, we are into the highest, the holiest, and the loftiest reality in all of time and eternity. Frankly, for man to rename God is like climbers ascending to the peak of a pristine and majestic mountain and leaving behind piles of human waste. Moreover, God assures us in His Word that He changes not. (Malachi 3:6) If that is so, neither does His name, for names in the Bible represent who the named one is. To change His name is to change God. Apparently no Religious Humanist in all of this even begins to realize what he is doing.

Our calling regarding God's name is stated in Psalm 45:17,

**"I will cause Thy name to be remembered in all generations;
therefore the peoples will give Thee thanks
forever and ever."**

How on earth can we make sure that the following generations will remember His name when we multi-change His name from year to year. After a while, no one will know who in the world He is or what His name is. Disaster!

Moreover, these substitute names for God are not names, but attacks upon His Divine nature and character. They both depersonalize and degrade Him. How? They characterize Him as a pan- theistic god, i.e. a god who is the universe. They identify Him as essentially one with creation and not as the Creator. They completely misrepresent Him.

More specifically, let's take a closer look at just a couple of these triads. Instead of the Father, the Son, and the Holy Spirit, you may want to consider: **"SUN, LIGHT, AND BURNING RAY."** Sounds like a name for the latest sun-block product. But what it would mean therefore is that when you are worshipping God the Father, you are worshipping the "Sun." By the way, worshipping the sun is not anything new. The ancient Egyptians were poly-theists. They worshipped approximately 2000 gods and goddesses. But there were a few top guns – a few top gods. One of them was "Horus" who was the "Sky God." Sky King! But above Horus was "Amon-Ra" who was the "Sun God." He was worshipped as the lord of the universe. Numero Uno! He was the hottest thing going in terms of gods. I am sure that the ancient Egyptians and modern sun-worshippers would feel right at home with God the Father being named the "Sun."

When you worship God the Son, you had better wear your sun glasses, for you are now worshipping the "Sun's Light." Of course, He is not "Sun-Light." He is "Son-Light." He is the eternal Son of God in whom there is no darkness at all. (I John 1:5) That is why Jesus calls Himself, "The Light of the World." (John 8:12) Apart from Jesus men walk in spiritual darkness all of their life long, and in that darkness they are without God and without hope in this world. Life apart from Jesus is dark and meaningless. He alone illumines the sin-darkened souls of men, takes the scales off from their spiritually-blinded eyes, and in His light they see light. All of life for the first time makes glorious sense.

When you are worshipping God the Holy Spirit, you had better cover yourself with factor 30 sun-block, for you are worshipping the "Sun's Burning Ray." Watch out for the Holy Spirit and those dreaded "UV-HS Rays." Sad to say, the Holy Spirit throughout church history has always been devalued, and here He is demoted again. Laelius Socinus, an Italian theologian of the 15th century, denied both the Deity and personhood of the Holy Spirit. Instead, Socinus believed that the Holy Spirit is the power through which God accomplishes His work. The Holy Spirit as "Burning Ray" comes very close to Socinianism. "Burning Ray" likewise is but an influence or power of the "Sun." This name does nothing to affirm and everything to deny the Divine Personhood of the Holy Spirit.

What is really behind this brazen assault on the Trinitarian nomenclature by the modern Religious Humanism Church? Self! The undenied self! Short and simple! Allow me to explain. Canon Charles Raven once said to a student audience, "I pity the man who does not find God more interesting than his own soul." (22) So do I because I was pitifully there once upon a time. We could also put it this way, "I pity the man who does not find God more interesting than himself."

When self is centralized, as Schuller desires, man will be bored with himself. When God is at the center of life, man will be thrilled with God. Come now, I mean walk around the human self a couple of times, in fact once will do, and you have seen it all. Walk around God eternally and you will only ever just begin to discover His infinite glories. Man compared to God is a dreary disappointment, an anthill compared to a mountain range. W.B.J. Martin writes: "The young boy rebelled against the intense evangelicalism of his home and became an agnostic. But in later life he wrote in his journal: 'What a bore it is to wake up every morning the same old person.'" (23) Exactly! The same old self!

Yes, of course, the self-life – Same-O, Same-O! Boring! Being self-centered is solitary confinement. Being self-focused is walking through life blind-folded and unable to see the glory of God.

W.B.J. Martin, quoting from the *Journal* of Andre Gide the French author, relates Gide's observations about his visit to Italy which included in his journal the following: "I found Rome most boring, but that was because I did not find myself interesting there." (24) The fact is that when man is mired in self, it will make all of life boring, including God, Rome, and every other person and place in the world!

It should come as no shock to us therefore that even religious man can be, as they say, bored out of his gourd. He will be bored with God as well when he is focused on self. So to jazz up his religious self-centered life, he has to continue to put new and gaudy racing stripes on his Religious Humanism theological motorcycle. Vroom! Vroom! He will even go so far as to try to hype up God by giving Him dazzling and flashy new nomenclature like Sun, Light, and Burning Ray. Give God a new look. Spice God up with new names. Spruce God up with a new set of clothes. Zataran religion! Religious jambalaya!

When self is the focus, everything and everyone including God must be pumped up and given new zip. When you refuse to deny self to follow Christ and obey His Word, you can never experience how infinitely glorious and amazing Christ is. One of Christ's Biblical names is given to us in Isaiah 9:6 (KJV),

"And His name shall be called Wonderful Counselor...."

That means exactly what it says – He is always full of wonder. He is astonishingly, staggeringly awesome. But you cannot be full of self and full of "Wonderful" at the same time. And you will never come to realize Wonderful's wonder unless you obey Him as your Counselor.

What the entire modern church desperately needs is to be emptied of self and filled with the Holy Spirit. Modern Christianity is immersed (baptized) in self, and it needs to be immersed (baptized) in the Holy Spirit. (Acts 1:5) There you are, now we are talking truth. Why? Because of what we read in John 16:14 where Jesus says about the Holy Spirit,

"He shall glorify Me...."

When you are not filled with the Holy Spirit but with self, you have to change Jesus' name to entertain your bored-out-of-your-gourd religious self. But when you are filled with the Holy Spirit, you can't mention the name of Jesus without getting goose bumps. The Holy Spirit puts the wonder in Wonderful. Selfianity takes it out. Religious Humanism has to change the name of Jesus. Spirit-filled Christianity adores the name of Jesus and can't praise Him enough. Praise You Jesus!

Allow me one more triad. The modern Presbyterian Church USA nomenclatures have concocted other designations for the Holy Trinity, such as: "**THE COMPASSIONATE MOTHER, THE BELOVED CHILD, AND THE LIFE-GIVING WOMB.**" So now it is permissible to refer to God the Father, God the Son, and God the Holy Spirit in the baptismal pronouncement in this way, "I baptize you in the name of the Compassionate Mother, the Beloved Child, and the Life-Giving Womb." Sounds like a maternity ward at the local hospital.

This is also the spirit of self-centered Feminism on the loose – The Compassionate Mother! If God was required to apply for a driver's license, the Religious Humanist Fems would demand that at the least He should check both gender boxes. The transgender God! God need not be called Father. He can be called Mother, too. He is not only "Abba Father!" He is now "Dear Mommy!" We used to sing, "This is my Father's world." Now they want us to sing, "This is my Mother's world." It would not have gotten onto the parking lot of my boyhood church! Furthermore, if I ever even tried to refer to my dad as my mother, knowing him, he would have warned me once, and the second time he would have tanned my filial hide with the uncompassionate palm of his very unfeminine, masculine hand.

As for the "Beloved Child," this also is a pathetic perversion of the Trinity. It makes Jesus appear as only a pre-adolescent kid. How cute! A very lovable little child! Neutered, too! Non-specific, generic little Jesus! Not even the "Beloved Son." The Fems love that!

However, when Matthew 28:19 refers to Jesus Christ as "The Son," it is referring to Him as the eternal and only begotten Son of the Father. Never forget that there was never a time when the eternal Father did not have His eternal Son, and there was never a time when the eternal Son of God did not have His eternal Father. The Father has never been Sonless, and the Son has never been Fatherless. His name "The Only Begotten Son of God" has nothing to do with incarnation, Christmas, or sweet little Jesus child. The Son of God did not begin at Christmas. Historic Christian theologians have referred to the mystery of the Son of God's begottenness as "Eternal Generation." In fact, the Son of God did not begin at all. He is eternal!

Yes, thank God that the Son of God entered time and became a male child for our salvation. Sorry Fems, the Savior was not Joseph and Mary's daughter. He was their son. But that is not what the baptismal designation of "The Son" is about at all. When we baptize new converts to Christ in the Name of the Son, it is in the Name of the Everlasting, Almighty, and Infinite Divine Son of God.

As for the Holy Spirit being renamed the "Life-Giving Womb," this is also a depersonalizing, humanizing, and feminizing of the Holy Spirit which turns Him into a pregnant woman's womb! So was my wife's mother! She was far more than that, but she was a life-giving womb! She gave birth to thirteen children. She was a bountiful life-giving womb if I ever saw one. But she was not a goddess. She was dear and sweet Jennie, my wife's precious mom. No, the Holy Spirit is God! The Holy God! The Holy Spirit of the Triune Godhead! Not a woman's womb. (I know that they were thinking of the Spirit's rebirthing role in our lives.)

All of this ought to make Presbyterians really angry. It has! Steven Poole writes: "The Rev. Mark Brewer, senior pastor of the Bel Air Presbyterian Church (Los Angeles, CA) is among the 2.3-million-member denomination unhappy with the additions. He said, 'You might just as well put it: **HUEY, DEWEY, AND LOUIE.**'" (25) Steven Poole continues: "It reminds me of the names for movements in the Chinese martial arts. How about 'White Crane Spreads Its Wings - Green Dragon Emerges From The Water - Step Back To Ride The Tiger.'" (26)

When churches tamper with and thereby desecrate sacred realities, it opens the door wide for the world to walk right in and have a good old irreverent heyday at God's expense. Some have responded to Steven Poole's critique of the Presbyterian Church USA's renaming the Triune God and have suggested other designations in response to the entire fiasco with other triads such as, "Lock, Stock, and Barrel," "Lions, Tigers, and Bears, Amen," "Rock, Paper, and Scissors," "Bell, Whistle, and Gong," "Olive Oil, Sweet Pea, and Spinach," "Santa Claus, the Easter Bunny, and the Tooth Fairy," "Groucho, Chico, and Harpo," "Moe, Larry and Curly," "Fire, Ice and Lukewarm Water," "The Father, the Son & Goalie Host," "Black, White & Read All Over," and "God-0-, God-1-, God-2." See what you open up when you violate God! Give the Devil a crack and he will come in and desecrate the entire temple.

THE BIBLE DECODERS

The never able-to-be-satisfied human self is not only discontented with Who God is, but it has also become discontented and bored with the Bible of historic Christianity. No big surprise! If they attempt to jazz up God's name, it is but one small step to spicing up His inspired and infallible Word as well. If they in their self-obsession are bored with God, they will be bored with His Word, too. Keeping these self-centered Religious Humanists spiritually juiced up is like keeping little children entertained for an entire week. Drug addicts aren't the only ones who are looking for the rush. The religious self is always searching for a bigger rush, too! In fact, self is the original rush addict. And like children, self is always begging for more in the midst of plenty. Entertain me! Thrill me! Dazzle me! Stimulate me!

Satan is more than willing to accommodate. Along comes Michael Drosnin's book, *The Bible Code*. Drosnin does not believe in God. He does believe that space aliens wrote the Bible and encoded within the Scriptures events predicted thousands of years before they happened. Bill Clinton as President! Moon landings, spaceships, and Apollo 11! Hitler the Nazi! Kennedy and Dallas! He believes that hidden under the Bible in the Hebrew text are encoded futuristic revelations that criss-cross the Hebrew text like some sort of intergalactic crossword puzzle. You know, like 6 across, 21 down, as well as 14 diagonally. More than that, the Hebrew cross-word puzzle, which can only be deciphered by sophisticated computer programs, reveals catastrophic earthquakes coming to Los Angeles in 2010, as well as earthquakes, fires, and economic collapse in Japan. On and on it goes!

Sure enough, wouldn't you know it? This most recent "Bible Scrabble Game," ends up being promoted by the Trinity Broad-cast-ing Network as in fact Bible truth. TBN has jumped on "The Bible Code" bandwagon from a faith perspective. It is also known as "Equidistant Letter Sequence," or "ELS." A man by the name of Yacov Ramsel has been the TBN Bible decoder. We no longer just have Bible scholars and exegetes. Too old fashioned! Now we have Bible decoders as Bible commentators.

Anton and Janet Hein-Hudson of "Apologetics Index" quote G. Richard Fisher who observes, "The book's success (The Bible Code) has also afforded Drosnin guest appearances on popular television broadcasts such as Oprah. Other notables within Christian circles, including Paul Crouch, Hal Lindsey and Grant Jeffrey, have also jumped on the ELS bandwagon."(27)

As has been noted, we no longer have just those who rightly divide the Word of Truth. (II Timothy 2:15 KJV) Now we have those who are rightly cracking the code of truth. A whole new department could be opened up in seminaries across the land. To qualify as a Doctor of Codology, you must be very good with words, spelling, and foreign languages such as Hebrew and Greek. And you must get your Doctor of Divinity Degree in Scrabbleology and Crossword Puzzleology.

Remember the television series *Startrek* where you meet all sorts of science-fiction freaks from formerly unheard of planets? There are still Startrek groupies today. You haven't seen anything yet. Welcome to Codetrek! Fiction being dramatized as Biblical fact! You think that Startrek's inter-galactic creatures were far out. Codetrek will make Startrek look like Sesame Street, and John's Revelation look like Lassie.

Each week Starship Enterprise flew the devoted TV Trekkies to distant planets where they encountered some of the strangest outer-space weirdoes ever imagined. They were constantly being caught in interplanetary warfare along the way. Well now, welcome to Codetrek's "Codeship Fantasy", in which you will be flown *Back To The Future* where the New York City Twin Towers, 9/11, and Manhattan have supposedly been encoded and decoded in the Hebrew Text of Isaiah 30. Only Code Trekkies know what awaits those who fly on Codeship Fantasy. TBN has already produced a film based on the Bible Code movement called *The Omega Code*, which was attended mostly by "Bible Code Trekkies." The Roman Catholic Church has its Popery, and Religious Humanism now has its Codery. My reaction to the entire thing is, "Beam us up, Jesus."

Why such a serious warning against the "Bible Code Movement?" First of all it is a corrupting of the Holy Scriptures by adding to the Bible. In fact, it is another bible and an attempt to give this new, bogus bible Divine authenticity and sanction. It is so deceptive because it seems to be taken from the Bible. God does not speak in some secret and imagined code when in the plainest of words He condemns adding to and subtracting from the Holy Word of God. God says to us through Moses in Deuteronomy 4:2,

> "You shall not add to the word which I am commanding you, nor take away from it, that you may keep the commandments of the Lord your God which I command you."

God also says through John in Revelation 22:18-19:

> "I testify to everyone who hears the words of the prophecy of this book: if anyone adds to them, God shall add to him the plagues which are written in this book; and if anyone takes away from the words of the book of this prophecy, God shall take away his part from the tree of life and from the holy city, which are written in this book."

The gravest of all warnings in the Bible! Those who add to or subtract from

God's Word no longer have any access to the Tree of Life. They are also banned from ever entering the Holy City, the New Jerusalem. The horror of this cannot be exaggerated, for their sentence of damnation is irreversible and out of the reach of Divine mercy and salvation both now and forevermore.

God's Word is not a religious laboratory for self-appointed pseudo-theological chemists to experiment in. That is what these modern Bible decoders have turned the Holy Bible into, a test tube of human formulas and experimentation for the purpose of producing new and shocking revelations that will mesmerize the religious masses for the purposes of profit from their books, CDs etc. Dear Lord, we have enough profiteers already. Please give us true prophets of God.

Second, we would be remiss if we did not point out that man has always had a most uncanny ability to make things say what he wants them to say for his own purposes. For instance, man has done so by adopting what has come to be known by some code fanatics as, "The Devil's Code." In "The Devil's Code" the alphabet is numbered backward from zero, i.e. Z=0, Y=1, X=2 etc., and then when multiplying each letter by six, the late fundamentalist leader Jerry Falwell's last name is made to equal 666, which is the mark of the beast in the book of Revelation. Falwell's liberal and anti-God opposition just loved "The Devil's Code." When the dear brother in the Lord, Ronald Wilson Reagan, was elected president, "The Devil's Code" enthusiasts pointed out that each of Ronald Wilson Reagan's names had six letters – 666. (28)

Our minds have a propensity to organize and formulate any imagined reality in any way we wish to. It is a well-known fact that you can empty a bag of marbles on the floor and by selectively ignoring certain marbles and keying on others you can find any pattern you wish. You can also do so with the cloud formations as you take pictures of the imagined fluffy figures, and publish it all under the notion that God is sky-writing and sky-painting special messages in "Cloud Codes." Little children have been known to find words spelled out in their alphabet soup at lunchtime as noodle letters float into position in the soup broth. Others read tea leaves and human palms. Cloudology, noodleology, teaology, palmology, and now codology! What next? Stay tuned! And this bored self-generation will continue to eat up the latest codology and all the exciting "Ologies" yet to come.

Of course, the huge problem with all of this is that you can find the same code-carnival in other books that we know for sure were not encoded by space aliens or by the Holy Spirit. Writes G. Richard Fisher, quoting from Peter T. Chattaway, in his article *The Bible Code – God's Fingerprints?* "For one thing the Bible is not the only text in which computers may find coded prophecies.

Orthodox rabbi, Shlomo Sternberg, together with Australian mathematician, Brendan Mckay, claims to have found the names of Indian Prime Minister, Indira Ghandi, and Nicaraguan President, Anastasio Somoza, in the text of Moby Dick, overlapping such phrases as 'the bloody deed' and 'he was shot.'" (29)

Need we say more? Nothing but incidental scraps of Hebrew, for that is all this Bible Code stuff really is. Insignificant chancy but high-sounding disconnected, disassociated and discombobulated trifles! Ooooh, did you notice, there is my name? Did you see it, discomBOBulated? It must be God! The code has been cracked again. Better yet, we can crack the name code in Webster's Dictionary. And because my name in discomBOBBulated is found on the same Webster Dictionary page with the words disco and disfavor, it must be that Bob is involved in dirty dancing which will put him in disfavor with his church. I'll bet that is what God is trying to tell us about Bob. Wait until I tell my wife? Hear me, neither Ruth nor I can dance a lick. Have you had enough? I have! Let's get out of here!

Third, God does not reveal Himself in Scripture or communicate in one word verbal grunts and burps, or in more prolonged sneezes of two or three words. Yes, the Bible does record Jesus saying on the cross "I thirst" and "It is finished." But always in the context of complete narratives and teachings which are the modus operandi of the Holy Spirit! The Bible Code so-called revelations are completely out of sync with the entire rhythm, style and flow of Holy Scripture. God does not paint by number, or reveal Himself in criss-crossword puzzles. The Holy Spirit never breathed into any Bible writer a mere spelling book or word book of names, places, or things. The Holy Bible is not a thesaurus, but God's love letter of redemption and forgiveness to a lost-in-sin world.

RELIGIOUS HUMANISM – THE PATH OF LEAST RESISTANCE

God alone in His infinite wisdom knows how to bring the most glory to Himself from the lives of His children. In one case, a man's healing will bring glory to God through a powerfully restored body, and a grateful and praising heart. In another case, an afflicted or handicapped person brings God glory through a miraculously sustained joyful and patient spirit, and a Divinely bestowed physical enabling that transcends natural ability.

Many Religious Humanists totally reject this truth, because it doesn't suit their self-convenience. Nonetheless, this is exactly why the Apostle Paul's thorn in the flesh was not taken away by God, and the "why not" is clearly explained by Paul in II Corinthians 12:7, 9 (KJV),

"...to keep me from exalting myself...,"

and,

"...for my strength is made perfect in weakness...."

First, Paul was given the big pain to keep him from getting the big head. Paul gets humbled! Second, the glory of God's power was magnified by enabling a physically afflicted Paul to live in such a triumphant way that it could only be explained as a supernatural empowerment. God gets glorified!

It is right here where Religious Humanists have a fit, because the comfort and ease of self does not receive first place, but God's glory does. Kenneth Copeland, a modern health and wealth pusher on his radio and television ministries called *The Believer's Voice of Victory*, goes so far as to say that: **"GOD HAS NEVER USED SICKNESS TO DISCIPLINE HIS CHILDREN."** (30) Or again, Copeland declares: **"AIDS IS 'ABSOLUTELY NOT' GOD'S WAY OF PUNISHING IMMORAL PEOPLE."** (31)

Oh really? We read in Hebrews 12:6 and11,

"For those whom the Lord loves He disciplines, and He scourges every son whom He receives."

"All discipline for the moment seems not to be joyful, but sorrowful; yet to those who have been trained by it, afterwards it yields the peaceful fruit of righteousness."

We must read with these Scriptures the following words of Lam-entations 3:33 where we are told about God sending affliction and grief into our lives:

"For He does not afflict willingly, or grieve the sons of men."

Vast segments of Religious Humanism teach contrary to the Bible about God:

"For He does not afflict period."

No matter what Scripture says, they hold stubbornly to their position, and blame all human afflictions either on the Devil, or on sin in the afflicted one's life, or on the lack of faith.

The verb "To Scourge" in Hebrews 12:6 literally means "To Whip" or "To

Flog." Big time affliction! We are not talking here about a Divine slap on the wrist or a few Divine spanks on our bottoms. God puts His children through some heavy physical pains and afflictions, so that being disciplined by them, they will be perfected and bring forth in their lives fruits of righteousness which in turn create peace all around.

Right here is where Religious Humanists have fits, big ones, and have caused untold damage to and confusion in the lives of countless people. Nonetheless the Psalmist says in Psalm 119:71,

> **"It was good for me that I was afflicted, that I may learn Thy statutes."**

So much for this nonsense that God doesn't use affliction to mold and mature us in the Holy Spirit!

We are told by Kenneth Copeland that God does not use sickness and affliction in our lives to discipline us. We read about God in Exodus 4:11 asking Moses questions and giving him but one answer to all of His questions:

> **"And the Lord said to him, 'Who has made man's mouth? Or who makes him dumb or deaf, or seeing or blind? Is it not I, the Lord?'"**

Who makes some men eloquent, sighted, and sound of hearing? God does! Who makes other men dumb, deaf, and even blind? God does! Why? So that, according to the Bible, the child of God can praise Him through and even for the scourge, knowing that as he trusts and serves God through it, the end result will be a purified, productive and righteously transformed life. But Religious Humanists cannot stomach any of this, for their God is a God who produces only ease and therefore can have nothing to do with disease. Their God is not the God of Scripture, but of their own invention.

Kenneth Hagin Sr., founder of Rhema Bible College in Broken Arrow, Oklahoma, once made this statement about his childhood heart malady and God allowing it: **"SOME OF THESE CHRISTIANS TRIED TO TELL ME, 'WELL, NOW MAYBE GOD DIDN'T DO IT. BUT NOW HE PERMITTED IT AND HE'S GOT SOME PURPOSE IN ALL OF THAT.' I SAID, 'IF YOU'RE THAT KIND OF GOD – ME A LITTLE INNOCENT BABY – IF YOU'RE THAT KIND OF GOD I'D RATHER GO TO HELL THAN TO BE WITH YOU!' AND I MEANT EVERY WORD OF IT! AND I STILL MEAN IT!"** (32) Some of the most God-defying and blasphemous words I have ever read! Either God must have nothing to do with childhood disease and deformity either in causing or allowing them, or if He does, then it would be better to go to Hell with the Devil than spend eternity with such a fiendish God in Heaven. This is how outraged and irrational people can become when they dictate to God the perimeters they have set for Him.

What about AIDS in the lives of homosexuals? God has nothing to do with physically punishing people for their wickedness!? Wrong! What God are we talking about here? Not the God Who put boils on man and beast throughout the pagan land of Egypt, which was ruled over by proud and obstinate King Pharaoh. (Exodus 9:9-10) Not the God who sent fiery serpents among the murmuring and rebellious Israelites, so that they bit the people and many of them died. (Numbers 21:6) Not just serpents, but fiery ones. Flaming serpents with hot bites! Wouldn't just plain venomous snakes be adequate? This is the very same God who says about Himself in Deuteronomy 32:39,

> **"See now that I, I am He, and there is no god besides Me; it is I who put to death and give life, I have wounded, and it is I who heal; and there is no one who can deliver from My hand."**

To say that God no longer heals is a lie. To say that God only heals is a lie. Lies never work.

It makes me think of Helen Keller. In a Sunday magazine supplement, Helen Keller was brought up in the question and answer section. Someone wrote in and asked, "I've just read a reference to a book written by Helen Keller. This must be an error, because Helen Keller was deaf, mute, and blind. Isn't there some error?" In the answer, the editor replied, "No. You're correct that she was deaf, mute, and blind. But she is not only the author of that book; she is the author of nine books. She wrote in Braille. She also wrote slowly in longhand. She graduated from Radcliffe College. She contributed $2 million to a foundation to help others." That God's strength is perfected and glorified in weakness could be illustrated over and over again.

Religious Humanists cause such harm and embarrassment to the Body of Christ in this regard. When Billy Graham came to a particular city to conduct one of his evangelistic crusades, a certain man wrote Billy Graham a letter and rebuked Billy for something that simply cannot be fathomed. This critic also read his letter publicly over one of the local radio stations in his city, broadcasting his rebuke to Graham so that the public would be party to it. In the letter, which now had become headline news, he rebuked Billy Graham for, of all things, allowing Joni Erickson Tada to sit on the platform with him and give her testimony to the goodness and the grace of God in her life. Why? The answer is that the Religious Humanist would not and could not accept the fact that a physically challenged person in a wheelchair could bring glory to God. The only way that men can really bring glory to God is if everyone is healed, prosperous, comfortable, and living the Religious Humanism false definition of the abundant life.

The Apostle Paul, Helen Keller and Joni Erickson Tada have brought more glory to God in their weakened, blinded, and paralyzed state than they ever could have in a naturally strong, sighted, and mobilized state. Do you know why a river winds its crooked snakelike path? It does so, because a river always takes the path of least trouble and resistance. That path not only makes rivers crooked, it makes people crooked and twisted, too. It also twists and corrupts their theology. Billy Graham's critic was the twisted and crooked one. His critic was the detractor of God's glory. Joni Erickson was the reflector of God's glory. In Billy Graham's crusade she praised the Lord her God Who had turned what looked to some as a tragedy into a magnificent triumph. She had been proven through trial and testing, while the Religious Humanist critic flat-out flunked the test. He stumbled and fell on his face while Joni in her wheelchair was walking nimbly in victory.

In Christianity, the mountain many times must be climbed and conquered rather than removed. It brings to mind the story of Sir Edmund Hillary. The first time he had tried to climb Mt. Everest, he failed. Hillary was subsequently invited to address the Parliament in London, England. When he walked in, there before him was a massively enlarged picture of Mt. Everest. Without delay he went right up to the picture and said: "**MT. EVEREST, SINCE THE LAST TIME I SAW YOU, YOU ARE NOT GETTING ANY BIGGER. BUT SINCE THE LAST TIME YOU SAW ME, I HAVE BEEN GETTING BIGGER INDEED.**" Precisely the point! Mt. Everest was not getting any larger. But Edmund Hillary was. And eventually he did climb to the top of Mt. Everest, and he did realize conquest.

If God would always shrink the mountain, or remove the mountain entirely, what would happen? It is then that we would miss the greatest miracle of all, and that is the discovery of the miracle that God's grace and strength are greater than any obstacle in our lives. If God were to remove every mountain, we would never have the thrill of experiencing the awesome enabling and gracious empowering of God. That is why we read that God scourges every one of His children. There it is! True Christian character is always in each and every one of our lives formed by climbing Everest's trying and difficult steeps. Always!

Resources:

1. Dynamic Preaching, "Does it make a difference Who Jesus is?" (Seven Worlds Corporation, Knoxville, TN, July/August, 1995, Volume XI, No. 7) page 41

2. Bishop Katharine Jefferts Schori, "New Life Out Of Death: A Message For Easter," Episcopal News Service, April 8, 2007 (Quoted By Permission From Rev. Canon C. K. Robertson, PhD, Canon To The Presiding Bishop)

3. Let Us Reason Ministries, Mike Oppenheimer, "Internet Christian Bookstores: Havens For Non-Christian Materials"

4. Way of Life Literature, David Cloud, "A Worldly Baptism," Friday Church News Notes, October 5, 2007" (Baptist Press, September 25, 2007)

5. Ibid.

6. Let Us Reason Ministries, Mike Oppenheimer, "The Seeker Friendly Church Model" (W.E. Vine, "The Collected Works")

7. Dynamic Preaching, "A Most Unlikely Evangelist" (Seven Worlds Corporation, Knoxville, TN, March, 1996, Volume XI, No. 3) Page 9, Jim Wideman, Illustration Digest, March-April, 1992

8. Apologetics Index, Anton and Janet Hein Hudson, Publishers (Rick Blinson of KneePrints, Inc., "Contentment: The Antithesis of Prosperity Teaching."

9. Paul Kengor, "Carrying the Cross in Iraq" (Quoted By Permission, International Christian Concern-ICC, 2020 Pennsylvania Avenue N.W. #941, Washington, D.C. 20006-1846)

10. Apologetics Index, Anton and Janet Hein Hudson, Publishers (Rick Blinson of KneePrints, Inc., "Contentment: The Antithesis of Prosperity Teaching")

11. Dynamic Preaching, "Weeds in the Garden" (Seven Worlds Corporation, Knoxville, TN, July/August, 1996, Volume XI, No. 7) Pages 17-18

12. Biblical Discernment Ministries, Rick Miesel, John Beardsley (Gary Gilley, "The Word of Faith Movement") Robert Tilton, Trinity Broadcasting Network, 1990 (Charismatic Chaos, p. 285)

13. Dynamic Preaching, "Get Out of the Boat" (Seven Worlds Corporation, Knoxville, TN, July/August, 1996, Volume XI, No. 7) Page 3, "To Verify..." Leadership, 1996, Page 79

14. Let Us Reason Ministries, Mike Oppenheimer, "Creflo Dollar, A Name That Has A Ring to It" Pt.3 (Creflo Dollar, TBN, July 20, 1999)

15. Ibid.

16. Dynamic Preaching, "I Have Been Baptized" (Seven Worlds Corporation, Knoxville, TN, January, 1995, Volume X, No. 1) Pages 17-18, Wall Street Journal, Fall September 12, 1994

17. Let Us Reason Ministries, Mike Oppenheimer, "Benny Hinn's Romance with Necromancy," Pt. 2 (Benny Hinn, Trinity Broadcasting Network, December 9, 1990)

18. Let Us Reason Ministries, Mike Oppenheimer, "How Many False Prophecies And Teachings Does It Take To Make One A Liar And A False Prophet In God's Eyes?"

19. R. Albert Mohler, www.AlbertMohler.com, "The God Who Names Himself," Wednesday, June 21, 2006 (Permission Granted By Lawrence Smith, VP for Communications, The Southern Baptist Theological Seminary)

20. Ibid.

21. Ibid.

22. W.B.J. Martin, "Little Foxes That Spoil the Vines" (Abington Press, Nashville, Tennessee, 1968) Page 31

23. Ibid, Page 30

24. Ibid, Page 31

25. www.crookedtimber.org, Steven Poole, "Framing God," Friday, June 30, 2006

26. Ibid.

27. Apologetics Index, Anton and Janet Hein-Hudson (The Bible Code: Prophetic Insight or Fertile Imagination, G. Richard Fischer)

28. Dynamic Preaching, "With Your Head In The Clouds" (Seven Worlds Corporation, Knoxville, TN, February, 1996, Volume XI, No. 2) Charles R. Swindol, "Come Before Winter And Share My Hope" (Grand Rapids, MI, Zondervan Publishing House, 1985).

29. Apologetics Index, Anton and Janet Hein-Hudson (The Bible Code: Prophetic Insight or Fertile Imagination, G. Richard Fischer)

30. Biblical Discernment Ministries, Rick Miesel, John Beardsley, "Kenneth Copeland – General Teachings/Activities (Believer's Voice of Victory, 9/89)

31. Ibid, (Believer's Voice of Victory, 8/88)

32. Forgotten Word Ministries, Robert E. Wise, "Ken Hagin – False Prophet/Teacher (Ken Hagin, Ministry Tape, "You Can Have What You Say)

Chapter Five

THE CORRUPTING GODS IN MODERN CHRISTIANITY

††††

"None Provoking The People To Idolatry Ought To Be Exempted From The Punishment Of Death. The Whole Tribes Did In Very Deed Execute That Sharp Judgment Against The Tribe Of Benjamin For A Lesser Offense Than Idolatry."
~John Knox

Many of us oldies recall how the mild-mannered reporter Clark Kent of *The Daily Plant* went into a telephone booth, and there he was instantly transformed into the man of steel – Superman. One gets the feeling today within the ranks of Religious Humanists that when they get into their "Faith Booth," they experience in their world of spiritual superness what the man from Krypton experienced in his world of fiction. Religious Humanists in many instances actually believe that by having enough faith, they can right every wrong, catch a speeding bullet with their bare hands, and stop a powerful locomotive dead in its tracks. If you will, through faith, they enter into "Super-Being" status. Faith is to the Religious Humanist what Kryptonite was to Superman.

However, the analogy of Superman and Religious Humanists falls short. For Religious Humanists believe that having enough faith not only transforms them into supermen, but into gods. Yes, that is correct! You may remember the film *The Planet of the Apes*. Well now, Religious Humanists take us to *The Planet of the Gods*. In the former, apes monkey around with humans while showing themselves superior beings to all other life forms. In the latter, human beings strut around claiming to be gods and showing themselves superior to all other life forms on earth. More like *The Lost Planet of The Gods*, for if these Religious Humanists are gods, then we live on a lost and hopeless planet indeed.

Of course, the idea of men being or becoming gods is not original with modern Religious Humanists. It has ancient pagan roots. In 44 B.C., the Roman Emperor Julius Caesar had a statue erected in his honor with the inscription, "The Unvanquished God." In that same year Julius Caesar was assassinated by some of his citizens who wanted to see Rome return to its earliest republican ideals. The Roman god was vanquished after all! Those who play god always end up being "degoded" in the end.

The Mormon Church teaches that the worthy among them shall become gods who one day shall create, rule and receive worship from the domains that they shall be lords over in eternity. Patrick Zukeran is one of the contributing writers of Probe Ministries, and a great internet resource for the scholarly study of the cults. He writes: "Christianity has taught monotheism from its foundation, the belief in the existence of one God. Mormonism believes in the existence of a plurality of gods. According to Mormonism there are an infinite number of planets like earth in the universe, each with their own god or gods who were once men but who have evolved into godhood." (1)

In the same Zukeran article, Mormon theologian and apostle Bruce McConkie is quoted as follows: "(A) plurality of gods exist...There is an infinite number of holy personages, drawn from worlds without number, who have passed on to exaltation and are thus gods."(2) Religious Humanists outdo the Mormons in this regard. They hold to the teaching that the Kingdom of God is full of gods here and now on planet earth. In fact, for many Religious Humanists the Kingdom of God is really the kingdom of the gods.

This has been Satan's strategy from the beginning of time, to dupe men into believing themselves to be gods! Well, let's put it this way, that there has never been any greater trophy of deception in Satan's trophy case than this. In short, convincing men that they are gods is Satan's masterpiece of deception.

In this regard, Religious Humanism joins with other satanically deceived people such as Deepak Chopra and Oprah Winfrey and other New Age Mystics who teach that each one of us is our own god (divine spirit), and that whatever we say is truth. That divine-spirit being inside of us is the same as the Being that suffuses every atom of the cosmos. "Big B" and the "little b's." And so the god-man beat booms louder and louder. We are about to see that Religious Humanism is much closer to New Age Mysticism than it is to Christianity. God and the gods!

Let's bring it down to the mundane for a moment. The fact of the matter is that many Religious Humanists, far from being gods, are more like the used car salesmen of the modern world. You have probably met one or two of them during your lifetime. There are those less-than-ethical used car salesmen who want you to think that it is a 2006 Pontiac, when in fact it was produced in 2005. They want you to believe that it is in mint condition, when in fact there have been rust spots filled in and painted over. They suggest that you take a spin down the city street to see how smooth the ride is. However, if you took it instead for a ride down the highway, you would suddenly discover that there is a bad shimmy at 60 miles an hour. The car isn't what it appears to be.

The Religious Humanists are not what they try to pass themselves off as being either – gods. I realize that likening them to used car salesmen is a cruel analogy, because there are honest and moral used car salesmen. But for the sake of making the point, I beg the trustworthy used car salesmen's forgiveness and understanding. Speaking of cars, it is far past the hour for the gods of Religious Humanism to be driven out of Dodge. If you hang around them for 60 seconds, their godness will begin to badly shimmy and sway as well.

RELIGIOUS HUMANISM'S SILLY GOD-SYLLOGISMS

We must now examine some of the illogical logic that Religious Humanists use in order to try and convince people that as Christians they are gods. Those who hold to the view that believers are gods include such names as the late Earl Paulk, Creflo Dollar and many others who we shall note as we go along. These names again are not what are important. However, to be thoroughly informed about and guarded against the destructive delusions of this self-deification belief, we must know where and who it comes from.

Religious Humanists start from the premise that everything produces after its kind. Says Creflo Dollar, Pastor of World Changers Church International in College Park, Georgia, whose services have been broadcast regularly on TBN: **"EVERYTHING PRODUCES AFTER ITS KIND. THAT'S THE LAW OF GENESIS. EVERYTHING PRODUCES AFTER ITS KIND. WILL GOD SET A LAW IN MOTION AND THEN NOT FOL-LOW THAT LAW THAT HE SET INTO MOTION? ABSOLUTELY NOT! WHERE DID YOU COME FROM? WHO DID YOU COME FROM? EVERYTHING PRODUCES AFTER ITS KIND. HORSES GET HORSES AND DOGS GET DOGS, AND GOD PRODUCED GODS...."** (3)

Likewise the late Earl Paulk, founder of Cathedral at Chapel Hill in Decatur, Georgia, states: **"JUST AS DOGS HAVE PUPPIES, AND CATS HAVE KITTENS, SO GOD HAS LITTLE GODS. SEED REMAINS TRUE TO NATURE, BEARING ITS OWN KIND."** (4)

To call people little gods is as ridiculous as to speak of miniature giants. Short skyscrapers! Finite infinity! Retarded omniscience! Partial omnipotence! God and His little gods! More than that, you talk about anti-climactic! When you've come to know God, who gives a flip about little ones? That is about as exciting as kissing your sister. Forgive me sis!

Little gods? It is like trying to bring both ends of a contradiction together – miniature and massive. There is no such being as a little god. If he or she were little gods, they would therefore immediately be god dropouts. There is nothing little about God. Everything is infinite and immeasurable about God. The fact is that God cannot be spelled with a small "g."

ѡ absolutely incumbent upon us to shred the god-player's clever-ιg but totally false logic. What logic? The syllogism that Religious ᴨumanists use to prove man's supposed godness goes like this:

"Everything produces after its kind." (Major Premise)

"<u>Dogs have puppies, cats have kittens</u>." (Minor Premise)

"Therefore, God has little gods." (Conclusion)

It all sounds so reasonable and logical to the undiscerning and the spiritually gullible, of which the religious world is full today. To rid them of their faulty logic is like trying to get deeply embedded gum out of your child's hair. Of course, you can always cut the hair off and it will grow back. But you cannot cut off someone's little god-head, for it will not grow back. This is not going to be as easy to fix as jiggling the toilet handle I tell you. Their minds just keep on running with this illogical logic. But we must try.

First of all, this syllogism is completely false because the major premise lumps together and equates the Creator with the creature, the infinite with the finite, the eternal with the temporal, and the Divine with the human and the sub-human in the same comprehensive noun – everything. God lumped with dogs, cats, horses etc. When you really think about it, considering how many gods (believers) God has produced, they make Him look like a rabbit. You know, God and the gods, rabbit and the bunnies.

Every syllogism succeeds or flops, rises or falls depending upon the validity or invalidity of its major premise. If the major premise is erroneous, which this one grossly is, the entire syllogism is a failure and falls flat on its face. This one does just that! Splat! To equate and align the Creator God with every creature from cats to dogs to horses to man, not only continues the hideous affront to and assault on Almighty God, but it makes this syllogism totally illegitimate. Listen, for it to be legitimate, everything that is included would have to fulfill the requirement of equality. It does not nor can it, for nothing and no one is equal to God. That is why we read over and over again truth like this in Isaiah 40:18,

**"To whom then will you liken God? Or what likeness will
you compare with Him?"**

In other words, the disparity is so immeasurable, that Creator and creature in terms of essential being cannot be equated in the same breath, or in the same universe, or in the same premise. It is like equating a five course meal with leftovers. It is about as idiotic and silly as the following likewise goofball syllogism:

"Everything produces after its kind." (Major Premise)

"God produces gods." (Minor Premise)

"Cadillacs Produce Roller Skates." (Conclusion)

Second, if God could produce other gods, as the Religious Humanists contend, He would then not be the Creator. He would be creature, for only creatures can produce after their kind. That is what the Creator designed them to do, as the first chapter of Genesis makes clear throughout. Genesis 1:24 states:

"Then God said, 'Let the earth bring forth living creatures after their kind: cattle and creeping things and beasts of the earth after their kind; and it was so."

But when it came to God making man, it states in Genesis 1:26,

"Then God said, 'Let Us make man in Our image, according to Our likeness...."

He did not say:

"Let us make man after our kind."

Creatures bring forth after their kind. God created man after His likeness. Two totally different realities! Two totally different meanings! The Hebrew word for "Kind" is "Zan" which means "Species." In other words, where we read the phrase, "After their kind," it could also be translated, "After their species." God created horses, dogs, cats etc. to be able to reproduce after or within their species. However, when God created man, He did not "zan" him, that is, make him another species of Godness. No, God made man in His "Tselem – Image," according to His "Demuth – Likeness!" Man was made as a likeness of God, not as a species of Divinity. Religious Humanists have their "zans" and their "demuths" all goofed up. Come to think about it, they pretty well goof up everything they touch.

Third, the entire line of reasoning is errant simply because there are certain things that God cannot do or have. God cannot lie! God cannot begin! God cannot have birthmarks. God cannot end! God doesn't have to make funeral arrangements. God cannot deny Him-self. More than that, God cannot beget other gods. Why? If He could, he would not be God, for there cannot be more than one God. **EXCLUSIVITY IS THE ESSENCE OF DIVINITY.** There simply cannot be two or more Divinities. There cannot be two "Originals." There cannot be two "Ultimates." There cannot be two "Every-things." If you are all and have all, there cannot be another all, not even another know-it-all.

God does not work well on a committee, let alone a committee of other gods. God unequivocally states about Himself in Isaiah 45:21-22,

> **"...And there is no other God besides Me, a righteous God and a Savior; there is none except Me. Turn to Me, and be saved, all the ends of the earth; for I am God, and there is no other."**

Sorry world, if you don't believe in God, you have run out of options. No god except God! Not even little ones! Not even a hint of another god. The God-field is narrowed down to One. No other gods allowed! No other gods possible! No one need apply. So much for assistant gods! For that matter, since when does God need assistance? God is the monotheistic God. Christianity is therefore monotheistic. Religious Humanism is polytheistic.

Fourth, to answer Creflo Dollar's question when he asks, "Will God set in motion a law and then not follow that law that He set in motion?" The obvious answer to that question is absolutely yes in each and every case. Elementary Watson! The supernatural God is not subject to any natural law. That is what being supernatural means! The only law that God is subject to is the supernatural law of His own being. What is that? Simply this, that because He is the only, eternal God, He must of necessity be the only, eternal God. He cannot not be God, any more than man cannot not be man.

God created all kinds of natural laws into His creation and is subject to none of them. When God goes flying with our Christian U.S. Air Force pilots, He does not have to wear a parachute or a seatbelt. God needs no contingency plans. God created the law of gravity which we have all been forced to acknowledge and obey. If we don't, we will meet "Mr. Gravity" in the form of the "Mr. Big Hurt." But seeing God set in motion the law of gravity, does that mean, as Dollar and Paulk state, that God is also subject to the same law? That is very difficult to affirm when the Bible tells us that God rides on clouds and walks on wind. We read in Psalm 104:3

> "…He makes the clouds His chariot; He walks upon the
> wings of the wind."

As a matter of fact, God not only stands in complete contradiction to the natural laws that He has established, but He seems to make a sport of defying and contradicting them.

While God rides in his cloud-chariot in the skies, men by comparison ride on their tricycles on earth and crash into each other. While God does His cloud dance in the sky, many of us can't even dance on earth without stumbling and falling all over ourselves. Every time I see the clouds moving and swirling, I think to myself that God is having fun in the sky today. While He walks upon the wind, we get blown over by it. The supernatural God dominates the natural, while man is dominated by it.

Every bush that I know of will be turned to ashes by fire that consumes it. That is just the law of nature with its natural elements. If every element is kept in its place, things go well. But if the elements get out of place, things don't go well, and then fire becomes an inferno and forests become charred embers and instant wastelands. Not so with God! He can be in a burning bush and not be touched by the flame. And for added effect, neither is the bush burned, let alone singed. (Exodus 3) Let the religious humanistic gods try that. Burn Center here they come.

The supernatural is always contrary to, above and outside of natural law. Does the supernatural God set into motion natural laws that He doesn't abide by? Indeed, each and every one of them! If the supernatural had to abide by the natural, it would not be super-natural now would it?!

VERY DIFFICULT BEING #2

It is terribly hard being #2. In 1849, financier Joshua A. Norton came to San Francisco with $40,000 and big ambitions. For five years he invested his money wisely until he was filthy rich. Then he took a gamble. He invested all of his money in the rice market. The market fell through and he lost every penny. No one saw him again for five years. Then in 1859, Joshua Norton walked into the office of the *San Francisco Bulletin* and told them to print a proclamation that he was Emperor Norton I, emperor of the United States. As a joke, the editor printed the proclamation. (5)

It is really hard being #2. In post-World War II Europe, once it was confirmed that Hitler had committed suicide, the intense hunt was on for another architect of Nazism – the infamous Gestapo chief by the name of Heinrich Himmler. After Germany had fallen, Himmler and two of his cronies tried to hide by disguising themselves as members of the Secret Field Police. Himmler's disguise was most ingenious – he shaved off his mustache and wore a black patch over one eye.

But Herr Himmler could not bear to be #2. He could not allow himself to be dressed up in the humiliating uniform of a lowly private, and therefore in his vanity he felt compelled to dress himself up in the uniform of a sergeant. However, the allied forces were under strict orders to arrest all members of the Secret Field Police beginning with the rank of sergeant. Himmler's inflated ego proved to be his downfall and led to his capture. Otherwise he might have escaped if he could have endured being a mere private. (6) The creature would have lived in perfect Paradise had he not aspired to be the Creator. But Herr Adam could not stomach being a lowly private either. Proverbs 16:18 states:

"Pride goes before destruction and a haughty spirit before stumbling."

What is the real driving force behind this Religious Humanism god-complex? It is not original with man or even unique to him. It is as close as you can get to the Devil himself, who is the originator of the entire "Wanna-Be-God" craving. You recall that it all started with Satan when he was yet known as Lucifer (light-bearer) in Heaven. Satan is recorded in Isaiah 14:14 as saying:

"I will ascend above the heights of the clouds; I will make myself like the Most High."

Nothing more or less than god-lust driving him to aspire to equality with his Maker! God refers to Satan in his sinless state as "Star of the Morning. (Isaiah 14:12) However, it was too disparaging for Satan to simply be a star. He wanted to be the sun. Satan said, "I Will!" God said, "You won't." More exactly God said to him in Isaiah 14:15,

"Nevertheless you will be thrust down to Sheol, to the recesses of the pit."

Hell apparently is a deep place, and the deepest depth and the black-est darkness is reserved for Satan.

That is how Lucifer the "Angel of Light" became the "Satan of Darkness," and the "Angel of Heaven" became the "Devil of Hell." He pushed the button on the elevator that read, "Top Floor – God's Throne." Down he went! Satan was thrown out of Heaven and from that day has gone into a Hell-bound free-fall from which there is no recovery. He became the original falling star. We all ought to have learned from Satan by now that those who try to raise themselves up to the highest position in Heaven will be sent down to eternity's lowest position in Hell. Not just Hell, but the darkest recesses of Hell. The first really are last!

Satan then went on to tempt man with the same "Wanna-Be-God" rush. He promised Eve that if she would eat the forbidden fruit, she would be as God. She must have conveyed this whopper of a lie to her hubby, Adam, even as Religious Humanists are conveying the same lie to people still stupid enough to listen. Anyone who tempts others with the "Can-Be-God" lie is setting them up for a terrible fall. Adam and Eve then craved Divine status for themselves, as well as omniscience in the understanding of good and evil. (Genesis 3:5) They ate the fruit and died and thereby became the antithesis to God. They became like the Devil who is called by Jesus a liar, a thief and "The Murderer" from the beginning. (John 8:44)

When Adam and Eve ate the forbidden fruit, they were infected with Satan's genes. They passed on to their offspring more than just the propensity for bad teeth. They passed on Satan's character to their children and the greater propensity for really bad hearts. The first woman-in-labor, the very first time around, gave birth to a brother-killer. And so their first son murdered their second son. I sure hope that she didn't look at her husband and then be dumb enough to ask the question, "Where did we go wrong, for we brought them both up the same way?" See what the "Wanna Be God Rush" got the human race! We've lived with serial murders ever since called BTKs and abortionists.

Remember this if you remember anything about Satan and that is that he is the master gamester in the "Who Wants To Be God" game. He never plays the game for less than all, and will draw us in to do the same. All the while he risks nothing because he has already lost everything, while man risks everything and in so doing ends up losing all, too. There are no winners in the "Who Wants To Be God," game, only eternal losers. What Satan is really after in promising us godness is to make us devils like himself.

Man by nature has been bitten and poisoned by Satan's "Wanna-Be-God" fangs and venom. Then when smooth preachers come along and falsify the Word of God by their cunning words and tell people they can be gods, it stirs all the more their prideful "Wanna-Be-God" juices. Every man alive wants by nature to be a god unto himself.

You might be saying to yourself by now that you cannot imagine an angel such as Lucifer, who had it all angelically speaking, attempting to replace God and mount the Almighty's throne! But really now, haven't you done that? Haven't I done that? We all have! We all by nature are closer to Satan than we think. Each time we want to run our own lives and go our own ways, we declare that we are our own gods. The fact is that we all have competed with God. The arrogance of the time in which we live is unprecedented. Everyone seems to be running – not for president, but for God. No one is winning. No one ever has! No one ever will!

Surely we have learned by now, haven't we? Surely you would think that the church would be filled with people who now know better. Yet when their pastors stand before them telling them the biggest lie they have ever heard, and that is that they are gods, they still fall for it hook, line and sinker and thereby become co-conspirators with Satan in the biggest grievance ever committed against God. It is one thing to change God's name. It is quite another to steal His name and pretend to be Him. The most arrogant case of identity theft in human history! The God impersonators! For that very thing, Satan was cast out of Heaven, and Adam and Eve were cast out of Paradise. To those of you who have become part of this god-conspiracy, are you sure that you still want to be associated with it in even the slightest way?

PRAYING TO YOUR GOD-SELF

The man tied his lawn chair to a bunch of weather balloons filled with helium. This fella strapped himself into the chair and he only planned to go up a hundred feet or so. He had an anchor rope with other ropes tied to the chair which were held by "friends" who were supposed to hang on to the ropes as he went up. The only problem was that friends as a practical joke let go of the ropes, and when he got to the end of the main anchor rope it snapped. Up, up, up this fella goes in his lawn chair, sneakers and shorts. He didn't go up 100 feet, but rather, he went up 16,000 feet. Jetliners were flying by and radioing in saying that they had spotted a UFO. Upon closer examination they discovered that the weird looking UFO was a guy in sneakers and shorts tied to a lawn chair which was tied to balloons.

At 16,000 feet its gets very cold! It just so happened that he had taken with him a BB gun and he shot out as many of the balloons as he could one by one. What he didn't notice was that he was now falling to earth at a high rate of speed. By the mercy of God, the remaining balloons got caught in some tree branches, and believe it or not, he was saved uninjured.

When the bad is not corrected, it will always go from bad to worse. One would think that praying constantly to God in humble dependency upon Him would help man maintain the "Most Superior God – Most Inferior Man" distinction. Wrong! The Religious Humanists have all of that corrupted also. Wouldn't you just know it? Man's "Wanna-Be-God" spark always gets more and more fanned and enflamed by Satan's "Wanna-Be-God" fuel. The fire eventually spreads out of control, as is the case we are about to see. Only God can shoot these high flying god-players down, for there is no end to the heights that they will let themselves go.

What now follows is what these "Wanna-Be-God" seeds planted in humanity can do. Kenneth Copeland alleges that God spoke to him and said the following: "**PRAY TO YOURSELF, BECAUSE I'M IN YOUR SELF, AND YOU'RE IN MYSELF. WE ARE ONE SPIRIT,' SAITH THE LORD.**" (7) It was bound to happen. Every falsehood will surely be attended by a long train of even greater absurdities. Can you imagine this? Catholics pray to saints. Religious Humanists pray to themselves. Roman Catholics believe in the invocation of saints. Religious Humanists believe in the invocation of self. Why? Because according to Copeland, God is in us and we are in God, so that praying to yourself and praying to God are one in the same thing. I mean, take a good long look at this bazaar scene of yourself praying to yourself, which is the same as praying to God. Does anyone feel the need to ask, "What is wrong with this picture?"

First, nowhere in the Bible or in the teachings of Jesus Christ are we told to pray to ourselves in God or to God in ourselves. Zero! Zilch! Zippo! What Jesus commanded us to pray is, "Our Father Who art in Heaven." Nowhere are we commanded or even slightly encouraged to pray, "Our Father Who art in us," or, "Our Us who art in the Father."

But why would anyone think up such a thing? I will tell you why. Anything to erase the infinite distinction between God and man! Get them on the same level, even in prayer, so that prayer is no longer vertical but horizontal. Now you can pray to God or to yourself. Hollowed be Thy name! Hallowed be my name! What is the difference anyway? God and the gods! We are one spirit! Choose your prayer direction!

Religious Humanists identify themselves so strongly with being gods on earth that they need no longer pray to God in Heaven. Praying to their god-selves on earth is the same as praying to God in Heaven. I know that this not only borders on lunacy, it crosses the line. For those of you who are thinking of starting a ministry entitled "Horizontal Prayer," I would strongly recommend that you see a good Christian counselor first, and surely don't quit your day job just yet.

Second, really now, it is one thing to go around talking to yourself. I will admit that I have done that from time to time. In some instances I encourage myself in the undertaking of some project far too big for me by saying something like, "Come on, Bob, with God's help and guidance you need not be afraid. I can do all things through Christ who strengthens me" Or at times talking to and chiding myself for some bone-headed act by saying something like, "Boy Bob, what are you, brain dead?" Perhaps you have talked to yourself a time or two in like manner. Talking to myself is one thing. But praying to myself is quite another. You talk about a psycho-spiritual quantum leap. I think it is time to call 911!

Third, yes we are told by God's Word in I Corinthians 6:17,

"But the one who joins himself to the Lord is one spirit with Him."

However, being one spirit with the Lord Jesus does not erase the distinction between God and the believer! Nor does being one spirit with the Lord allow us to conclude that praying to self is the same as praying to God. That would be like saying because the husband and the wife have become one flesh (Genesis 2:24), they are so one that they can make love to themselves and thereby make love to each other. It would be like me going about the house kissing myself and telling my wife that I am really kissing her and showing her great affection. Or it would be like me talking to myself, and assuring my wife that I am communicating with her. It really now is time to call 911!

Fourth, can you even begin to imagine how spiritually impoverishing this whole thing is? There is nothing like reverential praying to the exalted Heavenly Father God that will bring those holy, lofty impressions of God upon a man's spirit! Are we then to suppose that praying to ourselves or even having that notion, will cause the same Awesome-God impressions and in the same proportion? Praying to God will make us God-centered, while praying to self will make us self-centered. Praying to God will give us God-awareness, while praying to self will give us self- awareness. This notion of praying to yourself is not only stupid, it terribly harmful, for it will erase the sense of God as the "Holy Other."

THE ONE AND ONLY

Many Religious Humanists, particularly in the modern Charismatic communities and on television, hold to the belief that Christians are little christs and little gods on earth. So many of those who embrace the little god and little christ stuff are prominent TV personalities – the "television gods." Benny Hinn states: **"WHEN YOU SAY, 'I AM A CHRISTIAN,' YOU ARE SAYING, 'I**

AM MASHIACH' IN THE HEBREW. I AM A LITTLE MESSIAH WALKING ON EARTH…YOU ARE A LITTLE GOD ON EARTH RUNNING AROUND." (8) Benny Hinn tells Christians that they are little messiahs and little gods running around on earth. Why running around I will never know. I suppose these little gods run around while the big God walks around. Of course if you are a god, you certainly wouldn't have to run after someone or run to somewhere. Why? I mean, let's cut to the chase here. Because a god, even a little one, would have to be omnipresent, which means he would not have to run to anywhere because he is already there. Then Hinn commands his audience: "SAY, 'I'M A BORN-OF-HEAVEN GOD-MAN. I'M A GOD-MAN. I AM A SAMPLE OF JESUS. I AM A SUPER-BEING.'"(9)

Where do we start? God have mercy! Here we go again – little messiahs and little gods and god-men and super-beings. We have dealt already with the contradictory adjective "little" being placed before God. Remember? Short skyscrapers! Miniature giants! Little gods! The only place that "little" is appropriate is little men, if I may borrow the words from Louisa May Alcott. Jesus looked at His disciples as a mother would look at her brood and said to them in John 13:33,

"Little children…."

It is obvious by now that Religious Humanism is overrun by God's little gods, and has no place for God's little children.

Now we have added to the false teaching that Christians are little gods, the equally false teaching that Christians are little messiahs, that is, little christs. As distinguished from big Christs I suppose. If we are big Christs, then that would be a big no-no! But as long as we are little christs, that makes it okay. Sort of like the difference between a little lie and a big lie. Just don't get caught telling a big lie. But if it is a little one, well, then it's okay. Sorry, the fact is that to say we are little christs is a little lie, and to say that we are big Christs is a big lie. Either way it is a lie! Even if we called ourselves teeny-weeny christs, it still is a big fat lie.

The Hebrew for Messiah is "Mashiah," and the Greek counterpart of Mashiah is "Xristos" or Christ. Nowhere does the Bible refer to Christians as Xristoses or Mashiahs, whether big or little. True, we bear Christ's name as "Christians" because we are Christ's followers. Furthermore it wasn't Jesus Christ who called His disciples "Christians." It was the enemies of Christ who first sneeringly got the title "Christians" attached to the back of Christ's devotees in Antioch. (Acts 11:26) It was more blame than fame. It was more taunt than tribute. It was more sneer than salute. So be it, we are humbled and thrilled to be called by His name. Call us anything you want, but be sure to call us Christians. It is the highest compliment anyone could ever give to us.

However, there is only one Christ and only one Messiah. Peter had it right when he honored Jesus by confessing in Matthew 16:16,

"...Thou art the Christ, the Son of the living God."

When Peter confessed Jesus to be "The Christ," Jesus called him blessed because that advanced confession was given to him by the Father in Heaven. (Matthew 16:17) And did you notice that Peter declared, "Thou art THE Christ!" Not a Christ! Not one of the Christs. The one and only Xristos! Knowing Peter then, if Benny Hinn would have called him a little christ, or a little messiah, Peter would have cut off one of his ears if not both. The definite article cancels out all other additions, options or possibilities. But Jesus warned us, didn't He, about false Christs arising in the last days? He said in Matthew 24:24,

"For false Christs and false prophets will arise and will show great signs and wonders, so as to mislead, if possible, even the elect."

Also, we must hasten to add that Jesus Christ is the one and only "God-Man!" The title "God-Man" has always been exclusively reserved in the historic Christian church for the incarnate Son of God. There are no god-men! There is only one Who is fully God Who became fully man, sin excepted. His name is Jesus Christ – the God-man! To erroneously call Christians "god-men" is again an attempt to put believers on the same level with the incarnate Son of God. Sample Christs! Sample god-men! And if Christians are god-men, then they would have to be a bunch of incarnated deities (born from above) and not regenerated sinners (born again).

Quickly about this superman-superbeing status of the Religious Humanists! Allow me to handle it this way, because honestly, right now I am getting tired. I am not feeling real supermanish! Remember in "Superman-The Movie" when Superman first revealed his superpowers to the world? Lois Lane was left dangling from a cable, high atop the Daily Planet newspaper building. She was screaming at the top of her lungs. Just as she begins her long fall to earth, Superman changes into his flashy red, yellow and blue outfit and swoops up to catch her in midair. "Don't worry, Miss," he assures her, "I've got you!" She exclaims, "You've got me, who's got you?" My sentiments exactly! I couldn't have put it better or even that good.

THE GOD-PLAYERS – THE OVER-ACTORS

Did you ever notice that those who think that they are little gods and little messiahs and little god-men always try to carry themselves with phony, staged supernatural flare. Perhaps that is why they get all dressed up in white suits for crusades. They try to give them-selves that aura of other-worldly godness that they believe about themselves, and that they want others to believe about them, too. Image is everything!

When I attended Calvin Theological Seminary of the Christian Reformed Church back in the 1960s, the would-be pastors (seminarians) were taught in the Hermeneutics Class that we should wear the most subdued clothing possible when we preached and ministered the Word of God, so as never to draw attention to ourselves and away from God and His Word. Good sound advice! Good stuff!

Today we have preachers and evangelists who appear as if they have stepped out of some *Theological Esquire Magazine.* Some of them wear enough jewelry on their bodies to start a jewelry store chain. They have enough grease in their hair to give a lube job to several cars. They wear blinding garments to draw attention to their imagined godlike status. Jamie Buckingham told the story of a well-known southern preacher who wore red socks, sequined trousers and a flashy sport coat on the pulpit platform. Then he would begin his message by praying, "God, hide me behind the cross." Not likely when you resemble a 4th of July fireworks display.

More than that, Jesus never laid His hands on people, healed them, and then knocked them down and pulled them up repeatedly as if they were human yo-yo's. Never! Jesus wasn't a showman! He is God and doesn't have to show off. Nor did His apostles puppetize people! Christianity always becomes a Nintendo Game in the hands of those who are smitten with a "Divinity-Complex." That's what happens when little boys dress up like and try to play god. They always overstate the part. They always overact their role! People will do that when they try to prove themselves to be what they are not. They embellish and exaggerate and thereby blow their cover.

A lie will always be clothed in exaggeration and overstatement. The fact is, all that they are really doing is playing a "Religious Puppets On A String" god-game with other people's lives. In contemporary Religious Humanism, we are now finding ourselves in a 3rd rate Broadway play called "The God Players."

If they only knew how they really appear. We read a rather humorous story in the Bible when young David was courageously about to go out and fight the giant Goliath. King Saul took David into his tent and put his own heavy 250 pound suit of armor on this 125 pound kid. Can you imagine how David looked in this clumsy and grossly-oversized war attire which was far too big and cumbersome for him? David must have looked like some children do when they try to dress up in their daddy's and mommy's clothing. What a sight! What a hoot! Grab the camera and get some pictures of this hilarious moment. All of these "God Players" should be featured on "America's Funniest Videos."

Furthermore, we make terrible gods. You had better thank God than I am not God, and I had better thank God that you aren't God either, even a little one, which would be a big disaster in either case. If you want to see the asininity and calamity of man trying to be God, and if the Bible has been unable to convince you of both, then rent the DVD of the film *Bruce Almighty*, and allow Jim Carrey to bring you into the hilarious comedy of man trying to be God. Religious Humanists are just as hilarious, though they don't know it. They owe it to themselves to view this film. They would perhaps then be freed of going around victimizing themselves and others with their "God-Kick" by watching this "God-Flick."

I am reminded in all of this of the principal in a high school who had an administrative post to fill. He promoted one of his teachers with 10 years of teaching experience to the position. When the announcement of the choice was made, a non-chosen teacher became terribly upset. She complained to the principal that the teacher of choice had only 10 years of experience, while she had 25 years. The principal responded to her by saying that she was wrong, and that she did not have 25 years of experience – rather, she had one year's experience 25 times.

Well then, we will just let God have the position of being God, for He has had an eternity of experience. As for me, it takes everything that God has put in me just to be God's man, and I have had many years of experience trying to be one. As a child of God, I have been making progress in my maturing as a man of God. And I must confess that I have more than enough challenge being a man of God, let alone trying to be a god-man.

MAN CREATED EQUAL WITH GOD

The late Kenneth Hagin Sr. was one of modern Christianity's first to put forth the Man-God-Equality doctrine as truth. He didn't so much join the Man-God-Equality parade, but rather led it by making claims about Adam and God standing together on the same level. You might call Hagin the modern drum major of the "Adam-Equal-With-God Marching Band!" He wrote: "**[MAN] WAS CREATED ON TERMS OF EQUALITY WITH GOD, AND HE**

COULD STAND IN GOD'S PRESENCE WITHOUT ANY CONSCIOUSNESS OF INFERIORITY…MAN LIVED IN THE GOD REALM. HE LIVED ON TERMS EQUAL WITH GOD… [THE] BELIEVER IS CALLED CHRIST…THAT'S WHO WE ARE; WE'RE CHRIST." (10)

You might be asking, and I hope that you are, "He can't be serious, can he?" Yes, I'm afraid he is serious. We are to believe that Adam as created had no sense of difference from or inferiority to God? He lived comfortably in the God realm as a God himself. Eyeball to eyeball with God! Even Steven! If you will Adam, after Eve's being created as his rib replacement, instantly stood up, beat his chest in Divine exaltation like some Edenic deified Tarzan, looked at God and yelled the Tarzanian yell, "Me God –You God!"

The Bible nowhere teaches anything of the kind. We read in Genesis 2:7,

"Then the Lord God formed man of dust from the ground…."

First, feel those words! Let them sink in. Read them again. Once more! The Lord God! Man of dust! God formed dusty man, but dusty man never formed God. Man came from a dirt hole, but God dug it. Are those the realities that describe the state of two co- equals and co-supremes? Are those the words about God and man standing on the same level? No consciousness of inferiority to God? Those are notions that are as far from the truth as your toes are from your nose. Does dirt look at or up to the dirt Maker? Does clay look up at or up to the Potter? Do people look at or up to Mount Rushmore? We are talking here about the eternal God as contrasted with dusty man who the second before he was made from dust was nothing. Let alone standing in God's presence without a conscious inferiority; if it wasn't for God Adam wouldn't have a leg to stand on.

Second, as fruit is dependent upon the tree and the branches while hanging upon them for its very life, so Adam-man is dependent upon his Creator for his very life and the Creator is not dependent upon the Adam-man for His life. We read in Acts 17:28,

"For in Him we live and move and exist, as even some of your own poets have said, 'For we also are His offspring.'"

We are dependent upon God for our very lives, movements and continuance, while He is not the least bit dependent upon us for His life, movement and continuance. Adam-man lives, moves and has his being in God, but nowhere do we read that God lives, moves and has His being in Adam-man. God lives in the God realm, and Adam-man lived in man realm. God lives in the Creator realm, and Adam lived in the creature realm. Don't tell me that Adam and Eve weren't saturated with a deep awareness of the immeasurable God-man distinction, and a deep sense of their inferiority to their infinitely superior God from the mere standpoint of the "Maker" and the "made," the "Life-Giver" and the "life-given," the "Un-begun" and the "begun."

Let's use another analogy for the totally "Independent One" and the completely "Dependent One," as if we needed another. The Bible says in Genesis 2:7,

> **"...and breathed into his nostrils the breath of life...."**

Let's take a very deep breath together here for a second and then exhale it totally, but don't take in another breath. Exhale and don't breathe! Gasp! Now having done that, we must honestly answer the question, "Is the breathed-into breather inferior to the Breath-Giver?" Every time I breathe through my nose or mouth, I realize that there would be no air to breathe in or out had not God, my lung-Maker, first blown and continues to blow into my nostrils the breath of life. No Divine Breath-Giver, then no human breather. Of course, Adam the breathed-into piece of dirt had a staggering awareness of the awesomeness of his Divine breath-giver.

So must we! Isaiah 42:5-6 says it best,

> **"Thus says God the Lord, Who created the heavens and**
> **stretched them out, Who spread out the earth and its**
> **offspring, Who gives breath to the people on it, and spirit**
> **to those who walk in it, 'I am the Lord....'"**

So much for the notion that while God breathed into Adam and got the human breathing process started, the succeeding generations of human breathers, including ourselves, breathe on our own. Read it again! Isaiah does not say that God only gave Adam breath. Rather he says that God gives breath to all of the people on planet earth. Ongoing present tense! His words are inspired and chosen carefully by the Holy Spirit, Who Himself breathed His Word into Isaiah.

There, He just blew breath into you again. Praise God that He just gave you another snoot full of air. He constantly gives us mouth to mouth resuscitation, even as He did to Adam. We don't only live by God's oxygen supply from day to day, but from breath to breath. Let's face it, we are all on life support, and God is the "Supporter" and we are the "supportees." Without God, we wouldn't know where our next breath is coming from. So then, inhale that into your dependent lungs and breathe on it!

Third, if Adam and God were on equal terms, as Hagin believed, then God would not have told Adam what he could or could not eat. God ordered Adam as follows in Genesis 2:16-17,

> **"From any tree of the garden you may eat freely; but from the tree of the knowledge of good and evil you may not eat...."**

After all, where does God come off drawing up Adam's menu if they were co-dieticians? If Adam and Eve were co-gods and co-equals, the least God should have done was get a consensus of opinion from His co-divines. I mean to say, who does God think he is telling His co-god what he may have for lunch and what he may not? If that was the case, Adam should have said to God, "Hey, since when do I need your approval for my eating preferences and habits? I will eat what I jolly well want, thank you." In fact, that is exactly what Adam did do, and he was not only immediately tossed out of the kitchen, he was tossed out of the house. The "Divine Approver" disapproved of the "Human Approvee's" meal selection, and kicked him out of "Eden Garden." Hey God, how can you do that, after all co-gods have co-ownership of Paradise! Since when does a God evict other gods?

Fourth, if Adam was on an equal basis with God, how could Satan have had such success in tempting him to be as God? Satan is despicable, but not dumb. Why would he try to lure man into what he already had? Absurd! Of course Adam and Eve had a deep consciousness of their inferiority to God. That is why Satan used it to bring them into that deadly covetousness of Godness. Once again Religious Humanism flies into the face of Scripture and crashes.

ADAM – SUPERMAN – ASTRONAUT

How can we help Religious Humanists drop their heretical God-self and Christ-self claims, and get them enrolled in Jesus' disciple-ship class for developing godliness and Christ-likeness? In order to do that we must go down deep to the taproot of their false belief system and yank it out. Easier said than done, because that rooting is strong and deep! We have already probed the taproot, but what follows shows its true shape not only, but how far this root grows once it gets started.

It goes all the way back again to their false claims about Adam. Follow along now! Benny Hinn states about Adam: "**(ADAM) WAS THE FIRST SUPERMAN THAT REALLY EVER LIVED...HE USED TO FLY...HE FLEW TO SPACE – WITH ONE THOUGHT HE WOULD BE ON THE MOON.**" (11) Well now, isn't that just super-duper! The prefix "Super" in the English language means "Above." Adam is called here the first "Superman." That is, the first "Above-Man" to walk on earth. Adam as created was not a mere man, a mere human. He was far above humanness according to certain Religious Humanists. Hence Superman – Adam the Above-man! Religious Humanism has a very serious case of "Super-Duper Adamitis." All of that, of course, to put forth the notion that all of those who are in Christ the second Adam, have above-man, super-man status, too! That is how it all fits together!

First, all of us in this modern society have overused, misapplied, and worn out the prefix "Super" to the extent that we don't have the slightest idea anymore what it means and to whom it alone truly and rightfully belongs. We all know how the super-phrases go: "Isn't that just super-duper! Oh, it was just so super-cool! He is such a super-guy. Let me tell you, he is super-fast. How are you? – Oh I am feeling super! Great, how about you? I am doing super, just super! You can really get some super-deals there!" Today we have super-sized burgers, superhighways, and oh yes, super-egos. Isn't that just super-neat? In Christianity as well, according to Religious Humanists, we have supermen and not just men. The entire concept of superness has been so abused and misapplied that it has become meaningless.

Let's get back on track here! In Biblical Christianity the prefix "Super" is exotic, not commonplace. It is rare, not random. It is exclusive property – it belongs to God alone. God alone is super-natural. God has the realm of the supernatural cornered. In fact, He is super-everything and man is super-nothing. That is why we read about God in Ephesians 4:6 (KJV),

"One God and Father of all, Who is above all, and through all, and in you all."

In order to be authentically super and thereby have supremacy over all as the only Super-Being, one has to be "Above all." God alone is the "Above All One!" He alone is the "Super-God!" If man was super-anything, then God would not be Super-everything and there-fore not Super-God. You simply cannot have two "Above Alls," for then neither would be the "Superior One."

Religious Humanists can add all of the super-duper descriptions to Adam that they want to. I have no doubt that Adam's ability and understanding before his fall into sin were vast and keen. But always human, limited, and never omniscient, omnipotent or omnipresent! All that Religious Humanists are doing is super-imposing upon man what alone belongs to God.

Second, you might even say that Adam was a "Common Garden-Variety Man." In fact, Adam, so far from being a super-man, was appointed by God to be the gardener and caretaker of the very dirt from which he was taken. How appropriate! We read in Genesis 2:15,

**"Then the Lord God took the man (Adam) and put him
into the Garden of Eden to cultivate it and keep it."**

God gave the first man his first job. Adam was ordered by God to cultivate and maintain the Garden of Eden and keep it in edenic splendor. He was the world's first landscaper and horticulturist. That was his distinguishing badge! Nothing wrong with that! I wish I had more of a green thumb myself. For Adam before the fall, it must have been a beautiful garden landscape to cultivate. Stunning fields! Lush meadows! Rich vineyards! No eyesores there! No unsightly weeds. No thorny bushes. Well, at least we will give him this much, he was Eden's super-intendent.

Third, more than that, Adam the Superman according to Benny Hinn became history's first astronaut, and with one super-thought he could fly to the moon. Have thought, will travel. All that Adam had to do was think, "Fly me to the moon," and he was there. Eden was earth's first Cape Canaveral! Roger, Eden!

The reasoning that is often used for this is that because Adam was given by God dominion over every living creature including birds (Genesis 1:26), therefore he certainly should be able to do what they do, but do it even better – out-fly them etc. With that kind of logic, and I use the term loosely, seeing that Adam had dominion over fish, I suppose that he was able to swim upstream with all of the sockeye salmon, arrive first at the spawning grounds and out-spawn them all. I really do smell something fishy around here. Ludicrous! There is nothing in the Bible to even faintly suggest that Adam could space-fly and space-walk, or that he was the first super-astronaut on the moon. You talk about adding to Scripture! We are back to Religious Humanism's fantasyland again.

THE GOD CLASS

Yet, Kenneth Copeland persists: "**MAN WAS CREATED IN THE GOD CLASS, NOT CREATED IN THE ANIMAL CLASS. HE'S IN THE**

GOD CLASS. HE HAS A UNIQUENESS ABOUT HIM THAT EVEN ANGELS DO NOT HAVE…ALL RIGHT, WE ARE GODS. WE ARE A CLASS OF GODS." (12) Like Satan, Religious Humanists will not allow themselves to be outclassed, not even by God. Tragic but true in this regard: **"WHILE CHRISTIANS ARE GOD-CONSCIOUS, RELIGIOUS HUMANISTS ARE GOD-CLASS-CONSCIOUS."**

According to Copeland, all you have to do to find God is to look Him up in the yellow pages under the classified-ad section entitled "Gods." There you will find Him listed amongst all of the other gods. However, there is just one huge problem here. Webster defines a "Class" as "A group of individuals ranked together as having the same status!" But God summarily declassifies Himself when He says in Isaiah 45:21,

> **"…and there is no other God besides Me, a righteous God and a Savior; there is none except Me."**

Then He states in Isaiah 45:22,

> **"…For I am God, and there is no other."**

No God-class exists. God is too singular, distinct and incomparable to be confined to or included in any classification whatsoever. There is no God class. There is only God!

According to Copeland, there were only three classes of beings in creation – the "Animal Class," the "Angel Class," and the "God Class." There was no "Human Class" of beings in creation! Even though God said, "Let Us make man in Our image." (Genesis 1:26) He did not say, "Let Us make gods in Our genus." However, for Religious Humanists, you were either created a dog, an angel or a god. God, the gods, the angels, and the dogs!

Now you are seeing where all of this heresy comes from and where it leads. Jesus did not die for humans who had fallen into sin. No, no! He came to earth to restore the fallen and disgraced gods to their god-class once again. In Christianity, Jesus restores sinners to fellowship with God. In Religious Humanism, Jesus restores the ex-gods to equal godness with God.

THE GODS WILL FALL

Think about this for a moment, in Secular Humanism men make and worship their gods, while in Religious Humanism men are the gods. Some of the gods that Secular Humanists have worshipped for years are money, financial institutions and financial markets. These man-made monetary gods of the Secular Humanists have now been brought into the church and are being worshipped by Religious Humanists as well. These money gods have begun to rot and fall apart like decaying, rotting wood.

Isn't it a remarkable sight that we are seeing these days? As the monetary class of gods of Secular and Religious Humanists are falling over and breaking their necks like ancient Dagon in the Bible, the financial priests of President Obama, led by the High Priest and Secretary of the U.S. Treasury, Timothy Geithner, are trying to prop the money-gods up. Sacrificing on the altars of the money-gods the multiplied trillions of dollars of present and succeeding generations of taxpayers, their hope is that their gods will rise up strong again. This tottering money-class of gods remind us of the craftsman of an idol-god of whom Isaiah 41:7 says,

"...And he fastens it with nails that it should not totter."

America now has a president and a regime who do not have a clue as to what America really is, what her true spiritual roots are, and what has made her so blessed over the centuries. It reminds me of the meeting of investors and the guest lecturer who said, "I want you to stop and think of the greatest single factor in the success of the United States." One man stood up and said, "Mass production – the assembly line – Henry Ford." Another man jumped up and said, "The mass information through the computers – Thomas Watson – IBM." Typical answers! Wrong, a thousand times wrong. The basis for all of America's freedom and prosperity is the God of the Bible Who she embraced and served from her very birth. He has been the greatest single factor in the success of America! She is now faltering because Washington D.C. and much of grass-roots America have turned their backs on God. Now we have a president who summarily disassociates America from the God in Whom she once trusted.

The God of Christianity, the God of historic America, the God to end all gods, doesn't allow competition. America and the world will be hearing from Jesus shortly. The day is fast approaching when God shall judge all idolaters, and put their idol-gods to shame. The money class of gods of Secular and Religious Humanists will totter and fall. In that day their former worshippers will throw away their financial gods like bad pennies. All of the failed money-gods of secular and religious America will finally be rejected by their former devotees who run in terror from the God. We read in Isaiah 2:20-21,

"In that day men will cast away to the moles and the bats
their idols of silver and their idols of gold, which they made
for themselves to worship, in order to go into the caverns of
the rocks and the clefts of the cliffs, before the terror of the
Lord and the splendor of His majesty, when He arises to
make the earth tremble."

What about that branch of Religious Humanism where men are the gods. They, too, shall totter and fall from their self-made thrones. In that great and terrible day, not one shall be left standing, but with Tom Hanks in *Castaway*, they will be forced to say, "I had absolutely no control over anything." Of course they never did. They just talked liked they did. The God and Father of our Lord Jesus Christ in the end shall be the only God left standing and ruling as God over all, blessed forever!

GODS DON'T DIE

Benny Hinn states: "IS HE GOD? ARE YOU HIS OFFSPRING? ARE YOU HIS CHILDREN? YOU CAN'T BE HUMAN! YOU CAN'T, YOU CAN'T!" (13) Again Hinn states: "GOD CAME TO EARTH AND TOUCHED A PIECE OF DUST AND TURNED IT INTO A GOD...ARE YOU A CHILD OF GOD? THEN YOU'RE DIVINE! ARE YOU A CHILD OF GOD? THEN YOU'RE NOT HUMAN." (14) Why not go all the way, seeing you have come this far? So Hinn states: "I AM NOT PART OF HIM, I AM HIM! THE WORD HAS BECOME FLESH IN ME. ARE YOU READY FOR SOME REAL REVELATION KNOWLEDGE...YOU ARE GOD." (15)

The Apostle Paul writing to Timothy states about God in I Timothy 1:17,

"Now to the King eternal, immortal, invisible, the only
God, be honor and glory forever and ever. Amen."

First, God is eternal, that is, He has no beginning and He has no end. He was never born, and He will never die! From everlasting to everlasting is how the Bible puts it. Psalm 90:2 states:

"...Even from everlasting to everlasting Thou art God."

God never started being and He will never stop being. Therefore anyone who claims Divinity must be beginningless, endless and deathless. If you will, he must be eternal.

We are told here by Hinn that as Christians, "You can't be human, you can't, you can't" Not only that, but we are told that we are God! Well then, we must conclude, "We can't die, we can't, we can't." For God cannot die, He is eternal, and if I am Him, I cannot die either. The problem is that these falsely divinized humans are without exception characterized by starts and stops, beginnings and endings, births and deaths. That is true of believers and unbelievers alike.

Read the birth announcements and the obituaries in the church bulletin. These god-mimics all one by one, through their eventual and inevitable deaths, prove themselves to be just a bunch of god-failures and god-dropouts one by one. Gods are dying every minute of every day, which is something that good little gods just don't do. They shouldn't even take naps, for God neither slumbers not sleeps. (Psalm 121:3-4) There is nothing more embarrassing and annoying than a sleeping, sucking air, snoring god fast asleep. After all, a god should be giving his children sleep (Psalm 127:2), and not keeping them awake. You just shouldn't have to shout to a sleeping, snoring god, "Honey-god, you're snoring, please roll over."

Are you ready for some real Bible-revelation knowledge? We read in Hebrews 9:27,

"Inasmuch as it is appointed unto all men to die once and after this the judgment."

That means that, "We can't be gods, we can't, we can't." Why? Because the Bible says about all men, "We must die, we must, we must." Not only that, we shall all be judged. Gods should never be judged, for God is the Judge.

Remember when you were a child and you watched *Sesame Street*! One of those *Sesame Street* shows aired on Thanksgiving Day and dealt with the subject of death, so as to try and explain the death of one of the Sesame Street's characters. The special show was televised on Thanksgiving Day so that both moms and dads could watch with their children. In one segment, Big Bird walks in on camera and says to the cast, "I just drew pictures of all my grown-up friends on Sesame Street and I'm going to give them to you." He passed out sketches and the cast members responded with their oohs and aahs over the remarkable likenesses.

Big Bird was left with Mr. Hooper's picture. Big Bird said, "I can't wait till he sees it. Say, where is he? I want to give it to him." One cast member explained, "Big Bird, don't you remember? We told you...Mr. Hooper died.

He's dead." Big Bird said, "Oh yeah, I remember. Well…I'll give it to him when he comes back." Another cast member got up from her chair, touched Big Bird and said, "Big Bird, Mr. Hooper is not coming back." Then Big Bird asked innocently, "Why not?" A cast member explained, "Big Bird, when people die, they don't come back." (16) I've got news for you, yes they do, every one of them in the resurrection to eternal life or eternal death.

TV personalities take on a kind of mystical, eternal quality to children. To adults, too! But the grim reaper got Mr. Hooper, too. Death is the universal leveler. So, too, all self-appointed gods shall be proven to be but men in the end. All in all, it is so tragic watching so many in Religious Humanistic circles counterfeiting Divinity. And then after all of their god-strutting and god mumbo-jumbo, they die as their grand climax! Death always makes short and final work of the god-players.

Second, I Timothy 1:17 tells us that God is immortal. That means that He is forever imperishable and incorruptible. He is never in decline. He never decays, weakens or shrivels. No fillings, braces, crutches or wheel chair. There is no death process in God. How man frets over his failing body. We have been for some time now in an aerobic frenzy in America. Man trying to sweat, pump, and grind himself into immorality. It is a losing battle. Truly man cannot run from his mortality for he is rotting while he is running. Everyone drops dead in the run for their lives. Well at least give them credit that they died trying.

Some years ago a group called "People Forever International" was founded by a certain Charles Brown. At one time, this organization had adherents in 16 countries. PFI members believed that they could cheat death, and like gods, live eternally. This Charles Brown fellow experienced what he came to refer to as a "Cellular Awakening" while engaged in some sort of meditation. Brown claimed that we are a species that has the ability to perpetually renew itself. His idea was that by tapping into the intelligence of our cells we can prolong life indefinitely. Of course, he was quick to add that this rejuvenation is an individual process, and that some are more adept at it than others. (17)

Yeah sure! The problem was that the PFI membership had to be constantly replaced because the "Forever People" proved to be temporal after all – they all continued to fall apart and die. Practice does not make perfect! Their name was declared a misnomer by each wake which took them from PFI to PUM – "People Universally Mortal." Thank God for the glorious promise of I Corinthians 15:53 for every believer in Christ,

"For this perishable must put on the imperishable, and this mortal must put on immortality."

Third, God is invisible. I Timothy 1:17 says so! We read about Jesus Christ in Colossians 1:15,

"And He is the image of the invisible God, the first born of all creation."

What part of invisible don't we understand? We read in John 4:24,

"God is spirit, and those who worship Him must worship in spirit and in truth."

Benny Hinn, Kenneth Copeland and the Mormons contradict these express givens of the Bible. They teach instead that God is visible and physical. Benny Hinn asks and answers the question: **"WHAT DOES GOD THE FATHER LOOK LIKE? LIKE THAT OF A MAN...GOD HAS THE LIKENESS OF FINGERS AND HANDS AND A FACE."** (18) Kenneth Copeland describes God as follows: **"A SPIRIT BEING WITH A BODY, COMPLETE WITH EYES, AND EYELIDS, EARS, NOSTRILS, A MOUTH, HANDS AND FINGERS, AND FEET."** (19) It all sounds pretty much like Mormonism which teaches the following: **"FIRST, WE BELIEVE THAT GOD IS A BEING WITH A BODY IN FORM LIKE A MAN'S; THAT HE POSSESSES BODY, PARTS AND PASSIONS; THAT IN A WORD, GOD IS AN EXALTED, PERFECTED MAN."** (20)

Of course the Bible talks about the face of God. (Psalm 27:8) It speaks of the nostrils of God. (Psalm 18:15) It refers to the feet of God. (Psalm 18:9) How can man relate to an invisible Spirit? That is not easy! We are such five-sense creatures. Therefore, God speaks to us in anthropomorphisms to help us relate to Him – God conveyed in human terms. God throughout His word coos to us as babies! He condescends to us in human-word pictures. Jesus called Himself the door of the sheep. (John 10:7) That does not mean that He is a literal door hanging on hinges to be opened and shut at the whims of men. He likens Himself to the door because He alone opens to us the safety of His sheepfold and eternal fellowship with God.

Religious Humanism does more than a nip and tuck on God. It gives God not only a nose job; it attaches imaginary prosthetics to His imaginary body. God looks just like us. Pardon the pun, but now we are on equal footing. When you've seen one god, you've seen them all! Where do we get such notions from? Not from the Bible I assure you.

Here again is what is behind this. When you humanize Divinity, you are then in lock step with those who deify humanity. If you will put a man's face on God, you are in lock step with those who put God's face on man. All distinctions between God and man are then erased. Divinity is humanized and humanity is deified. Now you're getting it!

Christ and Christians are look-alike gods. That way when God pulls you over for sinning, you can flash your god-card with your god-picture. God then says, "He can't be wrong, he's my co-god." And even as there is honor amongst crooks, there is a mutual respect and understanding amongst the gods. God, His holiness, His righteousness, and His justice are no longer impressive or imposing when you are a god yourself. The fear of God becomes non-existent. That is why confession of sin and asking God for forgiveness in the "We Are Gods" church services is seldom if ever done anymore. After all, the gods seldom blow it anyway. For the most part they live sinless lives. And if they do goof up, they will just shake hands as gods with God, and the rare infraction is forgotten.

TO BE LIKE JESUS – OUCH!

We are saved to be Christ-like! Paul says in Romans 8:29,

> **"For whom He foreknew, He also predestined to become conformed to the image of His Son, that He might be the first-born among many brethren."**

Not being conformed to the world, but being conformed to and entering into the character of Christ is the process as well as the grand purpose of our being made new creatures in Him. It is the ultimate purpose of man being saved. Only then can we glorify God! That is what maturing in the Christian life is all about. The old song puts it best:

> **"To be like Jesus, to be like Jesus, all I ask is to be like Him; all through life's journey, from earth to glory, all I ask is to be like Him."**

Listen to what God demands of us in II Peter 3:18,

> **"But grow in the grace and knowledge of our Lord and Savior Jesus Christ...."**

How then do we mature into Christ-likeness? By coming to know Jesus more and more intimately day by day! No spiritual growth hormones will get the job done. And every bit of spiritual growth in our lives which results in Christlikeness comes from gracious revelations to us about Jesus Christ by the Holy Spirit through the Word of God. Every time there is a spiritual growth-spurt of Christ-likeness in our lives, it is because by God's grace we have come to know Jesus better on a much more personal and deeper level. The point being that the more we come to know Jesus personally, the more personally we become like Jesus.

However, becoming Christ-like and claiming to be little christs are two totally different realities. The former is Christianity, while the latter is Religious Humanism. They are two completely different belief systems. Not only that, but Christianity is by far the most difficult of the two. Why? Claiming to be Christ is instant self-deification – the shortcut to godness. However, there is no shortcut to and nothing instantaneous about becoming like Christ. It is a lifelong process, and it is painful at the very least. Christ's character has never been built into a believer in a day, and never without a great deal of spiritual molding, chiseling and sandpapering by God on our lives. Ouch!

When the contractor builds a house, he comes with all the various tools of the trade, like a hammer, a saw, a chisel, a planer, and lots of sandpaper. Listen to the noise, and see the sawdust fly. So, too, the Master Divine Contractor – God the Holy Spirit, as He builds us into Christlikeness, cuts away with His skill-saw of sanctification all of our unsightly protrusions – zzz, zzz, zzz, zzz. zzz. Sometimes through severe trials and stern rebukes from others, He literally chops those protrusions off. Oh that smarts! To enable us to fit the Christ-pattern, He continues sawing and in the process often hits knots of resistance and rebellion in us. He applies the needed pressure to cut through the hardness in us, and oh does that smart! Then some sandpaper applied to those rough spots in our personalities. Miss Sandpaper at your place of work rubs you the wrong way. God put her there so that you can learn how to manifest the love and forgiveness of Christ where and when it really counts. Miss Sandpaper is never alone. The construction crew includes Johnny Jab, Priscilla Poke and Harry Hammer. No pain, no gain in the process of Christlikeness! All that we might be to the image of Jesus Christ. (Romans 8:29)

It is like the time that Lucy says to Charlie Brown, "Adversity builds character Charlie Brown. Without adversity in life, a person could never mature or face up to all the things in life." Charlie Brown then asks Lucy, "What things?" Lucy responds, "More adversity." Lucy is right! We all are a work in progress and the process will go on all of our life long. May the beauty of Jesus be seen in me, all his wonderful passion and purity; O Thou Spirit Divine, all my nature refine, till the beauty of Jesus be seen in me.

Religious Humanists think that they can skip the entire molding and maturing process of being built into Christ-likeness, and just jump right into being little gods, little christs, little messiahs! It is much easier that way. "Insty-Gods!" "Insty-Christs!" How convenient! Just claim to be Christ and blow your God-trumpet with-out having to practice your musical scales or strengthen your pucker.

And blow their god-horns they do! No sound has ever been so shrill and discordant on earth or to Heaven as these sounds are today. Listen to Benny Hinn blow his messianic horn with the same noisome and abrasive sounds that have become all too familiar to us by now. He blares: **"WHEN YOU SAY, 'I AM A CHRISTIAN,' YOU ARE SAYING, 'I AM MASCHIACH' IN THE HEBREW. I AM A LITTLE MESSIAH WALKING ON EARTH."** (21) Speaking of walking on earth, the Bible tells us that Enoch walked with God. (Genesis 5:22-24) You see, Christians walk on earth with God, while Religious Humanists walk on earth as gods. Christians walk on earth with Christ, while Religious Humanists walk on earth as christs. In summary, Christians are **"IMITATORS OF CHRIST."** Religious Humanists are **"IMITATION CHRISTS."**

Biblical Christians walk with God through prayer! Religious Humanists walk as gods through pronouncements. Biblical Christians pray humble petitions. Religious Humanists issue divine fiats. Have you ever noticed that? Perhaps you have felt uneasy about it, but you couldn't quite lay your finger on why. If for instance you watch Evangelist Richard Roberts closely on his nightly television program entitled *The Hour of Healing*, you will discover something very revealing. What he calls prayer for the sick is very interesting. He may begin to pray with his eyes shut, but in a matter of a few seconds, his eyes are opened wide and what began as prayer is suddenly turned into giving orders and commands to the sickness to leave. A huge segment of Religious Humanists have replaced praying to God with giving orders as gods. They call it prayer, but it isn't. They have totally lost the art of praying, i.e. supplication, entreaty, and petition! They really don't know how to pray anymore, for it is something that gods just don't do.

But we must yet ask the question, "Can people actually grow into Christlikeness?" You respond, "I don't think I could ever pray a prayer of forgiveness for those who crucified me." Jesus, according to Luke 23:34 prayed on the cross that seemingly unthinkable prayer for those who were killing Him. He prayed,

"…Father, forgive them; for they do not know what they are doing…."

He asks His Heavenly Father to deal with His killers mercifully in forgiveness and not wrathfully in judgment. He wanted His murderers to be saved, and for them He was praying and dying so that they could be. He loved His enemies, and if we are Christlike, we will love our enemies and pray for God to deal with our enemies in mercy, too.

For Jesus to pray this prayer for forgiveness meant that He had already done so in His heart! What good does it do to lift a prayer to God's throne of grace in Heaven for the forgiveness of our enemies when our spirits are the contradiction to it on earth?

But can believers in their heart of hearts ever rise to that level of Christlikeness? Some would say, "My, my, Jesus is a tough act to follow." First of all it wasn't an act, and secondly God would never require us to be like His Son unless He was sure that His grace would enable us to be so. And that is why Jesus cuts us no slack in Matthew 6:14-15,

"For if you forgive men for their transgressions, your Heavenly Father will also forgive you. But if you do not forgive men, then your Father will not forgive your transgressions."

God so uncompromisingly requires us to be like His Son in this regard that He has made the forgiveness of our enemies the indispensable condition of His forgiving us.

If our goal is to be more and more like Christ, we will never here on earth reach the point where we can say, "This is it. This is as far as I can go in being Christlike. I am so much like Christ now that I am another christ." In this great quest, there is never a winding down, only and always a moving on. It is a long and a severe discipline. The most dedicated and wisest of God's children have found it to be the chief and most formidable task of their entire lives.

The Christian life is not just easing down the road into Christlikeness. Those who say about the Christian life, "No problem," are not living in reality. There will be setbacks, and at times the enemy of our souls will trip us up and cause us to speak and act more like him than like Christ. There still are days that I look more like a wounded warrior being carried by stretcher bearers, beat up by Satan and my lingering carnality, than I do a mighty conqueror in Christ. Therefore, no matter what, as my dear friend Pastor Burt Evans often said, "We must grab ourselves by the nap of the neck." We must ask God to forgive us and then we must get tough on ourselves and determine with the Apostle Paul in Philippians 3:14 to press on toward the goal of Christlikeness. And as Paul states in Ephesians 4:13,

> **"Until we all attain…to a mature man, to the measure of the stature which belongs to the fullness of Christ."**

THE POWER OF LOVE – OR – THE LOVE OF POWER

You know what it is all driven by don't you? Power! The lust for power! It is all about power! Religious Humanism is saturated with the love of money and the love of power. It is power that is the deciding issue in every situation. Lucifer knew this and as He watched God manifest His omnipotence, it made him power-mad.

Religious Humanism is driven by the same power-hunger. Listen again to Benny Hinn: **"SAY 'I'M A BORN-OF-HEAVEN GOD-MAN. I'M A GOD-MAN. I'M A SAMPLE OF JESUS. I'M A SUPER-BEING.'"** (22) And again: **"I'M BENNY JEHOVAH."** (23) Once more: **"WE ARE ALL LITTLE GODS…WITH ALL THE POWER OF GOD…EVERYTHING THAT JESUS EVER WAS."** (24)

We have at length examined the God-complex of Religious Humanism. But I want you to feel the power-hunger here. Anytime we hear people who refer to themselves as "Super-Beings," what is being stated is that they view themselves as "Super-Powers." To the extent that they will actually say about themselves things like Benny Hinn says about himself, "I Am Benny Jehovah." And, "I am a little god with all the power of God." In other words, "I Am An Omnipotent One." Power-lust is the strong driving force behind this pretense. Christianity believes in the power of Godliness. Religious Humanism believes in the power of godness.

At this point, I must tell you a Bible story which illustrates man's lust for spiritual power. It happened in the 1ˢᵗ century A.D., where we find one of the early Religious Humanists of church history. The Apostles in Jerusalem had heard that people in Samaria were accepting Jesus as their Savior in response to the miracle-filled ministry of an evangelist, Philip by name. The Holy Spirit was accomplishing astounding things through Philip. Those who were possessed with demons were being delivered, and the paralyzed and lame were being healed. (Acts 8:7) The Bible tells us in Acts 8:8 that there was much rejoicing in that city.

When the church at Jerusalem heard that the Samaritans were accepting the

Word of God, they sent Peter and John to Samaria to assist Philip's evangelistic crusade by praying with the new converts to Christ, as well as bringing them into the baptism and fullness of the Holy Spirit. As they laid their hands upon the new disciples of Christ and prayed for them, these baby Christians were powerfully filled with the Spirit of God.

What happened was apparently most demonstrative in the lives of those people. So much so that a man by the name of Simon, a magician, who had been amazing the people of Samaria with his witchcraft and black magic for some time, saw that the Holy Spirit was powerfully coming upon the people of Samaria through the laying on of the hands of Peter and John. We read about Simon's reaction to all of this in his words to Peter and John in Acts 8:18-19,

> "…**he offered them money**, saying, 'Give this authority to me as well, so that everyone on whom I lay my hands may receive the Holy Spirit."

Simon the magician coveted this miraculous Holy Spirit power so strongly that he eagerly wanted to buy it. We cannot buy anything from God. This is always the glaring and tragic error in Religious Humanism, namely, that the role of money is prominent in order to become the recipients of the miracle blessings of God. Always! Peter and John came down hard on Simon the Magician for thinking that he could buy the power of God, or any other blessing of God for that matter. Peter said to him in Acts 8:20,

> "…**May your silver perish with you**, because you thought you could obtain the gift of God with money."

Never have more pointed and relevant words ever been spoken. Like a laser-guided missile they strike today at the heart of modern Religious Humanism.

Simon's magical prowess had so impressed the people of Samaria that we are told in Acts 8:10 that they called him:

"THE GREAT POWER OF GOD."

This is a Religious Humanist's dream come true, i.e. being called "The Great Power of God!" Religious Humanists live on these Divine-power steroids. It made Simon the Magician one of the headliners on the Samaria Strip, and one of the hottest tickets in town. If you were in Samaria, you just had to take in "Simon's Magic Show." "The Great Power of God" was being given top billing.

He was the 1st century David Copperfield of Las Vegas. Oh yes, Divine power! Raw power! All power! Power-power! The Great Power of God! Simon ate up the accolades, and in so doing sent up a challenge to the omnipotent God.

God has His ways! Lately Simon had been out-miracled and over-powered by God through Philip and the signs and wonders that followed Philip's ministry. Simon couldn't keep up with or compete with Philip. Simon, "The Great Power of God," had become "Simon the Also Ran," and even worse, "Simon the Has Been."

We must see right here that the greatest weakness of Religious Humanism is its obsession with power. That which more than anything makes vast segments of Religious Humanism a counterfeit Christianity is its power-madness. In Religious Humanism, God is power. In Christianity, God is love. (I John 4: 8-16) Nowhere do we read in the Bible that God will ask us in the final judgment about how many acts of power we performed. Not a word! Not a syllable! Not a whisper! That cracks the Religious Humanist's measuring stick for true Christianity completely in half.

Jesus said in the Sermon on the Mount, Matthew 7:22-23,

> **"Many will say to Me on that day, 'Lord, Lord, did we not prophesy in Your name, and in Your name cast out demons, and in Your name perform many miracles? And then I will declare to them, 'I never knew you; depart from Me, you who practice lawlessness.'"**

Do you see what is happening here? The religious were sure that God embraced them as His own because of all of their mighty acts done in His name. Surely they would have their pictures in Heavens Hall of Fame! They were sure that their mugs would be featured on the Heaven's Wall of Fame reserved for the greatest "Miracle Home Run Hitters" of all time. When it came to serving God, they thought that they were top-notchers. As it turned out, God didn't even know their names. Oh of course He did, for He knows everyone's name, but not on a personal basis. In that sense He had never heard of them. In their self-estimate, that was as unimaginable as the modern baseball gods never having heard of Babe Ruth, or the modern church world never having heard of Benny Jehovah.

What we are told loud and clear by Christ is that in the judgment we will be confronted with how many acts of love we did or did not do, i.e. whether or not we clothed the naked, fed the hungry, showed hospitality to the stranger, and visited the sick and imprisoned. (Matthew 25:31-46) The judgment will be so mundane to the mighty! The whole point being that God is not first of all interested that we have His hand of power, but that we have His heart of love. And again, the infallible test of true Christianity is the power of love, while the infallible test of Religious Humanism is the love of power.

CHRISTIANS – INCARNATIONS OR REGENERATIONS

It was Michelangelo who prayed, "God, grant that I may always desire more than I can accomplish." A worthy prayer indeed! There is another and equally urgent prayer that must be prayed these days in the modern church, "God, grant that I may never claim to be more than I am, or someone that I am not." Religious Humanists are the antithesis to that prayer.

Speaking about claiming to be what I am not, listen to these claims by Kenneth Hagin Sr., "**EVERY MAN WHO HAS BEEN BORN AGAIN IS AN INCARNATION AND CHRISTIANITY IS A MIRACLE. THE BELIEVER IS AS MUCH AN INCARNATION AS WAS JESUS OF NAZARETH**." (25)

New Agers like Shirley Maclaine and Hindus believe in reincarnation. It is another lie! God tells us in Hebrews 9:27,

> **"And inasmuch as it is appointed for men to die once and after this comes judgment**."

We live once, we die once and we are judged once. Then it is either eternal Heaven or eternal Hell. God offers each one of us just one try at life. If we had nine lives to live, this one would lose its significance. A man can be very nonchalant about this life if he expects a shot at others. He can make up for the mess the next time around. Sorry, no rain checks on a sin-drowned life.

Religious Humanists believe in incarnations and not just "The Incarnation of the Son of God." We as believers are all gods and like the Son of God we have become incarnate gods. The same thing holds true for incarnationism as it does for reincarnationism, and that as if there are multiple incarnations, the incarnation of Jesus Christ not only loses its significance, it becomes totally indistinct. Then Jesus is just one of the incarnated gods.

I wouldn't deal at length with this heresy except for the fact that it is rampant though subtle in its manifestations. I bumped into something like this recently at a funeral home of all places, where a very religious fella came up to me out of the blue and said, "You know don't you that we existed with God in eternity and entered into a covenant with Him before we came to earth." I said, "No, I hadn't noticed!" I was there to express my sympathy to the bereaved, and not get into a discussion or argument with an incarnationist.

To the reincarnationists I must say, "There has never been a prior you, and there will never be a genetically altered you in this world after your death in the shape of an eagle or a beagle." To the incarnationists I must say, "There has never been an eternally prior you, let alone a pre-existent Divine you. You are not incarnations." Our only pre-existence was in the mind of God! And there has only been one incarnation, and that was the Son of God becoming the Son of Man. Only one! There has never been and never will be another incarnation.

And while we are at it, if Hagin wants to talk about himself and every Christian as an incarnation, he and they would have to have been conceived and born of a virgin. Hagin would then be the divine-human offspring of a virgin conception and birth. Today's DNA testing would disprove every incarnation. Furthermore, they would have to be born without sin if their incarnations were to be authentic. Then they would not have to be saved by Jesus seeing that they are sinless. That is exactly why you will hear these incarnate christs say things like, "I can't remember the last time I sinned." How about right now, for you just lied your brains out.

Only the Son of God was incarnated, i.e. God clothed in human flesh and blood! We read of it in John 1:14,

"And the Word became flesh, and dwelt among us, and we beheld His glory, glory as of the only begotten from the Father, full of grace and truth."

Christians are not incarnations. Christians are regenerations. Religious Humanists talk about being incarnated. Christians talk about being regenerated. Religious Humanists talk about being incarnate Christs. Christians talk about being regenerated in Christ. Only Jesus Christ came from Heaven to earth. Christians are sinners who the incarnate Christ saved from Hell for Heaven.

Only God came to earth in human form. He left Heaven's marvel and entered earth's misery. That is what the word "Advent," which we use so often at Christmas, actually means – "To Come To." God the Son came to us from Heaven as a man named Jesus, and lived for 33 years in what we refer to as the "Holy Land." We call it the "Holy Land" because the Holy Son of God was incarnated there, lived there, walked there, ministered there, died for human sin there, arose from the dead there, and ascended into Heaven from there. No one else ever has or ever will have an "Advent." No one else ever has or ever will transform any earthly real estate into a "Holy Land." Every land that man has set his foot on has become unholy.

Mark Connelly in his classic play *Green Pastures*, has the angel Gabriel walking on the stage with his horn under his arm, and he approaches the Lord Who is in deep thought. God is troubled about what is happening to His people on earth. God is also troubled because He had sent his prophets and messengers who the people refused to listen to. God is troubled about humanity's sinful ways. Gabriel then offers to blow his horn – the final trumpet – and end the whole thing. But the Lord brushes the horn away from Gabriel's lips. Gabriel then presses the Lord as to what He is going to do. God says to Gabriel, "I am not going to send anybody this time. I am going Myself." (26) How dare they cheapen and disgrace the super-gracious incarnation of God by calling themselves incarnate christs?

FAITH – MATERIAL SUBSTANCE OR SPIRITUAL DYNAMIC

At the outset of now an extended discussion about faith, you must sense by this time that Religious Humanism is all about equating Christians and Christ. So we are not surprised by the false proposition about faith that Religious Humanists put forward, and it is this, that God lives and works by faith and Christians live and work by faith. There it is! Everything God does is faith-based and everything Christians do is faith-based. These are the internal wheels that move this entire misguided theological system. This is the epicenter of Religious Humanism, i.e. presenting the gods of faith and the God of faith as faith co-equals.

Now then, Kenneth Copeland states: **"FAITH WAS THE RAW MATERIAL SUBSTANCE THAT THE SPIRIT OF GOD USED TO FORM THE UNIVERSE."** (27) Laying aside for the moment the statement that the Spirit of God faith-formed the world, which we will address at length later, faith is defined here as **"RAW MATERIAL SUBSTANCE."** Raw is a word which suggests something like unprocessed crude oil! Material substance sounds like some sort of faith tablet that the pastor can prescribe to a parishioner who is struggling with doubt. You know, "Take two of these faith tablets every four hours and call me in the morning." Faith by this definition is something that you can see, feel and handle. I am surprised the Religious Humanists don't come up with faith pills that people can send for like prayer cloths, of course with an offering "tucked in" your request letter. Placebo religion!

Words are critically important. Don't be misled by such words about faith. Why? Because the fact is that faith is a spiritual dynamic and not a raw-material substance. That is why we read in II Corinthians 4:13,

"But having the same spirit of faith…."

213

It does not say: "But having the same raw-material substance of faith." Faith is a spiritual dynamic produced in us by the working of God's Spirit in our spirits. And when we are full of the Holy Spirit we will also be full of the spirit of faith. We read in Acts 11:24 about a man named Barnabas,

"for he was a good man, and full of the Holy Spirit and of faith...."

Those who are Holy Spirit-filled are faith-filled. Those who are not fully of the Holy Spirit will not be faith-filled.

To call faith a raw-material substance is to grotesquely distort Christian faith beyond recognition, even as to put a human face on God grotesquely distorts Him. Let's "face" it, to put a nose a mouth, ears and hair on God is even more degrading than putting an ape's head on man. But it should not surprise us that a material God would then require a material faith in order to make contact with Him. In both cases, the spiritual is materialized. Religious Humanism not only renames, replaces and redesigns God; it renames, replaces and redesigns faith.

The noun for "faith" in the New Testament Greek language is "pistis" which most literally means "faithfulness," and "steadfastness." The verb for "to believe" in the New Testament Greek is "pisteuo" which most literally means "to adhere to," "to rely on," and "to trust in." Faith is both noun and verb. It is something that we must both have and do.

How does the Holy Spirit produce faith (steadfast trust) in the heart of man? Nothing abracadabra here! No hocus-pocus or sleight of hand. No sending in for faith pills. No money orders for faith. We receive that steadfast adherence to, reliance upon and trust in God through the hearing of the Word of God. We read in Romans 10:17,

"So faith (pistis) comes from hearing, and hearing by the Word of Christ."

Newsweek and *Time* magazines and most of the major TV networks will prevent faith, and if you already have faith, they have the great potential to weaken and even destroy your faith. Wolf Blitzer and Anderson Copper of CNN aren't exactly "Swift Boat Veterans For Truth" or "Faith Boosters." The evolutionistic Discovery Channel is more interested in what cavemen wrote on cave walls than on what God wrote on the tables of stone. Today's news and documentary channels are nothing more or less than faith traps, and once they get a hold of you, God will seem more and more remote, the narrow path less and less discoverable, until you barely have anything left of God in your life. We are told that 70% of Christian young people who go to secular colleges and universities have their faith severely weakened or destroyed. Nor will a message from the current president strengthen your faith in or draw you closer to Jesus Christ.

Only staying in the Bible, having prayer and fellowship in true Bible churches, and listening to pastors who preach the whole counsel of God, will birth and strengthen faith in you in the midst of these anti-faith, anti-God apostate last days. The Word of God is the only "Safe-Faith Refuge." Today's "Socially Correct" and "Culturally Correct" Religious Humanism churches will by diluting and cherry picking the Word of God prevent truth faith and corrupt the faith that you already have.

GOD OF FAITH OR FAITH IN GOD

The teaching that God lives and works by faith is so twisted that you do not need much light in order to discover its deformity! Those that believe this false teaching ought to blush in the dark for doing so. Nowhere does the Bible teach, suggest, or even hint that God has faith, lives by faith, or operates by faith. It is a total Religious Humanism fabrication. The fact of the matter is that if God has faith, and if God lives and acts by faith, then God is not God, for that makes Him a believer and not the to-be-believed-in One.

According to Hebrew's 11:1,

"Now faith (pistis) is the assurance of things hoped for, the conviction of things not seen."

Let's start with the latter half of the Bible's definition of faith first – faith is the conviction of things not seen. We read about God in Hebrews 4:13,

"And there is no creature hidden from His sight, but all things are open and laid bare to the eyes of Him with whom we have to do."

Everything is seen by God. All things! Nothing is hidden from God. There are no hiding places from God. Adam and Eve played the first hide-and-go-seek game with God. (Genesis 3:8) They even tried to cover their nakedness with fig leaves sewed together. (Genesis 3:7) What a wasted camouflage! The hiding was over before the seeking began, and their camouflaged pants and skirt went out of date before they had been sown together. It may be fun to play hide-go-seek games with your kids, but God's kids find out very quickly that there is no fun in playing hide-go-seek games with God. Every place we hide He is there already.

When God called out to Adam in Genesis 3:9, "Where are you," He was not saying to him, "Come out, come out, wherever you are!" What He wanted Adam to admit to himself was where in his sinful state he now was in his relationship to God – cut off from His Creator! So visible is everything and everyone to God, that the Bible tells us that everything and everyone is wide open and laid bare before Him.

Faith therefore has no place in God! They are contradictions! Why would God Who sees all things need faith which is the conviction of things not seen? Thinking of God with faith is like picturing Him as a blind man walking with His seeing-eye dog named Faith. The requirement laid down by God for Christians in this time-space dimension is stated in II Corinthians 5:7,

"For we walk by faith, not by sight."

It must be said of God in the eternal dimension on the other hand that,

"He walks by sight, not by faith."

Faith for God would be a totally useless and demeaning thing. In fact why would God need faith when He not only sees all things, but sees through them, too?

But our discussion of faith is not yet complete. According to Hebrews 11:1, faith is not only the conviction of things not seen, but it is the assurance of things hoped for. God neither lives by faith or by hope. It makes no sense in either case. Hope is the only thing that can take a man out of a dismal present into the promise of a brighter future. God is not in a dismal present awaiting and hoping for a brighter future. God is eternal light, and in Him there is no darkness! God never has a dark day hoping that things will brighten up tomorrow.

More than this, there is no future to God, for God is eternal. There is no yesterday or tomorrow in eternity, and therefore there is no past nostalgia or future hope with God. God is eternal, and eternity is timeless. It is truly mind boggling that everything is already fully and perfectly accomplished before God. He sees the beginning, the middle and the end all at once. So we read words like these in Romans 8:24,

"…but hope that is seen is not hope; for why does one also hope for what he sees?"

Therefore God does not need hope. He sees His fully accomplished ends as well as His perfectly begun beginnings, and everything in between that may look like a hodgepodge to us, but makes total sense to Him. He hopes for nothing. He does not reminisce about the good old days. Nor does He hope for better days ahead. Hope therefore has no place in God!

Our faith and hope are in God Who assures us in Ephesians 1:11 that He,

"…works all things after the counsel of His will."

The "Counsel of God" never has emergency meetings to figure out what went wrong and to see if there is anything that can be done. The "Counsel of God's Will" is the perfect blueprint of permanent success for God and His people. No one but God has ever read His "Secret Counsel Strategy Manual." He knows exactly what He is doing, and does exactly what He knows.

History is not moved along by a chancy, impersonal force or some fiendish power. There is always the overarching, all-wise loving purpose and awesome power of God at work. Don't think for a moment that anything, no matter how catastrophic it may appear, dams the stream of God's purposes from flowing through history to completion. God will work, and nothing and no one will stop Him.

Disappointed in prayer? Don't be! The Lord works it all out and He never has and never will fail. We have every reason to be totally hopeful and optimistic, and therefore have a dynamic faith! God is working everything for good to those who love Him! (Romans 8:28) That is why Paul can state in Romans 8:24,

"For in hope we have been saved…."

Hope in God has always been the anchor of faith and of the human soul! As the Palmist states in Psalm 71:5,

"For Thou art my hope; O Lord God, Thou art my confidence from my youth."

GOD'S FAITH-FORCE

Now we must examine more closely what Kenneth Copeland teaches as to what faith is and how it works. In short, he teaches that faith is not only material substance, but that it is also a force. Says Kenneth Copeland: "**GOD DID NOT CREATE THE WORLD OUT OF NOTHING. HE USED THE FORCE OF HIS FAITH**." (28) News Flash! CNN's "Breaking News!" We interrupt the regular scheduled programming with the following report! Here is Religious Humanism's correspondent, Ken Copeland, reporting, "God did not create the world out of nothing! He created it by His raw-material substance called faith-force!"

First, the Christian Church throughout the ages has always rightly taught creation "Ex Nihilo," a Latin phrase which means "Out Of Nothing." Copeland says that the world was not created from nothing. True, the couplet "Ex Nihilo" is not literally in the Bible. However, it is taught literally in the Bible, as we read in Hebrews 11:3,

> "**...so that what is seen was not made out of things which are visible**."

We also read in Romans 4:17 that God,

> "**...calls into being that which does not exist**."

He called all things to come forth from nothingness. It was God's "Creation Call." We call our kids for supper and they don't come. God calls an entire universe to come into being, and there it is. God called everything that exists out of nothing, and before Him nothing existed but Himself. Nothing called Him into being for He always was. He called everything into being that had never been. He called out to nothing, and boy oh boy did it become something. We call to something and we get nothing. Not only our children, but sometimes our dog won't even come when he is called.

But in Religious Humanism, "From Nothing" has been replaced by "Material-Substance-Faith-Force." This is more of a concoction than the Theory of Evolution. Evolutionists believe in the "Big Bang." It is predicated upon the notion that matter is eternal, and matter got so dense that there was an explosion, and after the dust settled there was a perfectly formed and ordered universe. It is also called the "Super Dense Theory" because you have to be super dense to believe it.

Religious Humanism believes in the "Big Force." Faith force! Sorry, there was no faith or force involved. The entire faith-force thing is the "Theory of Faith-Forcealution." Let alone there being no force, I don't even think there was a fuss, let alone a "Big Fuss." The Bible tells us in Genesis 1 that God simply "Said."

Romans 4:17 tells us that God simply "Called." I can hear the faith-force theorists say, "Well at the least He must have shouted." Why would He? There was nothing to shout at, and even if He did, there was nothing and no one to listen anyway.

What then is point of all this faith-force business? The point is that in Religious Humanism's power lust and power priority, everything has to be powered, forced, and exploded! Not with God. Not in the least. When you are God, you don't have to force anything. Who needs a "Big Bang" or a "Big Force" when you are "Almighty God?" Then You are the "Big Bang" and the "Big Force," and You whisper if you so choose and it happens just like that.

Second, nowhere in the Bible is God said to have faith, and nowhere in the Bible is faith defined as Divine force. The word faith is not used in the Old Testament. The main Old Testament word for faith is "batach" which means "to trust, to lean on, and to be confident." "Batach" of the Old Testament is the "Pisteuo" of the New Testament which means "to adhere to, to rely on, to trust in." Faith is therefore defined for us in the Old Testament long before we get to the New Testament. It is trust in God. Religious Humanism completely redefines and falsifies Biblical faith from trust to force.

The Psalmist David expresses his faith over and over again. One of King David's favorite prayers is when he declares that his trust, not his torque, is in God. We read about David's trust in God in the following Scriptures from the King James Version of the Bible, such as Psalm 31:1,

**"In Thee, O Lord, do I put my trust; let me never be
ashamed: deliver me in Thy righteousness."**

Or as David declares in Psalm 56:4,

**"In God I will praise His word, in God I have put my trust;
I will not fear what flesh can do unto me."**

Do you see it? David speaks of God before he speaks of his trust. He doesn't say, "I put my trust in God." Rather, he states, "In God I have put my trust." I like that! I always have! It has caught my eyes many times throughout the years. He does it over and over again. God is the priority in the faith (trust) life, and not faith itself. In Christianity, it is "God our Trust" that receives the primary focus. In Religious Humanism, it is "Faith-Force" that receives the spotlight.

Why then this complete distortion of faith, and the falsifying of faith as being a force? The reason for Religious Humanism's mass appeal is that people love the thought of being in control. If faith is a force, and God has faith and we have faith, then we do not have to live by childlike trust in God, but by blunt force as gods ourselves. There you go!

Simply put, faith-force puts man in control, while faith-trust puts God in control. What Religious Humanists crave is control! Control of their lives! Control of the universe! Control of all circumstances! Christians pray, "Lord, I humbly beseech You by faith." Religious Humanists command, "By faith, I declare it, I command it, I order it, I speak it, and it is so!" Christians pray in faith. Religious Humanists force by faith. Christians then say the "Amen" of trust in God! Religious Humanists expect a sonic boom from their faith-force fiats. Christians conclude their prayers looking to God as their Jehovah Jireh – Provider with "Amen!" Religious Humanists shout their faith-force fiats as producers, directors and ringmasters and expect cosmic boom as the climax. Bang!

FAITH-FORCE FIATS

Copeland then goes on to explain how God's faith-force works in the following quotation: "**GOD USED WORDS WHEN HE CREATED THE HEAVEN AND THE EARTH...EACH TIME GOD SPOKE, HE RELEASED HIS FAITH – THE CREATIVE POWER TO BRING HIS WORDS TO PASS.**" (29) Kenneth Copeland in the above refers to creation, and when he does he declares as a Biblical fact that God created the world by faith-force. Moreover, he states that God released His faith-force through words, and that His creative words were empowered by His faith-force.

Religious Humanists of the Copeland brand teach that God spoke "Faith-Force Words," and thereby realized the miracles of the six-day creation. So likewise Religious Humanists tell us that believers, who also live by faith as gods, create and control circumstances through their "Faith-Force Words" as well. Even as the great and only God said, "Let there be," and there was, so Religious Humanists teach that believers as gods can likewise say, "Let there be," and there will be.

I was sitting at a Christmas gathering some time ago, and out of the blue someone who is caught up in this delusion came up to me and said, "You know don't you that we can create with our words?" I sat there with a mouth full of teeth. I had never been approached by anyone before in my life with this shocking statement, let alone at a Christmas gathering. The speaker stood there proclaiming to be a co-creator with God through faith-force-words. Like he was about to pull off a 7th day of creation before my very eyes! And the gods rested on the 8th day! I remember feeling weirdness coming over me and thinking that I had better look into this far-out stuff soon. So now I have! I have discovered and am sharing with you what has come to be known over the years as "**THE WORD OF FAITH MOVEMENT.**"

States Kenneth Copeland: "**THE VERY FAITH THAT GOD USED WHEN HE CREATED... IS THE FAITH THAT IS BURNING IN YOUR SPIRIT...WELL, HE CREATED ALL THE PLANETS, HOW COME YOU CAN'T CREATE SOMETHING? YOU DON'T KNOW AS MUCH AS HE DOES. HE HAS GREATER WORKING KNOWLEDGE OF THAT FAITH THAN YOU DO. BUT WE'RE LEARNING. OUR TIME IS COMING. AND IN SOME WAYS IT IS ALREADY HERE.**" (30) There you pretty much have it. Taking Copeland's quotes together, many Religious Humanists teach that even as God created by faith-force released through His words, so believers can create by faith-force released through their words. God just happens to be better at it, for after all He has had more experience and practice operating in faith-force word creativity.

But then again, stop making excuses, for we are gods, too. Hop to it! The little men-gods are catching up with God. It just takes time! Practice makes perfect! Their time is coming. Just stay with it until you get the real hang of it. I guess you have to attend Kenneth Copeland's faith-force-word training classes for apprentice-gods to get really good at it. Regular people train dogs. Religious Humanists train gods.

The Religious Humanism syllogism at this point should be carefully outlined. It would go like this:

"**Christians are gods**." **(Major Premise)**

"<u>**God created through faith-force words**</u>." **(Minor Premise)**

"**Christians can create through faith-force words**." **(Conclusion)**

The only problem with this syllogism is that the major premise and the minor premise are both false, and therefore the entire syllogism reaches an equally false conclusion.

For just a moment, imagine getting caught up in all of this, namely, that faith is a force, and that this faith-force is released through the words of your mouth to create what you want to create, to affect what you want to affect, and to get what you want to get. Can you imagine the tremendous power of suggestion that this has in the lives of the spiritually gullible and naive, and the excesses to which this could lead, not to mention the messes that people could get themselves into through it?

Of course, embedded in all of this is the great potential for what must be called sins of presumption. Under the windshield wiper of his car which was now parked illegally, the driver, a man of faith, stuck this note, "I have circled the block for 20 minutes. I am late for an appointment. If I don't park here, I'll lose my job. I believe that God forgives all our sins. Forgive us our trespasses." When he came back from the appointment, he found a parking ticket under his windshield wiper with this note attached, "As a policeman I've circled this block for twenty years. It I don't give you a ticket, I'll lose my job. Lead us not into temptation."

And again, when you are faith-force gods, you can call forth riches and stuff, too. All men by nature want it all, and now with faith-force you can have it all. After all, gods should have it all, don't you think? That really is no different from those, however, who do not pay much attention to God, but who think that they are gods, too. Ted Turner has had his wealth and phenomenal business success. When he sold his television network to Time Warner, he was quoted as saying, "The only thing I hate about it is I'll never be the wealthiest man in America now." Oh don't feel bad, Teddy boy, just get some faith and you can have God and have it all again, too. That is how modern Christianity works.

I have actually seen and heard these "Faith-Force-Sayers" declaring their faith for a new house, and declaring in faith with their mouths that God was now going to make a way where there seemed to be no way, money where there was no money, and a house where there was no house. After all, they gave Him no options. What choice did He have? The gods had spoken, and He had to agree. They had "Faith-Force-Spoken" it, and now it simply had to become. My, my, what an absolutely handy and hands on arrangement. Simple, easy, clean! No downside or disappointments!

Then, upon the basis of their faith-force declarations and their faith-mouth proclamations, they wrote checks on faith for their new house, with the totally presumptuous assurance that God would now provide the funds which they by faith had declared, and which at the time they did not have. God didn't provide, and the police had another name for it all – "Hot Checks." Their checks bounced higher than a goofy-ball. That is only one tragic example of Religious Humanism being carried out in a "Faith-Force Word-Fiasco."

I have heard again and again of Religious Humanists trying to exert their faith-force and their mouth-might, and it turned into a huge disaster as well as into hearts of doubt and disillusionment. In a Religious Humanist church in Nebraska, the pastor died of cancer. Of course, this should not happen to a pastor in the land of the gods, especially an ordained god. When it came time for his funeral, the people coming into the funeral service were all informed at the door that this would not be a funeral, but rather a resurrection service. As the memorial wake unfolded, the pastor did not awaken.

The service lasted for hours, as people prayed, cried, and shouted faith-force-words of the binding of death, and faith-force-words of the release from death for the corpse, as the dead body was commanded in Jesus' name to rise from the dead and climb out of his casket. Over and over again they commanded the dead pastor to get up, but he didn't obey. All he could do was to just lie there, dead as a doornail. Of course it wasn't him, it was his shell. Hopefully he was in Heavenly bliss, and they were trying to bring him back down to earth's mess by their verbal-faith-bluster.

The motionless corpse after many hours of faith-force-fiats finally stopped the resurrection service dead in its tracks. The end result was not only were the dead man's earthly remains buried, but the misguided faith of many of his parishioners was buried with him. The church disbanded, and the people scattered everywhere, some of them to other churches, and some of them to no churches at all. This complete and deadly falsification of faith makes people lose their minds, their faith and their church.

The time-tested truth is this: **DISILLUSIONMENT IS THE CHILD OF ILLUSION.**" Such are the twisted and confused remains of a church that gets caught up in "The Word of Faith Movement," which has also come to be known as "Blab It And Grab It," or "Name It And Claim It," or "Speak It And Tweak It."

SAY TO THIS MOUNTAIN – MOVE!

The "Word of Faith" people base their theology upon words such as those of Jesus to His disciples when He said to them in Matthew 17:20,

> "...**for truly I say to you, if you have faith as a mustard seed,
> you shall say to this mountain, 'Move from here to there,'
> and it shall move; and nothing shall be impossible to you**."

It is one of the most glorious, powerful, and hopeful promises ever made to the followers of Christ. I believe every word of it, but in the context of the verse. Religious Humanism is infamous for violating basic principles of Bible exegesis by taking texts and isolating them from the context in which they are found. Isogesis! That way you can make the Bible say anything that you want it to say!

First, when Jesus made this dramatic promise to His disciples about speaking to mountains and moving them from here to there, it was in the context of their inability to cast a demon in a demon- possessed boy from in to out. Hear it! Getting rid of demons from people's lives is likened by Jesus to moving a mountain. We must understand this from the get-go before we can order a demon to get out of someone. Demons do not leave easily. They have to be involuntarily evicted. Did you ever try to move a mountain in your own strength? I wouldn't advise it! Instant double hernia and ruptured discs!

Plus, the demon was a mean cuss, as the boy would often be thrown into the water and into the fire by the evil spirit that had taken control of his life. By the way, all demons are very bad tempered. They all have rotten attitudes, especially about God and those created in His image. I do not say this as cursing, but the fact is they are all literally mad as Hell, for Hell is the essence of eternal madness. You and I don't want to go there! You won't find one person or demon who even gives so much as a hint of liking you.

The boy was demonized. He was also very ill. The father called is son a lunatic. Bound by demonic powers and sickened! On top of all of that, the demon was viciously attempting to either drown this boy or burn him to death. Satan has declared war on the human race, whether young or old, and he will use all of his devilish powers to bury us under mountains of torment and pain.

We are not dealing with something merely annoying or bother-some here. We may not trifle with the words of Jesus. This young lad was being crushed under the mountainous weight of hellish bondage and suffering. A huge percentage of Jesus' earthly ministry was spent in demon exorcism from the lives of the demon-inhabited. If the church is really following Christ, so must its ministry be in the deliverance of the demonically oppressed and possessed, of which the world is full. There are some even in the church now and then.

Second, we read in Matthew 17:18,

"And Jesus rebuked him (the demon), and the demon came out of him (the boy), and the boy was cured at once."

How glorious! When Jesus spoke words of rebuke to the demon, the demon was moved from being in the boy to being out of the boy. The boy's mountain of crushing torment was removed from him. This young lad had been in the solitary confinement of a torture chamber. He was set free, just like that. Glory to God! He was delivered and healed.

We have been privileged to witness Jesus doing the same in our ministry over the years. Like the young woman whose body was grotesquely twisted and disfigured, spit constantly running out of her mouth and her mind insane. Then on occasion in the mental institution she would jump out of her wheelchair, get ahold of a nurse or orderly and literally throw him or her down the hallway. Then she would snap back into her contorted state. This was not human strength, but demonic power. You should have seen her the day that Jesus set her free. She was the most beautiful gal imaginable, fully clothed and in her right mind. Unrecognizable! Jesus does make all things new.

When the disciples saw that Jesus had driven the demon from the boy, they were frustrated and puzzled to say the least. Why? They had encountered this demon-possessed boy earlier. The boy's father had brought his son to the disciples in the hope that they could help him. They couldn't! The demon didn't budge an inch. So after Jesus had freed the boy, they went to Jesus in private and asked Him in Matthew 17:19,

"…**Why could we not cast it out**?"

Good question! And very revealing! The reason for their failure becomes immediately evident. Their focus had been on themselves and on their own ability, or should we say on their own inability. Why couldn't we? At this point in their discipleship journey they were Religious Humanists. Trusting in one's self is trusting in nothing. In other words, their faith failed to deliver the boy of the demon because their faith was in their ability (inability) rather than in God's ability. Religious Humanists do the very same thing today by putting faith in their faith. Jesus tells us in Mark 11:22,

"…**Have faith in God**."

But it wasn't just that they were trusting in themselves to be able to order the demon to come out of the boy. They wanted it out presto! Nope! No go! It doesn't work that way. They forgot some basic fundamentals of spiritual warfare. They didn't pray and fast which are two of the mightiest weapons in our spiritual arsenal. Jesus spent many all-nighters in prayer, and fasted for as many as forty days and forty nights. That is why His ministry on earth was so powerful. He took out His "Demon Exorcism Training Manual" for His disciples and we read in Matthew 17:21,

"**But this kind does not go out except by prayer and fasting**."

We had better beseech God before we bark at demons. We had better fast as well before we attempt to free someone. Otherwise all that may happen is that the demon laughs at and pukes on our rebukes. The point being that if prayer and fasting make Christians powerful in spiritual warfare, they had better stop trying to war against Satan in their own strength as a bunch of impotent, embarrassing, feeble flunkies. Vast segments of the modern church have never once heard a sermon on prayer and fasting for spiritual warfare. Some have never fasted once in their entire lives, let alone for the purpose of demon exorcism. They do however major in church suppers, potlucks and couldn't scare a demon out of a pig or a chicken if they tried.

Third, Jesus was not talking here about the ability willy-nilly to speak to and remove anything and everything in our lives that we find to be an inconvenience or a hindrance to our comforts. That is what Religious Humanists do with Scriptures like Matthew 17:20. They are drawn to such Scriptures like moths to the flame, and they create the incurable itch in many parts of the Body of Christ of indiscriminate "Mountain Movingitis." They are constantly shouting at this, that, and the next thing to move or be removed, as if God has given them an unrestricted license to change the landscape of life at will.

However when God by His Holy Spirit gives us discernment that we are dealing with demon possession, He has authorized us to move that mountain as He did in Mark 9:25,

> "...**He rebuked the unclean spirit, saying to it, 'You deaf and dumb spirit, I command you, come out of him and do not enter him again.'**"

In other words, "Get out and don't come back." After some protest from the demon and some rumbling and shaking in the mountain, the demon came out of a possessed boy. That sovereign Divine power is available through faith in God still today.

POSITIVE CONFESSION – NEGATIVE CONFUSION

Religious Humanists are of the persuasion that there are two words that have killed more dreams and hopes than anything else they can think of. The two words are, "Be Realistic." They have dumped the words "Reality," "Realism," and "Realistic" from their minds and their vocabularies. They have not only replaced all negative thinking with positive thinking, but have also replaced reality with unreality by embracing the practice of what has come to be known as **"POSITIVE CONFESSION."**

What is really being advocated here by the Religious Humanist positive confessors in the nitty-gritty of life? Allow me to illustrate. When someone is sick with cancer, then the positive confessors will tell the ill person that he should never confess the fact that he is sick with cancer! Don't ever take the word cancer on his lips! Rather, he should by faith positively confess the opposite, namely, that he is not sick, but totally healthy.

Why do they teach this? Because it says in Isaiah 53:5 (KJV),

> "….and with His stripes we are healed."

Therefore they tell the cancer-ridden man that by faith he is to confess that his body is healed and healthy in the name of Jesus. Of course this would mean by the same token that I should not admit or confess my sins, but simply confess that they don't exist and that I am sinless, even as I am sickless. Why? Because it says in Psalm 103:2-3,

> "Bless the Lord, O my soul, and forget none of His benefits;
> Who pardons all your iniquities; Who heals all your
> diseases."

Don't confess the negative, but only confess the positive, and to confess your sins would make you a negative confessor. If you should not confess your sickness, then you shouldn't confess your sins either. Do you see where this stuff leads? Let me tell you, negative confession or confessing the negative in many cases is good, really good. God says in I John 1:9,

> "If we confess our sins, He is faithful and righteous to
> forgive us our sins and to cleanse us from all
> unrighteousness."

Well now, the reason that people fall for this is that "Positive Confession" does have a wholesome and virtuous ring to it. It sure seems to beat "Negative Confession" by a verbal mile. And more than that, it is a way of never having to deal with negative facts or the tough realities in life. Extremely appealing! You know, kind of like the old song says, but with a bit of a different twist: "**HOME, HOME ON THE RELIGIOUS HUMANISM RANGE, WHERE THE WORD-OF-FAITHERS AND THE POSITIVE-CONFESSORS ROAM; WHERE NEVER IS HEARD A TRUTHFUL WORD, AND THE STORMY SKIES ARE DECLARED SUNNY EACH DAY.**"

The avoided fact in all of this positive appeal is that speaking or admitting the truth has never been and will never be a negative confession. That would turn an age-old adage on its head, and require it to be rephrased with the words, "Honesty is the worst policy," and, "Dishonesty is the best policy." Furthermore, Jesus said in Matthew 5:37,

> **"But let your statement be, 'Yes, yes' or 'No, no'; and anything beyond these is of evil."**

Jesus never even intimated that at times our "Yes" should be "No," and at other times our "No" should be "Yes." Jesus would call "Positive Confession" evil, for it requires "Yea" to be "Nay," and "Nay" to be "Yea." It confesses presence as absence, and absence as presence. It presents truth as falsehood, and falsehood as truth. It declares reality to be unreality, and unreality to be reality.

Furthermore, positive confession presents faith and facts as incompatible. As if living the life of faith means that you must deny the facts of life. This is what gives the church the reputation of being filled with escapists and neurotics. The Christian life, Christian prayer and Christian decision-making are not hot-air balloon rides. All of the basic disciplines of life are made within the context of the real stuff of life! And positive confession makes God appear like He cannot handle the stuff of life because He is simply not up to snuff.

How would you like to have a child who when you say no to him, he does it anyway because he only thinks yes? And then when you ask him why he did what you said he may not do, he tells you that his positive thinking overruled your negativity. And so you spank the positive little liar, and he looks at you with a grin on his face and tells you that what you are doing really feels good and that he hopes you will do it again soon. You know for a fact that it hurts because your spanking hand feels like it is being stung by bees, yet he makes it sound like all you are doing is making honey.

This is not and cannot be of God for the following reasons. First of all, because God cannot lie! We read exactly that in Titus 1:2,

> **"In the hope of eternal life, which God, Who cannot lie, promised long ages ago."**

Second, because God is not a God of confusion. We read in I Corinthians 14:33,

> **"For God is not a God of confusion but of peace...."**

MODERN CHRISTIANITY CORRUPTED

Lies are falsehoods that mislead, disappoint, and cause great pain, confusion and disillusionment to yourself and to others. Positive confession therefore is not just a little innocent avoidance of the truth. It is the very antithesis to God, and terribly injurious to people's mental, emotional and spiritual health.

Third, it makes the church look and sound ridiculous and not to be believed. I am convinced that when man tries to be God, he obviously has to try too hard, and therefore gets himself into all kinds of folly. Sort of like the duffer golfer who tries too hard and hits the ball with all of his might, and the ball hooks or slices far out of bounds in every errant direction rather than straight down the middle. So it is with the positive confessors, in trying to be duffer gods, they always try and swing too hard. They always over swing, and they find themselves deep in the rough of the out-of-bounds, and pardon the golf pun, "In A Very Bad Lie."

That is where Religious Humanism always leads you, out-of-bounds and in the tall weeds of denial, as you kick the ball back in bounds when nobody is looking, deceitfully attempting to turn a negative into a positive. Have you ever seen a golfer cheat his way out of difficulty? Isn't it a tragic sight? Have you ever heard a positive confessor lie his way out of reality? Isn't it a tragic sound?

Fourth, what bondage and disasters this leads the positive confessor into! I have known throughout the years those who were caught up in this faith-force and positive confessing. They often refused to get health insurance or life insurance, for to do so would be to confess the negative realities of sickness and death. Then when they fell sick, the hospital and doctor bills became insurmountable.

Or again, I have been with a young wife whose dear husband was at the door of death from a terminal disease, but she was under the weight of guilt when she felt the need to talk about or even make tentative funeral arrangements. Why? Because she had been told by a Religious Humanist church that that would be negative confession, and she was led to believe that this would be claiming death and therefore could bring about her precious husband's premature passing away Positive confession has and is leading multitudes into the cruelties of confusion, fear and guilt.

Resources:
1. Patrick Zukeran, "Mormon Doctrine of God – Monotheism or Polytheism" (Probe Ministries, Richardson, TX)
2. Patrick Zukeran, "Mormon Doctrine of God – Monotheism or Polytheism," (Probe Ministries, Richardson, TX,) Bruce Mc Conkie, "Mormon Doctrine" (Salt Lake, Bookcraft, 1991) 576-577

3. *Forgotten Word Ministries, Robert E. Wise, "Creflo Dollar – False Preacher/Teacher" (Creflo Dollar, "The Creative Ability of Word," Tape From His Ministry, Product Number 8432091)*

4. *Biblical Discernment Ministries, Rick Miesel, John Beardsley, "What Joyce Wants, Joyce Gets" by Bob Waldrep, Watchman Fellowship of Alabama (Earl Paulk, "Satan Unmasked," p. 96)*

5. *Dynamic Preaching, "The Triumphant Christ" (Seven Worlds Corporation, Knoxville, TN, April, 1995, Volume X, No. 4) Page 31, Joyce Madison, "Great Hoaxes, Swindles, Scandals, Cons, Stings, and Scams" (Penguin Books, New York, NY, 1992) Pages 49-53*

6. *Dynamic Preaching, "It's Hard To Be Number Two" (Seven Worlds Corporation, Knoxville, TN, January, 1996, Volume XI, No. 1) Page 16, Life, Special Issue Commemorating 1945 and World War II, Page 82*

7. *Let Us Reason Ministries, Mike Oppenheimer, "Kenneth Copeland's Land of Biblical Revelations" (Kenneth Copeland, "Believers Voice of Victory" Feb. 1987, p. 9)*

8. *Let Us Reason Ministries, Mike Oppenheimer, "The Recent Anointed Actions of the Charismatic Movement's Leading Man Benny Hinn" (Benny Hinn, Praise-A-Thon, TBN, November 6, 1990)*

9. *Ibid (Benny Hinn, Praise The Lord, TBN, December 6, 1990)*

10. *Apologetics Index, "Resources on Religious Movements, Cults, Sects, World Religions and Related Issues," Anton and Janet Hein-Hudson, Publishers (Kenneth Hagin Sr., "Zoe: The God-Kind of Life" 1989, Pages 35-36, 41)*

11. *Let Us Reason Ministries, Mike Oppenheimer, "Touch, Tilt, Topple" (Benny Hinn, Praise The Lord, TBN, December 26, 1991)*

12. *Let Us Reason Ministries, Mike Oppenheimer, "The Image of God in Man" (Kenneth Copeland, Praise the Lord, TBN, 2/5/86)*

13. *Ibid (Benny Hinn, "Our Position In Christ" #2, 1990, Audio Side 2)*

14. *Ibid (Benny Hinn, TBN, December 1, 1990)*

15. *Let Us Reason Ministries, Mike Oppenheimer, "Touch, Tilt, Topple" (Benny Hinn, "Our Position in Christ" Tape # A031190-1)*

16. *Dynamic Preaching, "A Message from Big Bird" (Seven Worlds Corporation, Knoxville, TN, March, 1995, Volume XI, No. 3) Pages 27-28*

17. *Dynamic Preaching, "Reality Maps and Rolling Stones" (Seven Worlds Corporation, Knoxville, TN, April, 1995, Volume X, No. 4) Page 27 (National & International Religion Report, October 3, 1994) Page 5*

18. *Let Us Reason Ministries, Mike Oppenheimer, "The Image of God in Man" (Good Morning Holy Spirit, p. 82, Benny Hinn, Word, 1991)*

19. *Ibid (Kenneth Copeland Ministry Letter, 21 July 1977)*

20. *Ibid (Brigham H. Roberts Conference of the Mutual Improvement Association of the Salt Lake Stake of Zion, August 18, 1901, published in both the Desert News and the Improvement*

21. *Let Us Reason Ministries, Mike Oppenheimer, "The Recent Anointed Actions of the Charismatic Movement's Leading Man Benny Hinn" (Benny Hinn, Praise-A-Thon, TBN, November 6, 1990*

22. *Let Us Reason Ministries, Mike Oppenheimer, "The Recent Anointed Actions of the Charismatic Movement's Leading Man Benny Hinn (Praise The Lord, TBN, Dec. 6, 1990)*

23. *Ibid (Spiritual Warfare Seminar, May 2, 1990)*

24. *Ibid (The Berean Call, 1992 Media Spotlight Report, Feb. '94*

25. *Apologetics Index, "Apologetics Research Resources on Religious Cults and Sects," Anton and Janet Hein-Hudson, Publishers (Kenneth Hagin Sr., "The Incarnation," The Word of Faith, December, 1980, Page 13)*

26. *Dynamic Preaching, "Learning from A Little Child" (Seven Worlds Corporation, Knoxville, TN, December, 1995, Volume X, No. 12) Page 16, Mark Connelly, Green Pastures*

27. *Let Us Reason Ministries, Mike Oppenheimer, "I Have What I Think and Say I Have" (Kenneth Copeland, Authority of the Believer II, Fort Worth: Kenneth Copeland Ministries, 1987, Audiotape # 01-0302 Side 1)*

28. *Let Us Reason Ministries, Mike Oppenheimer, "I Have What I Think and Say I Have" (Kenneth Copeland, "Spirit, Soul and Body," #01-0601, Tape # 1)*

29. *Let Us Reason Ministries, Mike Oppenheimer, "Kenneth Copeland's Land of Biblical Revelations" (Kenneth Copeland, The Power of the Tongue, Fort Worth: KCP Publications, 1980, Page 4)*

30. *Let Us Reason Ministries, Mike Oppenheimer, "I Have What I Think and Say I Have" (Kenneth Copeland, John Hagee Today, August 18, 1999)*

Chapter Six

THE CORRUPTING RESULTS OF MODERN CHRISTIANITY

†††

"A Lie Travels Around The World, While Truth Is Putting On Its Boots."
~Charles Spurgeon

An old man was attempting to lead an obstinate and contrary donkey down the road. A passer-by stopped him and commented on the way that the donkey was misbehaving. The owner responded, "Oh, I can make him do anything I want him to do with just a kind word." The passer-by sneered and said, "It doesn't appear that way to me." The owner said, "Sure, I can!" Whereupon he climbed off the donkey, picked up a two-by-four from beside the road, and smacked the animal with it on the head. He then explained to the shocked onlooker, "Before he will respond to a kind word, I have to get his attention first."

Such is the day in which we live. Most church people just drift along until something really hits them between the eyes. Then they may take notice. Otherwise not! Multitudes in the Christian church world need a rude awakening, a Martin Luther confrontation that is like a two-by-four up against the side of their heads to get their attention.

The philosophy of Religious Humanism has played upon the minds of the unsuspecting, and anesthetized their thinking into a kind of stupor. Self-gratification and earthly pleasures are being presented with a slick religious veneer as if they are the very heart of Christianity. Hundreds of thousands of church folks, even the most spiritually minded, have been inundated and brainwashed by a counterfeit gospel. Once Religious Humanism has gotten inside of them and taken over, it is very difficult to cure them of its fatal disease. It requires powerful spiritual antibiotics of truth to cleanse them of it and heal their souls.

It has been taking place for far too long now, and the roots of Religious Humanism have been growing deeper and deeper with every passing day. The modern church is in grave danger, and does not realize it. I am sure you have heard of or read the illustration of the frog in the tea kettle. We are told that if you put a frog in boiling hot water, which of course is unthinkable, but if you did, the frog would immediately attempt to hop out of the hot water. However, we are also told that if you put the frog in comfortable water and increase the water temperature very gradually, the frog will continue to swim around in the water even though the water has reached the boiling point. Experts tell us that it is due to the phenomenon known as "Habituation." The frog does not sense its perilous plight because it has become habituated to its environment.

Much of the modern religious church and television audience has already been habituated to the presence of Religious Humanism's falsehoods that are being passed off on people as truth by adding to, subtracting from and twisting Scripture. A constant deluge of corrupting Religious Humanism TV programming has bit by bit been accepted as Gospel truth. Habituation! People would be much safer and learn far healthier lessons and even some Biblical principles by watching reruns of "The Andy Griffith Show" on the TV Land Channel, than by viewing what the Religious Humanism TV net-works are airing today.

THE HOLY SPIRIT – HEAVEN'S MUSCLE

It is impossible to faithfully or effectively preach the Gospel of Christianity without the Holy Spirit of God going ahead to prepare the way to reach the hearts of sinners. Yes, He is "The Comforter." (John 14:26 KJV) But that is not the Holy Spirit's complete personality profile. It is not His chief M.O. Not by any means!

We read of Him in John 16:8,

> **"And He, when He comes, will convict the world concerning sin, and righteousness, and judgment."**

In Religious Humanism the Holy Spirit's complete personality profile has been for the most part hidden. He is known affectionately by most as the "Comforter." However the Holy Spirit comes to trouble us before he soothes us. He comes to convict us before He comforts us. He is God the "Great Discomforter." He shames us with our sins before Jesus saves us from them. All people hide themselves from themselves with disguises of self-righteousness and their public properness, so "Heaven's Convictor" has to strip us bare before we can be clothed in the righteousness of Jesus Christ. Man walks around like Dr. Jekyll, and then the Holy Spirit comes along and horrifies us by introducing us to our Mr. Hyde. It is exactly that the Psalmist prays for in Psalm 83:16,

> **"Fill their faces with dishonor, that they may seek Thy name, O Lord."**

The Greek word for "Spirit" is "Pnuema." Religious Humanism has replaced the aggressive Holy Spirit of God with a far less offensive and a far more "Passive Pneuma." The spirit of Religious Humanism doesn't rattle anyone's cage, or rub anyone the wrong way. As I have referred to previously, we hear it again and again from pastors and teachers in the self-friendly churches and TV networks, "We should not tell people that they are sinners, for they already know that. After all, people out there are hurting, and they need to be told that God loves them, that He has a glorious purpose for their lives, and that Jesus is the way to their success and destiny."

Religious Humanists by the hundreds of thousands will no longer put up with a repent-of-your sins message that offends them. They are now above that. Such preaching is an offense to their presumed superiority. When is the last time, or even the first time, that you heard a John the Baptist preach in your church words like those in Matthew 3:2-7-8,

> **"Repent, for the kingdom of heaven is at hand...You brood of vipers, who warned you to flee from the wrath to come? Therefore bring forth fruit in keeping with repentance."**

Dear Lord, how to make enemies and turn off people! You brood of vipers, or, "You offspring of snakes." He called his audience, which included Pharisees and Sadducees, descendants of very poisonous serpents. John the Baptist definitely has their attention now.

Whoa, John! I can hear and see them hissing and flashing their fangs at him. They thought that they were safe from the judgment because of their well-polished surface religion. Repent! Turn from your rotten fruits of unrighteousness, and bring forth fruits of repentance. It's all there in the Baptist's preaching – sin, righteousness and judgment, and in the most abrasive and confrontive words imaginable. They are all now looking at him like a bunch of John McEnroes after an unfavorable call by the head linesman.

If John the Baptist preached in the majority of today's churches, he would have his head lopped off all over again. They want prophets who sound more like fortune tellers. After all, the Religious Humanism devotees are investing their hard-earned money, and they are demanding a positive, up-beat product. They won't admit it, but what they really want is the lust of the flesh, the lust of the eye and the pride of life. And they are getting it week after week. They didn't get it from John the Baptist who according to the prophet, Isaiah, was making ready the way of the Lord. (Matthew 3:3) Religious Humanism preachers are making ready the way for a fake gospel and a false messiah who will elevate their listener's financial and social standing.

A pastor on any given Sunday morning has no idea what and who are really sitting out there. Many have hidden but deadly sins, and the longer they are put to sleep under this Religious Humanism sedation, the stronger and more killing their sins become. They are hooked on their pills, their booze, their cigarettes, their pornography, their sex addiction, their materialism, their adultery, their perversion and who knows what else. They can't stop because they are so sin-enslaved. They would rather watch *Entertainment Tonight* for a nightly half hour of sexual garbage and gossip than read the Word of God. They must hear John the Baptist's thundering "Repent," and they desperately need to hear the voice of Jesus in John 8:36,

> **"If therefore the Son shall make you free, you shall be free indeed."**

But instead they hear,

> **"If you give, He will make you rich."**

And I guarantee you of this: **"WHILE THESE RELIGIOUS HUMANISM PREACHERS ARE ASSURING THEIR SIN-BOUND PARISHIONERS OF SUCCESS AND HEAVEN, THEY ARE IN FACT PREPARING THEM FOR FAILURE AND HELL."** True Gospel preachers are called by God first of all to be spiritual surgeons, not self-boosters and success cheerleaders. If the church is to keep people's consciences sensitive, it must keep them pricked. Tragically today, the "sheep" are sitting in their cozy, comfy church pews Sunday after Sunday, while their goat-selves are running all over the place during the week.

The man was consulting with his psychiatrist, and told him that he had a terrible problem. He said, "Lately I have been misbehaving and it seems to be getting worse every day. My conscience is troubling me deeply and I was wondering if you could prescribe something that would help me." The psychiatrist said, "Oh, I see, you want some-thing that will strengthen your will power." The man said, "No, you don't understand. I want something that will weaken my conscience." I have several churches I could recommend that will do the job for him.

It is impossible to bring sinners to conviction without "Heaven's Convincer." The Holy Spirit is the One Who burns into the hearts of men the deep conviction of sin, righteousness, and eternal judgment. It is being put in the

Holy Spirit's super-heated furnace of conviction that alone can melt the sin-frozen heart of man. Thus the Holy Spirit prepares the way for the triumph of the saving Gospel of Jesus Christ. But it is also a fact: **"THE LESS A MAN FEELS HIS SINS IN THIS WORLD, THE MORE HE SHALL FEEL THEM IN THE NEXT."** This is the most terrifying result of Religious Humanism!

It is so awesome to see people convicted of their sins and have a hunger and thirst for righteousness for the first time in their lives. Fornication is rampant in America, and yet from the pulpits of Religious Humanistic churches there is little preaching against it. A young woman came forward in one of my evangelistic crusades with many other young people to accept Christ as their Savior. She sought me out privately later, and under the conviction of the Holy Spirit asked me if having sex with her boyfriend was a sin. I said, "Yes it is." She then asked me, "What is that sin called in the Bible?" I answered, "It is called fornication." She said, "Well then, now that I am saved, I am going to quit doing it." Then she added, "Do you see that good-looking young man sitting in the pew out there alone?" "Yes," I said." She went on, "That is my boyfriend, and would you go tell him that we can't have sex together any-more?" I said, "No, that is your job, and God will help you."

The young woman was in her early twenties, and she honestly didn't know whether pre-marital intercourse was a sin, or for that matter what the name of that sin was. Now she was saved from her sins and committed her life to Christ and to living and loving in righteousness.

If this powerful Holy Spirit convicting triad of sin, righteousness, and judgment is not being preached in your church, get out! Now! You are breathing in the sweet-smelling but poisoned air of the false gospel of the modern apostate humanistic church. Sin, righteousness, and judgment just do not fit the "Feel-Good Gospels" that have become the darlings of so much of contemporary Christianity. And if that is the false gospel that is being preached, you can and must conclude that the Holy Spirit is not doing the preaching in your church.

JUDGMENT OR JACKPOT RELIGION

Let us set the record straight! The message of the Gospel of Jesus Christ is not a message of bad news, but of good news, not of judgment, but of salvation. Jesus said so! Jesus says in John 12:47,

"...For I did not come to judge the world, but to save the world."

God does not salivate when the subject of the judgment of sinners is brought up. He does not want to judge anybody, but to save everybody. (II Peter 3:9.) But eternally judge the rebellious and unrepentant sinner He must, for He is a just God. He is both a God of justice and a God of salvation. In fact, the latter would be unnecessary if it were not for the former. The King James Version of the Bible says in Isaiah 45:21 about God that He is,

"...a just God and a Savior...."

Not anymore. In much of the modern, humanistic church He is not a just God and a Savior. Today He is just a Savior, but not from sin, but from poverty. He is not a God of justice and mercy. He is only a God of mercy. He is not a God of wrath and love. He is just love. Listening to many modern preachers, one almost gets the feeling that it would be unjust for God to be just. The truth of God's Word however stands. God is both the God of justice and the God of salvation.

Justice! Judgment! Who hears that old time religion stuff anymore? I mean to say, it is only the Amish who go to church in horse and buggy and listen to that kind of stale and antiquated preaching. We live in Amish country, and there are mornings that I feel strongly inclined to follow the horse droppings to an Amish house church, rather than go to another Religious Humanistic church service and hear that if I give liberally in the offering, I will hit the jackpot. Religious Humanism preaching is about baiting the honey hole. Bible preaching is about giving your heart to Jesus or be dumped forever in the Hell-hole. Honey-pot preaching or Heaven and Hell preaching! The latter is now rare and difficult to find, unless you can find a blessed horse-manure trail to truth.

When Religious Humanists get done with you, you will no longer think of Christ in terms of salvation, but rather in terms of a "Savings & Loan." When you think of Heaven, it will not be about a throne, but a bank vault, not a judgment throne. Nevertheless, the Bible tells us there is a very big day coming. It fact, we must expect it any moment. As they say, "The Big One Is Coming." Or the more down home, "The BigUn Is Acomin." That same alert has been used for years about the biggest of all earthquakes that is coming to the West Coast. Now it has been expanded to an act of terror that will make 9/11 look small by comparison. Whether in Los Angeles or Lower Manhattan, we don't know just where! May God give America a man in the While House who has a dynamic faith in Jesus Christ if and when those "Big Ones" hit.

However, none of those "BigUns" can compare to the "Biggest One Of All" that will soon be here. For the Christian it will be the "Big Terrific." For the unbeliever, it will be the "Big Terrible." Sadly many church folks talk and act as if God's white glove inspection will never really happen. When you talk to them about the soon coming King and the judgment day, they look at you with a blank stare and they really have nothing to say. I can tell that their bags aren't packed for the rapture of the church. For those who ardently believe the Bible's eschatology, the Son is rising to come for His church and the eastern sky has become bright with His approach. For so many others who are very religious about their religion, eschatology never progresses beyond a dimly lit, hazy horizon.

I often find that those in the church, who have wandered off into the political land of the far left, are also those whose minds seldom wander to Beulah land and their eminent arrival there. But then why would they, for if God's Word is not taken seriously as regards to killing babies, homosexuality, same-sex marriage and God's entire created order, why would they become excited about the rapture and the judgment? Only those who take sin seriously take the judgment seriously, too.

Daniel 7:9-10 pictures a day and a scene that we seldom hear about anymore. It is the red hot judgment day which Daniel described as follows:

> **"I kept looking until thrones were set up, and the Ancient of Days took His seat; His vesture was like white snow, and the hair of His head like pure wool. His throne was ablaze with flames, its wheels were a burning fire. A river of fire was flowing and coming out from before Him; thousands upon thousands were attending Him, and myriads upon myriads were standing before Him; the court sat, and the BOOKS WERE OPENED."**

First of all, get a load of the God to end all gods! Is this the God that is being presented to the lollipop churches of modern Christianity? Glistening in white! Sitting on a flaming throne! A river of fire flowing out from before Him like burning molten lava! Thousands upon thousands of angels attending Him! God is then rolled out on a throne with wheels of burning fire. Strange! Burning fire! What fire isn't burning? Isn't that redundant? No! Nothing about God is redundant. It is a wild scene! His throne and the wheels of His throne are shooting out towering plumes of flames. And so much for the guy who says to his buddy about his brand new sports car, "Wow, those are the hottest wheels!" He hasn't seen anything yet, and I pray that he never does! This is not hotwheels.com. This is hotwheels.heavensjudgmentthrone.com.

Men think that their death is the end of them forever. No matter how they lived, they are eulogized at their funeral, and then honorably and lovingly interred. The books are closed on their lives, as the final chapter is supposedly written in green grass over quiet graves. However, the books of their lives are not closed, but in point of fact they are yet to be opened.

By "The Books" in Daniel 7 is meant the omniscience of God in which each and every detail of peoples' lives are kept infinitely more clearly and comprehensively than if they were written down in literal earthly ledgers. Concerning those who did not repent and turn from their sins and accept and serve God's Son as their Lord and Savior, God will then open "The Books" of His omniscience, and every secret and known sin of each unbeliever will be exposed from "The Books" as they stand before God. The multitudes before the throne will not be judged anonymously nor their sin dealt with generically. So much for the Las Vegas television come-on to sin that whatever happens in Vegas stays in Vegas! The Bible dissolves that false hope quicker than an ice cream cone on the Vegas strip in July.

Myriads of them! Myriads upon myriads! Myriad means countless. An innumerable multitude of people standing before the Ancient of Days Who is seated on His flaming judgment throne, with a river of fire flowing from His throne which will carry them into Hell! What an unspeakably horrifying sight! Luke 12:2 assures us that there is nothing covered up that will not be revealed, and hidden that will not be known. It's all in "The Books."

Religious Humanism is rewriting the Bible and "Cooking the Books." Apostate pastors are spewing forth their no-Hell heresies in increasing numbers and in a few cases are being driven out of their churches by faithful and Bible-believing parishioners. It happened recently in my son's church in Colorado where he and his family attend. Hell-denying shepherds must now be driven from the flock of the Good Shepherd as the heretics that they are. It is all a result of the Emerging Church Movement which was spawned by Religious Humanism.

For those truly repentant sinners who are saved through the blood of Jesus Christ, their names and their sins do not appear in the "The Judgment Books" of God's omniscience, even as the promise in Hebrews 10:17 states:

"And their sins and their lawless deeds I will remember no more."

Because of the precious and powerful sin-cleansing blood of Jesus Christ, God miraculously blots out the believer's sins from His omniscience. Glory hallelujah! When it comes to the bad things born-again believers have done on earth, in the judgment there will be no record of their ever having done them. There is that much wonder-working power in the blood of Jesus!

Not only are their names and sins blotted out of the "The Books," but the names of the repentant and believing sinners turned saints, according to Revelation 21:27 are written instead in "The Lamb's Book of Life." We can be sure of this, and that is that our names will either be in "The Books" or in "The Lamb's Book." Fact: "**IT IS NOT A QUESTION OF WHETHER OR NOT WE HAVE BEEN ETERNALLY BOOKED! RATHER, THE CRITICAL QUESTION THAT WE MUST BE ABLE TO ANSWER NOW IS IN WHICH BOOK ARE WE BOOKED!**"

Eternity is not about "Who's Who!" The rather humorous but true story is told about how some years ago, the then Senate Majority Leader Senator Robert Dole, got caught in a very embarrassing situation. It just so happened that his office sent a two and a half page letter inviting a man named Bosko Struminikovski of Memphis, Tennessee to accept membership in the distinguished "Republican Senatorial Inner Circle." The letter explained to Bosko Struminikovski that the "Republican Senatorial Inner Circle" was made up of individuals who discuss national and regional topics in a comfortable mix of business and social gatherings. He was also informed that the next meeting of the "Inner Circle" would be held in Washington D.C. The problem was that as much as the invitation honored Bosko, he was unable to accept the invitation to join Dole's "Inner Circle," seeing that he was at the time an inmate at the federal penitentiary in Memphis. (1)

Earth is always about "Who's-Who?" You know what I mean! It is about the rich and the famous as contrasted with the poor and anonymous. Of course, the invitation was mistakenly sent, but there will be no mistake when the thief on the cross who was crucified next to Jesus, and who asked for mercy and Divine remembrance, will be sitting at the head table with Jesus Christ in Heaven's banquet hall. Jesus said so! (Luke 23:43) "The Books" and "The Lamb's Book of Life" will turn earth's inner and outer circles of "Who's-Who" and "Who's-Not" inside out and upside down.

THE NO-DANGLE-OVER HELL THEORY

Religious Humanists tell us today that we should never threaten people with Hell in our preaching and witnessing, nor should we ever dangle them over Hell's fires in our sermons. Joel Osteen, pastor of the very large Lakewood Church in Houston, Texas is of this school of thought. He states: "**LISTEN, DON'T DANGLE PEOPLE OVER THE FIRES OF HELL...LISTEN,**

THAT DOESN'T DRAW PEOPLE TO GOD."(2) Rather what we should preach and witness about is the goodness of God. Says Osteen: "**WHAT YOU GOT TO DO IS TALK ABOUT THE GOODNESS OF GOD. LISTEN, IT IS THE GOODNESS OF GOD THAT BRINGS PEOPLE TO REPENTANCE.**" (3)

This would leave Jonathan Edwards with little if any possibility, if he were alive today, of being given a position on Joel Osteen's pastoral staff. After all, Edwards preached that most published sermon in church history entitled, "Sinners In The Hands Of An Angry God." If most modern pastors preached today like Jonathan Edwards preached, the result would be, "Pastors In The Hands Of Angry Parishioners." Or even, "God In The Hands Of Angry Sinners."

So many church people today are described by Isaiah in Isaiah 30:9,

"For this is a rebellious people, false sons, sons who refuse to listen to the instruction of the Lord."

"Stop," they demand, "stop this sin, righteousness, judgment, Heaven's glory and Hell's fire preaching. We don't want any more of this heavy stuff." Instead, they want the "Slurpee Gospel" which must be constantly handed out to the faithful "Slurpee Slurpers" if they are to continue to give their tithes and offerings, i.e. buy Protestant Indulgences. They don't want to come to a church which serves strong meat. They want Forrest Gump's box of chocolates. They are false sons, and not sons of God. They are the tragic results of Religious Humanism.

We are told by Joel Osteen that we should not dangle people over Hell's fire in our preaching or teaching, for it won't draw people to God! In one sentence, he makes the Holy Spirit irrelevant and obsolete. More than that, God in His Word not only dangles the readers over the fires of Hell, but He takes them in His Word in Luke 16 into the very horrors and anguish of Hell. Christ thrusts them into the flames of Hell through His story of a wealthy pagan who on earth had been successful, prosperous, and a scrooge. He totally ignored a poor man at the bottom of the food chain who is covered with sores and lying at his gate day after day, hoping to receive some crusts and crumbs from the land of plenty just inside the gate where they are always eating far more than they need. Those who live by their insatiable wants will always disregard others in their needs.

The wealthy man's name is not given, and though he was no doubt well-known on earth, he will forever remain anonymous in the fires of Hell as if he never existed. The relatively unknown pauper is identified as a man named

Lazarus who becomes one of Heaven's celebrated trophies.

What burns the Religious Humanist's "No Dangling Over Hell" theory into ashes even more is that this "Successful Failure" is pictured by Jesus Himself as crying out from Hell across an unbridgeable gulf to father Abraham in Heaven. He first begs Abraham to send Lazarus from Heaven to Hell with some water to soothe his burning tongue. In Hell all of the "richies" who ignored the poor will ironically become the beggars. He also begged Abraham to send a messenger to his five brothers in his father's house on earth in order to warn them so that they would not come into Hell's torments, too. (Luke 16:27-28)

The rich Hell-dweller now has the awful realization that he is immersed in eternal flames and that there are no fire trucks, hoses or water in Hell to put them out. This flaming wretch could not be given the tiniest drop to relieve his burning thirst. And even if someone could give him some water, it would be stolen before he could drink it. Hell is full of rich and poor crooks and the crime rate there, if there were things to steal, would be a 100%.

How paradoxical! In Hell, they are asking for more sermons about Hell to be preached to the unbelievers on earth. In earth's Religious Humanistic churches, we are being told by the "No Dangle Theorists" that such sermons must be banned. The fact is: **"PEOPLE TODAY ARE SAFER LISTENING TO SERMONS FROM HELL THAN THEY ARE LISTENING TO RELIGIOUS HUMANIST'S SER-MONS ON EARTH."**

This wealthy, damned man wanted his brothers to be dangled over Hell's belching flames so that they would be scared out of their wits and make their lives right with God before it was too late. It appears that his five brothers were so sin-hardened that they were fearless when it came to eternal realities. In Luke 16:31 Father Abraham says that they would not be persuaded even if someone came back from the dead and warned them. People on earth can become so impenetrably hardened in their unbelief, that a resurrected Hell-dweller would not by his warnings make the smallest of dents in their steely hearts. I have personally met them.

Joel Osteen also tells us that we are to preach only about the goodness of God, for it is the goodness of God that leads sinners to repentance. Is that so? Wrong! It is not confessing the goodness of God that will save a sinner, but each sinner confessing his badness and turning to Jesus Christ for forgiveness and power to resist the Devil. Even John McCain's and Sarah Palin's "Joe The Plumbers" and "Joe Six Packs" will say at times things like "Somebody Up There Loves Me," or "The Old Man Upstairs Was Watching Over Me." But do the lost-in-sin Joe's of life repent of their sins, and turn from them to Jesus for their salvation? Not the last time I checked. While these good-ole Joes believe in this good ole beneficent, bearded God up there somewhere, they just keep on plumbing, six packing and cussing a blue streak.

The modern Osteens of Religious Humanism would have us to believe that those who preach that old time Gospel of sin, salvation and service are really out to lunch when it comes to successful preaching and mega-church building. They completely break ranks with the John the Baptist preachers of thousands of years like Jonathan Edwards and Billy Graham who called sinners – sinners, sin – sin, hell – hell, and Heaven – Heaven. Instead they now tell people how terrific they are while they hold their hands, pat them on the head, and kiss them on their way out so that they go home feeling like a million bucks until their next false feel-good gospel fix. It is a modern-day pulpit debacle. It is not only the modern no-spank theory brought into the church, but the no-tongue lashing policy as well. The idea is that rewards work better than punishment. People aren't really being saved from their sins, just salved into self-approval.

But we also have here an exegetical zoo yet again. The text that Osteen no doubt uses to prove that preaching the goodness of God leads to repentance is found in Romans 2:4 which says:

"Or do you think lightly of the riches of His kindness and forbearance and patience, not knowing that the kindness (goodness) of God leads you to repentance?"

What is Paul talking about here? What is the context? Very briefly, in Romans 2:1-3 Paul under the inspiration of the Holy Spirit is addressing those in the church at Rome who are judging and condemning others, while they are doing the same things that they are judging others for. We have all done it at one time or another. He tells us that those who do this will not escape the judgment of God. Here comes the Judge! As a matter of fact, the only reason that God has delayed pouring out judgment upon these hypocritical self-appointed judges in the church at Rome is because of His kindness (goodness) and forbearing patience. In other words, it is because of God's being rich in kindness (goodness) and the patient holding back of His wrath upon these judgmental hypocrites that they still have the opportunity to repent of their own sins and their condemnatory spirits toward others.

Now then, that is what Paul is talking about. If you will, it is only because of the goodness and kindness and patience of God that He hasn't clobbered them already. I have seen churches so judgmental over the years that they literally have gone out of existence. Their candlestick has been removed. But Paul is not saying that we are only to preach the goodness of God as the sole subject that leads men to repentance. If you will, preaching a God of all mercy and no judgment, all love and no wrath. That is not what this text is saying at all! That is not the Bible! What we are seeing here again is a complete rape of the Bible, rampant isogesis, and a false religion that is spreading over the land in the name of Christ.

GOODIES GOSPEL OR GOOD NEWS GOSPEL

Today's syrupy sermonizing sickeningly reminds me of the 1963 Hollywood film entitled Under *The Yum Yum Tree*. This rampant brand of "Confectionary Christianity" has tragically and disgracefully turned the cross of Jesus Christ into a candy cane. The "Goodness Gospel" or "Goodies Gospel" could well be called "The Yum Yum Gospel!" Today if the gospel being preached isn't sweet enough, it fails the Religious Humanism taste test.

Religious Humanism has turned Jesus into a "Pinata" hanging from a tree being beaten and bloodied while the candies and toys just keep on falling. It ought to make us outraged. It ought to make us cry. Religious Humanists have turned the Christian Gospel's bloody tree into a "Yum Yum Tree" under which man can ply God for all of the goodies that his heart desires. Religious Humanism is perverting the true Gospel, cheapening the Cross, trampling on Jesus' blood, minimizing sin, and imperiling the modern masses. All of these tragedies are the results of Religious Humanism's "Yum Yum Gospel."

The Christian Gospel is not the "Goodies Gospel." It is the "Good News Gospel." What good news? Oh, let me assure you that it is the best news that you ever have heard or ever will hear! Allow me to illustrate the true "Good News Gospel" by sharing with you the story of the young man who had a bitter argument with his father. Their relationship had steadily deteriorated until after one big explosion between them, in great anger the son left home and was away from his parents for many years. During that long period of separation, he heard nothing from his father, but his mother carried on correspondence with him. He would write to his mother and ask her, "Has father forgiven me? Has father forgiven me?" His mother would always reassure him by saying, "Yes, I am sure that he has forgiven you."

One day the son wrote to his mother and said, "If my father has forgiven me, I want to come back home. But please mother, be certain." Wanting to be sure, the young man's mother wrote back to him and said, "You know that big oak tree at the back of our lot right by the railroad tracks? If your father has forgiven you, there will be a big white cloth on that tree so that you can see it from the train window as you pass by on your way into town. If you don't see the white cloth, stay on the train and go on."

As the train approached the young man's hometown that day, and as it came to the place of the big oak tree in the backyard of his boyhood home, the young man could not bear to look. He asked his friend who was seated beside him, "Do you see a big oak tree?" He described the tree and the property to his buddy. The friend replied, "Yes, I see the tree." He then asked his friend, "Is there a white cloth on the tree?" His friend was silent for a moment. The young man's heart was close to breaking. Then the friend blurted out, "There is not only one white cloth, there is a white cloth on every branch."

Christianity is about white robes of forgiveness and righteousness hanging on Calvary's tree for sinners like you and me. What a relief the Christian Gospel alone brings to sinners. A glorious reconciliation to God after a life of sin and hostility! Like the glorious new life of springtime after the long coldness of a wintry heart dead in sin. A dreadful fear of wrath gives way to the warmth and tenderness of Divine grace. For sure: "**NOTHING BRINGS A DEEPER SENSE OF GRATITUDE AND PEACE THAN FULLY-DESERVED JUDGMENT THAT IS UNDESERVEDLY AND FULLY REMOVED.**" You can now get off the train of doubt, uncertainty and fearfulness. Welcome home to God the Father's loving arms of forgiveness! The "Good News Gospel" of our Lord Jesus Christ!

SINNIE THE POOH

I am sure that some of us still recall the name of the cartoon character "Winnie the Pooh!" The lovable fictional bear was created by A.A. Milne. The cuddly and endearing bear who was stuffed with lots and lots of fluff first appeared in the children's books *Winnie-the-Pooh* (1926) and *The House at Pooh Center (1928).* Winnie the Pooh, or Pooh Bear, had an insatiable appetite for honey, his favorite fare to feed that constant "Rumbling in his Tumbling." Pooh became a favorite of young and old alike, as well as a mainstay in Walt Disney featurettes.

The modern church has given birth to another cuddly little creature, namely, "Sinnie the Pooh." He is a cute little churchgoer who is also stuffed each Sunday with lots of fluff. Sinnie the Pooh has in recent years multiplied into thousands upon thousands of "Church Pooh-Bears" who each Sunday feed on a steady diet of the "Honey Gospel" to satisfy the "Growlies in Their Soulies."

Allow me to enable you to become more thoroughly familiar with Sinnie the Pooh. Sinnie the Pooh-Pew Bear, the modern church "Stuffed-With-Fluff" parishioner, no longer has the realization that he is by nature desperately sinful. Rather, he has the inner conviction that he is really quite huggable, and at his worst merely mischievous, i.e. benignly and playfully naughty. Not really a full-blown sinner, just a "Sinnie." There you go! A really cute little church teddy who will play with you as long as the church den- father or den-mother continues to serve up lots of honey – sweetsies for his dear little heartie.

If Sinnie the Pooh is such a cute little teddy bear, why are there those times that suddenly he becomes Grumpy the Grizzly? A young mother and her little son were driving down the street one day, and we all know how disarming little kids can be. Out of nowhere he asked his mother, "Mama, why do the idiots only come out when Daddy drives?" Someday the little boy will understand that Daddy's anger is more about Daddy than it is about the quality of the other drivers on the road. Cute Sinnie the Pooh can become a raging grizzly bear given the wrong set of circumstances.

Hey, come on, admit it, put Sinnie the Pooh in hot water (heated circumstances) and you will see a bear of a different color – brown bear. When a tea bag is put in hot water, the brown color comes into the hot water. The hot water didn't put the brown color into the tea bag. The hot water simply brought it out, for it was there all the time. And let me tell you, given its dwelling in the hot water for enough time, it will be the strongest tea you ever drank. When the heated pressure is on, Sinnie the Pooh more often than not becomes a snarling and growling bear of an altogether different sort.

But how then did Sinnie the Pooh church bear get his name? Oh, it is very simple. He attends a church and listens to a preacher who pooh-poohs sin. For the multiplying "Sinnie the Poohs" today, there is a surplus of this "Sin Pooh-Poohing Gospel" and these "Sin Pooh-Poohing Churches" and these "Sin Pooh-Poohing Preachers" that are no longer designed to produce the conviction of sin, but rather the affirmation of self. As a result, Religious Humanism is filling the church with "Sinnie the Poohs." It is not the church of the Lord Jesus Christ.

Listen to this official statement of the United Methodist Church for instance concerning homosexuality: "**HOMOSEXUAL PER- SONS NO LESS THAN HETEROSEXUAL PERSONS ARE INDIVIDUALS OF SACRED WORTH. ALL PERSONS NEED THE MINISTRY AND GUIDANCE OF THE CHURCH IN THEIR STRUGGLES FOR HUMAN FULFILLMENT, AS WELL AS THE SPIRITUAL AND EMOTIONAL CARE OF A FELLOWSHIP THAT ENABLES RECONCILING RELATIONSHIPS WITH GOD, WITH OTHERS AND WITH SELF.**"

"**THE UNITED METHODIST CHURCH DOES NOT CON- DONE THE PRACTICE OF HOMOSEXUALITY AND CONSID- ERS THIS PRACTICE INCOMPATIBLE WITH CHRISTIAN TEACHING. WE AFFIRM THAT GOD'S GRACE IS AVAILABLE TO ALL, AND WE WILL SEEK TO LIVE TOGETHER IN CHRISTIAN COMMUNITY. WE IMPLORE FAMILIES AND CHURCHES NOT TO REJECT OR**

CONDEMN LESBIAN AND GAY MEMBERS AND FRIENDS. WE COMMIT OURSELVES TO BE IN MINISTRY FOR AND WITH ALL PERSONS." (4)

First of all, I appreciate the spirit of love and compassion in the United Methodist Church's official statement concerning homosexuals. I know that they want to bring all people to Christ as their Savior and Lord. The loving spirit manifested is commendable. The desire to minister to all people is laudable.

But it all falls apart from that point on, for in their desire to be fair to all they can't give what the Bible calls an abomination (Leviticus 18:22) a failing grade. It comes out to be about a C- at worst. Not sinners, just sinnies. Religious Humanists always make sure somehow that most sinners stay ahead of the moral curve. So on Saturdays, many church folks now have to choose between all-church invitations to a wedding where the man and the woman are entering their third marriage, or to the wedding between two lesbians who are entering their first. In the first they will support serial polygamy, and in the second they will sanction perversion. Welcome to the modern ecclesiastical "Dark Ages of Ecclesiastical A-morality."

Second, did you notice that they call homosexuality a practice and not a sin? The Bible calls homosexuals unrighteous, i.e. sinners! (I Corinthians 6:9-11) Doctors practice medicine. Attorneys practice law. Now we are to believe that gays and lesbians practice homosexuality? It almost makes homosexuality sound like a vocational career. Hardly! Unfaithful spouses do not practice adultery. Sexually active singles do not practice fornication. Thieves do not practice robbery. Gays and lesbians do not practice homosexuality. They are all sinners living in unrighteousness.

Since when are sinners no longer sinners, but instead merely practitioners? This entire way of camouflaging sin is the shame of Religious Humanism, and the total subversion of morality. Mark these words, that those who are no longer confronted with the shamefulness of their sins will be completely shameless in their sinning. This is exactly why the Psalmist says what he does in Psalm 36:2 (KJV),

"For he flattereth himself in his own eyes, until his iniquity be found to be hateful."

Third, the United Methodists tell us that they do not condone homosexuality. The Christian Bible tells us that God condemns homosexuality. Not to condone is passive disapproval. To condemn is active denunciation. Not to condone in Religious Humanism is but mere criticism which Methodists hope will not lead to hurt feelings or alienation. To condemn in the Christian Bible is to pass a sentence of spiritual and eternal death unless there is a turning away from sin to God.

We have but to remind ourselves of the homosexuals that came from all over the cities of Sodom and Gomorrah demanding of Lot that he send out the male guests in his house for the purpose of perverse sexual relationships. Lot's guests were in fact angels in the form of men. The homosexuals were so filled with perversion and seething lust that they tried to beat the door down of Lot's house to get at them, even after they had been stricken by God's angels with blindness. There these blinded homosexuals were, pounding away at the door making all kinds of ruckus until they wore themselves out. Now they were so tired that their sin-sick sex drives went into neutral for the moment. We know what happened to the cities of Sodom and Gomorrah. God destroyed them with brimstone and fire out of Heaven. Why? The angels said to Lot in Genesis 19:13,

"For we are about to destroy this place, because their outcry has become so great before the Lord that the Lord has sent us to destroy it."

Fourth, did you also notice that homosexuality is characterized as being incompatible with Christian teaching? No! Certain homosexuals may find themselves incompatible with other homosexuals. But homosexuality is not a mere incompatibility with God. It is a flagrant sin against God's holy and revealed will.

Perhaps United Methodists may want to rethink their stand. In Religious Humanism, **"HOMOSEXUALITY IS PRESENTED AS A PEDAGOGICAL IMCOMPATIBILITY."** In the Christian Bible, **"HOMOSEXUALITY IS PRESENTED AS AN ABOMINABLE INIQUITY."** Radical difference! According to the United Methodist Church, homosexuals are not sinners, just incompatibles. The result being that in the worst case, they are not "Sinners," but merely "Incompatible Sinnies."

Fifth, the United Methodists are also told by their church leadership that as families and churches they are not to reject their lesbian and gay members and friends. Of course, that all sounds so laudable and loving. Without a doubt we are to love our gay neighbors, whoever and whatever they might be, as we love ourselves. But not without calling them to repentance, and telling them unless they turn to the Lord and turn away from their perversion, they are and will be forever outside of the Kingdom of God.

There is no such thing as a homosexual Christian church member. There is no such thing as a Christian community of heterosexuals and homosexuals. To talk about practicing homosexuals as church members is to create sex-preference-optional churches, sort of like clothing-optional beaches. Come now, quit dressing it up with politically and socially correct baloney. What you really have is a queer church and a nude beach.

When United Methodist leadership talks about "gay church members," it is just another one of modern Religious Humanism's blue-ribbon oxymora of our day. God says in I Corinthians 6:9-10,

"Or do you not know that the unrighteous shall not inherit the kingdom of God? Do not be deceived;
neither fornicators,
nor idolaters,
nor adulterers,
nor effeminate,
nor homosexuals,
nor thieves,
nor the covetous,
nor drunkards, nor revilers,
nor swindlers, shall inherit
the kingdom of God."

Gay Christian Church members!? Lesbian Christian church members!? There is no such thing. Converted to Christ ex-gay Christian heterosexual church members! Converted to Christ ex-lesbian heterosexual Christian church members! Now you are talking Bible truth. Yes indeed, and the Corinthian Christian church was blessed to have them as members and rejoiced over the victory of Christ in their lives. They were now by the miracle of rebirth in Jesus Christ, heterosexuals. I have seen again and again homosexuals totally broken and helpless before God, confessing their sinfulness and perversion, repenting of their abominable lifestyle, and trans-formed by the blood of Jesus and the regenerating Holy Spirit into heterosexuals with holy, heterosexual desires.

SATAN THE POOH, TOO

It becomes more shocking when we find that Religious Humanists do not even want to offend Satan, or make him feel uncomfortable or rejected. Larry King on "Larry King Live" interviewed Pastor Joel Osteen on Monday, June 20, 2005. Poor Satan the Pooh! Larry King got into the subject of whether or not we are supposed to love the Devil. A no-brainer when you really think about it, and even if you don't think about it. That part of the interview went like this as recorded by "Forgotten Word Ministries:" King – "**I ASKED REVEREND GRAHAM IF GOD LOVES THE DEVIL. DIDN'T – COULDN'T – HE'D NEVER BEEN ASKED IT BEFORE.**" Osteen – "**I NEVER THOUGHT OF IT EITHER. I DON'T KNOW.**" King – "**HE (GOD) LOVES EVERYTHING. DOES HE LOVE…?**" Osteen – "**I DON'T KNOW. I'LL LEAVE THAT FOR DR. GRAHAM.**" (5)

To ask the question whether we should love or hate Satan is about as astounding as asking the question whether we should love or hate God, for that flat out was King's question. Where does such confusion come from? It is really very easy to understand, for wherever you have lost sight of the absolute antithesis between good and evil, you will then have the synthesis of total opposites. That is exactly where such questions and answers on "Larry King Live" are coming from. The fact is that it is as damnable to love Satan as it is to hate God.

The Bible tells us that Jesus loathed the Devil so much, that He came to crush Satan's head. (Genesis 3:15) Not a very affectionate thing to do! Here's a heads up for you – Satan's head was smashed by Jesus at Calvary and the empty tomb! No love lost by Christ there! The feelings were mutual. It was Satan who was the instigator of the crucifixion of our precious Savior. Satan was there at the very beginning of Jesus' ministry to tempt Him and bring Him down. Then at the end of Christ's ministry all that was done by the hateful instruments of His arrest and suffering was done by Satan's direct instigation, as we read in Luke 22:53 what Jesus said to the chief priests, officers of the temple, and to the elders:

"**…but this hour and the power of darkness are yours.**"

Satan's finger prints were on the crown of thorns that was smashed down unto Jesus head. Satan's finger prints were on the nails that were pounded into our Savior's hands and feet. Satan's finger prints were on the sword that was thrust up into our Savior's lungs. Now are we supposed to look with loving eyes on the prince of darkness? No! Not a chance. Think again! This is truly the one instance that we can feel justified in saying with the Psalmist in Psalm 139:21

"**Do I not hate those who hate Thee, O Lord? And do I not loathe those who rise up against Thee?**"

But instead, not only do we now have "Sinnie the Pooh" pastors, but now we have "Satan the Pooh" pastors as well. Not only soft on sin, but soft on Satan! It was bound to happen in all of this Religious Humanism drivel and mush. For when you become soft on sin you will become soft on sin's originator. Billy Graham then can't help you! Jesus either!

And of course if churches don't hate sin as sin and Satan as Satan, then it is no wonder that many churches today send out fewer and fewer missionaries every year. Because they do not recognize sin, they do not recognize Satan, and they do not believe in Hell, eternal judgment and eternal punishment. There goes the urgency of the Gospel message. Religious Humanism is undercutting the very mission of the Christian Church.

THE GOSPEL OF UNIVERSALISM

Before leaving the Larry King-Pastor Joel Osteen debacle of June 20, 2005 on CNN's "Larry King Live," we must ask, "How could the answers to Larry King's elementary and straightforward questions have had such pathetically botched answers?" Larry King's interview did not require Pastor Osteen to pass some sort of spiritual SAT exam. A Sunday school kid in any solid Christian Church could have answered King's questions with Biblical clarity, decisiveness and definitiveness. But all that really happened was that Christianity was made to look like a foggy, hazy, nondescript, wishy-washy, indeterminate religion.

Here is another part of the interview which from a Christian perspective staggers the mind and imagination: King – **"WHAT IF YOU'RE JEWISH OR MUSLIM, YOU DON'T ACCEPT CHRIST AT ALL?"** Osteen – **"YOU KNOW, I AM VERY CAREFUL ABOUT SAYING WHO WOULD AND WHO WOULDN'T GO TO HEAVEN. I DON'T KNOW…"** King – **"IF YOU BELIEVE THAT YOU HAVE TO BELIEVE IN CHRIST? THEY'RE WRONG, AREN'T THEY?"** Osteen – **"WELL, I DON'T KNOW IF I BELIEVE THEY'RE WRONG. I BELIEVE HERE'S WHAT THE BIBLE TEACHES AND FROM THE CHRISTIAN FAITH THIS IS WHAT I BELIEVE. BUT I JUST THINK THAT ONLY GOD [WILL] JUDGE A PERSON'S HEART. I SPENT A LOT OF TIME IN INDIA WITH MY FATHER. I DON'T KNOW ABOUT THEIR RELIGION. BUT I KNOW THEY LOVE GOD. AND I DON'T KNOW. I'VE SEEN THEIR SINCERITY. SO I DON'T KNOW. I KNOW FOR ME WHAT THE BIBLE TEACHES; I WANT A RELATIONSHIP WITH JESUS CHRIST."** (6)

Robert E. Wise of "Forgotten Word Ministries" states: **"SINCE THIS INTERVIEW, JOEL OSTEEN HAS APOLOGIZED TO HIS CONGREGATION FOR HIS FAILURE TO EXPRESS WHAT HE REALLY BELIEVED. IF JOEL DIDN'T ACTUALLY BELIEVE THE**

STATEMENTS ABOVE, THEN WHY DID HE SAY THEM TO START WITH? THE TRUTH BE KNOWN, JOEL HAS A REAL PROBLEM ON HIS HANDS THAT HE IS HIDING FROM THE PUBLIC AND HIMSELF. I BELIEVE THAT HE ACTUALLY DOES BELIEVE WHAT HE SAID DURING THE INTERVIEW, BUT BECAUSE OF THE CRITI-CISM HE RECEIVED FOR MAKING THEM HE GAVE AN APOLOGY." (7)

Allow me, before we go any further, to try and blow away at least some of this Religious Humanistic fog that is spreading over the ecclesiastical landscape of America and the world, and is getting thicker by the moment. First, the phrase "I don't know" was stated over and over and over again ad nausea by Joel Osteen during the interview. Nothing will subject Christianity to contempt by the world as the ignorance of it's fundamentals on the part of its supposed leaders. Also, the people then under their charge are left unprotected by blind watchmen on the walls of Zion. Nothing will expose men to error and heresy like the ignorance of truth. Spiritual leaders must take heed to the words of Hosea 4:6,

> **"My people are destroyed for lack of knowledge...."**

It was Larry King looking lost in the dense Religious Humanistic fog of "I don't know." All that would have had to be said to Larry King and the vast viewing audience are the well-known, unmistakable, clear-as-crystal Gospel words of John 3:16,

> **"For God so loved the world that He gave His only begotten Son, that whoever believes in Him should not perish, but have eternal life."**

Second, speaking of other religions such as Hinduism which Joel Osteen referred to, the Hindu religion does not believe in Jesus Christ, the only begotten Son of God. They therefore categorically do not love God. How can you love someone you don't even believe exists? Hindus believe in anything and everything else. Hinduism's main god, the god or divine reality that is above all else, is named Brahman. Underneath Brahman, there are gobs of other gods. Some have estimated that the Hindu religion has hundreds of millions of gods. Many of their gods are the manifestations of natural realities such as fire as well as the elements that make up storms. They make idols out of deified cows! However, all of their idol-gods are but expressions of the one chief god – Brahman. No, they do not believe in the Christian Trinity, and they do not believe in or worship Jesus Christ, without Whom they are doomed. Hinduism has nothing in common with Christianity or Christianity's God. They do not love God! They love false gods!

As for Islam, referred to in Larry King's question, it teaches that the Koran is the Word of God, not the Bible, and that God is Allah. President Obama often quotes from the Koran as he is a closet Moslem on his way out of the closet. Also, Moslems believe that Mohammed is the messenger of Allah. Their mantra is, "There is no God but Allah and Mohammed is his messenger!" Islam does not believe in the truth of the Trinitarian God – Father, Son, and Holy Spirit, but utterly rejects it. Christianity declares, "There is no God but the Triune God and Jesus Christ is His messenger." Islam has nothing in common with Christianity, even though there are those today who say otherwise, and are promoting the merger of the two under the name "Chrislam."

As for Judaism, they reject Jesus as God's promised Messiah and Savior of mankind. The Jews believe in Jahweh, the Jehovah of the Old Testament. The Jewish people were used by God to give us a Savior, and they rejected what He gave to them and to all mankind. We read Jesus' powerful and scathing words in John 15:24,

"If I had not done among them the works which no one else did, they would not have sin; but now they have both seen and hated Me and My Father as well."

The Jews in their rejection of the Christ could not and cannot argue innocence from the lack of proof. It was not a blind rejection in that regard. All of the miracles that Jesus did affirmed Him to be the Messiah in capital letters. They saw Him day after day as He shone in all of His Messianic brilliance and power, but in their sin and unbelief they chose to stare down the Son. As the result, they remain spiritually blind as a people to this very day.

Mike Oppenheimer of "Let Us Reason Ministries" states: **"WHEN JOEL OSTEEN WAS ON BILL O'REILLY'S SHOW, HE WAS ASKED IF HE BELIEVED WHETHER JESUS WAS THE WAY, THE TRUTH AND THE LIFE, THE ONLY WAY TO GOD. OSTEEN IGNORED THIS QUESTION, SAYING THAT HE DOESN'T GET INTO THAT. THAT EVASIVE ANSWER IS INDICATIVE OF HIS BROAD POSITIVE APPROACH THAT ATTRACTS THE MASSES."** (8)

Joel Osteen's answer to Larry King's inquiry about the universal necessity of believing in Jesus Christ was that he (Joel) wants a relationship with Jesus Christ. That is not what he was asked. King asked about those who don't accept Jesus

Christ, and he got a song and dance run-around answer. So did Bill O'Reilly. Osteen's straight-forward answer should have been that you must accept Jesus as your Savior and your Lord to go to Heaven, and if you don't you will go to Hell. It was as simple as 2+2 = 4. But he didn't, not even close! The tragic results of Religious Humanism is that it left Larry King spiritually dead on "Larry King Live," and it left Bill O'Reilly without the Gospel facts on "The Factor."

Sure enough! The implication is clear! Here it comes! Wouldn't you just know it? Aw shucks, why not just include everybody. Inclusiveness! Religious Humanists are turning Christianity into an all-inclusive resort, drinks included! It was inevitable that what now follows would evolve.

This is where the gospel of Religious Humanism also will ultimately lead, namely, smack dab into, "**A GOSPEL OF UNIVERSALISM.**" All-inclusiveness! That is to say, no one will be judged, but everyone will be saved, whether or not they believe in Jesus as their Lord and Savior. That includes Hindus, Muslims, Jews, believers, unbelievers, and you name it. No inferno for anyone, and paradise for everyone. This gospel of universalism is another horrific result of Religious Humanism.

This is exactly what happened to Rev. Carlton Pearson who pastored the Higher Dimension Family Church in Tulsa, Oklahoma! He had often been a guest preacher on Trinity Broadcasting Network. He stopped believing in Hell and started preaching a gospel of universalism, i.e. that everyone will be saved. Hell is only something that many people suffer on earth, but they all will be delivered from it and live in Heaven forever.

Pastor Pearson was removed from the Church of God in Christ, which is a Pentecostal Fellowship estimated to be the sixth largest denomination in the United States. His church which once numbered 5000 worshippers dwindled to a few. This is nothing more or less than one of the tragic results of Religious Humanism. And it is spreading! Coming soon to a church near you!

The Biblical truth is that the Gospel of the Bible is, "**A GOSPEL OF EXCLUSIVISM.**" In other words, only those who believe in and serve Jesus as their Lord and Savior will enter into eternal life, while those who did not believe in and serve Jesus as their Lord and Savior will enter into eternal destruction! Those who give their lives to Jesus are the forever included, and those who do not are the forever excluded. The former in the Bible are called sheep. The latter are called goats. In that regard, the entire world is made up of either sheep or goats that now live together on the same planet, and sometimes in the same church. But in eternity, the sheep will live forever with the Good Shepherd in Heaven, and the goats will die forever with Satan the rebellious goat-leader in Hell.

We read in Matthew 25:31-33 the revealing words about the coming of the Lord Jesus,

"But when the Son of man comes in His glory, and all the angels with Him, then He will sit on His glorious throne. And all the nations will be gathered before Him; and he will separate them from one another, as the shepherd separates the sheep from the goats; and He will put the sheep on His right, and the goats on the left."

Then we read in Matthew 25:34,

"Then the King shall say to those on His right, 'Come, you who are blessed of My Father, inherit the kingdom prepared for you from the foundation of the world."

However we read in Matthew 25:41,

"Then He will also say to those on His left, 'Depart from Me, accursed ones, into the eternal fire which has been prepared for the devil and his angels.'"

THE GOSPEL DESTINATION CHANGED

This is it! The ultimate! The end all and be all! The grand finale! The beyond which there is no more! The mountain peak which towers above all others! It is written in bold letters throughout the Bible. It is the upper case destination for Christians. Everything else is lower case. The true Gospel destination is, **"DESTINATION GOD!"** The Apostle Peter puts it this way in I Peter 3:18,

"For Christ also died for sins once for all, the just for the unjust, in order that He might bring us to God...."

Jesus Christ died, the sinless for the sinful, the just for the unjust, to afford us one overwhelming and indescribable ecstasy, and that is to bring sinful, forgiven man into fellowship with the Holy God.

To bring man to God! It should not baffle us that the means to such an inestimably glorious end would have to be very elaborate astounding, as stated by the words, "The just for the unjust." We must remember that because of sin, man's way back to God had been blocked. God is so holy that He cannot even look at sin! (Habakkuk 1:13 KJV) Sinful men, which included all of us, were blocked from God's presence forever. We were all Hell-bound with a one-way ticket. Unlike Moses, we would never even get a glimpse of the Promised Land, let alone go there. Cut off from God for eternity is a nightmare that will never end.

The only time that we would see God would be in a courtroom scene before the Judge of all the earth and the sentence would be eternal suffering and death without parole. Condemned to die eternally! No possibility of a mitigated sentence. There we stand before the righteous Judge of Heaven and earth. We have looked bad before, but never as bad as we do now standing before perfect righteousness. There is a horrid sense of inescapable finality that was never in our lives before. No indulgences will get us out of this one. We thought we could buy our way out again, for the Religious Humanists had saturated the entire earth with a pay-as-you-go gospel that would always make everything alright. But it is despairingly evident that no indulgence-based absolution will be able to save us from this one. We are doomed!

I Peter 3:18 never looked this good! We must fully realize, in so far as it is humanly possible, that to bring sinful us back to the sinless God, which because of our sins we could never do for ourselves, God would have to become a man to die for man's sins which were man's unsurpassable barrier to fellowship with the Almighty. But to die for man's sins, not only would God have to be a man, but He would have to become a sinless man. For if He had sins of His own, He could not die for the sins of other men. Thus were required the supernatural intricacies of the virgin conception and birth of the sinless child, Jesus, by the Divine intervention of the Holy Spirit – the incarnation. The sinless man would also have to be God, for no man or angel, not even a sinless one, would be able to endure the wrath of God against humanity's sin and survive it. That is why no archangel could do the job, for it would wipe him out, too. Man! Sinless Man! God! Man could not hope for fellowship with God upon the basis of any other terms or provision. The Just for the unjust!

That has always been and always will be the surpassing magnificence of the Christian Gospel, though today it is being smothered under so much humanistic trash and materialistic junk. Religious Humanism's gospel pales in comparison and appears so drab and dismal in the full light of the Gospel of the Lord Jesus Christ. Religious Humanism is diverting the church from its true destiny with the trifling and plastic notions that Jesus died on a cross to bring us to bangles and beads, tinsel and trinkets. As a result, it has completely changed the Gospel destination. What to? To success avenue! To easy street! Do you think that I am kidding? Please read on.

Now read the words of Jesse Duplantis: "**THE VERY FIRST THING ON**

JESUS' AGENDA WAS TO GET RID OF POVERTY. WOULD YOU LIKE TO KNOW WHY SOME PEOPLE, INCLUDING MINISTRIES, NEVER GET OUT OF POVERTY? ... IT'S BECAUSE THEY'RE NOT ANOINTED. IF YOU'RE NOT ANOINTED, POVERTY WILL FOLLOW YOU ALL THE DAYS OF YOUR LIFE. HIS FIRST OBJECTIVE WAS TO GET RID OF POVERTY." (9)

In short, Religious Humanism cons people into believing that the Christian Gospel is all about Jesus being mockingly crowned with thorns and thistles, that men might be lavished with wine and roses. Human nature sucks this up and today nurses at the breasts of Religious Humanism's prosperity gospel like a nursery of sucking infants. Because of man's natural and voracious appetite for the material, his carnal cravings find Religious Humanism's material and temporal gospel irresistible. Oh yes, just mention riches and they start to feel the "anointing."

The gospel of Religious Humanism is about "**GOD-PLUS**." Not just to bring us to God? Oh goodness no! That is good for starters, but it certainly is not enough for Religious Humanists. A Gospel that only brings us to God simply does not get the job done. Religious Humanists want more than God. They want God-plus. God is not really the destination at all, but only a means to their much more longed for destinations – health, enlargement, power, riches, and lots of toys. They demand a package deal. Who wants to get stuck with merely God?! How drab! The Gospel that brings us only to God leaves the Religious Humanist melancholy and with a terribly discontented spirit. They feel that they are being short-changed unless they are brought to God with a whole bunch of extras thrown in. A Gospel that is God-Only is a rip-off. God alone! Oh God no! God-plus! Now we're talking.

The gospel of Religious Humanism is a "**GOD-PLUS RELATIONSHIP**." The Gospel of Christianity is a "**GOD-PERIOD RELATIONSHIP**." That is the consistent and unchangeable Gospel of Jesus Christ throughout the Bible. God-period! For you see, a God Who by and of Himself does not totally fulfill man is not much of a God at all. A God who has to be a God-plus God is really a God-minus God. God-plus speaks of a deficient God. No, God is in Him-self everything and more than man could ever need or want.

All of this is why we read the words that we do in Psalm 16:11,

> "...**In Thy presence is fullness of joy; in Thy right hand there are pleasures forever**."

It's all there! It is in the present tense. It is all there forever. It is the eternal tense. In God's presence! All the joy that we could ever want! Fullness of joy! All the pleasures and more than we have ever dreamed of! Pleasures unlimited! To be sure then, no man can be said to have enjoyed himself fully in life who is not fellowshipping at the right hand of God.

Comparing the pleasures of God's presence to the material pleasures of the world is like comparing the pleasures of the angels in Heaven to the pleasures of hogs on earth. It is like comparing hallelujahs to oinks. If you will, it is like comparing Heaven to a pig sty. There is no pleasure comparable to that which comes from God's presence. That is why the Psalm of Asaph states in Psalm 73:25,

"...And besides Thee, I desire nothing on earth."

And again, Psalm 73:28,

"But as for me, the nearness of God is my good...."

When God's Old Testament Church was in slavery in Egypt, God sent Moses to give the following fiat to King Pharaoh of Egypt on behalf of Himself in Exodus 5:1,

"...Let My people go that they may celebrate a feast TO ME in the wilderness."

God said, "Pharaoh, this is an order! Let my people go! Let them come to worship and celebrate Me in a sacred feast. I want My people all to Myself. Let them come to Me Pharaoh, yes, let them come to Me!" You may recall that at that point Pharaoh really got his dander up and abused the Israelites with harder slave labor than ever before.

I am convinced that Satan isn't upset about people simply going to church, especially to a Religious Humanistic church. I know he takes sick pleasure in that. What makes Satan really upset is when people begin to enjoy God and God alone. He realizes that this is where and only where he will lose man forever. There is nothing that the Devil fears more than when a man gets all wrapped up in God and God alone. Then he has lost man forever and will never get him back. I can hear him say to his demons, "Don't let people get caught up in those "God-Period Churches." Keep them from that upper-case faith. Rather, encourage them to get involved with those God-plus, lower-case churches and TV programs that are so plentiful today. Then they can yet be ours forever!"

The Christian Gospel is consistent throughout Scripture. In Exodus 19:4 God commands Moses to remind the sons of Israel of the one overriding purpose of their deliverance from Egyptian bondage when He said:

"You yourselves have seen what I did to the Egyptians, and how I bore you on eagles' wings, AND BROUGHT YOU TO MYSELF."

Short! Simple! Eternal! Profound! Listen up now! God did not ultimately bring Israel out of Egypt so that they might be set free from slave labor in Pharaoh's brickyards. That was only a means to the Divine end. Nor did God set them free from the tyrant Pharaoh so that He might bring them into Canaan land which was flowing with milk and honey. Oh, says the Religious Humanist, there it is – milk and honey – for that the Passover Lamb was slain in Egypt. No, it was not for something so trite as "Milk Duds" or "Honey Buns. God brought the Israelites out of captivity by the blood of the Passover Lamb for one grand and glorious purpose, namely, that He might bring them to Himself.

It is again so dramatically captured in the story of the distribution of and portioning off of the "Promised Land" by God to the tribes of Israel. When the tribe of Levi's turn came to receive their inheritance, they received no share of the land. Not one acre. Not even half an acre. Zero real estate! God simply said to them in Numbers 18:20,

"...I am your portion and your inheritance...."

The priestly tribe of Levi was a type of the believer's priesthood in the New Testament church. The Holy Spirit tells New Testament believers in Revelation 1:6 that Christ has made us,

"...priests to His God and Father...."

All that the Levites received for their portion was God and ministering to Him in the tabernacle and then in the temple! They received no earthly claim. All that we receive as Christian priests is God, and serving and ministering to Him. He is everything! Eternally and infinitely more than enough!

HIS DIVINE MAJESTY HAS GONE MISSING

The psalmist says about God in Psalm 104:1,

"Bless the Lord, O my soul! O Lord my God, Thou art very great; Thou art clothed with splendor and majesty."

The Psalmist here sees God clothed in all of His heavenly and kingly regalia. The Divine King of Heaven and earth, the grandest Potentate of time and eternity, is here being worshipped in response to and with the deepest sense of His royal splendor and majesty. Splendor refers to his unmatched beauty. Majesty refers to the grandeur of His sovereign, universal Kingship. The King of Heaven is clothed in both. Heavenly splendor and majesty are His eternal wardrobe.

Then for His royal robe, so to speak, we read of God in the following words in Psalm 104:2,

"Covering Thyself with light as with a cloak...."

His royal robe is shimmering light, the brilliance of His blinding purity. God lights up Heaven all by Himself with His eternal and dazzling holy luminescence. When John the Revelator tries to describe the luster of the New Jerusalem, the capital city of Heaven, he says in Revelation 21:23,

"And the city has no need of the sun or of the moon to shine upon it, for the glory of God has illumined it, and its lamp is the Lamb."

I Can Only Imagine! One can feebly try to imagine God Almighty sitting upon the throne of Heaven, clothed in His Kingly garments of dazzling splendor, with the majestic scepter of sole sovereignty in His right hand, and His entire being ablaze in spectacular light. It all defies description! It staggers our puny minds and notions.

We may try to take our point of reference from earthly kings and potentates, but the comparison of the King of Kings and the Lord of Lords to any earthly ruler is infinitely and ridiculously disproportionate. It is not possible to reference the temporal to illustrate the eternal, or to point to the earthly as an analogy for the Heavenly. That would be to dishonor God's Kingship, for all earthly rulers and magistrates pale in comparison, and standing alongside of the King of Heaven they appear as but safety patrols at school crossings.

Something has happened in the modern Christian Church that has devastated the deep and reverential awe of the blazing splendor, sovereignty, majesty and holiness of God. The church has been invaded by Religious Humanism which has infected much of the modern Christian community with an inflated and even ostentatious concept of humanity, and a thereby deflated and demeaned awareness of Divinity.

An oversized humanity will always result in an undersized Divinity. John the Baptist recognized this inescapable principle, when he said in John 3:30,

"He (Jesus) must increase, but I must decrease."

In order for the former to happen, the latter must take place. Notice the order of the Baptist's "Must Principle." We must first see the awesomeness of the King, before we can see the commonness of ourselves as His subjects. Only by knowing and seeing His magnificence can we know and see how miniature and bland we really are. All true worship in the church has always risen out of John the Baptist's "Must Principle."

Conversely, what is in fact happening in the modern Religious Humanistic churches across the land is this:

"Man has increased, and God has decreased."

As a result, man has become one of the gods, and God has become one of the guys. This can be illustrated in many ways. The inverting of John the Baptist's "Must Principle" has permeated the modern religious world. For instance, a Los Angeles company called "Teen Millionaire" produced and sold T-shirts on which is written the slogan: **"JESUS IS MY HOMEBOY."** The company knew something about the current religious-humanistic mindset in America. The shirts originally retailed for about $25.00, and they sold like hot-cakes. Not just teens and hipsters, but Christians of all ages as well, loved the "Jesus Is My Homeboy" T-shirts.

If you will, Jesus is just one of the boys around our house. We just love having that boy around here. He is welcome here anytime. I get the drift of it. Adults as well as young people want Jesus to be simply one of the fellas. You see, that way they don't have to deal with His Divine splendor, sovereignty and majesty. That is all too threatening to modern religious man and makes him far too accountable as a subject of the King of Kings and Lord of Lords. So modern religious folk take false comfort in imagining Christ's domesticated boyishness! That way we can be more relaxed around Jesus, for after all, boys will be boys and Jesus is now one of them. Hey Jesus Homeboy, You just make yourself at home in our house and relax, and we will make ourselves at home in Your house and relax as well. Groovy! Coffee and donuts during the sermon anyone? Cafe Latte Christianity!

A "Casual God" meeting with "Casual Christians" in a "Casual Atmosphere!" I have seen with my own eyes a pastor on a Sunday morning conducting the morning worship service in Bermuda shorts, sandals, and a gaudy colored and patterned shirt. The guy looked like he was either going golfing or had already been. Instead of worship-ping the Triune God, I felt like shouting, "Four!" In short, the God of majestic holiness is no longer the point of reference in Religious Humanism. Rather, fleshly self-interest and self-comfort has become the guiding principle. Just make sure that "God's House" has all of the comforts of home.

I have seen in these same Religious Humanistic environments women coming to church dressed in halter tops and shorts to worship Jesus the majestically splendid and holy King of Glory. Lady Liberty in New York Harbor is dressed with more modesty and reverence than today's tank-top male and halter-top female church-goers. Oh, I know that many are already jumping all over this, and are shouting at the author of this book that man looks on the outward appearance, but God looks at the heart. That is exactly the point, for by the same token the condition of the heart is revealed in part by how we conduct and clothe ourselves in the worship of the holy, majestic God.

It has all taken place within a few short years of recent church history. Before my tear-filled eyes, I have witnessed magnificent church orchestras and church choirs being completely dismantled and summarily replaced by a synthesizer, a few guitars, and a small group of singers called worship leaders or teams. It is all comparable to replacing the New York Philharmonic Orchestra and the Mormon Tabernacle Choir with The Beatles. It is not possible to counterfeit the worship of His majesty. Psalm 150 calls for every instrument to be used in the praise of the Lord. It calls for everything that has breath to praise the Lord. His magnificence cries out for magnified praise. It is not what man prefers, but what God demands. Psalm 150 informs us what alone will be suitable in the worship of His splendor and majesty.

All of this brings to mind one of the most astonishing events in the sacred history of God and the Jewish people. Who could have ever dreamed what the people of God were capable of, and are capable of today? God had revealed His staggering power on behalf of His chosen, but enslaved people in the land of Egypt. He displayed His infinite potency ten times. They are better known as the ten plagues. Heaven's Monarch and Potentate rolled back His royal sleeve, reached down His omnipotent arm, and put on a display of the most prodigious manifestations of His power and wrath ever witnessed by human eyes.

On top of all of that, no sooner had God sliced the Red Sea in half like a big watermelon, that the Israelites constructed and deified a golden calf and worshipped it. But that doesn't adequately convey the madness of what they had done. They substituted a golden calf for the King of Heaven. They took God off from the throne of His Heavenly majesty and replaced Him with a cute, cuddly little golden calf on an earthly pedestal. So benign and non-threatening! So manageable! It was Divine-human compatibility through calfability. A nice, manageable, little moo-cow god in the place of the majestic God! And not just a little calf-idol! Oh no! A little gold-god as well – a Religious Humanist's dream come true! It not only grossly blasphemed Divinity, but it shockingly illustrated how devoid the people of God can become of the deep sense of God's transcendent majesty and glory.

The major point being in all of this is: **"THERE IS NO GREATER AFFRONT TO THE SPLENDID AND MAJESTIC GOD THAN TO LOWER OUR NOTIONS OF HIM, AND THEN TO REDUCE OUR WORSHIP OF HIM TO THE DEGRADING LEVEL OF THOSE NOTIONS."**

GOD'S GRACE IS BEING DISCARDED

We must never underestimate the incredible power of the media. Day after day and night after night around the world, millions upon millions are seeing on religious TV a false face put on God. Before their very eyes and ears His "Grace Face" is being defaced and replaced with a "Business Face." His "Mercy Face" is being replaced with a "Money Face." American religion is being shaped by Religious Humanism TV programming. As a result, when the world rides by American churches on Sunday morning, many of them still called "Grace Church," they look at each other as they pass by and ask, "I wonder what they are selling in there this morning."

Christians are no longer sinners saved by grace. Rather, when it comes to them and their dealings with "Business God," they are only worth their weight in gold. It won't be long and they will have engraved on their tombstones, "I Made It To Heaven The Old Fashioned Way, I Earned It." As a result, God's grace is not nearly as amazing as it once was. In fact, God's grace has been disgraced by the entire Religious Humanism system.

Many modern Religious Humanists will not admit to the fact that they teach what they teach. In fact, they will deny it. John 1:16 tells us that we live from grace to grace. However, their merit-to-merit philosophy is hiding around every corner. The Christian sings, "Nothing in my hands I bring, simply to Thy cross I cling.” Religious Humanists, though they would deny it, are singing, “Something in my hand I bring, partly to Thy cross I cling.”

Sometimes it is not veiled at all, as in these words of TV speaker and fund-raiser Mike Murdock: **ANYTHING IN YOUR HAND** (money given to Murdock) **WILL CREATE ANYTHING YOU WANT IN THE FUTURE**.” (10) It's what is in your hands that is primary, and not what is in the grace-filled, nail-pierced hands of Jesus. Our future is not in the grace-filled hands of the Divine Creator and Redeemer, but in the money-filled hands of the human creature.

There are those rare glimpses of Heaven that we are given on earth. Perhaps you too have had one of those grace moments when someone unexpectedly gives you something valuable. You quickly reach for your wallet or purse, and the grace-giver says, “No, no, your money is no good around here. Just enjoy it as our love-gift to you.” That is as close to authentic Bible-Grace-Based Christianity as there is. When it comes to any and every blessing of God, we cannot buy one of them. Not one! God says to us, “No, no, your money is no good around here. Just enjoy it as Our love gift to you.” When it comes to receiving any and all blessings of the Triune God, our money is as worthless as a three dollar bill. Your might just as well try to buy something down South with Confederate money, or up North with Union money! So it is in the Kingdom of God, whether north, south, east or west, we don't live from dollar to dollar, but from grace to grace. The only currency that Heaven recognizes is Divine Grace.

Religious Humanism's favorite color, green, takes on different forms. Sometime ago I attended a funeral of a young wife and mother who had died of cancer. The pastor eulogized her as one who loved gardening and grew better sweet corn than the Jolly Green Giant ever could. She so unselfishly and faithfully provided her family with gifts from her garden. That is how he paid tribute to her, along with noting some of her other motherly and wifely virtues. Those were the main points of his message, and upon that basis we were assured that she was now one of Heaven's chief gardeners.

In that funeral there was not a word about the grace and blood of God's forgiveness in His crucified and resurrected Son. Not a word about her commitment to and love for Christ while on earth. Maybe she did love Him, maybe she didn't. Apparently all of that was irrelevant. But we were all assured that she was now one of the most beautiful gardeners, or should we say gardenias in Heaven's Glory Garden. Sound familiar? It was her green thumb and not Christ's bloodied hands. If you will, it wasn't the Divine Giver of grace for His children, but the human grower of greens for her family that really mattered and made the eternal difference. .

I remember distinctly during the horticultural eulogy that my mind wandered to the nursery rhyme the words of which are well-known: "Mary, Mary, quite contrary, how does your garden grow? With silver bells and cockleshells and pretty maids all in a row." Contrary Mary! Hmmm! What was that all about? I asked myself, "Why contrary Mary?" Contrary Mary and her garden, according to some theories, refer to Queen Mary I of England, also known as Bloody Mary who murdered Protestants. Hence, her garden was really a graveyard made up of row upon row of corpses. Silver bells and cockleshells were thought to be instruments of torture, and her maidens were guillotines used for beheading. Contrary Mary indeed!

There I sat at a Religious Humanistic wake, taking a mental journey from a sweetcorn garden of a deceased wife to a gruesome graveyard garden of another gardener named Bloody Mary who planted Protestant corpses. I believe that it was the Holy Spirit who was doing some gardening in my soul. The truth being that Bloody Mary's garden of sin and murder was more relevant to the moment than the dead woman's garden of sweetcorn.

Then the Holy Spirit took me to yet another Garden scene. For like Bloody Mary, all of us sinners are totally dependent upon another garden drama. In fact, the only garden that really matters for all of us is the Garden of Gethsemane where the Savior cried out to His Heavenly Father in Matthew 26:39,

> **"...My Father, if it is possible, let this cup pass from me; yet not as I will, but as Thou wilt."**

I believe to this day that the Lord at that dead woman's top-soil, under-the-soil debacle was preaching to me the sermon that He really wanted preached, and that the Religious Humanism minister never came close to preaching. It was because the only begotten Son of God submitted Himself to His Father's will in the Garden of Gethsemane, that we can pass from eternal death into eternal life and enter into the Paradise of God and not the Hell of Satan. However, during that entire memorial service, we never once came close to Jesus' Garden of amazing grace and precious blood that He already there began to sweat for sinners like ourselves.

"Bloody Mary and bloody sinners," you respond! Isn't that mere sensationalism? No! Come now, we have all killed someone at one time or another. The Bible tells us in I John 3:15 that if you and I hate our brother, we are 1st degree murderers. I guess we have all had our Bloody-Mary moments in that regard. In and of ourselves we are all condemned murderers. Oh thank God for the forgiving grace of God! And thank God for teaching us this, that what man calls merit is nothing, and that what God calls grace is everything. And even more than this because we live from grace to grace, not only are the repentant forgiven by His pardoning grace, but we would go back to our sins like a dog to his vomit if it weren't for His preventing grace. Grace for pardon! Grace for prevention! Grace upon grace upon grace! Heaven will be the eternal celebration of God's grace.

Still, everyone left the funeral not the least bit hungry for Christ's forgiveness for sinners, but instead with a craving for sweet corn. It took me a long time to ever be able to eat sweet corn again. It will for sure take a long time to forget the message preached to my heart by the Holy Spirit. Frankly, I don't think I will ever forget it. God more than made up for the total waste of those moments.

We read about Jesus in Ephesians 1:7,

> **"In Him we have redemption through His blood, the forgiveness of our trespasses, according to the RICHES OF HIS GRACE."**

Redemption! Blood! Forgiveness! Grace! The true Gospel of our Lord Jesus Christ! A small boy was consistently late in coming home from school. His parents warned him one day that he had to come home on time that afternoon. Nevertheless he arrived home later than ever. His mother met him at the door and said nothing. His father met him in the living room in complete silence and said nothing to him either. At dinner that night, the boy looked at his plate. There was a half of a slice of bread and a glass of water. He looked at his father, but his father remained silent. The boy was crushed in his spirit, and began to cry. The father waited for the full impact to sink in, and then quietly took the boy's plate and placed it in front of himself. He took his own plate of meat and potatoes, put it in front of his son, and smiled at him. The boy never forgot that moment or the lesson that it taught him. When the boy grew up, he said, "All of my life I've realized how good God is, how bad sin is, how costly the gift of God's grace was, that Jesus took my place for my sins, and gave me His riches of forgiveness and peace." (11)

The entire doctrine of Divine Grace must again be restored in the church, and pastors must wax eloquent on the grace of God once more. Perhaps it is not too late to rescue the souls of men from the false gospel of Religious Humanism, and put back the amazing into the grace of God. So that people can truly be saved and blessed the old fashioned and only way – Jesus paid it all, all to Him I owe.

HAKUNA MATATA – THE PROBLEM-FREE PHILOSOPHY

Surely you remember it, don't you? It was in Walt Disney's film *Lion King* that a meerkat named Timon and a warthog named Pumba comforted a lion cub name Simba with a song that celebrated their problem-free philosophy, "**HAKUNA MATATA**." Hakuna Matata is Swahilli, which most literally means, "**NO WORRIES OR CONCERNS HERE**." *Lion King* took the animated film industry by storm with record-breaking mass appeal. Released in June of 1994, its first summer weekend viewing netted more than 41 million dollars. Millions of people came to be part of a film that portrayed a land of no problems or worries for the rest of their lives.

Religious Humanism has also taken the media and local church world by storm and continues to net its millions of dollars. Hakuna Matata could very well be called the theology of Religious Humanism. There are a vast number of Religious Humanist preachers who constantly preach Hakuna Matata to their church congregations and their TV audiences. They just do not call it that. But that is exactly what it is. Today's "Hakuna Matata Preachers" tell their followers that if they give generously enough, if they believe strongly enough, if they think positively enough, and if they command authoritatively enough, they can turn all the negatives into positives, they can turn all disease into ease, they can turn their meagerness into wealth, and they can make all of the rough places smooth. Hakuna Matata! Timon and Pumba were right, it is no passing craze.

This is the picture of Christianity that the Hakuna Matata preachers try to convey to people in their churches and TV ministries. Television pastor Fred Price does this all the time as he lures people with his own Hakuna Matata message and lifestyle. You have to give him this much, at least he practices what preaches. He boasts: "**IF THE MAFIA CAN RIDE AROUND IN LINCOLN CONTINENTAL TOWN CARS, WHY CAN'T THE KING'S (CHRIST'S) KIDS?**" (12) He boasts some more to his congregation: "**I'VE GOT 25 MILLION DOLLARS IN MY FINANCIAL STATEMENT, FREE AND CLEAR, I HAVE NO DEBT. I LIVE IN A 25 ROOM MANSION. I HAVE MY OWN 6 MILLION DOLLAR YACHT. I HAVE MY OWN PRIVATE JET AND I HAVE MY OWN HELICOPTER AND I HAVE 7 LUXURY AUTOMOBILES AND I NEVER GET BORED HAVING TO DRIVE THE SAME CAR MORE THAN ONE TIME IN ANY GIVEN WEEK**." (13) Well now, "Halleluna Hakuna Matata!" Whether on land, on sea, or in the air, when you go with Christ, you go in style.

Destination panacea! Destination utopia! Destination the good life! That's the destination to which Christ wants to lead all of His followers according to Price, and Fred Price himself is Christ's show-and-tell. He states to his people:

"THE WHOLE POINT IS I'M TRYING TO GET YOU TO SEE – TO GET YOU OUT OF THIS MALAISE OF THINKING THAT JESUS AND HIS DISCIPLES WERE POOR AND THEN RELATING THAT TO YOUR THINKING THAT YOU, AS A CHILD OF GOD, HAVE TO FOLLOW JESUS. THE BIBLE SAYS THAT HE HAS LEFT US AN EXAMPLE THAT WE SHOULD FOLLOW HIS STEPS. THAT'S THE REASON WHY I DRIVE A ROLLS ROYCE. I'M FOLLOWING JESUS' STEPS." (14)

Mike Oppenheimer of "Let Us Reason Ministries" says: "BUT IT IS PRICE AND THE OTHER PROSPERITY TEACHERS WHO SEEM TO ENJOY THE BENEFIT OF THIS DOCTRINE, CERTAINLY IT IS NOT THE MAJORITY OF HIS CHURCH. AND IT WILL STAY THAT WAY." (15)

Peggy Noonan was at one time a writer for Dan Rather, and later for President Ronald Reagan, as well as for President George H. W. Bush. She says what the Religious Humanists cannot and will not express, and she says it so well with these words: "WE HAVE LOST THE KNOWLEDGE THAT HAPPINESS IS OVERRATED. IN FACT, LIFE IS OVERRATED. OUR ANCESTORS UNDER- STOOD AND BELIEVED IN TWO WORLDS...." Religious Humanists grossly overrate this world. Our Godly ancestors didn't. Not by any means! That is why they seemed far too heavenly minded to me when I was young. They lived in this world, but as with my parents and my wife's parents, they passionately longed for the next. Heaven! Their disparaging comments about this life turned me off. That was because of my youthful overrating of life here and now. But that is normal for young minds. Full of youthful idealism and optimism! I would never die! At least not in my lifetime! Only wrinkled and frail old people do that. Though my overestimating of this life was already shaken as a teenager when a high school senior was killed in a car accident after the junior-senior banquet! But I slowly discovered as I grew older that Peggy Noonan was right when she refers to earthly life as: "THIS SOLITARY, POOR, NASTY, BRUTISH AND SHORT ONE...."

Peggy Noonan continues: "OURS IS THE FIRST GENERA-TION TO BELIEVE THAT HAPPINESS IS TO BE FOUND ON EARTH. AND IN THE SEARCH FOR IT, WE HAVE EX-PERIENCED UNHAPPINESS." (16) It indeed is also the first time in church history that the religious world has so grossly overrated this earth and this present life in such delusional proportions. The early Christians knew nothing about Hakuna Matata. They instead knew a great deal about the realities contained in the following words:" THLIPSIS – STENOCHORIA – DIOGMOS – LIMOS - GUMNOTES – KINDUNOS

- **MAKAIRA**." What in the world is all of that about? More Hakuna Matata lingo? More Swahilli? Speaking in tongues? No, not quite! They are all Greek words transliterated into English letters which mean: **"TRIBULATION-DISTRESS-PERSECUTION-FAMINE-NAKEDNESS-PERIL-SWORD."** What the first century Christians experienced is recorded for us in Romans 8:35-36,

> **"Who shall separate us from the love of Christ? Shall tribulation, or distress, or persecution, or famine, or nakedness, or peril, or sword? Just as it is written, 'For Thy sake we are being put to death all day long; we were considered as sheep to be slaughtered.'"**

Those of you who think of Christianity as Hakuna Makata have either been duped or doped. What you have just read took place in the lives of 1st century believers all day long, every day of the week. Reality! The enemies of the infant Christian Church persecuted, chased, and killed Christians non-stop. The Christians came to view themselves as the Good Shepherd's "Slaughter-Sheep." It was the first century "Christian Holocaust" under Emperor Nero. They had to run to the next city without a change of clothing or food. Run to escape martyrdom? No, rather, to escape death so as to be able to carry on the work of the Gospel for as long as possible! Flee to the next village or city to do as much damage to the Devil's kingdom as they could before they died for Christ. Keep on moving and keep on witnessing for Christ and save as many souls as possible as long as you have the breath of life. We read in Acts 8:4,

> **"Therefore, those who had been scattered went about preaching the word."**

The Christian Church from its very inception until this day has never been characterized by the plush and pamper of Religious Humanism which today tries to pass itself off as Christianity. Religious Human-ism is a mockery of Christianity. From the first ages of the Christian Church, the apostles and followers of Jesus Christ planted the seeds of the Gospel by their preaching and witnessing, and watered those seeds with their blood. For a man or woman to profess Christ not only meant turning their backs on earthly possessions and pleasures, but saying goodbye to their earthly lives. Hakuna Matata! Not quite! Christianos ad leones! Christians to the lions!

That is original authentic Christianity! Not this health, wealth, gum-drops and sweet-treats myth that is casting dishonor upon Christ and His martyrs, and terribly sickening the contemporary church. Oh yes, martyrs! For an individual to list his name amongst Christians is to enlist in the Army of Christian Martyrs. To be a witness for Christ and to be a martyr for Christ are synonymous. To live for Christ is to die for Christ. By the way, that is what it means to be a witness for Jesus. The Greek word for "Witness" in the New Testament is "Martus" from which we derive the English noun "Martyr."

Then it was with torches, swords and crosses, while today it is with guns and machetes. Christians are being martyred in modern times for their commitment to Christ in staggering numbers across the entire earth. The heathen press and media simply ignore it. Some estimate that 160,000 Christians are martyred for their faith every year around the world. The brave Army of Christian Martyrs is powerfully marching into battle and the Gospel of Jesus Christ is mightily moving with them around the world.

I foresee Christian martyrdom coming to North America more and more in my lifetime. Christians will be treated wrongly when they are right. They will be punished when they are not guilty. They will be more and more gunned down in their churches and schools during worship services and classes. The only real hate in the phony "Hate Crime Legislation" in America is hatred for Christians. It has always been that way and always will be, for Jesus said in John 15:19,

> "...but I chose you out of the world, therefore the world hates you."

Christian living has never been, nor is it ever going to be some sort of charmed "Hakuna Matata Utopia" because we follow Christ. And furthermore, we must remember that nothing shall ever separate us from the ongoing love that Christ has for His own – neither death nor life. (Romans 8:38-39)

Martin Luther observed: "**WE LEAK THE GOSPEL AND IT NEEDS TO BE BEAT INTO OUR HEADS OVER AND OVER AGAIN**." The true Gospel is leaking out of many churches, and a false gospel is taking its place. As a result, this false gospel of Religious Humanism is producing generations of religious people in America who are totally unaccustomed to sacrifice, and who for the most part are totally unwilling to make sacrifices for Jesus Christ. Not only that, but they are being taught that God's will for them is to indulge themselves, rather than give up themselves totally for Christ's sake. They have no awareness any longer that we cannot wear the crown if we do not bear the cross. They are being told that Christ's priority for them is Hakuna Matata.

All of this presses us to ask the question: "Are today's Christian parents joyful when their sons and daughters serve on the dangerous and risky missions fields of Africa, the Philippines, India, Indonesia, China, Iraq, Pakistan, Turkey, the Balkans etc.?" And all of that not to bring glory and fame to self, but to their Lord and Savior Jesus Christ! Are we as parents as elated and proud to see our young sons and daughters bringing the Gospel of salvation to some backward, uncivilized, strife-ridden third-world country, as we are to see them on the football field of some major university, and setting school and personal records that are broadcast across the nation? Are we as willing risk their lives in Africa for Christ as we are to risk their lives in athletics for fame? To the point, do our hearts swell with as much pride when because of our children, Christ's name is praised in some remote bush land, as when our children's names are being praised on the athletic fields of American colleges and universities?

It calls to mind the story of William Kelly who was a devoted student of the Bible, whose scholarship and spirituality made him a real power for God in Great Britain at the close of the 19th century. Mr. Kelly helped a young relative prepare for Trinity College in Dublin, Ireland, and in that way William came to the attention of the professors there as well. They encouraged William Kelly to take up work at the college and thereby distinguish himself. When William Kelly showed a complete lack of interest and enthusiasm at the thought of working at the college, they were very much taken back. One of the professors said to him, "But Mr. Kelly, aren't you interested in making a name for yourself in the world?" To which William Kelly provokingly responded, "Which world, gentlemen?" That is the question, isn't it? I add to that question another, "Not only which world, but whose name?"

GOD THE MAGIC GENIE

The movie world abounds with fascinating and entertaining mythological figures past and present. Whether it is Puff the Magic Dragon, Wonder Dog, or Superman, they were always there to save the day. America has historically had a love affair with these mythical messiahs. It seems harmless enough, and I have rather enjoyed a few of them myself. Some of my childhood favorites were "The Lone Ranger" as well as "Sergeant Preston" and his dog "Yukon King."

It quickly loses its innocence when the mythological super-hero world of make-believe is dragged into religion and passed off on to thousands upon thousands of gullible people as reality. Now much of American religion is having a love affair with another made-up figure – "**God The Magic Genie**." In Religious Humanism, the church has been turned into Aladdin, who if he rubs his lamp properly, i.e. if faith is exercised sufficiently and authoritatively, then and then only will the Genie-God be released from faith's lamp of dreams to grant the Aladdin Church whatever it wants. Then the Genie-God appears and says to the Aladdin Church, "What is your wish, Master?"

I have watched this played out over and over again. Apparently, Religious Humanists must believe that at times the Genie-God is preoccupied or taking a snooze, for their faith-force dictates are often delivered with ever-increasing volumes of shouting, arm waving, and even foot stomping to awaken their Genie-God. You know, kind of like a "Clap-On Clap-Off God."

Listen! If God was a "Magic Genie God," and we could make Him do anything that we want Him to do, we would mess everything up real bad. We would be pulling intellect on the only omniscient God Who if He gave us everything that we "smartie pants" desire, it would destroy our lives and His entire created order. We would not like the results at all!

I am reminded of the story about three men who were walking down the beach and they came across a lamp buried in the sand. So they picked it up and began wiping it off. Suddenly a genie popped out of the lamp and said to them, "I can grant each of you your biggest wish in life when you rub my lamp of dreams. What do you really wish for the most, just tell me, and I will make it come true?!" We are back to imagining, dreaming and wishing again. The first man rubbed the lamp and whispered, "I wish that I was ten times smarter than what I am." The genie announced, "You are now ten times smarter." The second fellow took the lamp, rubbed it and whispered, "I wish that I was a hundred times smarter than I am." The genie said, "You are a hundred times smarter." The third man rubbed the lamp and said, "I wish I were a thousand times smarter than I am." The genie pointed at him and declared, "You are now a thousand times smarter, and you are now a woman."

Now hang on tight. We have to back up a bit here to see and understand all of this in context and how it developed. All the way back to the Garden of Eden and the creation account! Fred Price asks: **"WHY DID HE LEAVE IT UP TO A PUNY MAN TO GIVE THEM THE NAMES TO THE ANIMAL KINGDOM, THE PLANT KINGDOM, AND THE VEGETABLE KINGDOM? BECAUSE THEY BELONGED UNDER THE CONTROL OF ADAM AND NOT OF GOD! WHY? HE HAD DOMINION. NOT GOD, ADAM."** (17)

Whoa, horse! We are told that because God gave Adam dominion over the beasts, birds and fish etc. (Genesis 1:26), and because he assigned Adam to be the caretaker of the Garden of Eden, and to give names to the beasts of the field, the cattle, and the birds of the air (Genesis 2:19-20), the Religious Humanist with his hugely inflated man-obsession says that this makes man the Lord of the earth and not God. If you will, God is King over the Kingdom of Heaven, and man is

King over the Kingdom of earth. God has the upper Lordship, and man has the lower Lordship. Co-lords of Heaven and earth!

Follow now closely! So then when it comes to earth, God is in man's domain, and God must do what man, earth's landlord, dictates. So that God is really Aladdin Man's genie-god here on earth. God does His Earthmaster's bidding. Now you are getting the hang of it. Here is where this Genie-God thing begins!

More illogic! Simply because God commanded Adam to give names to the animals, birds and fish does not mean that man owns and runs the zoo. Sort of like if you as parents were to tell your daughter to watch the house and baby sit the younger kids for the evening, and when you come home she tells you that the house and the family are now under her control and authority, not yours!

Then Price goes on to say: "**NOW THIS IS A SHOCKER! BUT GOD HAS TO BE GIVEN PERMISSION TO WORK IN THIS EARTH ON BEHALF OF MAN....YES! YOU ARE IN CONTROL! SO IF MAN HAS CONTROL, WHO NO LONGER HAS IT? GOD...WHEN GOD GAVE MAN DOMINION, THAT MEANT THAT GOD NO LONGER HAD DOMINION. SO GOD CANNOT DO ANYTHING IN THIS EARTH UNLESS WE LET HIM. AND THE WAY WE LET HIM OR GIVE HIM PERMISSION IS THROUGH PRAYER.**" (18) Well now, how does that grab ya? Does it sound a tad out of line? How about a whole universe out of line?

First if you will, without our strong faith-praying, that is, without rubbing the faith lamp adequately with potent faith, God is trapped in the Genie Lamp forever. Poor Genie God! Totally bottled up by man! He can't do a thing! Unless of course we pop the top with top-popping faith-prayer! Then we can release God to do our bidding. Otherwise, He is trapped. Hogwash! All of it! Get a load of this! Psalm 135:6 states:

> **"Whatever the Lord pleases, He does, in Heaven and in earth, in the seas and in all deeps."**

Notice, He does what He pleases not just in Heaven, but in earth as well as in the oceans. Or get a second load of the same in Psalm 115:3,

> **"But our God is in the heavens; He does whatever He pleases."**

Man doesn't let God do anything! God does not need our faith-prayer permission slip. Christians do not hand out permission slips to God by their prayers. It is God's grace that permits us to pray. Who in the world are Religious

Humanists fooling? Nobody but themselves! All they are doing with this ranting and raving is howling at the moon. Whatever God pleases He does! Listen, it is not our prayer permission to God, but it is God's own good pleasure that is His all-sufficient reason and permission. Or as is asked in Job 9:12,

"...Who could say to Him, 'What art Thou doing?'"

We are talking about the complete denial and rejection of the sovereignty of God in modern Christianity. It is a disaster of incredible proportions that corrupts theology and distorts people's thinking, leading them into all the extremes that we are now dealing with. There are basically two ecclesiastical camps in all of this. First, I still have friends who are Calvinists. As a Christian I consider myself in terms of theological categories a Calvinistic Pentecostal. But not a hyper-Calvinist! What's that? To hear them talk and to read their periodicals, one immediately realizes that they view the world as a stage. And on that stage God does absolutely everything. In short, God writes the script and the dialogue, and we go through the motions and mouth the words. Puppets on strings! When a hyper-Calvinist falls down the steps and survives, he says, "Boy, I am sure glad that's over."

On the other hand, and on the other far end of the spectrum, where Religious Humanism is, God gets the play started by getting the curtain up. Then God goes off for coffee somewhere and everything on stage is improvisation. He will come back to bring the curtain down one day, but until then, the faith-gods write the lines, push the buttons, and run personal and world history. As a matter of fact, the only way God can reinsert Himself into earth's drama is by human permission called prayer. This is where Religious Humanism has taken much of modern Christianity causing people ungodly deception, disillusionment and defeat. It is another Religious Humanism mess that has to be cleaned up with the cosmic broom of Daniel 4:35,

"And all the inhabitants of the earth are accounted as nothing, but He does according to His will in the Host of Heaven and among the inhabitants of the earth; and no one can ward off His hand or say to Him, 'What hast Thou done?'"

Of course the truth is that life on a daily basis is Divine-human interaction. God works through us, in us, and with us. He allows us to make a big difference in the circumstances if we do what He tells us to do, and not what we tell Him to do. If you or I did everything for our children, then we would bring them into another kind of slavery – irresponsibility. So, the only way for us to be free and be all that God desires us to be is for God to work and for us to work. Sometimes we renege on our obligation and we get ourselves into a humanly un-solvable mess. Then it is too late for Divine-human interaction. The only way out is Divine intervention, and He has graciously done that for me, and I suspect for you, a goodly number of times.

Let me summarize in this way. Christianity can best be captured by the words of Daniel Webster: "**THE GREATEST THOUGHT I HAVE EVER HAD IS MY PERSONAL RESPONSIBILITY TO GOD.**" Religious Humanism can best be captured by the absolute opposite: "**THE GREATEST THOUGHT GOD HAS EVER HAD IS HIS PERSONAL RESPONSIBILITY TO ME.**"

Second, in Religious Humanism, they just keep playing "Now Top This!" And Price does just that when He says: "**YES! YOU ARE IN CONTROL. SO IF MAN HAS CONTROL, WHO NO LONGER HAS IT? GOD.**" (19) Whoops! If God does not have control, then He is not God. Simple as that! If man has control, then He is God. Oh yes, we are back to that again. Shucks, we thought that we had that Religious Humanist persistent god-complex corralled. Nope! It just keeps jumping over the fence. Religious Humanists are incessantly trying to trade places with God. In fact, when it comes to confusing man with God, they are just plain out of control. God is never out of control, and in fact is in control of all. We read in Psalm 103:19,

> "**The Lord has established His throne in the heavens; and His sovereignty rules over all.**"

Third, in Religious Humanism, God needs the prayers of man. In Christianity, man needs prayers to God. Nowhere is it even hinted at in the Bible that God needs us to pray to Him. Everywhere it indicates that we need to pray to God. If God needed our prayers, then He would be the deficient one and we would be the sufficient ones. Crazy stuff! But that is exactly what Religious Humanism does to the minds of men. It makes them believe crazy things.

When men pray thinking that they are giving God license to be and act like God, they are mocking God. Their words are empty and vanish into thin air. They are wasting their time, and they talk at Heaven for nothing. But when men passionately crave God in prayer, and are utterly dependent upon Him in humble petition, they not only reach His ears, but His heart. King David is called by God in I Samuel 13:14, "A man after His own heart." The heart is where David's prayers came from. We read in II Samuel 7:27 (KJV) about David's prayer life, "O Lord of hosts...therefore hath thy servant found in his heart to pray this prayer unto thee." Listen, heartfelt prayer alone reaches the heart of God, but headstrong pronouncements to God don't get past our noses.

Staying now with the subject of prayer, Religious Humanism puts man in a horrible dilemma. He is taught by the Religious Humanists that if he faith-rubs his Genie-God lamp adequately, God will each time abundantly satisfy him for so doing, and give him the exact answers to his prayers that he wants to receive. After all, he has to because man is "Earthlord" and has all authority as to what must go on down here.

What if the answer from God is different than the one that was desired and prescribed by "Earthlord?" Pardon the pun, but therein is the real rub. So often what happens is that when someone has the Religious Humanist mindset, and he doesn't receive what he has claimed to be his rights from God, his faith is literally rubbed out. Like a spoiled little kid, if Genie-God doesn't do what he wants, he throws his lamp away and goes home. He has never been taught properly in Religious Humanism that God is the absolute sovereign God of Heaven and earth, and that He does what He pleases in both realms. (Matthew 6:10) Then, befuddled and dismayed by the whole experience, he feels betrayed by his Genie-God and becomes totally disillusioned.

I have seen it happen too often. Some of these disillusioned victims of Religious Humanism become spiritually bankrupt and very depressed. They then pawn their faith for some other wacky religion, or they become agnostics. They come out of the entire experience like the financially bankrupt man who switches brokers, from stockbroker to pawnbroker.

This entire disaster stems from Religious Humanism's teaching that prayer is the faith-manipulation of God. People then become terribly misguided, because they fail to realize this prime lesson about prayer which is that if prayer does anything, it teaches us that man is not in control, God is. God alone knows all! He knows what we think the problem is. He alone knows what the problem really is. He knows what we think the only solution can be. He alone knows what the solution must be. We read these humbling words in I John 3:20,

"...for God is greater than our heart, and knows all things."

God is infinitely greater than man and He knows exactly what he needs. We can see only what is immediately in front of us. God can see from everlasting to everlasting. God has the long view. Man has a view that goes only to the end of his nose. God's vantage point and man's vantage point are as different as 20-20 vision and blindness. Nonetheless, Religious Humanists say to God, "Solve this and solve that, and here is the only way to solve it and solve it now." Prayer to them is like turning on the TV, the only difference being that they don't even give their Genie-God time to warm up.

What is prayer really? Simply but profoundly it is partially this: "**PRAYER IS DARING TO OPEN UP EARTH'S PROBLEMS TO HEAVEN'S SOLUTIONS**." That can be downright shocking, for God answers the petition and solves the problem according to His perfect knowledge and wisdom. Therefore, when we pray to the Bible's God, we are not praying inside earth's limitations, but rather, we are reaching outside of earth's boundaries and upward into Heaven's limitless wisdom, power and possibilities. So don't be surprised any more that you are surprised by God's answers and ways. But be assured of this, that when a child of God prays for a matter with loving and humble submission to the Divine will, let not that man or anyone else doubt that God will answer in the way that will secure the glory of God and man's eternal good.

MORAL TANGENTIALISM

When Religious Humanism begins to make inroads into the church community, it becomes harder and harder to maintain the truth, but even more difficult to be maintained by the truth. I would have never dreamed in a million years that I would be writing the book that I am writing, and seeing what I am seeing in the modern church scene. It is a sad fact that you just don't know anymore what you are going to find when you walk through the doors of a so-called Christian Church. Life is suspenseful and dangerous enough in this murder-mad, identity-theft world without having to be on our constant guard for hidden spiritual booby traps when you walk through church doors as well.

But sad to say, today we must be acutely wary, sharply spiritually discerning, and always on guard! Going to church in many instances today is a dangerous proposition. There are deadly religious IEDs all over the landscape of modern Christendom. And what you hear is the "Amen" of deceived parishioners who blindly affirm and applaud every man-made bomb that the preacher is planting in the minds of the undiscerning.

Sometimes even presidents are having their brains blasted by Religious Humanism! President Gerald Ford passed away on Dec-ember 26, 2006, and at the memorial service at Grace Episcopal Church in his home town of Grand Rapids, Michigan, President Jimmy Carter was one of the eulogists invited by the Ford family to pay tribute to his friend and predecessor in the White House.

It was a beautiful service of praise to God and tribute to the 36th President of the United States of America. Presidents Ford and Carter were friends and brothers, as they shared together a common and eternal bond in their personal faith in Jesus Christ as their Lord and Savior. There was so much that was good and pleasing to God about the eulogy given by President Carter. The spirit of a strong faith in God along with an enormous sense of American patriotism gave me goose bumps as well as a lump in my throat and tears welling up in my eyes again and again.

With all of that said, there were some striking words uttered by President Carter that were deeply troubling, and tarnished those endearing moments of presidential honor and remembrance. President Carter made this observation: **"CHRISTIANS SHOULD NOT BE DIVIDED OVER SEEMNGLY IMPORTANT, BUT TANGENTIAL ISSUES, INCLUDING SEXUAL PREFERENCES AND THE ROLE OF WOMEN IN THE CHURCH, THINGS LIKE THAT."** Interesting word – Tangential! The "Tangential Issues" that he was referring to included homosexuality and women in ecclesiastical positions of authority and leadership. He said these issues, and others like them, were only seemingly all-important, but were in fact merely tangential. Moreover, President Carter stated that these tangential issues should not be allowed to divide Christians.

I knew when I heard the word "Tangential," that it is derived from and included the word "Tangent." A tangent is simply a digression from the usual or the norm. In other words, sexual preferences and women's ecclesiastical roles are merely digressions from the more traditional path and not moral or theological issues. One can only imagine what else he was referring to when he said, "Things like that." I have no doubt that this included abortion which is not a tangent, but is murder. Things like that!

Every unborn baby in America is a target for the abortionist now more than ever. President Barack Obama stands for unlimited abort-ion rights even through the last trimester – partial birth abortion. His stand on abortion was clear before the election, in that he could not say when human life began. He stated that such a question was above his pay grade. No not really, but it was above his moral grade. It is open season on all unborn babies in America! The culture of killing the innocent will now grow even more. It doesn't call it killing. No, no, it speaks of the quiet, easy deaths of abortion and euthanasia, the legal disposing of the young and the old.

Secular and Religious Humanists voted for President Obama and in so doing furthered the ACLU crusade for women's rights over Divine righteousness. According to President Carter, President Obama is merely on a tangent. There are biologists today who say that infanticide (including killing babies) is as natural as the sex drive. They tell us that all animals, including man (get that –

we're now animals) practice it. What a rationale! Animals do it and so we can too. Hear me; very few animals kill their own. There are a few, but they are few in number, and now we have a predator-president leading the human pack of baby killers. I guess animals are far less tangential than man.

All of this of course in the name of tolerance and acceptance of those who take a different, tangential path from the more traditionally traveled one. Religious Humanism is more concerned about being loosely tolerant of what is vogue in society, than it is about being strictly obedient to what is the clear voice of God in the Bible. Religious Humanism caters to varying cultures, while Christianity submits to unvarying Divine commands. Religious Humanism majors in options while Christianity majors in mandates. We are back to mush versus must again! Religious Humanists attempt to take the guilt out of sin by giving it a much more benign label. While President Carter stated that sexual preferences are merely **TANGENTS**, God states that gays and lesbians are committing **TRANSGRESSIONS.** The Lord does not say about men,

"All of us like sheep have gone on tangents."

Rather He does say in Isaiah 53:6,

"All of us like sheep have gone astray...."

Alternative routing and straying are not synonymous. Not even close! The former simply means to take a different path which leads nonetheless to the same destination. Perfectly legitimate! To stray or to go astray is to leave the right path and take a wrong way which leads to a totally different destination. Religious Humanists tell us that homosexuals and abortionists are merely into religious diversification and alternative routing. Christianity tells us that homosexuals and abortionists are into moral disobedience and on the wrong road to eternal destruction. In short Religious Humanism calls certain sins tangents, while Christianity calls sins – sins.

In American churches, moral tangentialism versus moral absolutism is yet another fierce conflict that can be traced right back to the multi-headed monster called Religious Humanism and its corruption of modern Christianity.

Resources:
1. Dynamic Preaching, "Come to the Feast" (Seven World's Corporation, Knoxville, TN, September, 1995, Volume X, No.9) Page 5 (Parade Magazine, October 28, 1990)

2. Let us Reason Ministries, Mike Oppenheimer, "Preaching a False Positive with a Smile" (Joel Osteen, "Sermon: What the Resurrection Means To Us As Believers")

3. Ibid.

4. The Book of Discipline of the United Methodist Church, 2004 Copyright, "Social Principles: The Nurturing Community – Human Sexuality," Paragraph 161 G, Used By Permission

5. Forgotten Word Ministries, Robert E. Wise, "Joel Osteen – False Preacher" (Larry King Interview of Joel Osteen, CNN, June 20, 2005)

6. Ibid.

7. Ibid.

8. Let Us Reason Ministries, Mike Oppenheimer, "Preaching a False Positive"

9. Let Us Reason Ministries, Mike Oppenheimer, "Prosperity of the Faith Teachers (Paying the Pipers)," (Nov. 1997 Voice of The Covenant Magazine, p. 5)

10. Let Us Reason Ministries, Mike Oppenheimer, "The Magnanimous Money Message of Mike Murdock" (Mike Murdock, LeSea Broadcasting, April 26, 2002)

11. Dynamic Preaching, "Dressed For the Wedding" (Seven Worlds Corporation, Knoxville, TN, September/October, 1996, Volume XI, No. 8) Page 38

12. Let Us Reason Ministries, Mike Oppenheimer, "Fred Price, Is 'The Price Is Right?' Or Is The Price Wrong?" (Faith, Foolishness or Presumption, P. 34)

13. Let Us Reason Ministries, Mike Oppenheimer, "Fred Price, Is 'The Price Is Right?' Or Is The Price Wrong?" (Audio #CR-A2 "Ever Increasing Faith Program" TBN Dec. 9, 1990)

14. Let Us Reason Ministries, Mike Oppenheimer, "Fred Price, Is 'The Price Is Right?' Or Is The Price Wrong?" (God Stuff Video)

15. Let Us Reason Ministries, Mike Oppenheimer, "Fred Price, Is 'The Price Is Right?' Or Is The Price Wrong?"

16. Peggy Noonan - Ben Haden, Changed Lives, "Why Jesus Didn't…" (Ben Haden Evangelical Association Inc., Chattanooga, TN, 1993) Pages 4-5

17. Let Us Reason Ministries, Mike Oppenheimer, "Fred Price, Is 'The Price Is Right?' Or Is The Price Wrong?" (Ever Increasing Faith Program, May 3, 1992)

18. Let Us Reason Ministries, Mike Oppenheimer, "Fred Price, Is "The Price Is Right?' Or Is The Price Wrong?" (Frederick Price Quoted From – "Christianity In Crisis" By H. Hanegraaff, 1993)

19. Let Us Reason Ministries, Mike Oppenheimer, "Fred Price, Is "The Price is Right?' Or Is The Price Wrong?" (The Word Study Bible, 1990, P. 1178)

20. Let Us Reason Ministries, Mike Oppenheimer, "The Church Losing Her Salt" (Pulpit Helps, 1987)

POSTSCRIPT

†††

Religious Humanists are by far the most subtle, slippery and persistent conveyers of untruths into the minds of modern men that I have ever met in my lifetime. But the fact remains that while the fisherman may tantalize and play the bait before the fish, he cannot force the fish to swallow it. A lie cannot be believed but under some fake appearance of truth. That is Religious Humanism!

I pray to God that *Modern Christianity Corrupted* has enabled you to be able to say victoriously, "Though I now recognize very clearly how Religious Humanists have been fishing around in my mind, I am thankful to report that they have caught nothing and they never will." I also pray to God that if you have already bit on some or all of the Religious Humanist lures, by the Holy Spirit's power you will be able to spit them all out of your souls. He that has an ear let him hear what the Holy Spirit is saying to the modern Christian Church.

May a glorious and desperately needed 21st century Protestant Reformation break forth throughout America and the world! Martin Luther is once again nailing his ninety-five theses to the church doors. Only this time they must be nailed to Protestant church doors. It is time for Bible- believing Christians to stand up for the infallible truth of God's Word, not just in the world, but especially in the modern Christian church.

It won't be easy, it never is! Among 7,441 Protestant pastors asked if they believed that the Bible is the inspired, inerrant Word of God, 87% of Methodists said NO, 95% Episcopalians said NO, 82% of Presbyterians said NO, and 67% of American Baptists said NO…As the leadership goes so goes the church. (20) More than that, Religious Humanism monopolizes religious television worldwide. It is far from being a level battle field. By the same token, Roman Catholicism monopolized the 16th century world. However, just one God-fearing Martin Luther is a majority.

It is way past time for those of us who embrace the Bible as God's inspired, inerrant Word not only to stand up but to fight for truth, the whole truth and nothing but the Bible truth, so help us God. The Reformation call is strongly and urgently again going out to all of Christ's followers to rediscover, reaffirm, defend and propagate the truth of God's Holy Word, and rescue the Gospel of Jesus Christ from corrupting Religious Humanism. President George W. Bush right-fully declared the "Global War On Terror." The enemy of our souls has declared his own GWOT – "Global War On Truth." We must declare and carry out a GWOH – "Global War On Heresy."

Jude 3 calls to us,

**"Beloved, while I was making every effort to write you
about our common salvation, I felt the necessity to write to
you appealing that you contend earnestly for the faith
which was once for all delivered to the saints."**

Not only for our sakes, but for our children's children, and for the sake of those who must yet to come to Christ. I appeal to you to tell everyone you can about this book, and tell them that they can order it by calling **Father's Press** at **816-600-6288**. You will also be able to order this book from my **Whole Truth Help** website at www.wholetruthhelp.com God graciously bless you, powerfully use you, and protectively keep you as you obey Him in contending earnestly for the faith which was once delivered to the saints.

ACKNOWLEDGEMENTS

†††

Without the scholarly and exhaustive research of the following ministries, this book could not have been written. Our deepest thanks to Mike Oppenheimer of Let Us Reason Ministries, Robert Wise of Forgotten Word Ministries, David Cloud of Way Of Life Literature, Rick Miesel and John Beardsley of Biblical Discernment Ministries, and Anton and Janet-Hein Hudson of Apologetics Index. Never did so many of us owe so much to so few.

So many more to thank! My wife and I are indebted to Mike Smitley who is the founder and president of Fathers Press, and whose heart beats with ours for the need of a new reformation in the modern Christianity. We thank God for Mike's faith, vision and dedication.

We also express our special thanks to those who helped us in getting this new reformation project off the ground. Sheila, Sharon, Kim, Clenda, and countless others. We bless the Lord for your giving hearts and unfailing friendship. This book would not have been within our reach without each and all of you. It has been said that a brother is not necessarily your friend, but a true friend is indeed your brother. We thank God for our friends, brothers and sisters everywhere. All of you are true family to us.

I want to give the loving thanks of all to my dear Ruthie who pours her heart into everything that the Lord calls me to do. Because of her love, prayers and encouragement, she is the personification in my life of the words of Scripture, "I can do all things through Christ who strengthens me." For her can-do Christian spirit, her positive and loving criticism, and her faithful editing and constant encouragement, the goal was always in sight, even when it seemed overwhelming at times. Thank you my wife!

Above all thanks be to God who gives us the victory through our Lord Jesus Christ. May His name forever be praised and His Word cherished, obeyed and protected by His blood-bought church. And may a new "Protestant Reformation" sweep across the modern Church and across the world in this eternally defining final hour.

ABOUT THE AUTHOR

Bob Klingenberg is married to Ruth who is his dear wife of 48 years. Bob and Ruth have 4 children and 10 grandchildren. Bob is a retired pastor/evangelist in the Assemblies of God Fellowship, and has been in the ordained ministry since 1966. He is a graduate of Calvin College and Seminary in Grand Rapids, Michigan. His pastorates have been in Michigan and New Jersey, and his evangelistic crusade ministry has been conducted in Great Britain, Germany, Netherlands, Jamaica, Aruba, Curacao and across America. He has conducted guest lectureships in Continental Theological Seminary in Brussels, Belgium. He is the author of *Is God With America?* and *Modern Christianity Corrupted.* Bob's website is Whole Truth Help at www.wholetruthhelp.com. His email address is bobwk@centurytel.net.

CPSIA information can be obtained
at www.ICGtesting.com
Printed in the USA
LVOW12s2300150816
500437LV00002B/2/P